# The political interests of gender revisited

# The political interests of gender revisited

## Redoing theory and research with a feminist face

Edited by
ANNA G. JÓNASDÓTTIR &
KATHLEEN B. JONES

## United Nations University Press

TOKYO • NEW YORK • PARIS

*Published by* Manchester University Press in the UK, Europe, Australia and New Zealand
Oxford Road, Manchester M13 9NR, UK
www.manchesteruniversitypress.co.uk

*Published by* United Nations University Press in North America and its
Dependancies, Japan and Geneva, Switzerland
United Nations University Press
United Nations University, 53-70, Jingumae 5-chome,
Shibuya-ku, Tokyo 150-8925, Japan
Tel: +81-3-5467-1212  Fax: +81-3-3406-7345
E-mail: sales@hq.unu.edu general enquiries: press@hq.unu.edu
http://www.unu.edu/unupress

United Nations University Office at the United Nations, New York
2 United Nations Plaza, Room DC2-2062, New York, NY 10017, USA
Tel: +1-212-963-6387  Fax: +1-212-371-9454
E-mail: unuona@ony.unu.edu

United Nations University Press is the publishing division of the United Nations University.

Printed in the UK by the MPG Books Group

ISBN   978-92-808-1160-5   hardback
ISBN   978-92-808-1161-2   paperback

*Library of Congress Cataloging-inPublication Data*
The political interests of gender revisited : redoing theory and research with a feminist face / edited by Anna G. Jónasdóttir and Kathleen B. Jones.
      p. cm.
   Includes bibliographical references and index.
      ISBN 978-9280811605 (hardback) — ISBN 978-9280811612 (pbk.)
   1. Feminist theory.  2. Political science.  I. Anna G. Jónasdóttir.  II. Jones, Kathleen B., 1949–
   HQ1190.P64 2008
   306.201–dc22                                                    2008034655

# Contents

# Figures and tables

## Figures

## Tables

# Contributors

*Berit Åberg*, Senior Lecturer in Gender Studies, Örebro University, Sweden

*Eudine Barriteau*, Professor of Gender and Public Policy and Head, Centre for Gender and Development Studies, University of West Indies, Barbados

*Sue Dunlap*, VP for External Affairs, Planned Parenthood of Los Angeles, CA, USA

*Ann Ferguson*, Professor of Philosophy, University of Massachusetts–Amherst, USA

*Anna. G. Jónasdóttir*, Professor of Gender Studies, Örebro University, Sweden

*Kathleen B. Jones*, Professor Emerita of Women's Studies, San Diego State University, USA

*Ingrid Pincus*, Senior Lecturer in Gender Studies, Örebro University, Sweden

*Ronnee Schreiber*, Associate Professor of Political Science, San Diego State University, USA

*Aili Mari Tripp*, Professor of Political Science and Women's Studies, University of Wisconsin–Madison, USA

*Maria-Barbara Watson-Franke*, Professor Emerita of Women's Studies, San Diego State University, USA

*Brigitte Young*, Professor of Political Science, Westfälische–Wilhelms University, Münster, Germany

*Gillian Youngs*, Senior Lecturer in Media and Communication, University of Leicester, UK

# Acknowledgements

We began working on this book in 2001, while still involved in the collaborative education and research project *Gender in the History and Practice of Democracies* between the (then named) Centre for Women's Studies, Örebro University and Department of Women's Studies, San Diego State University. This project was supported by a grant from the Swedish Foundation for International Cooperation in Research and Higher Education (STINT), which gave us a valuable start. For the continuation and completion of this volume the most important support came from Örebro University and the International Science Centre to which Kathleen Jones was affiliated as a visiting professor 2003–5.

Thanks to all the participants and their many useful comments at two different seminars: one at the Centre for Feminist Social Studies, Örebro University (2003) and the other at the Political Science Department's Feminist Theory Seminar led by Maud Eduards, Drude Dahlerup and Diane Sainsbury (2005).

Special thanks for Kathleen Jones's opportunity to present a version of chapter 2 at the kick-off conference for *Gendering Excellence (GEXcel): Towards a European Centre of Excellence in Transnational and Transdisciplinary Studies of Changing Gender Relations, Intersectionalities and Embodiment* at Linköping University in Linköping, Sweden (May 2007) and especially to Nina Lykke and Jeff Hearn for their helpful comments and feedback. We are also grateful for the invitation to Kathleen Jones to present chapter 2 at a seminar sponsored by the Sociology Department of Sydney University in June 2007, and for the thoughtful feedback she received from colleagues there.

For their close reading and insightful criticisms of the initial proposal and manuscript as a whole, we thank the anonymous reviewers. We are grateful to Anthony Mason, Lucy Nicholson and Jenny Howard of Manchester University Press for their enthusiastic support of this project.

For their willingness to publish their research in this collection, we thank each of the contributors.

A very special acknowledgement to Dr Amy L. Fraher, whose careful, painstaking editing of the whole manuscript allowed us to avoid many errors of substance and style.

# 1

# The political interests of gender revisited: reconstructing feminist theory and political research

*Anna G. Jónasdóttir and Kathleen B. Jones*

## Changed contexts/outmoded theories?

In 1988, in the preface to *The Political Interests of Gender*, we wrote that our work had been prompted by 'the desire to promote dialogue about the parameters of a truly international feminist theory and practice that represents the interests of gender in cross-cultural and historical perspective' (Jones and Jónasdóttir 1988: ix). Much has transpired in the decades since that book's publication, making dialogue about international feminist theory and practice both more difficult and more imperative. The terms 'feminist theory and practice' have undergone further fragmentation and contestation, as evidenced in the titles of several prominent collections of essays: *Coming to Terms, Conflicts in Feminism, Gender Trouble, Third World Women and the Politics of Feminism, Feminisms: A Reader, Is There a Nordic Feminism*? And the idea of the international itself has been subjected to rigorous criticism (Rosenau 1990; Mackie 2001; Naples and Desai 2002). At the same time, the pervasive impact of political-economic and social processes represented by the shorthand 'globalisation' has put questions about the interests of gender into circulation around the world and led feminist scholars to stress the relevance of gender to understanding the impact of globalisation in different political systems (Walby 2003).[1]

Globalisation, or global restructuring, can be considered both an old and a new phenomenon. Although its roots extend as far back as the European expansion of the fifteenth century, or even earlier, as a contemporary concept globalisation most frequently refers to a 'significant economic and political transformation [which] has been occurring since the 1970s' (Marchand and Sisson Runyan 2000: 4; Kelly *et al.* 2001: 3). The transformation signalled by globalisation includes major changes in the social relations and spaces of production, a widened gap between the techno-logical and economic resources of the relatively more industrialised

'North' and the relatively more impoverished 'South', environmental and ecological crises, increased population mobility, porous national borders and the undermining of national sovereignty, and the emergence of new supranational structures and ideological movements.

In the two decades since the publication of our last anthology two trends have characterised approaches to the concept of gender in political studies. On the one hand, feminist scholars in many fields including international studies, development studies, political economy, comparative political studies and social policy have made the political interests of gender central to their research and stressed the importance of gender to the study of topics such as the impact of new media and new technologies on gender relations; rights and citizenship; the restructuring of gendered roles, identities and relationships in different social contexts; political representation and governance; individual, family and household welfare; sexual trafficking; and the gendered dynamics of militarisation (Vishvanathan 1997; Walby 1997, 1999; Sassen 1998; Sainsbury 1999; Freeman 2000; Marchand and Sisson Runyan 2000; Green and Adam 2001; Kelly *et al*. 2001; Shade 2002; Ehrenreich and Hochschild 2003; Rai 2003; Banaszak *et al*. 2003; Lister 2003; Daly and Rake 2003; Enloe 2004, 2000). On the other hand, many of the most frequently cited texts of feminist theory, particularly those influenced by post-structuralism, have 'deconstructed' both the concept of 'gender' and the concept of 'interests' and urged researchers to discard one or both as 'essentialist'.[2]

Since the 1990s in particular, implicit tensions between these two approaches – the one strategically centring gender in social and political analysis and the other deconstructing gender – have become more explicit and pronounced. In our judgment, we have reached an impasse in the project of feminist political theory: the contention that the concept of gender is essential both to the adequate theorisation of politics and efforts to achieve a more egalitarian transformation of global power systems stands at odds with both the claim that gender is a suspect category and the argument that a more radical democratic project demands the overthrow of gender theory itself. Also, the claim that a sustainable democratic project on the local, national, regional, or global levels can be better articulated, investigated, and defended *with* an elaborated feminist interest theory stands against the rejection of the concept of 'interests' and interest theory.

This impasse constitutes a 'crisis' within contemporary feminist theory. While we borrow Butler and Scott's terminology of crisis (Butler and Scott 1992: xiii), we distinguish our meaning from theirs. Butler and Scott argued that the 'radical contestation' and destabilisation of fundamental concepts of feminist analysis, such as 'women', 'experience', 'subject', 'agency', etc. generated a productive 'crisis' in feminist theory (1992: xiv). Although 'all fundamental conceptualizations of self, other, world are contestable . . . such conceptualizations are nevertheless necessary or unavoidable for an adequately reflective ethical and political life' (White 2000: 8). Even though we agree that debates about the meaning of these concepts have been valuable, we contend that the crisis engendered by the current impasse in feminist theory is of a different order.

This crisis is not primarily about how to *think about what we can know* about gender, identity, or representation in the epistemological/linguistic sense. It is about how to *think about what we can do* about gender, identity, or representation in the ethical/political sense (Zerilli 1998). In other words, the contemporary crisis in feminist theory concerns how to think critically about conflicting action claims. Without both a historically and institutionally specific account of the 'workings of power' (Butler 1995: 137) and a substantive account of democratic projects and norms it becomes difficult to think, talk, and make judgments about broad strategies of collective and individual engagement and action.

What motivates us to assemble this anthology is to provide an account of the political interests of gender in theoretically coherent ways that push past this impasse and bridge the gap between discursive (post-structuralist, semiotic, philosophical, etc.) and socio-materialist accounts of gender relations and politics. How shall we conceptualise the key categories framing this project – 'the political', 'interests', and 'gender'? Before proceeding to a substantive account of these concepts we must first distinguish between levels of analysis at which to articulate such concepts.

Between meta-theoretical premises about these concepts and empirical studies of their operation of power 'on the ground' exists a rich array of social theories and methods. Figure 1.1 illustrates these distinctions.

At the meta-theoretical level, we locate fundamental philosophical premises about the nature of human existence (ontology), knowledge (epistemology) and methodological principles (methodology). At this level, theory postulates broad claims about social reality, historical change and human nature, as well as claims about what we can know and how. Using the concept of 'research tradition' derived from the work of Larry Laudan we can distinguish among meta-theoretical claims by viewing each set of claims as 'a set of general assumptions made about the *ontological* entities and processes in a domain of study, and about appropriate methods [and epistemological criteria] to be used for investigating the problems and constructing the theories in that domain' (Laudan 1977: 79).

Research traditions – such as historical materialism/realism, positivism, hermeneutics, semiotics, post-structuralism and post-humanism – provide a 'set of guidelines for the development of specific theories belonging to

**Figure 1.1** Levels of analysis

| Philosophy of science | Research traditions<br><br>• Ontological assumptions<br>• Methodological principles<br>• Epistemological criteria |
|---|---|
| Empirical sciences | Specific theories<br><br>• Basic<br>• Middle range |
| | Empirical studies |

that tradition'. Yet, such philosophical assumptions are 'neither explanatory or predictive, nor directly testable' (Laudan 1977: 81–2). Instead, they are postulates from which specific theories, both abstract and concrete, can be elaborated and tested empirically. By 'empirical' we mean the full range of data collected through a variety of methods, including discourse analysis, and distinguish it from the narrow use of the term in logical positivist research traditions.

Rather than constructing an epistemology- or exclusively 'method-driven' social theory, our approach calls for grounding theory in ways that better enable political engagement with the world 'by calling into question the institutional structures [and discourses] that generate the observable regularities of everyday society' (Shapiro and Wendt 1992: 213, 218). We consider this approach 'realist' because it 'tolerates the persistent epistemic uncertainty' that developing social science and social theory as question- rather than method-driven entails (Shapiro and Wendt 1992: 217). In other words, it is 'realist' in the sense that it refuses to ground social and political theory in a set of epistemological premises or constraining philosophical principles that either unduly limit social inquiry to the elucidation of the meaning of actions or automatically reject efforts to identify and explain social contingencies.

'Realism' is a term in wide use with controversial connotations in several fields. We consider realism to be a main research tradition, distinguishable from both logical positivism or empiricism and hermeneutics (or the interpretive tradition, which can include post-structuralism as one among a variety of ways to articulate meaning). Our conceptualisation of realism bears little resemblance to the caricature of 'realist theories' represented in some post-structuralist constructions of modernist thought. In other words, by defending a realist paradigm we do not suggest that researchers gain unmediated access to a world, or that 'facts' present themselves as transparencies. We accept the principle that all knowledge is mediated by, among other things, philosophical presupposi- tions, language, or varying social, cultural, and historical circumstances and remains subject to interpretation. Yet, to say that social inquiry is 'theory-laden does not mean that it need be theory-driven' (Shapiro and Wendt 1992: 198; Jónasdóttir 1994: ch. 1).[3]

At the outset we referred to the term 'globalisation'. Globalisation serves as the contemporary political horizon in the case studies and comparative political studies collected in this anthology. In order to iden- tify, explain, and assess the impact of globalised forces and social rela- tions on the possibilities for feminist democratic politics we need to sustain different levels of analysis in research about the political interests of gender in different contexts. The essays in this collection aim to model theoretical and empirical work that can elaborate, in detail, which par- ticular structures and dynamics create and sustain 'networks of power/ discourse' in which processes of linguistic 'resignification' *and* political representation and decision-making always occur. The first five chapters of the book provide a theoretical framework for the analysis of the key concepts anchoring this collection, while the following eight chapters shed light on one or more of these concepts through concrete case studies. Taken together, these studies document a variety of political responses to the changed context and shape of politics which globalisation signals.

## Politics and the political

Our conceptualisation of politics and the political links structural analy- sis of social relationships, activities and institutions to critical attention to narrative or discursive practices. Fundamental to such analysis is the con- ceptual or analytical distinction between discourse and social structure, and between linguistic resignification and political change, a distinction that resists reducing one to an epiphenomenon or mere by-product of the other.

To claim that 'discourse', as a system of meanings, 'constitutes' institu- tions or social structures in no way contradicts the materiality or relative durability and persistence of those institutions and structures. As Nicos Mouzelis (1988) noted in a critical review of Laclau and Mouffe's (1985) *Hegemony and Socialist Strategy* 'all institutional arrangements . . . are discursively constructed. But *there is absolutely no reason why one should link discursive construction with fragility and precariousness* – labelling any reference to institutional durability as essentialist. For the core institutions of a social formation often display such a resilience and continuity that their overall, extremely slow, transformation can be seen only in the very *longue duré*, needing to be assessed in terms of centuries rather than years or shorter timespans' (113–14). In fact, the claim that discourse constitutes institutions and structures begs the questions of why and how particular meanings constitute specific structures in particular ways. At the same time, to argue that social institutions and relations shape discourse is not to deny the materiality of discourse. Discursive representations of gender can persist and continue to shape social relations and structure social activities.

Chapter 2 provides an account of the relationship between critical epistemology and social theory and offers a way past the impasse in the further development of feminist political theory, which we identified in this introduction. In particular, this chapter offers a close, detailed reading and critique of the idea of 'the political' in post-structuralist theory. First, we trace the outlines of the shift in direction in feminist political theory toward the 'linguistic turn' or what Scott (1988) called the 'shift to literary paradigms among social scientists' (41). Next, we identify several distinguishing criteria or themes in post-structuralist social theory – the critique of meta-narratives, the critique of essentialism, the critique of the unitary, autonomous subject, and the critique of generalised norms – and assess the impact of these defining criteria on conceptualisations of politics, interests and gender in feminist theory. Finally, the chapter offers a way beyond the impasse in its articulation of the outlines of a critical feminist-realist theory of politics.

As we suggest in chapter 2, a *critical feminist-realist theory of politics* provides an explanatory, yet non-deterministic account of social structures and power relations, and understands such structures and relations as the conditioning situations enabling and constraining political action. This approach tries to answer feminist questions about different social conditions and politics with both empirical research, using multiple methods of investigation, and interpretive analyses. It brings identification of social structures and institutions of power together with elucidation of the norms and rules of language or discourse, explaining how these norms and rules shape and are shaped by specific social structures and relationships ordering social life, and yet are subject to change.

But what are feminist questions? In the wake of the epistemological emphasis on the 'instability' of categories such as 'women', 'gender' and 'feminism' one might hesitate to say that the most basic question feminists ask is 'why, in just about all societies, are women disadvantaged, politically,

socially, [sexually], and economically relative to men?' And, more concretely, do 'hierarchical gendered structures of inequality' support the
unequal distribution of prosperity in the global capitalist system (Tickner
2005: 6)? Naturally such questions beg others: What are the criteria for and
indicators of 'disadvantage'? What are the criteria for and indicators of
'hierarchical structures'? Are women the only ones disadvantaged by hierarchical gendered structures of inequality?

Two chapters in this collection approach some of these questions
through the lens of policy analysis, broadly defined. Exploring the relationship between gender and monetary policy in the European region,
Brigitte Young (chapter 12) shows how certain macroeconomic strategies
perpetuate gender systems and suggests strategies that might more effectively work toward achieving egalitarian goals. Stressing 'the active role of
institutions in creating systems of beliefs and norms' she advocates a 'constructivist approach' to understanding 'how the European Monetary
Union is involved in constructing identities and interests of member states
and groups within them'. She specifically connects analysis of 'the discursive construction of globalisation and European integration' with assessment of 'the effects of the EMU's monetary policy on the creation of new
norms and systems of beliefs . . . more commensurate with neoliberal
practice and discourse' to identify what could be called the 'social relations' implicit in EMU macroeconomic policy. Then, she uses this linkage
to consider how to make integrated monetary policy in the EU compatible with the goals of gender equality.

Gillian Youngs (chapter 13) provides an assessment of shifts in
Amnesty International's strategy regarding violence against women,
examining its expansion of definitions of public violence to include the
state's failure to protect women from violence even in the 'private' sphere
as a breach of women's human rights. She demonstrates how gender is a
complex system of social relations of power institutionalised in civil
society and the state, linking the domains of public and private. Her analysis of transnational efforts to broaden definitions of human rights to
include violence against women in the so-called private sphere as state-
supported structural violence raises important questions about the adequacy of state-based political strategies for redressing inequality without
rejecting the state as a critical arena of change.

A theoretical analysis of democratic politics must account both for the
potential for democratisation and identify the specific social forces and
relations operating in historically concrete structures and institutions,
which enable and constrain movements for democratic change. As the
essays in this collection demonstrate, researchers can use a variety of theoretical approaches to differentiate analytically yet map connections

between social institutions of power and discourses. These allow us to consider both the concrete ways that discourses shape and are shaped by how individuals and groups are 'named' and rename themselves, and how different individuals and groups articulate material/practical programmes of social transformation aimed at, among other things, feminist democratic goals.

In this anthology, two chapters on very different subjects illustrate different approaches to the politics of democratisation. In chapter 7, Ingrid Pincus turns her attention to a study of the factors blocking the implementation of gender equality policy in Sweden. Through a detailed study of the administration of equality policy in Sweden, she demonstrates how such policy challenges a division of power between men and women and, in turn, leads to its opposition among men tasked with the job of implementing it. 'The implementation of gender equality policy is not only about focusing the norms, structures and practices in these organisations – the aim of this policy is to change them – to the advantage of women.' Given this strategic goal – to alter the balance of power in organisational norms, structures, and practices – Pincus documents how men, who are expected to change a system that would disempower men, create barriers to such change.

In 'Pragmatism, Feminism, and the Linguistic Turn', published in the mid-1990s, Nancy Fraser (1995) noted that 'one of the most important – and most difficult – tasks for feminist theorising is to connect discursive analyses of gender signification with structural analyses of institutions and political economy' (160). Shifting to the terrain of contemporary US politics, Jones and Dunlap (chapter 9) illustrate another way to 'link historical, systemic analysis with critical analysis of discursive processes' (Jónasdóttir and Jones). Through a case study of the discursive and institutional parameters of protest politics within the context of the 1996 Republican National Convention (RNC) in San Diego, California, the authors analyse queer politics as 'a complex, multiple set of practices of political resistance . . . mobilized before, in, and around the site of the RNC, as well as the strategic challenges to traditional practices of politics . . . represented by the efforts of different marginalized groups to gain access to public space'. Distinguishing between queer as an identity category and as a political category they argue that 'Queer citizenship confounds citizenship's national, sexual, racial, gendered, and class parameters in the name of a different citizenship. This different citizenship has as its purpose the building of a different kind of democratic community that would be genuinely constitutive of the plurality, and hence, the "queerness", of the concerns raised by new social movements.'

## Interests

By the concept of 'interests' we do not intend to signal that feminist political theory represents only another version of 'interest group liberalism'. Yet, we do not dismiss the political significance of interest group activities for changing the structure and substance of gender power. After all, the lobbying efforts of so-called marginalised groups have led to key policy gains and important changes in the law in the arenas of work, sexuality, literacy, reproduction, and political rights at the local, national and international level.

As Jónasdóttir has argued elsewhere, the concept of interests has both a 'formal' and a 'content' dimension, both of which are taken up in different ways in several chapters in this collection (Åberg, Jones and Dunlap, Ferguson, Pincus, Schreiber, Tripp). Its formal dimension connects most directly to the concept of political agency, which goes beyond the legal right to access, while its content aspect refers to agency's aims. The struggle for formal presence, or the right of members of an excluded group to be included among the participating and influencing members of a political community, has been a significant part of the history of democratic politics, of which feminism is a part. Formal representation of those who had been excluded from decision-making not only included *more* groups in the democratic process, but also challenged the substantive content and formal aspects of politics itself.

Women and men have had historically distinctive experiences and situations of living, been represented among 'different activities, [worked] with different things, [had] different responsibilities, [been] involved with people in different ways' (Jónasdóttir 1988: 43). Consequently, their demand for political standing, or group representation, has signalled, at least in part, the demand for recognition that gender matters to how we define the ends or purposes of public life. In this respect, the formal and the substantive, or content, aspects of the category of interests remain interconnected. At the same time, evidence from even the most 'women-friendly' states shows that women's struggle for what Jónasdóttir calls 'controlling presence' is even harder to win than the 'simple' right to access.[4]

Taking up the question of interests specifically in connection with the politics of empowerment in development studies, Ferguson (chapter 4) provides a concrete illustration of the usefulness of the concept of interest as what we might call a bridging concept between politics and gender. Using a post-structuralist critique 'as a way to open the conceptual and political space for interpretations of empowerment and other relevant concepts (e.g. needs, interests and rights) from a feminist materialist perspective' her chapter demonstrates concretely how these theoretical paradigms can be combined usefully and applied fruitfully in the study of political interests.

Ronnee Schreiber (chapter 10) clarifies the distinction between formal and substantive interests in her analysis of conservative women's politics. Literature on the politics of the women's movement 'frequently conflates *women's* activism and policy issues with *feminism* [and] fails to explain the behavior of conservative women'. Using two US conservative women's organizations – Concerned Women for America (CWA) and Independent Women's Forum (IWF) in her case study, Schreiber demonstrates that there is no automatic link between identity and ideology, or between women's formal interest in politics and their substantive political interests. 'Conservative women are changing public discourse about women's interests; indeed one of the main goals of the IWF is to transform debates about "women's" issues by offering the viewpoints of conservative women.' By problematising the category of 'women's interests' through a study of non-feminist women, Schreiber provides a critical perspective on the concept of gender and the complexities of the politics of women's interests.

Aili Tripp (chapter 11) examines specific conditions which have motivated women's mobilisation and definition of their political interests in several African states. She compares two markedly different phases in women's political mobilisation in sub-Saharan Africa, which have taken place during the post-independence period, and fleshes out what is distinctive about women's collective action compared 'with other interest groups' in the African political landscape. She explains some of the main changes constituting the shift from the 'old model' of mass women's organisations, more or less closely tied to single-party states and claiming to represent the interests of all women, to a second generation of women organising and networking autonomously across the continent 'on an unprecedented scale'. Thus the main characteristics of women's mobilisation since the mid-1980s are heterogeneity of organisations, autonomy from both the state and traditional political institutions, and a new emphasis on political strategies and political participation, with women deciding on their own agenda and how to form a distinctive political presence. What is so fruitful in Tripp's chapter is that she combines an aim to 'identify a set of commonalities shared by a growing number of women's movements in Africa' with a clear emphasis on the plurality of interests and the internal disagreements and debates within the various organisations and institutions.

## Gender

A key argument put forth in this anthology is that it is possible to explore the production of gender differences without assigning gender an ontological or 'naturalised' status. In fact, the 'naturalisation' of the unequal power and status of different socio-sexual groups makes the historically varying material production of socio-sexual inequalities invisible. This naturalisation is the result of a political process manifest in both civil society and the state (Watson-Franke, chapter 5 in this collection). We may want to resist making 'gender a "women's issue"', and avoid limiting 'feminist analysis to soliciting the "women's perspective"'. But if we want to identify and explain the particular social institutions and structures of power and privilege that sustain socially constituted differences it becomes incoherent to talk about feminist politics without at least conceptually 'positing "difference" as its basis' (Disch 1999: 546).

We doubt that 'difference' is *the* most fundamental category of feminist theory (Jónasdóttir 1994: 196–9; Jónasdóttir and von den Fehr 1998; Carlsson Wetterberg 1998). Yet, to assert as an imperative that feminist theorists make 'difference a target of [feminism's] critique of power' (Disch 1999: 546) collapses distinctions between levels of social analysis. In other words, it confuses the theoretical utility of 'gender difference' as a social category in political analyses of inequality (such as in research on differences between women's and men's economic opportunities) with assigning gender an ontological or 'naturalised' status (such as in claims made that women are inherently more peaceful than men).[5]

In her exploration of 'the point where gender analysis meets . . . public policy and everyday life' in Commonwealth Caribbean societies Eudine Barriteau (chapter 6) criticises what she calls 'the abuse of the concept' of gender. Not taking feminist scholarship on gender inequalities seriously, Caribbean public policy fails to comprehend fundamental differences in the living conditions of women and men. Policy-makers argue that any focus on women's situation specifically, or even on the social relations of women and men, is ideologically biased. Instead, utilising an abstract concept of gender (instead of women or social relations of gender) in theory as well as public policy debates has led to two clear results: the promotion of 'knowledge without power' and a privileged focus on men.

Building on the insights that 'gender is produced as a specific social system of structural difference or inequality', in chapter 3, Anna G. Jónasdóttir reconstructs Marx's methodology in feminist terms to provide an account of the social process of the production and appropriation of 'love power'. She argues that Marx's variant of historical materialism can 'serve feminist theory' and that feminist theory can also make a major contribution to the more general debate on Marx and the adequacy of his method. This chapter builds on the theory of gender offered in Chapter 2.

Several chapters in this anthology contribute directly and indirectly to analysis of how different social organisations of activities constitute gender as a social system of difference and, under particular conditions, sometimes a structural system of inequality. In chapter 5, Barbara Watson-Franke shows how nation-state formation altered, or attempted to alter, social relationships of ethnicity and gender extant in three matrilineal systems – the Asante from West Africa, the Mosuo from Southwest China and the Minangkabau from Indonesia. In her counter-examples of societies where the 'politics of birth' and kinship relations are not male dominated, she provides indirect evidence for Jónasdóttir's thesis that the appropriation of women's love power by men sustains gender inequities in formally equal state-based societies.

Berit Åberg's study of the Swedish police in a local district (chapter 8) provides a case study of the reproduction of gender divisions in a work setting, despite formal equality of opportunity. She explores the production of gender as a system of social relationships through an analysis of how women and men are produced as gendered workers in the police interacting with social and organisational gender power structures. Her study offers an important illustration of the linkage between discursive representations of gender and social-structural dimensions through a study of workplace power hierarchies. Using the concept of gender structure 'as *an historically variable system of gendered relations among gendered practices* which produce gender relationships in societies and in organisations under specific conditions' she shows 'how certain apparently neutral organisational conditions within the police, such as the bureaucratic nature of the organisation and its mode of the professionalisation, support . . .masculinised gender practices to a greater extent than feminised gender practices' leading to 'internal sex segregation.' Her analysis connects meanings and practices, representations and roles, to articulate how gender power is reproduced in police work in Sweden, despite conditions of formal gender equality.

Taken together, then, this anthology is intended to provide richly concrete illustrations of how to formulate feminist political questions and elaborate feminist political theory, engaging with many of the political 'interests' of gender to which feminism variously responds. While its opening five chapters examine different dimensions of what we call a *feminist critical realist theory of politics*, articulating a theory of gender and politics linking historical materialist analysis with discursive analysis, the following eight chapters attend to the specificity involved in applying this theory to study the construction and transformation of the political interests of gender in specific contexts.

## Notes

1 For an overview of various contributions to the globalisation debate and an assessment of different theoretical approaches to globalisation, see for instance Ian Bruff (2005).
2 There are of course important distinctions among social theories of sexuality and gender, such as sexual difference feminism (Braidotti, Gatens, Grosz, Kristeva), post-humanist feminism (Haraway), queerfeminism (Sedgwick) and post-colonial studies (Spivak), which we cannot explore in this essay. For instance, sexual difference feminism conceives 'difference' in relation to 'the symbolic', i.e., as a 'relationship to power, language, and meaning' (Kristeva) while at the same time adhering to the epistemological principle that sexual difference is an identifiable, politically necessary and strategically useful analytical category. (Grosz 1989; Spivak). A close reading of several post-structuralist theorists is a focus of chapter 2.
3 There seems to be a growing interest among feminist scholars for the realist research tradition. See, for instance, Alison Assiter (1996) and Leslie McCall (2005).
4 Calling attention to ways that women have struggled for political standing does not mean gender interests are synonymous with women's interests. Yet we do claim the theoretical utility of 'gender' as a social category in political analyses of inequality (such as in research on differences between women's and men's economic opportunities).
5 The collapse of distinctions is evident in Joan Scott's analysis of nineteenth-century French feminist activists, whom Scott takes to task for their 'mistaken' view that they felt 'a sense of common experience' or had articulated a 'shared vision' (Scott 1996: 14). Her assumption seems to be that these feminists assigned 'women' and 'interests' an ontologically singular status. On a different reading, such feminists worked to detach women's political status from any arguments about 'women's proper place' based on ontology. That they argued against women's exclusion from citizenship, for instance, by calling attention to 'sexual difference' may be epistemologically paradoxical but it is hardly politically naïve.

## References

Assiter, Alison. 1996. *Enlightened Women: Modernist Feminism in a Postmodern Age*. New York: Routledge.
Banaszak, Lee Ann, Karen Beckwith and Dieter Rucht (eds). 2003. *Women's Movements Facing the Reconfigured State*. Cambridge: Cambridge University Press.
Braidotti, Rosi. 1994. *Nomadic Subjects*. New York: Columbia University Press.
Bruff, Ian. 2005. 'Making Sense of the Globalisation Debate when Engaging in Political Economy Analysis', *British Journal of Politics and International Relations* 7 (2): 261–80.

Butler, Judith. 1995. 'For a Careful Reading', in Seyla Benhabib, Judith Butler, Drucilla Cornell and Nancy Fraser (eds). *Feminist Contentions: A Philosophical Exchange*, pp. 127–43. London: Routledge.

Butler, Judith and Joan W. Scott (eds). 1992. *Feminists Theorize the Political*. New York: Routledge.

Carlsson Wetterberg, Christina. 1998. 'Equal or Different? That's Not the Question: Women's Political Strategies in Historical Perspective', in Drude von der Fehr, Anna G. Jónasdóttir and Bente Rosenbeck (eds). *Is There a Nordic Feminism? Nordic Feminist Thought on Culture and Society*, pp. 21–43. Philadelphia, PA: UCL Press.

Daly, Mary and Katherine Rake. 2003. *Gender and the Welfare State: Care, Work, and Welfare in Europe and the USA*. Cambridge: Polity Press.

Disch, Lisa. 1999. 'Judith Butler and the Politics of the Performative', *Political Theory* 27 (4): 545–60.

Ehrenreich, Barbara and Arlie Russel Hochschild (eds). 2003. *Global Woman: Nannies, Maids, and Sex Workers in the New Economy*. New York: Metropolitan Books, Henry Holt and Company.

Enloe, Cynthia. 2000. *Maneuvers: The International Politics of Women's Lives*. Berkeley, CA: University of California Press.

Enloe, Cynthia. 2004. *The Curious Feminist: Searching for Women in a New Age of Empire*. Berkeley, CA: University of California Press.

Fraser, Nancy. 1995. 'Pragmatism, Feminism, and the Linguistic Turn', in Seyla Benhabib, Judith Butler, Drucilla Cornell and Nancy Fraser (eds). *Feminist Contentions: A Philosophical Exchange*, pp. 157–71. London: Routledge.

Freeman, Carla. 2000. *High Tech and High Heels in the Global Economy*. Durham, NC: Duke University Press.

Gatens, Moira. 1995. *Imaginary Bodies: Ethics, Power and Corporeality*. New York: Routledge.

Green, Eileen and Alison Adam (eds). 2001. *Virtual Gender: Technology, Consumption, and Identity*. New York: Routledge.

Grosz, Elizabeth. 1989. 'Sexual Difference and the Problem of Essentialism', *Inscriptions* 5: 86–101.

Grosz, Elizabeth. 1994. *Volatile Bodies: Toward a Corporeal Feminism (Theories of Representation and Difference)*. Bloomington, IN: Indiana University Press.

Haraway, Donna. 1991. *Simians, Cyborgs and Women: The Reinvention of Nature*. New York: Routledge.

Jónasdóttir, Anna G. 1988. 'On the Concept of Interests, Women's Interests, and the Limitations of Interest Theory', in Kathleen B. Jones and Anna G. Jónasdóttir (eds) *The Political Interests of Gender: Developing Theory and Research with a Feminist Face*, pp. 33–65. London: Sage Publications.

Jónasdóttir, Anna G. 1994. *Why Women Are Oppressed*. Philadelphia, PA: Temple University Press.

Jónasdóttir, Anna G. and von der Fehr, Drude. 1998. 'Introduction: Ambiguous times – contested spaces in the politics, organization and identities of gender', in Drude von der Fehr, Anna G. Jónasdóttir and Bente Rosenbeck (eds). *Is There a Nordic Feminism? Nordic Feminist Thought on Culture and Society*, pp. 1–18. Philadelphia, PA: UCL Press.

Jones, Kathleen B. and Anna G. Jónasdóttir (eds). 1988. *The Political Interests of Gender: Developing Theory and Research with a Feminist Face*. London: Sage Publications.

Kelly, Rita Mae, Jane H. Bayes, Mary E. Hawkesworth and Brigitte Young (eds). 2001. *Gender, Globalization and Democratization*. Oxford: Rowman & Littlefield.

Kristeva, Julia. 2002. *The Portable Kristeva*. New York: Columbia University Press.

Laclau, Ernesto and Chantal Mouffe. 1985. *Hegemony and Socialist Strategy: Towards a Radical Democratic Politics*. New York: Verso.

Laudan, Larry. 1977. *Progress and Its Problems: Towards a Theory of Scientific Growth*. Berkeley, CA: University of California Press.

Lister, Ruth (ed.). 2003. *Citizenship: Feminist Perspectives* (2nd edn). New York: New York University Press.

McCall, Leslie. 2005. 'The Complexity of Intersectionality', *Signs* 30 (3): 1771–1800.

Mackie, Vera. 2001. 'The Language of Globalisation: Transnationality and Feminism', *International Feminist Journal of Politics* 3 (2): 180–206.

Marchand, Marianne H. and Anne Sisson Runyan (eds). 2000. *Gender and Global Restructuring. Sightings, Sites and Resistances*. London: Routledge.

Mouzelis, Nicos. 1988. 'Marxism or Post-Marxism', *New Left Review* 167:113–14.

Naples and Desai (eds). 2002. *Women's Activism and Globalization: Linking Local Struggles and Transnational Politics*. New York: Routledge.

Rai, Shirin (ed.). 2003. *Mainstreaming Gender, Democratizing the State? Institutional Mechanisms for the Advancement of Women*. Manchester: Manchester University Press.

Rosenau, James N. 1990. *Turbulence in World Politics: A Theory of Change and Continuity*. London: Harvester Wheatsheaf.

Sainsbury, Diane (ed.). 1999. *Gender and Welfare State Regimes*. Oxford: Oxford University Press.

Sassen, Saskia. 1998. *Globalization and Its Discontents: Essays on the New Mobility of People and Money*. New York: New Press.

Sedgwick, Eve Kosofsky. 1990. *Epistemology of the Closet*. Berkeley, CA: University of California Press.

Scott, Joan W. 1988. *Gender and the Politics of History*. New York: Columbia University Press.

Scott, Joan W. 1996. *Only Paradoxes to Offer: French Feminists and the Rights of Man*. Cambridge, MA, and London: Harvard University Press.

Shade, Leslie Regan. 2002. *Gender and Community in the Social Construction of the Internet*. New York: P. Lang.

Shapiro, Ian and Alexander Wendt. 1992. 'The Difference that Realism Makes: Social Science and the Politics of Consent', *Politics and Society* 20 (2): 197–224.

Spivak, Gayatri. 1988. 'Can the Subaltern Speak?', in Cary Nelson and Lawrence Grossberg (eds). *Marxism and the Interpretation of Culture*, pp. 271–313. Urbana, IL: University of Illinois Press.

Tickner, J. Ann. 2005. 'What Is Your Research Program? Some Feminist Answers to International Relations Methodological Questions', *International Studies Quarterly* 49 (1): 1–22.

Vishvanathan, Nalini, Lynn Duggan, Laurie Nisonoff and Nan Wiegersma (eds). 1997. *The Women, Gender and Development Reader*. London: Zed Books.

Walby, Sylvia. 1997. *Gender Transformations*. London: Routledge.

Walby, Sylvia (ed.). 1999. *New Agendas for Women*. Basingstoke: Macmillan.

Walby, Sylvia. 2003. 'Modernities/Globalisation/Complexities'. Paper presented to conference of the British Sociological Association, University of York.

White, Stephen K. 2000. *Sustaining Affirmation: The Strengths of Weak Ontology in Political Theory*. Princeton, NJ: Princeton University Press.

Zerilli, Linda M. G. 1998. 'Doing Without Knowing: Feminism's Politics of the Ordinary', *Political Theory* 26 (4): 435–59.

# 2

# Out of epistemology: feminist theory in the 1980s and beyond

*Anna G. Jónasdóttir and Kathleen B. Jones*

This chapter establishes a case for reconstructing feminist theory in critical-realist terms. It does so by engaging with post-structuralist theory through a close reading of critical texts situated in the framework of the history of ideas, which shaped its emergence. Through this close reading of the works of three key theorists – Judith Butler, Chantal Mouffe and Joan W. Scott – we hope to demonstrate the limitations of post-structuralist theories of gender and politics and to make an argument for more robust, multi-dimensional approaches to analyses of the political interests of gender. By suggesting ways to build bridges between material-ist and discursive theoretical frameworks we intend to foster what Nina Lykke (2007) has called a 'productive feminist pluralism'.

We published *The Political Interests of Gender* in 1988, at the beginning of the post-structuralist 'linguistic turn' or paradigm shift in feminist theory. We were writing its introduction in January 1987, a month after Joan Scott's essay, 'Gender: A Useful Category of Historical Analysis', appeared in the *American Historical Review*. In this essay, Scott (1986: 1062) defined gender as a 'constitutive element of social relations based on perceived differences between the sexes, and . . . [as] a primary way of signifying relationships of power'. Her contention that politics con-structed and was constructed by gender stimulated a lively academic debate about the uses of post-structuralist analysis in feminist history and politics.[1]

We found the insights of this version of post-structuralist analysis valu-able to theoretical efforts to widen the scope of conceptual lenses used in political research so as to take in the full range of conventions and insti-tutions that constructed gender and politics (Scott 1991; 1988). Yet, as we worked toward developing a theoretical framework that retained the idea of sex/gender with some specificity, trying to 'preserve gender as an inde-pendent *analytic* category' marking an '*analytically* distinct set of social relationships' (Jones and Jónasdóttir 1988: 7, 9 emphasis added) the lin-guistic/culturalist turn that Scott and others launched in history and social and political theory began to seem like the main, if not the only, direction feminist theory should take.

Post-structuralist feminist theory,[2] and what Scott (1996: 16) called its 'technically deconstructive' method, contested basic (semantic) concepts of feminist analysis through an epistemological premise that argued against the capacity of any concept or analytic category to 'represent' the experience or identity it 'names'. In its strongest version, post-structuralist theory drew the implication that the use of gender as an analytic concept and the identification of women as a 'subject for whom political representation is pursued' are theoretical strategies at odds with the development of a more radically democratic feminist political project (Butler 1990: 1). Similarly, this strong version portrayed analyses of politics in terms of socially based interests and interest representation as outmoded, orthodox and unitary (Marxist) notions and rejected them (Laclau and Mouffe 1985: 55ff.) because they 'conjured up a subject . . . what we would now call an essentialist conception of women' (Scott 1996: 110). Instead, post-structuralists represented democracy as the process of discursive struggle over the making of political identities and subjectivities.

The predominance of a discursive interpretation of 'gender' and 'politics' emerged at a moment of 'great epistemological turmoil' which took the form of 'a shift to literary paradigms among social scientists', and continued a debate at least as old as Marx 'between those who assert[ed] the transparency of facts and those who insist[ed] that all reality is construed or constructed' (Scott 1988: 41). As the literary, constructivist model took greater hold, debates about causes and explanations of social phenomena shifted to debates about the meaning of events and behaviour (Zalewski 2000: 73). Also, analysis of how social structures and mechanisms of power produced patterns of dominance and deprivation were supplanted by descriptions of how discourse produced subjectivities.

Discourse analysis became a central concern not only in history, but, increasingly, in other fields of social inquiry, including politics. A key impact in political theory was the substitution of a postmodernist linguistic or discursive account of politics for what came to be regarded as a naively materialist, anachronistic, even 'virtually useless' (Gatens 1992: 120) modernist account of 'social structures, relations and practices' (Segal 1999: 13). To quote Scott, post-structuralism was:

> A profoundly new way of thinking about history . . . The story is no longer about the things that have happened to women and men and how they have reacted to them, instead it is about how the subjective and collective meanings of women and men as categories of identity have been constructed. (1988: 6)

The roots of the shift from explanation to debates about meaning can be traced to trends in philosophy and social theory converging with sweeping political and economic changes. These historical changes reached an apex in the events leading up to and following the fall of the Berlin wall and the fragmentation of the former Soviet bloc, on the one hand, and the predominance of market systems of production and structural adjustment trends in the global marketplace, on the other. Such sweeping changes were accompanied by an increase in ethnic conflict, population mobility and displacement, a widened gap between the rich and the poor, rapidly emerging and spreading new technologies, the rise of new fundamentalisms in both the economic North and South, as well as the widened scope of transnational claims of human rights. Such changes mark the historical context of the shift in direction, or epistemological turn, taken in social and political theory, whose outlines we trace in this chapter.

In the following, we offer a detailed account of the evolution of this shift and assess its impact in order to situate post-structuralist premises within the history of ideas, which shaped its emergence. We also analyse the fundamental principles framing poststructuralist analysis, examining the impact of their adoption in feminist theory. Both our efforts to situate post-structuralism and outline its basic tenets are motivated, in part, pedagogically. We expect that students new to feminist theory, or coming into the debates about gender *in medias res*, will find this critical review useful as a guide to the often unarticulated premises of post-structuralism.

At the same time, our critical assessment forms the horizon against which we contrast our meta-theoretical premises and social theoretical postulates for reconstructing a critical feminist-realist framework for the study of gender and politics. Through this critical contrast we illustrate how different research traditions to studies bring different dimensions of gender and politics into relief. On the basis of this critical, comparative analysis, in the final section of the chapter, we suggest a way to bridge these differences.

It is important to stress here that our intention is not to reject discursive approaches to studying gender and politics, but to demonstrate their partiality. Our outline of a *critical feminist-realist theory of politics* is an attempt to push past unproductive polarities and 'negotiate a path between always impure positions – seeing that politics is always/already bound up with what it contests (including theories) – and that theories are always implicated in various political struggles (whether this is acknowledged or not)' (Grosz 1989: 99).

Throughout this chapter, we engage closely with the work of three scholars in particular – Judith Butler, Joan Scott and Chantal Mouffe – because they have been most prominently associated with the circulation of post-structuralist paradigms in feminist political and social theory. Their work has been cited frequently, influencing significantly the shape of feminist analysis of and research on gender and political interests since the 1980s. All three also cite each other, work together, and confirm similarities on various points about what inspires them, what preoccupies them, and what they defend. For instance, in *Feminists Theorize the Political*, a book co-edited by Butler and Scott, Mouffe (1992: 383) connects her work to Scott and considers Scott's way of dealing with 'the dilemma of equality versus difference' as 'inspired by a similar *problématique*' to the one Mouffe herself is defending. She also quotes Butler's *Gender Trouble*, suggesting an answer to Butler's own question: 'What new shape of politics emerges when identity as a common ground no longer constrains the discourse of feminist politics?' For Mouffe, Butler's question opens 'the possibility of a project of radical and plural democracy' (381ff.). In her chapter in the same volume, Butler expresses affinity with Scott's work and also with Laclau and Mouffe's *Hegemony and Socialist Strategy* on the issue of subject formation and politics (Butler 1992: 14, 20). Finally, Scott (1992: 39) cites Butler's work positively in a note in her chapter, 'Experience'.

All three theorists self-consciously take on what Scott (1988: 3) calls 'a preoccupation with theory', aiming to 'generate new and productive directions' for how to understand, but 'not to *settle*', a number of questions about the highly contested term 'theory', questions which they list as important for feminist debate. In their co-edited volume, Butler and Scott (1992: xiiiff.) warn the reader that this is not the place to discover 'what "poststructuralism" is'. Rather, they contend that, in this book, 'the value of poststructuralist theories is confirmed or contested in particular contexts'. However, their refusal to treat post-structuralism as a theory or paradigm of research with identifiable premises and principles of analysis extends beyond this one publication. In a subsequent section of this chapter, we describe these premises and principles.

### The post-structuralist shift

We begin with a clarification of distinctions between terms often used interchangeably. *Postmodernism* can best be understood as a historical or 'epochal term for . . . the period which allegedly follows modernity' (Best and Kellner 1991: 2). As with all periodisation theories, there is no precise dating of the phenomenon of postmodernity. Best and Kellner date the term's earliest appearance to 1870, when 'John Watkins Chapman spoke of "postmodern painting" . . . to designate painting that was allegedly more modern and avant-garde than French impressionist painting', and note a somewhat later use of the term by Rudolf Pannwitz 'to describe the nihilism and collapse of values in contemporary European culture'. Before Lyotard's (1979) coinage of the 'postmodern condition', the term postmodern underwent 'uneven development within several theoretical fields', beginning with its usage in historical studies in the 1940s and 1950s, followed by its incursion into social and cultural analyses in the 1960s and 1970s, and, finally, wide proliferation in the 1980s (Best and Kellner 1991: 5–6).[3]

Postmodernity implied a break, or at least a discontinuity, with earlier, modern forms of social and political organisation, modes of philosophy, systems of value, technologies, and other broad cultural trends. Consequently, different critics attached negative social or positive cultural assessments to its significance. But, what is most relevant to our discussion is the observation that the 'positive cultural discourse and the proliferation of postmodern cultural forms helped prepare the way for the reception of the discourse of the postmodern in the 1980s' (Best and Kellner 1991: 1). The greater impact culturalist discourses of the postmodern had on later postmodern theory meant 'sociohistorical discourses [of the postmodern] . . . were rarely noted or discussed' (Best and Kellner 1991: 1; Anderson 1998; Eagleton 2000, 2003).

As we argue below, this attenuation of the connection between postmodernity and analysis of socioeconomic and political developments to which it was in part a response has shaped the conceptualisation of the political in postmodern theories largely into discursive and semantic forms. Yet, dynamic processes of socioeconomic, political and cultural integration *and* fragmentation have characterised the decades since the 1970s, raising questions about the adequacy of linguistic/cultural analyses of politics to explain these apparently contradictory phenomena, or their relevance to feminist theory and practice. In other words, does post-structuralist analysis help us understand dynamic global/local processes and resistances to them, such as structural adjustment, the flow of international finance capital, nation-state fragmentation, increased militarisation, the spread of fundamentalist ideologies, the revitalisation of ethnic nationalism, increasing population displacement and migration or the connections between these processes and resistances and gender paradigms? Does it help locate specific points of feminist intervention or strategies for change? Put differently, does post-structuralist theory explain why sex/gender matters to democracy (Jones 1993: 102–41; Jónasdóttir 1994: 177–203; Webster 2002: 191–203)?

The term *post-structuralism* refers to a particular mode of postmodern theorisation, which took the insights of earlier French structuralist theorists, such as Saussure, Lévi-Strauss, Lacan, and Barthes, about how language structured meaning through psycho-social and linguistic systems of rules and codes and applied these insights more widely and in ways that broke fully with traditional theories of linguistic representation. Structuralists had argued that the 'subject' was constituted in and through language, and that meaning was not an effect of a subject's intent, but an effect of a culturally constituted language or semiotic system. Yet, structuralists accepted a categorical distinction between signifier (word, name, for example, 'woman') and signified (object, thing, for example, 'sexed body') and held that the relationship between them was determinate and relatively durable. By contrast, post-structuralists, such as Derrida, pushed the implicit cultural contingency of the relationship between signified and signifier to its logical extreme, making the 'signified . . . only a moment in a never-ending process of signification where meaning is produced not in a stable, referential relation between subject and object, but only in the infinite, intertextual play of signifiers' (Best and Kellner 1991: 21). As Derrida put it:

> What I call 'text' implies all structures called 'real', 'economic', 'historical', socio-institutional, in short: all possible referents . . . There is nothing outside the text . . . [means that] all reality has the structure of a differential trace . . . One cannot refer to 'the real' except in an interpretive experience . . . [that] yields meaning . . . in a movement of differential referring. (1988: 148)

Consequently, the 'signified' refers not to 'things' pre-existing in the world outside the text. Instead the relationship 'signified–signifier' becomes a relationship ('differential referring') among signifiers within discourse ('intertextuality'), which produces an inherently unstable signified through endless interplay among signs. In this perspective, the signifier antecedes the signified (Fridolfsson 2006: 41).

Despite its repudiation of typologies as necessarily simplifying, we can identify several distinguishing epistemological and ontological premises of post-structuralist social theory: the *critique of grand or meta-narratives* (anti-foundationalism), the *critique of essentialism* (anti-representation, anti-identity), the *critique of the unitary, autonomous subject* and subject-centred theory (anti-intentionality, anti-coherence, anti-identity politics), and the *critique of generalised norms* (anti-universalism). We acknowledge that the following survey underplays critical differences among the works of such theorists as Bourdieu, Baudrillard, Debord, Derrida, Foucault, Lyotard, and others. Nonetheless, we defend this general sketch as a useful heuristic.

### Critique of grand or meta-narratives

A key motivation in the development of post-structuralism was its premise that any effort to build general-level social theory or universalistic explanations of history inevitably foundered on the shoals of its own unarticulated partiality. All 'grand theory' or meta-narratives of history were 'false universals', whose conceptual scaffolding was derived from exclusionary practices of representation. By 'exclusionary practices' of representation post-structuralists signalled the impossibility that any analytic category – such as class, gender, race, nationality, ability, etc – can delineate or 'represent' the complexity of all possible cases falling within the category's definition. Categories, post-structuralists contended, were inevitably partial, unstable, and specific to a cultural space and time. To give one example, Laclau and Mouffe (1985: 77) wrote 'We will now attempt to demonstrate that these three theses [of classical Marxist theory] are false'. In their place they articulated a theory of democratic hegemony that, despite its hegemony, they claimed was not intended to be 'universal' but permanently partial (Mouffe 1992: 377ff.).

Human experiences varied culturally in infinite ways; any short-hand categorisation of such experiences was a representational fiction created by excluding whatever did not fit a theoretical model (allegedly) presumed true regardless of whether evidence supported it. Consequently, post-structuralists judged any theory purporting a general explanation of, for instance, the operation of modes of production, institutions of domination, forms of oppression/exploitation, or structures of subordination, or proposing a general programme for their transformation, to be distorted, at best, or a form of neo-colonialism at worst.

As an example, we cite Judith Butler's criticism of such exclusionary practices in feminist theory. Butler writes that:

> The notion of a universal patriarchy has been widely criticized in recent years for its failure to account for the workings of gender oppression in the concrete cultural contexts in which it exists. Where those various contexts have been consulted within such theories, it has been to find 'examples' or 'illustrations' of a universal principle that is assumed from the start. That form of feminist theorizing has come under criticism for its efforts to colonize and appropriate non-Western cultures to support highly Western notions of oppression. (1990: 3)

One of the strengths of post-structuralism has been to call into question the capacity of modern epistemic frameworks or knowledge systems to 'provide an adequate representation of things' (Benhabib 1990: 110). The resultant emphasis on the power of language or discourse as systems of meaning to produce and legitimate ways of being in the world, and even our understanding of 'world' itself, has contributed importantly to research on subjectivity. Yet, besides disclaiming the capacity of language to 'represent' the world, or ever fully describe what it names, post-structuralism extended its criticism to reject any ground or analytical 'foundation' other than the ever-shifting ground of power itself on which to rest knowledge claims, political judgments, or political theories.

Post-structuralists judged all 'grand theories' or meta-narratives negatively, including humanism, Marxism and any version of feminism that traced its roots to these traditions, for having written stories that followed a linear, univocal, progressive line, organising history into a systematic and coherent narrative and overlooking ruptures, breaks and exceptional cases which would have troubled its theory. As a result, efforts to identify 'oppressive' gender regimes and articulate criteria with which to evaluate gender systems in relation to feminist politics were stultified.

Not all post-structuralists adhered to the strongest version of this rejection of modernist 'truths'. Craig Calhoun (1993: 80) noted that some post-structuralists stressed how modernism's monological and rationalist universalism created 'truths' that 'were in some combination misleading, false and/or repressive'. By contrast, others, such as Michel Foucault, offered accounts of suppressed knowledges and silenced voices to reveal hidden 'tensions within seeming truths' in modernism, showing both how specific institutional and social forces constructed 'accepted truths, as well as the constant tendency of those truths to break down and reveal their internal inconsistencies and aporias' (Calhoun 1993: 80).

Interestingly, this version of the post-structuralist story, which stressed that tensions within stated truths 'derived not simply from textuality, but from interpersonal [social] struggles and fields of power' (Calhoun 1993: 80) converged to an extent with Marxist materialist methodology, as in Marx's analysis of social relations in the 'hidden abode of production' and the 'fetishism of commodities', or his claim that 'the ruling ideas of any age are the ideas of the ruling class'. It also shared a family resemblance with some feminist critiques, such as feminist criticism of the 'false universalism' of patriarchal representations of gender. Yet, such convergences largely remained unacknowledged. Ironically, post-structuralists portrayed modernity and modernist movements in ways that 'flattened out' the internal diversity, complexity and tensions within the modern tradition and its contemporary political heirs.

The more post-structuralists treated 'all aspects of culture and human action as texts', the more invisible social relations and institutions of power became in their accounts (Calhoun 1993: 80). Finally, the summary dismissal by Ernesto Laclau and Chantal Mouffe of Marxism as a deterministic and essentialist account of the democratic project, and their criticism of Foucault for maintaining analytic distinctions between the discursive and non-discursive, evacuated social relations into intertextuality even more completely (Laclau and Mouffe 1985: 107).

## Critique of essentialism

In 1985, Laclau and Mouffe published *Hegemony and Socialist Strategy* as a defence of radical and plural democracy, claiming to salvage the socialist tradition from essentialism and what they argued was the economic determinism of Marxism. At its core, they argued, Marxism was monistic, deterministic and essentialist, meaning Marxism adhered to an overly simplified view of history and social change, which gave primacy to the economic and failed as an account of social action or agency. By making the economy, or mode of production, determinant, they contended, Marxism reduced political and social complexities and social relations to the unvarying and automatic side effects of the development of economic or productive forces.[4]

The specific target of Laclau and Mouffe's critique was 'orthodox Marxism' which, they claimed, conceptualised the representation of the interests of the working class as the task of an authoritarian (Leninist) revolutionary party identifying the 'objective', 'real' or 'historical' interests of classes as socially constituted and identifiable in advance of any political struggle. This model of democratic socialism had been criticised by political theorists and social scientists long in advance of Laclau and Mouffe's intervention. Yet, their work made an important contribution to the debate about radical democracy by opening theoretical room for new social movements besides the traditional working class. In place of what they saw as a deterministic and working-class-based model of Marxist socialism, Laclau and Mouffe (1985: 153) defended a radical, plural model of democracy in which contingent, open and malleable 'discursive practices' 'produce' fluid, plural political identities or 'subject positions' whose articulation forms and reforms social relations. In their view, politics was best understood in general as the 'practice of creation, reproduction, and transformation of social relations'.

The implication of their argument, taken up by their followers, has been that understanding political activities in terms of socially or politically grounded interests, in contrast with discursively produced political identities/subjectivities, can only lead to an approach to political representation in the form of one or another of the 'essentialist paradigms' or authoritarian models with which Laclau and Mouffe set out to make a 'radical break' (77). Instead, the claim is made that the politics of radical democracy should signal 'articulatory practices' or the proliferation and rearticulation of new subject positions and new political signifiers identified with the multiple rallying points of new social movements demanding inclusion in a political community. Yet, if inclusion in the political community is the democratic goal, Laclau and Mouffe's theory of democracy lacked any structural components or determinants, distinguishing institutions, determinant agendas, or representative organisations. To put it differently, politics was everywhere and any moment of political intervention in the name of radical democracy appeared equal in impact to any other.

Although Laclau and Mouffe gave credibility to the radical potential of new social movements to proliferate new arenas, modes and strategies of democratic action, two further points deserve mention. First, in *Hegemony and Socialist Strategy* there is curiously little mention of feminist theorists' reconceptualisations of the political or of feminist revisions of Marxist theory. Yet, from the publication of Juliet Mitchell's *Woman's Estate* in the late 1960s through the extensive discussions of dual systems theory and beyond, a rich literature existed, which attempted to articulate a social theory of politics in the gap left by more orthodox Marxist interpretations (Jónasdóttir 1994; Jones 1988). Laclau and Mouffe's silence about this vast literature had the unintended consequence of ignoring how new social movements self-consciously defined their actions as struggles within a particular institutional context to control economic and social resources and transform social relations of production and reproduction. Second, Laclau and Mouffe's identification of Marxism with essentialism helped lay the theoretical foundation for further bracketing any institutionally grounded theory of politics. Subsequently, the dominant criticism of efforts to situate action in a context, as opposed to reading action as a text, was that such efforts reduced, reified or fixed the durability of institutions, instead of (properly) reading institutions as the mobile and mutable effects of discursive practices.

The result has been to eclipse social analysis of structures and institutions in political theory, including not only analyses of the market and the state, but also of kinship and family, social relations of intimacy, and other social networks of interaction, in favor of discursive analysis of texts, where 'texts' implies an inherent openness in 'structures'. This eclipse has had significant consequences for feminist political theory. By the time the charge of essentialism was transported to feminist theory, the imperative to treat as inherently suspicious all efforts to theorise gender as a specific system of social relations and material conditions, including embodiment, seemed unimpeachable.

### Critique of the unitary, autonomous subject

In his studies of the development of modern penal systems, scientific discourse, the history of sexuality, and ideas about madness, Foucault showed how systems of knowledge 'produced' subjects in particular ways. Using Foucault's theories about the dispersal, mobility and ubiquity of power and his analysis of how discourse produced subjects, post-structuralists expanded on these notions to develop a critique of 'the subject'. In place of unitary subjects they put 'subjectivities' defined as plural, shifting 'subject positions' constituted through the operation of regulatory regimes or networks of power/knowledge (unspecified except in Foucault's case), whose productive effects belied the idea that there was 'a doer behind the deed' (Butler 1990: 25). As Butler stated:

> Whereas the question of what constitutes 'personal identity' within philo-sophical accounts almost always centers on the question of what internal feature of the person establishes the continuity or self-identity of the person through time, the question here will be: To what extent do regulatory prac-tices of gender formation and division constitute identity, the internal coherence of the subject, indeed, the self-identical status of the person? To what extent is 'identity' a normative ideal rather than a descriptive feature of experience? (1990: 16)

By isolating the general process of subject formation in the 'regulatory practices of gender formation and division' post-structuralists, such as Butler, contributed importantly to earlier feminist analysis of how gender identity is constituted, sustained and subverted through a particular inter-polation of the 'sexed body'. Yet, carried to its logical extreme, some post-structuralists argued that since identity could not be defined outside of discourse without 'disavow[ing the definition's] own cultural location', any effort to 'fix' identity, including in liberatory theoretical paradigms repre-senting the political struggles of specific excluded groups, unnecessarily limited the subversive parameters of agency. This thesis led Butler (1990: 147), for instance, to locate agency *immanently* in discourse, that is, in the 'signifying practices that establish, regulate, and deregulate identity'.

To give another example, in her analysis of the history of French femin-ism Scott (1996: 3) wrote that 'In the age of democratic revolutions, "women" came into being as political outsiders through the *discourse* [italics added] of sexual difference' and 'the contradictions in the political *discourses* [italics added] [of individualism, individual rights, and social obligations] produced feminism'. Here it appears that the 'agency' of participants in social movements has been transposed to discourse (Varikas 1995: 97).

Some post-structuralists denied that making subjectivity into an effect of discourse, rather than its pre-existent 'ground' eviscerated the idea of agency (Butler 2004). Yet, most post-structuralist theories of subjectivity tended to treat political agency and political efficacy not as attributes or practices of subjects or actors, but as activities immanent in language, in discourse. In this view, the potential for another reality to exist different from the status quo is intrinsic to signification itself; possibility is 'always already' present in the excess of meaning, the *supplément*, to use Derrida's term, which words, terms or concepts try to contain by 'fixing' meaning. To quote Butler:

> The political efficacy of the signifier does not consist in its representational capacity, the term [such as 'women' or 'democracy'] neither represents nor expresses some already existing subjects or their interests. The signifier's efficacy is confirmed by its capacity to structure and constitute the political field, to create new subject-positions and new interests. (1993: 210)

Thus, in the discourse of post-structuralism, signifiers have efficacy; they structure, institute, constitute, sustain and subvert, in other words, they 'act'.

Does this amount to linguistic determinism? When pushed on this point, Butler responds with the claim that such a criticism is a symptom of being 'seduced by grammar':

> How can there be an activity, a constructing, without presupposing an agent who precedes and performs that activity? . . . It takes a certain suspicion toward grammar to reconceive the matter in a different light . . . The 'activity' of . . . engendering cannot, strictly speaking, be a human act or expression, a willful appropriation . . . it is the matrix through which all willing first becomes possible, its enabling cultural condition. In this sense, the matrix of gender relations is prior to the emergence of the 'human'. (Butler 1993: 6–7)

Yet even if this 'matrix of relations' is prior to the emergence of the human individual, how do we account for it historically or explain its relative persistence? Although this lack of explanation may not be problematic for ontology, it remains problematic as a principle on which to develop social and political theory that explains the persistence or change in the 'matrix of relations' as something more than an automatic by-product of discourse. Such a privileging of discourse sees it as a system of meaning that exercises 'a priori control inaccessible to the deliberate interventions of individuals. A system whose omnipotence and ubiquity mean that interventions – the intentions and plans – of speaking subjects are . . . of secondary importance' (Varikas 1995: 96).

Related to this post-structuralist critique of the autonomy of the subject is the assertion that subjectivity is always plural, fluid, incoherent and dissident. Consequently, post-structuralists argue that any effort to name subjectivity in terms of some identity marker – to identify subjectivity's constitutive features as if they were separable from one another – will necessarily exclude other dimensions of identity equally related to a subject's becoming *this* subject.

The importance of this critique is its recognition of the multiple determinants shaping subjectivity, which make even persons sharing a common background unique as individuals. At the same time, this strength can become a weakness from the perspective of social and political theory.

Laclau and Mouffe, for instance, define 'plurality' as a logically given point of departure for their analysis and a necessary pre-condition on the road to socialism, which they redefine as the hegemony of 'democratic practice'. In their view, no element for representing the social/political plurality of 'articulatory practices' (such as class, race/ethnicity, gender, sexuality etc.) of subjectivity should be seen as more theoretically significant than any other. Yet, emptied of specificity, it becomes difficult to understand to what any of these elements refer in particular and equally difficult to identify the specific systems of power that constitute them.

This lack of specificity is the result of confusion between levels of analysis. When post-structuralists postulate that discourse produces subjectivity, they state an ontological premise that they also treat as an epistemological premise: Discourse produces subjectivity; we know subjectivity by apprehending its meaning in discourse. Yet, the premise 'discourse produces subjectivity' cannot directly provide an explanation at the level of basic or middle-range social theory about how any specific discourse produces any particular set of meanings.

For example, to postulate that heterosexist discourses of sex/desire[5] produce heterosexuality as normative (hetero-normativity) through representations that vilify and reject (make abject) homoerotic sex/desire provides neither an epistemology of sexuality nor a specific account of the production of sexuality as such. In other words, this theory stipulates discourse produces sex/desire but does not explain what constitutes sex/desire as a conceptually distinguishable element of social being. To account for sex/desire as such, we need both a set of ontological and epistemological assumptions and a specific theory with which to distinguish sex/desire from other aspects of social being. We also need a specific theory to explain what particular activities and historical conditions generate its production and transformation. As Jónasdóttir (1994: 33–4) stated, 'if the purpose of theory is to describe and explain sex/gender-specific oppression . . . as the oppression women suffer as women' then 'women and men must be conceptualised as sex/gender groups (and not as groups determined by class, race, or something else)'. Ontological premises about desire can provide neither an account of sex/desire per se nor an explanation of its historical production and transformation.

### Critique of generalised norms

If subjectivity is produced discursively, and is plural and position-dependent, then, in post-structuralist terms, it followed that any evaluation of what constituted transformed, alternative or more progressive subjectivities should proceed on a non-normative basis or, at best, in terms of local and conditional norms. The celebration of local knowledges over universalistic criteria led to legitimation of localised normative criteria for evaluating the regulatory effects of discursive practices.

By contrast, universalist norms were considered to be necessarily exclusionary and even potentially imperialist. As Butler put it:

> Insistence upon the coherence and unity of the category of women has effectively refused the multiplicity of cultural, social, and political intersections in which the concrete array of 'women' are constructed . . . The anti-foundationalist approach to coalitional politics assumes neither that 'identity' is a premise nor that the shape or meaning of a coalitional assemblage can be known prior to its achievement. (1990: 15)

The one norm that escapes this critique is the imperative to transform or expand 'existing identity concepts as a normative goal' (Butler 1990: 15). Yet even if we agree with this goal, the criteria by which we should judge 'identity' concepts to further democratic ends or not remain unarticulated, unless one assumes that democracy refers to plurality only in the numerical sense of 'more', setting aside any attention to the content of the 'more' (White 2000: 89–95).

Here, Mouffe parts company with Butler, asserting that she does not agree with:

> Those forms of multiculturalism which defend legal pluralism – that is, which would allow different juridical-political systems to co-exist within one political association. A society cannot allow antagonistic principles of legitimation to coexist in its midst. There must be, at the political level, some agreement – a consensus – about which ethico-political principles are going to be the basis of shared life. (2001/2: 2)

In a liberal democratic society, she contends, those principles are 'liberty and equality for all'. Yet, Mouffe does not address how agreement on such principles is to be reached.

The radical critique of the premises of humanist philosophy, especially Marxist versions, led post-structuralists to shift attention from social theories of democracy, which included normative assessments of institutional arrangements and articulation of egalitarian political policies and programs, to an ontology of democracy. The essence of democracy was defined as the proliferation of subjectivities resulting automatically from alternative 'articulatory practices' and subversive 'resignification' of the terms of dominant discourses of power. As Laclau and Mouffe argued:

> What has been exploded is the idea and the reality itself of a unique space of constitution of the political . . . What we are witnessing is a politicization

far more radical than any we have known in the past . . . a proliferation of radically new and different political spaces. We are confronted with the emergence of *a plurality of subjects*, whose forms of constitution and diversity it is only possible to think if we relinquish the category of 'subject' as a unified and unifying essence. (1985: 181)

This insight was consistent with earlier feminist analyses of politics which expanded the 'space' of the political to include challenges to gender power in the arenas of domesticity, intimacy, media and the arts, to name but a few of the ways that feminists understood the phrase 'the personal is political'. New social movements, such as the women's movement and the civil rights movement, already had championed the development of a comprehensive theory of power's multiple institutional and ideological sources and criticised the narrowness of theories of oppression derived from economic analyses of the exploitation of labour. Yet, such movements also stipulated the importance of democratic transformation of both the norms *and* institutions of social interaction. By contrast, the more completely that post-structuralist theories about the constitutive power of discourse were lodged in social and political analysis, the more ill-defined, unspecific and de-institutionalised concepts of power and politics became.

## Post-structuralism in feminist theory

In feminist theory, the influence of post-structuralism was felt first in the fields of literary criticism and cultural studies. But, by the late 1980s it had become equally influential in history and social and political studies. In this brief review, we trace the influence of particular post-structuralist epistemologies in feminist political theory, distinguishing between strong post-structuralists, such as Butler, Mouffe and Scott, and those who attempt to take in the post-structuralist critique without discarding the entire framework of modernist thought, such as Fraser, Nicholson, Hekman and others.

As post-structuralist theory made its way into feminist political theory its critique of other approaches to political theory and political research depended upon a revisionist history of feminist political theory, which reduced that history's plurality, complexity, and self-critical reflection to a story about identity politics. Clare Hemmings (2005: 119) offered a similar criticism when she wrote 'one reason why I find unsubstantiated claims about the essentialism of feminist writing in the 1970s so aggravating is that they ignore the rich discussions about the relationships among gender, sexuality and race that took place in that decade'.

The story post-structuralists told about 'identity politics' in the women's movements and those movements' often bungled attempts at provisional unity leaked into poststructural representations of feminist theory. In this narrative, any attempt to conceptualise gender or gender systems as distinct, analytic categories, or to articulate a concept of interests, furthered a naïve, though not innocent, and essentialist ontology of gender. Butler, for instance, wrote that:

> The political assumption that there must be a universal basis for feminism, one which must be found in an identity assumed to exist cross-culturally, often accompanies the notion that the oppression of women has some singular form discernible in the universal or hegemonic structure of patriarchy or masculine domination. (1990: 3)

Butler did not provide evidence to substantiate her indictment that 'a universal basis for feminism . . . found in an identity assumed to exist cross-culturally' was the central feminist political assumption. In fact, despite what Butler wrote in *Gender Trouble*, feminist theorists in anthropology, economics, sociology, history and politics had been working with more nuanced theories of oppression for a long time.[6]

In part, the development of nuanced theories and political strategies challenging both the 'universal basis for feminism' and the singular form of women's oppression resulted from responses to criticisms made by both lesbians and feminists of colour, long in advance of Butler's writing. These criticisms led to efforts to address divisions in theory and practice. As Barbara Smith wrote in 1982:

> In my six years of being an avowed Black feminist, I have seen much change in how white women take responsibility for their racism, particularly within the last year. The formation of consciousness raising groups to deal solely with this issue, study groups, and community meetings and workshops; the appearance of articles in our publications and letters in newspapers; and the beginning of real and equal coalitions between Third World and white women are all phenomena that have really begun to happen, and I feel confident that there will be no turning back. (Smith in Anzaldúa 1990: 25)

Similarly, Scott's re-reading of the history of nineteenth-century French feminist struggles tended to eliminate other interpretations in favour of ones that 'read through paradox'. These feminists' efforts to achieve representation for women, Scott (1996: 2) argued, were trapped in a paradox: their pursuit of equality for women necessarily rested on an assertion of the difference they sought to undermine: 'A feminist history that takes for granted the inevitability of progress, the autonomy of individual agents and the need to choose between equality or difference reproduces without interrogation the terms of the ideological discourse within which feminism has operated.' Scott argued for maintaining 'analytic distance' from an ideology of gender that confused discursively produced 'sexual differences' with ontological essences, implying that deconstructive accounts offered the main way to achieve this distance.[7]

Although it may be true that some feminist theorists and activists continue to define gender in ontological terms, that is, as a category of being, it seems unfair to assert that proponents of gender theory subscribed to a 'metaphysics of substance' *tout court*. Why, then, was that assertion so persuasive? We think there are several reasons to explain why post-structuralist representations of feminist theory were convincing and led the way for post-structuralist paradigms to dominate in social and political theory.

First, other critiques about epistemology and 'exclusionary practices' in feminist theory had paved the way. Without drawing a genealogical line between them and post-structuralist theory, critiques made by feminist critics of science in the late 1970s and early 1980s about the partiality of mainstream scientific inquiry anticipated the post-structuralist turn in feminist theory. At the same time, a lively debate in feminist theory about the relationship between feminism and Marxism laid the groundwork for the gradual eclipse of materialist paradigms in feminist theory.

Sandra Harding's (1986) *The Science Question in Feminism* represented one such critical text whose legacy contributed to making the debate about epistemology central in feminist theory. The theory of situated knowledge, best represented by the shorthand 'standpoint epistemology', shared the claim with post-structuralism that 'a host of factors related to an individual's particular position in a determinate sociopolitical formation at a specific point in history' framed the situation of knowing (Hawkesworth 1989: 536). Still, standpoint theory differed from the radical scepticism of post-structuralism by adhering to the belief in the possibility of 'a more systematic and sophisticated conception of social and political life' (Hawkesworth 1989: 536), and by connecting such a conception to legitimation of the democratic political project, defined as the transformation of both institutions and discursive practices.

The post-structuralist shift also built on the critical work of feminists of colour and postcolonial theorists in political theory. Feminists of colour had argued that feminist theory ignored or marginalised certain voices and continued to call for attention to ways that 'differences' tended to be pushed aside. Chandra Mohanty (1991: 52) indicted mainstream western scholarship for either ignoring non-western women or analysing sexual difference from a position that privileged 'feminist interests as they have been articulated in the United States and Western Europe'. Writing in the late 1980s, Gloria Anzaldúa (1990: xix) argued that 'often white feminists want to minimize racial difference by taking comfort in the fact that we are all women and/or lesbians, and suffer similar sexual-gender oppressions . . . [White feminists] want a complete, totalizing identity'.

Yet, post-structuralism's radical critique of identity politics differed from the theory-building of these scholars by favouring a decontextualised and disembodied concept of the subject lacking any specificity in advance of that subject's discursive construction. Thus, although post-structuralist feminist theory finds antecedent for its epistemology in earlier feminist work, the critical difference is that in post-structuralist paradigms that epistemology displaced basic and middle levels of theoretical analysis of politics.

Second, women's movements contained a number of critical conflicts and divisions along the lines of race/ethnicity, class, sexual orientation, ability, region, age and civic status. In the 1980s, political-economic and cultural changes within the industrial north and the persistence of patterns of inequality between the north and south contributed further to the urgency within feminism of the discussion about what interests and problems should have priority in the feminist movement.

Post-structuralism offered one way to exit acrimonious debates by asserting that such debates were endless and undecidable because there were only 'paradoxes to offer'. In Butler's words:

> It is no longer clear that feminist theory ought to try to settle the questions of primary identity in order to get on with the task of politics. Instead, we ought to ask, what political possibilities are the consequence of the radical critique of identity categories. What new shape of politics emerges when identity as a common ground no longer constrains the discourse on feminist politics. (1990: ix)

Yet, apart from repeated appeals to 'coalitional politics' or 'action in concert' little analysis was offered to help answer the question 'what new shape of politics emerges?' or to think through the problematic of whose interests are served by whatever 'shape' politics takes.

Third, the rhetoric of post-structuralist arguments lent a degree of credibility to the claims made. For instance, assertions that all concepts were 'exclusionary' used a politically charged language to establish that feminist theoretical concepts were not only analytic heuristics but also were ideologically constructed ontological categories defining an 'essential' being of woman/women. The rapid circulation of the accusation of 'essentialism' in feminism led to the rejection of analytic concepts as useless.[8]

Similarly, the representation of post-structuralist theory as a necessary remedy depended on the caricature of all other approaches to social and political analysis as reductionistic, 'overly simple generalizations' that undercut more complex understandings of 'social causation' (Scott 1988: 59). For instance, Scott (1988: 42) wrote, 'Instead of a search for single origins, we have to conceive of processes so interconnected that they cannot be disentangled.' The words 'instead of' implied other feminist approaches are guilty of the 'search for single origins'. Yet, as Scott herself noted, 'positive definitions depend on negatives, indeed imply their existence in order to rule them out' (59). Ironically, the positive endorsement of deconstructive methods depended on the 'negative' representation of alternatives.

### 'Politics' in post-structuralist feminist theory

What kind of theory of politics then do feminist post-structuralists develop? What impact has this theory had on the use of central concepts such as 'politics', 'interests' and 'gender' in feminist theory and research?

Because they refuse to categorise what they are doing in any fixed terms, these theorists might respond to our first question – What kind of theory of politics do feminist post-structuralists develop? – by claiming that there is no such thing as 'a feminist post-structuralist theory'; there are only 'critical practices'. In the introduction to *Feminists Theorize the Political*, Butler and Scott (1992: xiii) write 'The theory under question is not a monolithic entity . . . indeed it is unclear whether, in the light of post-structuralism, theories constitute positions to be affirmed or denied.' Instead, they continue:

> 'Post-structuralism' indicates a field of critical practices that cannot be totalized and that, therefore, interrogate the formative and exclusionary power of dis-course in the construction of sexual difference . . . [Post-structuralism] asks how specific deployments of discourse for specific *political* [italics added] purposes determine the very notions used. (Butler and Scott 1992: xiii)

They claim post-structuralist theories are useful 'to the extent that they generate analyses, critiques, and *political* interventions, and open up a *political* imaginary for feminism'.

Butler and Scott (1992: xiv) deny that post-structuralism should be seen as '*a position* . . . from which one operates, a point of view or standpoint which might be usefully compared with other "positions" within the theoretical field'. Although they acknowledge 'strategic occasions' when this way of thinking about theory is justifiable, they consider such thinking trapped within 'the conventional grammar of theoretical debate' and reject it on principle, asserting that post-structuralism is 'a critical interrogation of the exclusionary operations by which "positions" are established'.

Yet, despite critical differences, 'strong' post-structuralists share common premises which structure their approach to politics and political theory: (1) the claim that feminist theory has based its ideas of democracy on an ontological concept of gender as a common identity, which narrows its vision of democracy to a 'representational politics' of 'interests' articulated by transparent, autonomous 'subjects'; (2) the claim that, because it is impossible to define 'identity categories' such as gender, race, class, sexuality, ability, etc. in non-essentialist or non-ontological terms, it is impossible to theorise political 'interests' in advance of action; (3) the claim that politics should be understood as an articulation process, that is, as a 'performative' or discursive practice without any pre-defined or delimitable institutional location or pre-conditions; and (4) the claim that post-structuralism provides the correct way to articulate a new politics of radical democracy as the proliferation of 'subject positions'. In what follows we consider the effects these premises have on the conceptualization and analysis of politics. As we discuss the operation of these claims in post-structuralist theory, it will be useful to refer to figure 1.1, p. 4 provided in our introduction (see also our discussion of these levels of analysis in our introduction).

Although post-structuralist feminist theorists connect their work to a radical democratic project, how shall we characterise their theories of the political conditions, institutions, or processes of democracy? In other words, at what level of analysis does their conceptualisation of 'the political' and 'politics' reside? A review of the use of the word 'political' or 'politics' in the work of Butler, Scott and Mouffe demonstrates that their conceptualisation is largely ontological or metaphysical. In other words, their articulation of a theory of politics as a productive process remains on the meta-theoretical level.[9] In different ways, all three theorists define politics as a 'performative' process or an effect of language rather than as a political 'representational' practice in the traditional sense. In other words, they locate politics immanently in discursive processes of signification and resignification rather than as the institutionally contextualised actions of self-conscious subjects.

In different ways each of these theorists argues for a 'new politics', not grounded in identity (practical interests) or limited to juridical forms of representation (formal/legal interests), and against seeing political representation as a 'set of practices derived from the alleged interests that belong to a set of ready-made subjects' (Butler 1990: 149). In this view, politics becomes a critical epistemological practice derived from an ontological premise (discourse produces effects) that opens up possibilities through a radical, immanent critique of identity categories and conventional modes of representational politics. Shifting from an analysis of politics as a set of practices and activities resulting from the representation of interests articulated by subjects to an understanding of politics as a critical epistemological project constitutes a major transformation of the concept of political representation. Altogether left out of this picture is a theory of politics at the specific level.

Here we must reiterate that we do not object to broadening the concept of representation to include the representational effects of language. Rather, we are concerned that this shift away from representation in the legal/institutional sense of a formal, egalitarian presence of subjects in public life to discursive representation constitutes a rejection of the political utility of any conventional understanding of representation. Although it is beyond the scope of this chapter to investigate the many, varied definitions of 'representation' in different fields of inquiry, we echo Jacques Derrida's (1982: 295) warning against a collapsed representational politics with representation as a principle in philosophy: 'Are we sure we know what [our word 'representation'] means today? Let us not be too quick to believe it.'

Scott (1988: 58) undertakes what she terms a reversal in 'the direction of our causal thinking' not simply 'from the economic to the political sphere' but towards 'political rhetoric', which she identifies as the locus of 'meaning' or 'the patterns and relationships that constitute understanding or a "cultural" system'. She endorses this reversal as a 'more radical' conceptualisation of politics. In place of politics defined as 'the goals of a collective movement aimed at formal participation in government or the state' Scott advocates a concept of politics as 'any contest for power within which identities . . . are created'. Scott claims that this conceptualisation of politics as a power contest about identities ('suggests that there is always a politics . . . in the operation of discourse') frees politics from being understood in 'essentially descriptive' terms (57).[10] Yet, the unfortunate and unintended effect of the conceptualisation of politics as any contestation of identity also frees a theory of democratic politics from any way to define and explain democracy's enabling conditions or institutional parameters.

Similarly, Laclau and Mouffe (1985: 58, 96–7ff.) paved the way for this kind of 'reversal' when they build their determination of the nature of the social as 'contingent relations' on a 'profound *potential* meaning' of one of Althusser's statements, arguing that 'everything in the social is overdetermined . . . that the social constitutes itself as a symbolic order'.

Taking up the question of political interests specifically, Scott (1988: 5, 56) asks, in whose interest is it to control or contest meanings, what is the nature of that interest or 'what is its origin?' 'There are two ways', she writes, 'to answer these questions . . . One, in terms of an objectively determined, absolute, and universal interest (economics or sexual domination, for example), the other, in terms of a discursively produced, relative, and contextual concept of interest.' Scott's preference is to define interests as discursively produced. 'We get nowhere by pursuing lines of inquiry that assume social causation because there is *no social reality outside or prior to language*' (italics added). Thus, for instance, class and class consciousness 'are the same thing. . . they are political articulations'.

Scott's (1988: 3) concern with politics as the discursive production of knowledge emerged, in part, from her 'sense of frustration at the relatively limited impact women's history was having on historical studies generally and [her] consequent need to understand why that was the case'. Poststructuralism emphasised 'the political nature' of the construction of knowledge and saw politics as 'the play of force involved in any society's construction and implementation of meanings' (4–5). It provided Scott (1996: 124) with a way to 'open a central chapter for feminism in the large histories of politics'. In any event, this may explain why Scott's account of a 'new politics' refers largely to a new politics of research in the discipline of history.

Butler shares Scott's concern to articulate a more radical vision of politics, but for different reasons. Butler (1990: ix) asserts that feminism needs a new politics, one that can take shape when the 'identity [of women] as the common ground no longer constrains the discourse on feminist politics'. She contends that the search for a common identity precludes a more 'radical inquiry into the political construction and regulation of identity itself'. Rather than turning on a 'political analysis that takes juridical subjects as its foundation', feminist politics ought to take as its subject the 'dual function of power: the juridical and the productive'. Instead of focusing only on how 'women might be more fully represented in language and politics', the task of feminist critique 'ought also to understand how the category of "women", the subject of feminism, is produced and restrained by the very structures of power through which emancipation is sought' (2).

In fact, the claim that power 'produces' subjects through practices of exclusion (of those who are not considered subjects in its terms) so overloads the concept of political representation with negativity that efforts to achieve representation in juridical, legal, or institutional terms are jettisoned in favor of non-juridical forms of political resignification or 'performative' politics. Instead of identity politics, rooted in the subject of women, Butler (1990: 1, 5) argues for a 'radical rethinking of the ontological constructions of identity' that might 'revive feminism on other grounds' as the *a priori* basis for a new feminist politics.

Yet, on what is Butler's (1990) claim that feminist theory has misidentified its subject based? The argument she offers in *Gender Trouble* conflates feminists' efforts to formulate concepts of gender and complex theories of gender systems with 'development of a language that fully or adequately represented women' (1). It implies that theorists assumed developing such a language was necessary, in an antecedent way, to foster a feminist project of political visibility, and implies that feminist theorists (who are not named) understood language in purely referential terms, that is, as if the categories of analysis they articulated were ontological instead of heuristic. In other words, Butler's argument depends on the premise that any theoretical articulation of a concept of gender at the level of specific theory is the same as constructing gender as an ontology.

If we accept this premise (theoretical concept = ontology) then we must reject any basic level social theory of gender and representational politics. In place of representational politics we have Butler's (1990: 5) 'new sort of feminist politics' (performative politics) that will 'contest reifications of gender and identity' and 'take the variable constructions of identity as both a methodological and normative prerequisite, if not a political goal'. As a result, discursive analysis and political analysis, and discursive contestation and political contestation become identical.

To illustrate her theory, Butler (1990: 17) argues that the 'subversive repetition' of dominant cultural configurations of subjectivity releases new 'cultural configurations' of sex and gender. By parodying dominant norms, a repetition of norms of femininity and masculinity, such as in drag, becomes 'subversive' because its appropriation and 'misuse' of those norms exposes and displaces those norms as not 'natural' but constructed. Butler identifies the 'failure' of marginalised 'identities' to conform to cultural scripts in persistent and proliferating ways as 'critical opportunities to expose the limits and regulatory aims' of 'the matrix of coherent gender norms'. Marginalised identities open up 'rival and subversive matrices' of gender within regulatory norms. Similarly, her later analysis of hate speech and pornography explores the resignified use of vilifying terms by the vilified. Although hate speech 'calls into question linguistic survival [and] . . . being called a name can be the site of injury . . . name-calling may be the initiating moment of a counter-mobilization . . . The word that wounds becomes an instrument of resistance' (163).

At the same time, Butler distinguishes between a 'speech act' and conduct, arguing that:

> When the scene of racism [or sexism in the case of pornography] is reduced to a single speaker and his or her audience, the political problem is cast as the tracing of the harm as it travels from the speaker to the psychic/somatic constitution of the one who hears the term or to whom it is directed. The *elaborate institutional structures of racism as well as sexism* [italics added] are suddenly reduced to the scene of utterance. (1997: 80)

Here Butler suggests the importance of situating speech and language in a social context in order to understand that a speech act's effects are 'socially contingent' on 'elaborate institutional structures' that precede the speaking subject and make speech efficacious (23). Yet, her analysis lacks any discussion of the 'broader institutional conditions' that produce contingencies such as inequalities or injustices to which democratic 'speech acts' respond. In fact, within the terms of post-structuralist critique, we lack any specific level theories that could identify or explain the 'elaborate institutional structures' of racism and sexism to which Butler refers.

Commenting on similarities in Scott's discursive analyses, Varikas (1995: 98) writes: 'If . . . "discursive boundaries change with historical conditions", how is this change to be explained?' Reliance on sources 'in which women are more often the objects of discourse than the subjects of discursive practices . . . tells us very little about the relationship of forces in which these discourses are established and about the extra-discursive conditions which might possibly transform them' (Tilly 1994: 128).

If the possibility for a dominant order to be transformed into something new is immanent in the process of signification itself as its inadvertent 'swerving' or 'turning' from its original purpose, and yet, to become materialised as 'the new', that possibility depends upon social contingencies that exceed the subject, we still need to explain and confront several thorny political problems.

First, how do we delineate the social contingencies and institutional structures that work to sustain particular 'regimes of power' despite the imaginative possibilities we can envision to overthrow them? Put differently, can we provide a *particular* account of the forces, interests, motivations, and purposes behind the specific 'regimes of power' that establish 'masculine hegemony and heterosexist power'? Second, if these regimes of power are multiple, how do we distinguish between them and articulate their points of convergence and dissonance? Third, what norms are available to distinguish between those repetitions leading toward a more 'capacious, generous and "unthreatened" ' (Butler 1995: 140) or democratic way of living and those that threaten democracy (White 2000: 93, 201)? Within the terms of post-structuralist critique, we lack a way to identify or explain institutional structures of sexism, heterosexism, racism, able-bodiedism, etc., and their inter-relationships.

This inability to theorise at the specific level about inter-relationships among structures of domination, oppression or marginalisation is the result, in part, of the lack of specific level theories of gender/sexuality, race/ethnicity, and embodiment. Instead, in certain versions of the metaphysics of post-structuralism, evidence drawn from empirical observation – about how 'identity' is produced and lived complexly and not unidimensionally – is used to support ontological arguments for intersectionality at the conceptual level in specific theory.

Post-structuralism rejected all theories of gender/sexuality, race/ethnicity and embodiment as essentialist except those that define subjectivities as an effect of regulatory discursive practices. This charge of essentialism resulted from the identification of any theorisation of social categories at the specific level needed to make sense of the terms gender/sexuality, race/ethnicity and embodiment, etc. as such, with ontology, and the simultaneous assumption that specific level theories of social categories are empirically descriptive of 'lived' experience. Theories of gender oppression, for instance, isolate gender as an identifiable category instead of recognising that 'because gender intersects with racial, class, ethnic, social, and regional modalities of discursively constituted identities . . . it becomes impossible to separate out "gender" from the political and cultural intersections in which it is invariably produced and maintained' (Butler 1990: 3).[11] Consequently, on philosophical grounds, one should dispense with a specific theory of gender.

Yet, the statement 'gender intersects with racial, class, ethnic, social and regional modalities of . . . identities' uses the ontological impossibility of separating dimensions of identity in concrete existence as evidence to support the epistemological claim that, at the specific-theoretical level, no conceptual distinction among such identity categories is possible. Yet, if there is no way to distinguish gender analytically from any other category then the statement 'gender intersects with racial, class, ethnic, social' itself becomes absurd, since intersection logically implies the coming together of 'parts' that are conceptually distinct from one another in some identifiable way (McCall 2005).

To assert the impossibility 'to separate out "gender"' leads then to abandonment of social theory at the specific level of generalisation, which could provide an account of gender as a system of social relations. In place of a specific theory of gender (or of race/ethnicity, embodiment, etc.) we have a conceptualisation of gender as a relation of signs in an endless and endlessly mobile chain of equivalences (Laclau and Mouffe 1985: 127ff.) or significations. This 'fetishism of signs' evacuates the concept of the social into the discursive and displaces politics onto the domain of (decontextualised) discursive practices. In other words, some model of the 'speech act' stands for politics, and some model of 'linguistic agency' stands for political agency. Definitions of political agency as performativity and political representation as reiteration remain inadequate as an 'account of the *actual practice* of freedom by subjects or groups of subjects in the political arena' (Webster 2000: 18).

Instead of theorising the activities, processes and institutional locations and structures of politics itself, and analysing individuals' and groups' social situations and political actions, along with interpreting discourse, post-structuralists use *active verbs that connote agency* – such as 'produced', 'constituted', 'initiated', 'founded', etc. – *to describe linguistic processes of 'subject-formation'*.[12] Such a theory of politics not only locates politics in discourse, but also reads the juridical dimensions of politics in exclusively negative ways. As a result, certain arenas of political action are refused because they expand state power.

For instance, Butler's analyses of hate speech concentrates on the prohibitive functions of the law in the arenas of censorship of various sorts, and leaves aside altogether the affirmative and transformative functions of the law in the area of welfare policy, equal opportunity policy, reproductive rights policies and the whole array of civil, political and social rights accorded by law to previously excluded groups. By focusing exclusively on the prohibitive/productive functions of the state/law, it binds such a theory of democracy almost entirely to 'non-juridical forms of opposition'.

Although it is true that 'strategies devised on the part of progressive legal and social movements . . . run the risk of being turned against [them] by . . . extending state power, specifically legal power, over issues in question' (Butler 1997: 24), this fact should not be construed as an argument to abandon efforts to provide a fuller account of state power in its affirmative and transformative aims (Young 2000: 158ff.; Fraser and Honneth 2003: 74). Nor should the assertion of the necessary 'risk' involved in the deployment of legal power automatically eliminate the use of judicial remedies to regulate or even prohibit certain activities.[13] Rather than eliminate the state (whether on the local, national or supra-national level) as a legitimate arena for political democracy, we need an account of state power that, at a minimum, recognises what Hannah Arendt called the 'right to have rights' as an essential feature of the democratic project.[14]

Equally troubling, the absence of any articulated normative criteria for evaluating institutions and practices means that the understanding of democracy implicit in these theories remains highly abstract and formalistic. As we have seen, particularly in certain strong versions of post-structuralist feminist theory, the linguistic turn has represented a turning away from efforts to explain how language or discourse is moored *in specific institutional contexts*. Yet, the forces and social relations of politics in the context of globalisation require us to identify and focus on specific institutions of power and their discourses, and to explore concretely how individuals and groups not only rename themselves, but also articulate practical programmes of social transformation aimed at feminist democratic goals.[15]

We continue to need political studies that identify which strategies work to advance democratic goals in what contexts for which groups.[16] To conduct such research, we argue that theorists must continue to treat social structures and relations of power as at least *analytically* external to 'subjects' who are of course shaped by them. The point is not to be mystified by one's concepts. In other words, theory must sustain a tension between concepts as useful analytic devices, or heuristics, and the social relations they cast in relief.

### Toward a new critical feminist-realist theory of politics

By way of summary, the key points we have made about the limitations or partiality of post-structuralist accounts of feminist politics are:

(1) *The rejection of any substantive account of gender* or definition of gender as social relationships (or dimensions of society) as necessarily reductionistic or essentialist. Instead, post-structuralists define gender as an indeterminate and dynamic matrix of signification without specifiable content or identifiable structure.

(2) *The lack of an institutional, systemic account of politics* in favour of an ontology of the political and politics. And ontology of 'the political' conceptualises 'the political' as the ever-present possibility of antagonism among humans (Mouffe), politics as any contest for power over identity creation (Scott), and political change as an automatic by-product of the built-in capacity for linguistic resignification or iterability of 'speech acts' (Butler). Without an institutional account of politics and the political we cannot explain the specific, historical conditions and.contingencies (institutions, structures, interests, identities) that enable and constrain political agency and both promote and limit the impact of political action.

(3) *The displacement of a robust, multi-dimensional theory of political action and agency by a politics of performativity or articulatory practices immanent in language/discourse.* Without a robust, multi-dimensional theory of action, the deliberate and deliberative efforts of individuals and groups to articulate interests in opposition to or in concert with others within the arenas of both state and civil society remain undertheorised.

(4) *The lack of any discernible evaluative criteria, articulated norms or theory of judgment* precludes any way to distinguish among a set of practices as more or less democratic. The absence of evaluative criteria reduces the political vision of democracy to a philosophical abstraction and brackets substantive efforts to achieve political representation, equality,

freedom, and justice in civil society and state contexts in favour of non-juridical forms of oppositional politics.

In response to these four limitations, we urge the reconstruction of feminist political theory based on the following basic elements:

(1) *A historical and materialist theory of gender* as a specific social system of relations and activities, produced in and through identifiable, historically changing social relations and practices, institutions and norms in specific cultural settings. This theory of gender connects ontological assumptions about gender to specific-level theories of its production and includes, but is not limited to, discursive representations of masculinities and femininities and theories of sexual difference.

(2) *An institutionally grounded theory of politics*, which locates politics spatially and temporally. *Politics is the systemically shaped set of actions self-consciously engaged by agents in an historically and institutionally conditioned context and oriented toward conflicts and resolutions regarding the scope, nature, and consequences of public life, including contestations about the boundaries between 'public' and 'private'*. In democratic systems, with which we are concerned, politics is people's struggle for freedom or for formal and substantive inclusion or presence in public life. With regard to decision-making in a polity, 'democracy enables participation and voice for all those affected by problems and their proposed solutions' (Young 2000: 10). Yet, participation and voice as normative democratic ideals are tied to the question of plurality not only in procedural, but also in substantive terms. In other words, 'one of the purposes of advocating inclusion is to allow the transformation of the style and terms of debate and thereby leave open the possibility for significant change in outcomes' (Young 2000: 12).

(3) *A multi-dimensional theory of political action and agency* as the deliberate and deliberative efforts of individuals and groups to gain presence (formal interest) and articulate claims (substantive interests) in the institutionally structured and historically changing arenas of both state and civil society. Any conceptualisation of political action must include, but not be limited to, activities in the arena of formal politics, or historically located 'state'-centred processes. It must also include activities in 'civil society' as a site of politics. Actions may be interpreted differently and have consequences in excess of actors' intentions. Yet, neither the unpredictability or uncertainty of action, nor the fact that 'agency' is realised (made real) through action undercuts the importance and motivating force of political consciousness. Consciousness of possibility – the perceived ability to begin something new (Arendt) – remains critical to the process of political mobilisation and change.

(4) *A theory of the normative/evaluative criteria for differentiating between democratic and non-democratic practices of representation.* This theory should include the double-normative of democratic freedom: inclusion in deliberation *and* outcome. 'Strong and normatively legitimate democracy . . . includes equally in the process that leads to decisions all those who will be affected by them' (Young 2000: 11), as a specific social system of relations and activities, produced in and through identifiable, historically changing social relations and practices, institutions and norms in specific cultural settings. The articulation of 'normatively legitimate democracy' requires, but is not limited to, the articulation of a theory of justice that addresses juridical and non-juridical elements of equality.

In the remainder of this chapter we will take up the first point in some detail – articulating theoretical principles for the development of an historical and materialist account of gender – as a way forward in this reconstructive effort. Through the case studies of particular political issues in specific contexts, the other chapters included in this anthology flesh out how to conceptualise the other points in concrete ways. We conclude this chapter with brief comments about the connections between this realist-materialist account of gender and the political interests of gender.

Earlier we argued for question-driven rather than method-driven theory development. It is perhaps time to ask again: What are the problems or questions with which feminist political theory is concerned? Among the problems to which feminist political theory responds are how to identify, explain, and transform 'regimes of power', which produce the inequalities, injustices, and anti-democracies sustained by patriarchal, heterosexist gender systems. Among the questions feminist political theorists have continued to ask are, what do women and men want, need, and demand in order to be equally present in public and private life, justly treated, afforded equal dignity and respect and become equally able to exercise control over the future?

One need not hold to a theory that assigns 'women' and 'men' a fixed identity to defend the political and democratic relevance of such questions. In fact, both post-structuralists and their critics agree that feminist theory is central to democratic theory. Both are committed to broader democratic processes and more equal access to power for different groups and individuals. How then do we bring their insights into conversation with one another?

We argue feminist political theory needs to take another 'turn', one that moves through, but *not without*, strategies of post-structuralist analysis. Rather than collapse institutions into discourse or reduce discourse to a by-product or effect of institutions, feminist theory should distinguish between, yet connect, discursive accounts of gender to systemic accounts of gender systems as an effect of institutional and structural power. To repeat the point made by Nancy Fraser (1995a: 160): one of the 'most important – and most difficult – tasks for feminist theorizing is to connect discursive analyses of gender signification with structural analyses of institutions and political economy'. How then can we do this? What theoretical frameworks are available with which to approach this task?

A central problematic of feminist theory, which marks it as a distinctive field of theory, has been to explain the persistence of systems of gender inequality in historically and culturally specific contexts. Here we offer some points for the further development of a feminist critical theory of politics in concrete and 'realist' terms. We expect a feminist theory of politics to link historical, systemic analysis of institutions with critical analysis of discursive processes. Or, as Sylvia Walby has put it:

> We do not need to abandon the notion of causality in the face of the complexity of the social world. We do not have to move from analysis of structure to that of discourse to catch the complexity; neither do we have to resort to capitalism as the sole determinant in order to have a macro-social theory. (1992: 48)

Earlier we argued that any effort to identify, explain, and assess the impact of globalised forces and social relations on the possibilities for feminist democratic politics would need to sustain different levels of social analysis. What do we mean by 'different levels of social analysis'? We distinguished between general levels of theory grounded in meta-theoretical (ontological, epistemological, methodological) assumptions about how to conceptualise a social process, and basic and middle-range or more directly empirically testable theories. This distinction calls attention to the fact that no meta-theoretical principle can provide conceptual schemes concrete enough to explain any particular social processes or social systems.

For instance, in their analysis of recognition and distribution as two types of or moral bases for political claims of social justice, Fraser and Honneth (2003: 3) both employ a multi-level analysis. They engage issues involved in their debate on 'three distinct levels': the moral-philosophical level (meta-theoretical premises for describing normative claims), social theory level (theorised relation among the elements of a social structure) and political analysis level (institutional arrangements, procedures, and outcomes oriented toward justice). To develop a feminist political theory of gender differentiation and equality, we require similar discrimination among levels of analysis.

The meta-theoretical premise that 'subjectivity' is produced through language is a useful postulate, but its social theoretical utility is limited. It cannot, on its own, explain which specific codes within language produce a particular kind of subjectivity or account for why. If, for instance, gender signals something about power, *what* it signals about power cannot be explained within meta-theoretical terms. Thus, any account of how gender is produced must instantiate meta-theoretical assumptions about social processes at the level of both basic and middle-range theory.

In other words, any account of the production or construction of gender that claims to offer more than a philosophical description of gender as an aspect of embodied being or as an element of subjectivity must be able to theorise gender as an identifiable, distinguishable, dimension of human existence. Without such a conceptually distinct theory of gender, we reduce gender to neo-biologism (Hird 2004: 223) or, at best, treat it as an indeterminate effect of the history of discourses about materiality. At the same time, any theory of gender must be accompanied by concrete, empirical studies of how gender is produced and transformed in specific social and historical contexts.

For us, the enduring questions for feminist political theory continue to be: How can we explain the production of gender in historically and culturally specific contexts? How can we identify, explain, and transform those 'regimes of power', which produce the inequalities, injustices, and anti-democracies sustained by patriarchal, heterosexist gender systems?

Fraser (1995b: 69) has offered one approach to the development of macro-social theory, arguing for a 'critical theory of recognition . . . which identifies and defends only those versions of the cultural politics of difference that can be coherently combined with the social politics of equality'. In her view, justice requires 'both redistribution *and* recognition' and she argues for a way 'to conceptualize cultural recognition and social equality in forms that support rather than undermine one another'.

Fraser (2003: 51) situates her attempt to solve the problem of redistribution and recognition 'within a broad social-theoretical frame. From this perspective', she writes, 'societies appear as complex fields that encompass at least two analytically distinct modes of social ordering: an economic mode [producing class-like modes of differentiation] . . . and a cultural mode [producing status differentiation]', both of which are 'mutually imbricated'. She takes distribution claims to be roughly analogous to economic modes of inequality and recognition claims as roughly analogous to cultural modes. Nevertheless, Fraser argues that some cases of status differentiation, such as gender subordination, demonstrate a 'two-dimensional' subordination. 'Neither simply a class nor simply a status group, gender is a hybrid category rooted simultaneously in the economic structure and the status order of society . . . Redressing gender injustice requires attending to both distribution and recognition' (19).

Yet, by tracing 'structural injustices' to 'socieoeconomic mal*distribution*' and defining the problem of cultural injustice as the assignment of inferior or lesser value to marginal groups, Fraser (1995b: 69, 75) misses the significance of post-structuralist emphases on social processes of *production*.[17] Even though we remain critical of how post-structuralist theory largely conceptualises production as a discursive process of subject-formation, we contend that analysis of social processes of gender production remains central to the articulation of a theory of gender differentiation and inequality.

In this regard, Butler's critique of Fraser's distinction between economic and cultural readings of gender and sexuality is instructive, though underdeveloped. 'It would be a mistake', Butler writes:

> To understand [the production of dominant and abject sexuality] as 'merely cultural' if they are essential to the functioning of the sexual order of political economy . . . The economic, tied to the reproductive, is necessarily linked to the reproduction of heterosexuality . . . This is not simply a question of certain people suffering a lack of cultural recognition . . . but . . . a specific mode of sexual production and exchange that works to maintain the stability of gender, the heterosexuality of desire, and the naturalization of the family. (1998: 42)

Notably, Butler alludes to a 'specific mode of sexual production', but does not develop this insight. In our analysis, the production of sexuality, or what we call socio-sexuality, is neither a feature of political economy (though sexuality has economic significance) nor a cultural effect (though sexuality has symbolic significance). Rather, the production of sexuality is an activity distinguishable from both 'labour' in the narrow economic sense and reproduction.

The key question is: *How is gender produced and under what conditions does it become a specific system of structural inequality?* What meta-theoretical assumptions about the production of social systems of power can we use to articulate a theory of gender inequality? How can these premises be used to develop basic and middle-level theories of gender differentiation and structural inequality?

We reconfigure historical-materialist/realist premises: namely, we begin with premises about 'real [embodied] individuals, their activity and the material conditions [including the materiality of embodiment] under which they live, both those which they find already existing and those produced by their activity' (Marx and Engels 1970: 42). These premises stress the centrality of productive activity in the creation of the means of life and of people themselves. Yet, instead of the traditional reading of 'productive activity' to connote only 'labour' or 'work' in narrowly economic terms, or expanded to include so-called cultural activities – such as the activities of speech and art – we claim a conceptualisation of productive activity that includes a 'specific kind of productive, or creative, process; a continuous and interactive process which goes on between' people as embodied socio-sexual beings (Jónasdóttir 1994: 219). This specific kind of activity is the process which produces gender as such in particular varying forms of 'political sexuality'.[18]

In this theory, 'sexuality' can be understood both in its everyday meaning and 'as a structural concept' roughly 'analogous to the concept of "economy"'. In their broader meanings economy refers to the social process of the production of the means of life while sexuality refers to the social process of the production of life itself, or the process in which people create people'. As a structural relationship sexuality is an organised process of human interaction 'in which people enjoy and create people (others and themselves), in which they give and take/receive, use and produce socio-sexual goods', sexed bodies, desires, needs, and pleasures (Jónasdóttir 1994: 228).

Understanding gender as produced through the social organisation of a particular kind of productive activity takes us to the level of specific theory and provides a way to distinguish gender as a dimension of society from other dimensions, such as class and race/ethnicity. At a necessary minimum, such a theory identifies 'a specific and "essential" sex/gender *relationship*, one that generates sex/gender specific *practice* or creative *activity*, a specific human development capacity or *power* over the use and control of which certain groups of people struggle'. In addition, it postulates that 'specific *institution(s)* are more central than others' in the reproduction of any sex/gender system in different historical contexts (Jónasdóttir 1994: 213). This does not imply that, existentially speaking, gender is experienced separately from other relationships, such as class, race, or nationality, or that it operates independently to structure a social system. On the contrary, it is the task of middle-level social theory to articulate and document the particular ways that gender is structured, experienced and transformed in different historical and cultural contexts (Jónasdóttir 1994: 333ff.).

But what specific activities produce gender or the sexed/gendered reality of human existence? Through the appropriation of what kind of power? According to what norms and principles of exchange? And what institutions are most central in this productive process? At the basic level of theory, these questions are trans-historical. Yet, the specific activities, modes and norms of appropriation and institutional locations of gender production varies in different societies over time.

To answer the first question – what activities produce gender – we hypothesise that it is the appropriation of love or love power in the

particular historical form institutionalised in a social order that constitutes humans as sex/gendered beings. 'Love refers to human beings'
capacities (powers) to make – and remake – "their kind", not only literally
in the procreation and socialisation of children but also in the creation and
recreation of adult people as socio-sexual *individuated* and *personified*
existences' (Jónasdóttir 1994: 221). The social and institutional location
and organisation of the appropriation of love power, then, produces historically specific patterns of gender differentiation. 'Love [power] is a
specific kind of alienable and causally potent human power, the social
organization of which is the basis of contemporary Western patriarchy'
(Jónasdóttir 1994: 221). From the general or meta-theoretical postulate
that the appropriation of love power produces people as specific sorts of
sex/gendered individuals in modern society, it then becomes possible to
develop specific level theoretical postulates about the historical conditions
shaping the production of gender in different systems.

Axel Honneth observes that, with the 'breakthrough to bourgeois-
capitalist society', a differentiation occurs among spheres of activity in
which humans gain recognition of themselves in their particularity. With
the advent of capitalism,

> The recognition form of love . . . became independent: the relations between
> the sexes were gradually liberated from economic and social pressures and
> this opened up to the feeling of mutual affection. Marriage was soon under-
> stood – albeit with class delays – as the institutional expression of a special
> kind of intersubjectivity, whose peculiarity consists in the fact that husband
> and wife love one another as needy beings . . . [who] reciprocally bring to
> this kind of relationship . . . loving care for the other's well-being in light of
> his or her needs. (2003: 139)

Yet, reciprocity in the activity of love was not guaranteed through the
structure of bourgeois marriage. Even the incursion of rights into this
sphere has not adequately addressed the fundamental problem of inequality lodged in the mode of appropriation. Just as the capitalist must appropriate labour power in order to be and remain a capitalist, so also, men
today must exploit women's 'love power' if they are to 'remain the kind of
men that historical circumstances force them to be' (Jónasdóttir 1994: 225).

The exploitative appropriation of women's love power makes heterosexuality function oppressively, both internally, in the form of women's
subordination to men, and externally, with regard to so-called 'marginalised' sexualities. The historical identification of bourgeois marriage and
its gender-oppressive patterns of appropriation of love with the legitimate
social organisation or mode of love produces a specific form of heterosexuality as normative. Moreover, this exploitative appropriation process

is not limited to the institution of marriage but also operates in the dynamics of heteronormative gender reproduction sustained by social relations in other institutions of civil society and the state, whether in the form of gender discrimination in patterns of employment, the vilification of other modes of socio-sexual relations, wage differentials, unequal civil and social rights, and inadequate political representation.

We have not advocated a theory of gender that is 'merely sexual'.[19] Instead we have suggested a conceptualisation of gender not grounded in a theory of identity, which offers fruitful possibilities for a materialist/realist critical feminist theory of politics. Our theorisation of gender as a set of social relationships produced by specific activities in particular institutional contexts links the production of gender to the reproduction of a political system of gender power without reducing gender either to the 'merely economic' or the 'merely cultural'. By focusing on relations of production of people as sex/gendered beings, this conceptualisation enables investigation of those particular activities and institutions in specific societies, which sustain gender inequality. It also supports analysis of how such activities and institutions interact with other dimensions of human activity to reproduce a social system in all its complexity.

What then are the political interests of gender? Recall that our earlier definition identified politics as the systemically shaped set of actions self-consciously engaged by agents in a historically and institutionally conditioned context and oriented toward conflicts and resolutions regarding the scope, nature, and consequences of public life, including contestations about the boundaries between 'public' and 'private'. By interests, we do not mean a set of concerns common to all members of a group. Rather, we mean the interest all members of a group have, where group refers to a socially structured position (Jónasdóttir 1994: 164–73; Young 2000: 136), in being among (recognition) those who can determine or have some control over a process or outcome. In this sense, interest is a 'means to social and political inclusion' and is clearly related to self-determination (Young 2000: 105; cf. Ferguson, chapter 4, this anthology).

We can now identify the political interests of gender as those actions emerging from conflicts over the appropriation of love power as these affect the scope, nature and consequences of public life. These actions are self-consciously engaged by those who seek to sustain or change a particular social organisation of the productive activity of love by altering the institutional structures and discursive practices conditioning the social organisation of the process of gender production. We advance the claim that actions leading to a more inclusive system of representation not only in the deliberative domain of democratic decision-making, but also in the administrative and judicial institutions of politics, whether at the local, national or regional level, must remain as central to feminist theories of democracy as expanded modes of communication and resignification.

Rather than declare the concepts 'women' and 'gender' essentialist fictions, perhaps the greatest feminist challenge today is to 'build or strengthen different forms of organised cooperation among women', which can 'articulate and deal with conflicts among women'. At the same time we need forms of organised cooperation between women and men to act collectively against patriarchy. 'Perhaps we can speak of a *differentiated solidarity* among women, a solidarity built on awareness of both common and different interests, a solidarity that also comprises the prerequisites for a cooperation with men, on women's terms' (Jónasdóttir 1995: 18).

## Notes

1 Aiming to push analysis further past descriptive accounts of differences between women's and men's political activities and attitudes, Scott's approach to the study of gender and politics put emphasis on gender as a signifier of power, presenting what could be called a 'culturalistic' model. We use the term 'culturalistic' parallel to the use of the term 'economistic' to signal a kind of reductionism in post-structuralist analysis of culture. See also Terry Eagleton, on a similar criticism of what he calls 'the modern-day culturalism' in postmodernists' reducing politics to culture (Eagleton 2000: chs 2, 43).

2 We recognise the pitfalls of using the generic appellation, 'post-structuralism'. As Lynne Segal (1999: 29) so aptly put it, 'It is hard to summarize the illuminations and provocations of academic feminism's current embrace of post-structuralist critiques of universalizing thought and emancipatory narratives . . . without courting the danger of homogenizing contemporary theorizing, much as it has erased the complexities of seventies feminism.' Yet, as we explore in greater detail below, it is not only possible, but also theoretically essential to identify particular tenets of post-structuralist theory in order to assess the impact of its epistemological emphasis on theories of politics.

3 This wide circulation of the term 'postmodern' in the period of the 1980s has a peculiar irony, given the impact, especially on the poor and economically vulnerable, of the deliberate and steady erosion of national welfare systems in major industrial states as reflected, for instance, in Reagan and Thatcher's neo-conservative policies. Consequently, the particularly virulent critique by left-leaning post-structuralists of modernity's 'falsely' universalistic norms occurred at the same time as right-wing policy-makers, who were gaining ascendancy in national and international arenas, were making arguments about the need to overthrow these same 'universal' standards in favour of deregulation and, in the US, 'states rights'. A concrete example of parallels between post-structuralist and neo-conservative paradigms is given in the similarity between Laclau and Mouffe's discarding of the concept of 'society' as totalising and

even anti-democratic (Laclau and Mouffe 1985: 95–6) and Margaret Thatcher's infamous declaration: 'there is no such thing as society' (Keay 1987).

4  It is beyond the scope of this chapter to consider in detail the ways that this characterisation of Marxism was itself essentialist and distorting. But, see Nicos Mouzelis (1988) for further discussion.

5  We use the term sex/desire to signal a particular aspect of political sexuality.

6  See for instance the work of Ann Ferguson, Michelle Zimbalist Rosaldo, Heidi Hartmann, Juliet Mitchell, Sheila Rowbotham, Zillah Eisenstein, etc.

7  The implication that post-structuralist theory is theory comes through particularly strongly in Scott's work, perhaps explaining the fact that her writing so often is taken to exemplify the post-structuralist tendency to a 'hegemonizing dismissal of theoretical frameworks not explicitly informed by post-structuralism'. See, for instance, Lynn Segal, *Why Feminism* (1999: 14); Susan Stanford Friedman, 'Making History', in *Feminism Beside Itself* (1995: 24, 32ff.); Kathleen Canning, 'Feminist History After the Linguistic Turn: Historicizing Discourse and Experience' (1997: 423ff.); Willie Thompson, *What Happened to History?* (2000: 66); and Catherine Hall, 'Politics, Post-structuralism and Feminist History' (1991: 207). Scott's elegantly written texts encompass quite a remarkable elaboration of modest, cautious formulations about post-structuralist theory *and* dismissive judgments about other ways of doing women's and gender history. See, for instance, Scott (1988: 42, 53; 1996: xi).

8  In her later work, Butler seems to sense the need to resurrect categories as provisionally useful, although, tellingly, she offers no way to make sense of, or define, what terms such as gender, race, class might mean, or to differentiate between 'resignifications' of such terms as more or less democratic.

9  Mouffe distinguishes between 'the political' as the ontological 'dimension of antagonism . . . constitutive of human societies' and 'politics' as 'the set of practices and institutions through which an order is created'. Nevertheless in her conceptualisation, politics is largely understood as an epiphenomenon of ontology. Perhaps nowhere is the trivialisation of the complexity of 'politics' more evident than in the way Mouffe discusses the obstacles to creating a democratic, multipolar world order: 'I do not want to minimize the obstacles that need to be overcome, but, at least in the case of the creation of a multipolar order, those obstacles are *only of an empirical nature*, while the cosmopolitan project is also based on flawed theoretical premises' (Mouffe 2005: 9, 118, emphasis added).

10  It is worth noting in passing that for all the efforts to move politics onto some territory other than identity, the prevalence of metaphors for politics as the proliferation of identities, subject positions or subjectivities suggests that not much of a shift may have occurred. Cf. Butler (2004).

11  Butler's refusal to 'separate out' gender is similar to Laclau and Mouffe's refusal to ascribe to 'class' any particular theoretical significance (on the premise that such a separation would imply a view of 'society' as 'closed'. The unwillingness to assign gender or class explanatory power precludes the development of any specific account of gender- or class-related power in society.

12 We are fully aware that the implication of our concept of 'individual's and groups' actions' implies that subjects initiate actions and formulate interests. But we reject the claim that because signification provides particular enabling conditions, rules and practices for subjects' actions to become intelligible, it becomes impossible to articulate a concept of political action as the action of subjects. In other words, we reject the claim that we must limit the definition of politics to the 'activity' of discourse.

13 For instance, although it increased the role of both the state and medical authorities in the arena of reproduction in the U.S., the Supreme Court's decision in *Roe v. Wade* also established important restrictions on state intervention in reproductive decision-making. One could argue that renewed efforts to overturn *Roe* in the U.S. are an indirect indication of how that law had altered gender power relations in the arenas of reproductive freedom.

14 See, for instance, both Ferguson and Youngs in this anthology.

15 See, for instance, Barriteau, Tripp and Youngs in this collection.

16 See, for instance, Pincus, Schreiber and Åberg in this collection.

17 In her discussion of 'remedies' that could address both problems of distribution and recognition, Fraser argues for a transformative approach to redistribution that depends on a 'deep restructuring of relations of production'. Yet, her analysis of justice as distribution gives no account of how to conceptualise gender inequality or other axes of inequality in ways other than narrowly economic or as sub-sets of class inequality (Fraser 1995b: 87).

18 In Chapter 3 of this anthology, Jónasdóttir takes up some of Marx's texts on method "to elaborate further some key ideas about the use-value of Marx's approach for feminist theory. The point is to show that a feminist use of Marx's method can both re-activate certain underdeveloped, constitutive elements of Marx's approach to the study of society and history and also bring forward others which are, in some sense, new".

19 See the debate between Fraser and Butler on the concept, 'merely cultural' (Butler 1998: 33–44; Fraser, 1998: 140–50).

## References

Anderson, Perry. 1998. *The Origins of Postmodernity*. London: Verso.

Anzaldúa, Gloria (ed). 1990. *Making Face, Making Soul: Haciendo Caras, Creative and Critical Perspectives by Women*. San Francisco, CA: Aunt Lute Foundation Books.

Benhabib, Seyla. 1990. 'Epistemologies of Postmodernism: A Rejoinder to Jean-François Lyotard', in Linda J. Nicholson (ed) *Feminism/Postmodernism*, pp. 107–30. New York: Routledge.

Best, Steven and Douglas Kellner. 1991. *Postmodern Theory: Critical Interrogations*. New York: Guilford Press.

Butler, Judith. 1990. *Gender Trouble: Feminism and the Subversion of Identity*. New York: Routledge.

Butler, Judith. 1992. 'Contingent Foundations: Feminism and the Question of "Postmodernism"', in Judith Butler and Joan W. Scott (eds) *Feminists Theorize the Political*, pp. 3–21. New York: Routledge.

Butler, Judith. 1993. *Bodies That Matter: On the Discursive Limits of 'Sex'*. London: Routledge.

Butler, Judith. 1995. 'For a Careful Reading', in Seyla Benhabib, Judith Butler, Drucilla Cornell and Nancy Fraser (eds) *Feminist Contentions: A Philosophical Exchange*, pp. 127–43. New York and London: Routledge.

Butler, Judith. 1997. *Excitable Speech: A Politics of the Performative*. New York: Routledge.

Butler, Judith. 1998. 'Merely Cultural', *New Left Review* 227: 33–45.

Butler, Judith. 2004. *Undoing Gender*. New York: Routledge.

Butler, Judith and Joan W. Scott. 1992. 'Introduction', in Judith Butler and Joan W. Scott (eds) *Feminists Theorize the Political*, pp. xiii–xvii. New York: Routledge.

Calhoun, Craig. 1993. 'Postmodernism as Pseudohistory', *Theory, Culture and Society* 10 (1): 75–97.

Canning, Kathleen. 1997. 'Feminist History after the Linguistic Turn: Historicizing Discourse and Experience', in Barbara Laslett, Ruth-Ellen Boetcher Joeres, Mary Jo Maynes and Evelyn Brooks Higginbotham (eds) *History and Theory: Feminist Research, Debates, Contestations*, pp. 416–52. Chicago, IL: University of Chicago Press.

Derrida, Jacques. 1982. 'Sending: On Representation', *Social Research* 49 (2): 294–326.

Derrida, Jacques. 1988. *Limited Inc*. Evanston, IL: Northwestern University Press.

Eagleton, Terry. 2000. *The Idea of Culture*. Oxford: Blackwell.

Eagleton, Terry. 2003. *After Theory*. New York: Basic Books.

Fraser, Nancy. 1995a. 'Pragmatism, Feminism, and the Linguistic Turn', in Behabib, Seyla, Judith Butler, Drucilla Cornell and Nancy Fraser *Feminist Contentions. A Philosophical Exchange*, pp. 157–71. New York and London: Routledge.

Fraser, Nancy. 1995b. 'From Redistribution to Recognition? Dilemmas of Justice in a "Post-socialist" Age', *New Left Review* 212: 68–93.

Fraser, Nancy. 1998. 'Heterosexism, Misrecognition and Capitalism: A Response to Judith Butler', *New Left Review* 228: 140–50.

Fraser, Nancy. 2003. 'Social Justice in the Age of Identity Politics: Redistribution, Recognition, and Participation', in Nancy Fraser and Alex Honneth, *Redistribution or Recognition: A Political-philosophical Exchange*, pp. 7–109. London: Verso.

Fraser, Nancy and Alex Honneth. 2003. *Redistribution or Recognition: A Political-philosophical Exchange*. London: Verso.

Friedman, Susan Stanford. 1995. 'Making History: Reflections on Feminism, Narrative, and Desire', in Diane Elam and Robyn Wiegman (eds) *Feminism Beside Itself*, pp. 11–53. London: Routledge.

Fridolfsson, Charlotte. 2006. *Deconstructing Political Protest*. Örebro, Sweden: Örebro Studies in Political Science 17.

Gatens, Moira. 1992. 'Power, Bodies and Difference', in Michèle Barrett and Anne Phillips (eds) *Destabilizing Theory. Contemporary Feminist Debates*, pp. 120–37. Cambridge: Polity Press.

Grosz, Elisabeth. 1989. 'Sexual Difference and the Problem of Essentialism', *Inscriptions* 5: 86–101.

Hall, Catherine. 1991. 'Politics, Post-structuralism and Feminist History', *Gender and History* 3 (2): 204–10.

Harding, Sandra. 1986. *The Science Question in Feminism*. Ithaca, NY: Cornell University Press.

Hawkesworth, Mary E. 1989. 'Knowers, Knowing, Known: Feminist Theory and Claims of Truth', *Signs* 14 (3): 553–7.

Hekman, Susan. 2000. 'Beyond Identity: Feminism, Identity and Identity Politics', *Feminist Theory* 1 (3): 289–308.

Hemmings, Clare. 2005. 'Telling Feminist Stories', *Feminist Theory* 6 (2): 115–39.

Hird, Myra J. 2004. 'Feminist Matters. New Materialist Considerations of Sexual Difference', *Feminist Theory* 5 (2): 223–32.

Honneth, Axel. 2003. 'Redistribution as Recognition: A Response to Nancy Fraser', in Nancy Fraser and Alex Honneth, *Redistribution or Recognition: A Political-philosophical Exchange*, pp. 110–97. London: Verso.

Jónasdóttir, Anna G. 1994. *Why Women Are Oppressed*. Philadelphia, PA: Temple University Press.

Jónasdóttir, Anna G. 1995. 'What Has Love to Do with Power and Political Interests', paper presented at the conference 'Macht-Frauenmacht-MachtFrauen-GegenMacht', arranged by the 'Arbeitskreis Politik und Geschlecht in der Deutschen Vereinigung für politische Wissenschaft', Heimfolkshochschule Springe, Germany, 3–5 February.

Jones, Kathleen B. 1988. 'Socialist Feminist Theories of the Family', *Praxis International* 8 (3): 284–300.

Jones, Kathleen B. 1993. *Compassionate Authority. Democracy and the Representation of Women*. New York: Routledge.

Jones, Kathleen B. and Anna G. Jónasdóttir (eds). 1988. *The Political Interests of Gender: Developing Theory and Research with a Feminist Face*. London: Sage Publications.

Keay, Douglas. 1987. 'Interview with Margaret Thatcher', *Woman's Own*, 3 October.

Laclau, Ernesto and Chantal Mouffe. 1985. *Hegemony and Socialist Strategy. Towards a Radical Democratic Politics*. London: Verso.

Lyotard, Jean-François. 1979. *The Postmodern Condition: A Report on Knowledge*. Manchester: Manchester University Press.

Lykke, Nina. 2007. 'Sexual Health, Embodiment, and Empowerment'. Paper presented at GEXcel Kickoff Conference, Linköping University, Sweden, 3–5 May.

McCall, Leslie. 2005. 'The Complexity of Intersectionality', *Signs* 30 (3): 1771–1800.

Marx, Karl and Friedrich Engels. 1970. *The German Ideology*. New York: International Publishers.

Mohanty, Chandra Talpade. 1991. 'Under Western Eyes: Feminist Scholarship and Colonial Discourse', in Chandra Talpade Mohanty, Ann Russo and Lourdes Torres (eds) *Third World Women and the Politics of Feminism*, pp. 51–80. Bloomington, IN: Indiana University Press.

Mouffe, Chantal. 1992. 'Feminism, Citizenship, and Radical Democratic Politics', in Judith Butler and Joan W. Scott (eds) *Feminists Theorize the Political*, pp. 369–84. New York: Routledge.

Mouffe, Chantal. 2001/2002. 'Interview', *Center for the Study of Democracy* 9 (1): 10–13.

Mouffe, Chantal. 2005. *On the Political.* London: Routledge.

Mouzelis, Nicos. 1988. 'Marxism or Post-Marxism', *New Left Review* 167: 107–23.

Scott, Joan W. 1986. 'Gender: A Useful Category of Historical Analysis', *American Historical Review* 91: 1053–75.

Scott, Joan W. 1988. *Gender and the Politics of History*. New York: Columbia University Press.

Scott, Joan W. 1991. 'The Evidence of Experience', *Critical Inquiry* 17 (4): 773–98.

Scott, Joan W. 1992. 'Experience', in Judith Butler and Joan W. Scott (eds) *Feminists Theorize the Political*, pp. 22–40. New York: Routledge.

Scott, Joan W. 1996. *Only Paradoxes to Offer: French Feminists and the Rights of Man*. Cambridge, MA: Harvard University Press.

Segal, Lynne. 1999. *Why Feminism? Gender, Psychology, Politics*. New York: Columbia University Press.

Smith, Barbara 1990 [1982]. 'Racism and Women's Studies', in Anzaldúa, G. (ed.) *Making Face, Making Soul: Haciendo Caras, Creative and Critical Perspectives by Women*, pp. 25–28. San Francisco: Anne Late Foundation Books.

Thompson, Willie. 2000. *What Happened to History?* London: Pluto Press.

Tilly, Louise A. 1994. 'Women, Women's History, and the Industrial Revolution', *Social Research* 61 (1): 115–38.

Varikas, Eleni. 1995. 'Gender, Experience and Subjectivity: The Tilly–Scott Disagreement', *New Left Review* 211: 89–102.

Walby, Sylvia. 1992. 'Post-post-modernism? Theorizing Social Complexity', in Michèle Barrett and Anne Phillips (eds) *Destabilizing Theory. Contemporary Feminist Debates*, pp. 31–52. Cambridge: Polity Press.

Webster, Fiona. 2000. 'The Politics of Sex and Gender: Benhabib and Butler Debate Subjectivity', *Hypatia* 15 (1): 1–22.

Webster, Fiona. 2002. 'Do Bodies Matter? Sex, Gender, and Politics', *Australian Feminist Studies* 17 (38): 191–203.

White, Stephen K. 2000. *Sustaining Affirmation: The Strengths of Weak Ontology in Political Theory*. Princeton, NJ: Princeton University Press.

Young, Iris Marion. 2000. *Inclusion and Democracy*. Oxford: Oxford University Press.

Zalewski, Marysia. 2000. *Feminism after Postmodernism: Theorising Through Practice*. London: Routledge.

# 3

# Feminist questions, Marx's method and the theorisation of 'love power'[1]

*Anna G. Jónasdóttir*

### Introduction[2]

Of all those who dealt with feminist theory before the de(con)structive gale of postmodernism swept over the world, almost everyone related to Marx in one way or another: they found him usable, or they let him go. I am one of those feminist theorists who did not let him go. But I took him on my own terms. Because of the kind of *feminist* premises I set, I have kept loose company with him ever since. Since 1985, and the influence of what might be called the P-P-D trinity (postmodernism, post-structuralism and deconstructionism) my elective affinity with Marx has endured and my belief that historically located feminist analyses of contemporary societies have much to gain from reading Marx has become even stronger. I do not claim that Marx, and Marx alone, can tell the truth, the whole truth, and nothing but the truth as to how feminist scholars should proceed; still less do I think he (or any one great thinker, male or female) can tell us how exactly we should deal with whatever problem we wish to study. Least of all do I think Marx has much to say, specifically, about the kind of feminist politics that would be appropriate in various parts of the world today. If, however, the main feminist question is *to theorise gender and power as ongoing, conditioned activities, relationships, institutions, and processes in historically located societies*, then Marx's approach, his *method*, is valuable.

How can my deliberately delimited but positive evaluation of Marx be grounded? In this chapter I pursue an extended argument concerning the developmental potential of historical materialism or, more precisely, Marx's variant of it. I consider Marx's materialism, his *method*, from the perspective of *whether and how it can serve feminist theory*. I contend that the materialist method can be employed, effectively, for radical feminist aims, if certain terms or *conditions* are set. By this I mean that certain choices must be made with respect to prevailing alternative views of what this method is, and how to use it. I wish to emphasise more clearly than I did in my earlier work that, by following the conditions set, such as treating radical feminist questions as a specific problematic or domain relatively independent from the theoretical domain of political economy, my feminist theory proposals have *implications* of considerable significance for historical materialism more generally.

I made almost no explicit textual interpretation of Marx in my earlier work. Rather, *Why Women Are Oppressed* (hereafter *WWAO* and Jónasdóttir 1994) presented the main results of my attempt to *use* him. In the second part of this chapter, I present some of Marx's texts on method in order to clarify how I read them and to elaborate further some key ideas about the use-value of Marx's approach for feminist theory. The point is to show that a feminist use of Marx's method can both re-activate certain underdeveloped, constitutive elements of Marx's approach to the study of society and history, and also bring forward others which are, in some sense, new. In the final part of this chapter I draw some conclusions concerning the relevance of my reinterpretation of Marx today.

### Using Marx's method: outcome, conditions and implications

#### Outcome

*WWAO* presented the main results of my attempt, as Heidi Hartmann expressed it, to 'put [Marx's method] to the service of feminist questions' (Hartmann 1981: 11; see *WWAO*: ch. 4). I began the work in 1980 as a contribution to what Alison Jaggar termed the 'distinctive theoretical project' of socialist feminism; a project which emerged as a broad theoretical movement in the early 1970s (Jaggar 1983: 118). My argument comprised an elaborated stance regarding the following two broad questions:

1  Given the ambitious aim of the 'distinctive' socialist – feminist theory project, what are the radical feminist questions that the 'Marxist method' might help to develop?
2  What *is* Marxist method and *how* can and should it be used for *this particular aim*?

In the process of answering these questions, I placed myself beyond socialist feminism and radical feminism in the sense that my translation of Marx's method into the field of sexuality and gender relations transcended both these branches of feminist theory. *WWAO* proposed, first, a reoriented feminist version of historical materialism seen as a realist *research tradition*, or – to borrow an important phrase from Marx – as a 'guiding thread for my studies' (Marx 1859/1977: 389). Although a metaphor, the phrase 'guiding thread' is a conceptual key to the stance I take regarding what Marxist method is or should be. By research tradition I mean, to quote Larry Laudan:

> A set of general assumptions about the ontological entities and processes in
> a domain of study, and about the appropriate methods to be used for
> investigating the problems and constructing the theories in that domain . . .
> A research tradition provides a set of guidelines for the development of
> specific theories belonging to that tradition [guidelines which are] neither
> explanatory, nor predictive nor directly testable. (1977: 79, 81, 82)

Second, I presented a draft of a *specific theory* derived from feminist and
historical materialist premises to why or how men's power positions with
respect to women persist even in contemporary western societies, 'where
women and men are seen as formally/legally equal individuals, where
almost all adult women are fully or partly employed, where there is a high
proportion of well-educated women, and where welfare state arrangements, which obviously benefit women, are relatively well developed'
(Jónasdóttir 1994: 1). I identified 'those mechanisms that hold together,
produce, and reproduce contemporary society when seen primarily as a
web of relations between the sexes' (Jónasdóttir 1994: 3). This specific
theory, then, is located *mainly* at the level of 'social being' or social existence; it is not concerned *specifically* with forms of consciousness.[3]

My theoretical project raised questions, with one eye, so to speak, on
Marx's method and the other on the feminist matter in question. My
'process of inquiry', to borrow well-known words from Marx, included
questions such as the following: What *is* specific about 'our oppression'? as
Juliet Mitchell put it, or, 'What is being done to us?' (Mitchell 1986: 92).
Why are *women* oppressed, and by whom? How has the concept of 'patriarchy' *actually been used* by radical feminists, and how can it be handled
from a feminist perspective more clearly informed by Marx's method?[4]
What is the valid ground for the feeling or 'sense' that 'our oppression'
(Rowbotham 1974: 24) is rooted mainly in something other than the
conditions and terms on which labour is organised and exploited? How can
we theorise *sexuality* as a field of individual agency (or performance) *and*
personal experience, as a complex web of socially and politically conditioned relationships, *and* as the consequence of what takes place in these
relationships? In other words, can we conceptualise 'sexuality' as a systemic
concept, much like the concept 'economy'? How can we develop a theory
of sexuality so that we keep *both* the criteria of materialist method *and* the
specific character of the field in focus? (Hartmann 1981: 29). How is *power*
understood and conceptualised as a part of sexuality in distinction from
power as dominance only or power merely as the effect of discourse?

Considering 'exploitation' not solely in the context of class and labour,
but also in the sociosexual context, in *which capacity* are women exploited,
and by *whom*? What is it to be exploited *as women*? How does *this particular* process of exploitation work? *Where* does it take place? And, to extend

the analytical questioning still further, *what* is it that is being exploited? In other words, *what* is being extracted, or appropriated, from women in their (socially and culturally formed) capacity as women? Here, the actualisation of 'love power' came into the picture for me, emerging as a result of my assumption that a crucial part of the theoretical analysis of women's exploitation must be done within the field of sexuality, and not limited to economy or work and also that the analysis had to be extended 'beyond oppression'. Yet, my proposal that contemporary patriarchy, or male dominated society, is produced and reproduced by means of appropriative practices or exploitation of women's love power was never intended to serve as a monocausal explanation. Rather, it was intended to supplement the explanatory power of feminist theories of women's oppression, male dominance and patriarchy. Practically all feminist theorists, radical and socialist feminist alike, who used Marxism as a 'method of social analysis' (Hartmann 1981: 11) have run into an impasse resulting either from what I call the 'work fixation', which often accompanies a 'total theory ambition' in socialist feminist theory, or the 'violence fixation' in radical feminist theory. Socialist feminist theory, which has been the main object of my critique, lacked all the main elements it needed for its analysis. To build a feminist realist approach to society and history and a theory of contemporary patriarchy appropriate to that approach, the necessary minimum of elements include the following: a specific, and in a certain sense 'essential' identification of the sociosexual *relationship*, along with a specific *practice* or creative *activity* generated in and occuring in this relationship involving a specific human developmental capacity or *power* over the use and control of which certain groups of people struggle. Without all these elements no sex/gender specific structure on the basic level of social being can be distinguished. Nor is it possible to determine clearly which institution(s) is/are more relevant than others in the production and reproduction of male power or patriarchy. The outlines of my constructive theses run as follows.

On the level of a research tradition, or 'guiding thread', I suggested an analytically distinct feminist view for the study of society and history. This view proposed a foundation of social existence, where *production (and reproduction) of life and living people, gender relationships (the social sexes)*, and the *organisation of love* take the place that *production (and reproduction)* of the *means of life, social classes*, and the *organisation of labour* hold in Marx's general social theory and view of history. The institution of *marriage* is seen as a central link between the state and society, meaning that its significance or status in my theory corresponds to the status of *private property* in Marx's theory.

On the empirically oriented and testable, specific level of a theory of contemporary western patriarchy, I argued that the basic structure of male dominance or patriarchy in formally/legally equal societies has been maintained in a conflict-filled process, where unequal energy or power transactions structure relations between women and men. Marriage, understood as historically changing and ideologically defined, is the key social and legal institution whose organisation and regulation keeps the process of male domination in action. The institution of marriage has a wide meaning. It refers not only to legally married or co-habiting couples, but also to the patterns of interaction which it establishes and prohibits between women and men, and between people as sexual beings (i.e., between and among women and between and among men) in society at large. What is crucial is men's possessiveness vis-à-vis women, that is, men's claims to access to women. In practice, men's 'rights' to appropriate women's sexual resources, especially their capacities for love, continues, even if (in many societies) no longer legally. The core of my theory is that women and men as sociosexual beings constitute the main parties of a particular exploitative relationship, a relationship in which men tend to exploit women's capacities for love and transform these into individual and collective modes of power over which women lose control.

## Conditions

What, then, are the conditions for the most effective use of Marx's method for feminist theory?

### Marx's and not Engels's method

We should adopt the materialist method as developed and used by Marx, rather than as summarised or reconstructed by Engels (Carver 1984). The point of appropriating Marx directly, rather than via Engels, is that Marx's work is much less affected by the all-inclusive philosophical materialism propounded by Engels, which is analogous to Hegel's all-inclusive idealism. Marx was clearly oriented towards the understanding and explanation of issues that are peculiar for the human social world and not towards any universal theory of 'dialectic materialism'. As a corollary to this, Marx had much less of the techno-economic determinism than can be found in Engels.[5]

### Marx's 'guiding thread': neither orthodoxy nor scientism

Marx's materialism should not be taken to be a *theory* in any strong sense of the word. Rather, it should be seen as a research tradition, which provides a set of guidelines and ontological assumptions for the development of specific theories. Research traditions, unlike the theories belonging to them, 'are neither explanatory, nor predictive, nor directly testable' (Laudan 1977: 81). This view of Marx's materialist method rules out the two classical or 'orthodox' Marxist doctrines; and it rejects the more recent scientistic or 'logicist' counterpart to the older two-sided orthodoxy as well, such as those suggested by Jon Elster and John Roemer (Elster 1985; Roemer 1988; Shapiro and Wendt 1992).

I include Habermas in this two-sided category of Marxist scientism or logicism, because he marks his own position on what historical material-ism is in terms of a '*theory of social evolution* awaiting empirical validation' (Habermas 1978: 47). Although Smith (1984: 513) is correct when he writes that: while 'For Cohen technological advance is the "motor" of history, pushing forward changes in the political, legal, and cultural spheres', whereas Habermas 'asserts that changes in the structure of moral-practical consciousness are at the center of historical development', both these 'opposite ends of the spectrum' take historical materialism to be a theory in the strong sense. In contradistinction to Habermas I think that the 'weak' view of historical materialism as a 'heuristic' guide to further studies is the view that should be taken. The 'weak or limited' (Habermas 1978: 47) interpretation of historical materialism as a research tradition (or 'guiding thread') implies that what can be *relatively strong* is the specific theories of concrete societies (or 'parts' of societies), which, according to this guiding thread, must be located and delimited in time and space.

## *The main interest: a non-formulaic Marx*
A third condition, also closely connected with the foregoing, is that the interest in Marx's work should focus on the 'mode of investigation' he developed in order to analyse, conceptualise, and explain 'the world'. Rather than providing concrete formulaic solutions to strategic feminist problems, or being of use 'as a manual for [feminist] revolutionaries' (James 1985: 143), I contend that Marx offers an unusually rich scholarly perspective concerning how social and political theory and analyses of history should be framed and conducted so as to render the composite and complex character of the subject matter as clearly as possible. In addition, I think that such a view of what scholarly work is for better ensures that such work will be useful for strategy and political action.

## *Political sexuality: a particular vantage point*
By preferring Marx to Engels on the materialist method, and by privileg-ing a certain kind of a 'weak or limited' *realist* view on historical mater-ialism, taking it to be neither a testable theory of the course of history nor instructions for political strategy or moral conduct, I arrived at a method-ological stance which accommodates radical feminist questions and Marx's method. This means that it should be possible to theorise (i.e.,

conceptualise and explain) the problem of patriarchy (women's oppression, or male dominance) from a fundamental perspective or *analytical vantage point*, and thus as a specific theoretical domain. Although guided by the same method, this vantage point does not fit within, nor is it plausible to derive it, as Jaggar claims, (1983: 135) from within the 'domain of political economy', i.e., from Marx's specific theory of capitalism, or from any economic or 'work-fixated' domain (Jonasdotir 1994: 208). I have labelled the specific domain in question 'political sexuality'.

## Implications

One crucial point I have taken as *a priori*: *it is the feminist questions, not the Marxist method, which is the subject that really matters*. This guided me throughout the work process on *WWAO* and still does, although now in a more qualified sense. Concretely this means that my aim was neither to supplement Marxism, nor to contribute to this or that underdeveloped area *in Marxism*, or to 'improve' the so-called unhappy marriage between Marxism and feminism. Rather, my aim was to help explain the problem why/how men's power vis-à-vis women is reproduced and augmented. Seriously considering the programmatic declaration of socialist feminists, I decided to ask radical feminist questions and see how far one could come translating the 'Marxist method' to feminist questions. My task was not to determine what Marx had written or not written about women, women's labour, or more generally, about the so called women's question. Instead, my task was to apply his method to contemporary feminist questions, while facing the fact that Marx had developed his mode of investigation in order to deal with 'economic questions' (Marx 1859/1977: 388) salient one and a half centuries ago. As I saw it, the point was to try to translate this method into an analytical domain both fundamentally different from and similar enough to Marx's concerns for the attempt of translation to be meaningful. In this regard, my project differed from other efforts, such as feminist standpoint theory (Smith 1974; Harding 1981; Hartsock 1983; Jaggar 1983) and those earlier efforts of Mitchell and Hartmann.

I realised that my theses, if they were valid, would have implications for the more general debates on 'problems of historical materialism' (Williams 1978; Soper 1979) that emerged in the 1960s and 1970s; debates which, although relatively marginalised at present, have not been silenced. If love, and not only labour, creates people/human social existence under conditions that can be called materialist, and if people produce society and make history by means of love, that is, by practising and using/consuming love power, then labour loses its absolute position as the singular concept in a materialist conception of history. If (gendered) sexual love is a specific alienable human material or exploitable capacity/power, which is vital for the production and reproduction of society, then the concepts of 'love' and 'love power' would be of immediate interest for the development of historical materialism more generally. 'Socially organised love' would serve to fill the 'potential gap' in the historical materialist tradition of thought. Such a gap opens up, according to Eric Hobsbawm, if or when 'comparable analytical discoveries' (that is to say comparable with 'labour's' status), actualised by the given process of history, can be identified. Such another, 'central analytical concept' would 'enable thinkers to reinterpret history' (Hobsbawm 1984: 41; Jónasdóttir 1994: 244).

Love as a *'practical*, human-sensuous activity'*, to quote Marx's 'Theses on Feuerbach' (1970: 122), would displace, or at least seriously compete with, other analytical discoveries with similar claims to the significance Marx ascribed to labour. My revision of Marx's materialism intervenes into the subject of this method, both by re-activating what is already there and by bringing in matter which develops it as well. In the following discussion I will concentrate on two related issues. First, I aim to show how I ground the relative independence, or distinctiveness, of sociosexual relationships as a contextual feature or part of society, fit for having a specific theoretical perspective founded on it: the domain of political sexuality. Second, I will look at the notion of 'activity' and 'human activity' in Marx. The questions are how inclusive these concepts can be, and whether anything in Marx's mode of thinking about human life and history justifies that the kind of sociality actualised in sexual love relationships can be conceived as having what McLellan described as 'world-creating capacities' (McLellan 1977: 75) and, therefore, a clear theoretical significance.

### Marx's method: a realist radical-feminist reading

When feminists look for formulations about Marx's (or Marxist) method, the usual place to start is with the following well-known passage in Engels's Preface to *The Origin of the Family, Private Property and the State* (hereafter *Origin*).[6]

> According to the materialistic conception, the determining factor in history is, in the final instance, the production and reproduction of immediate life. This again is of a twofold character: on the one hand, the production of the means of existence, of food, clothing, and shelter and the tools necessary for that production; on the other side, the production of the human beings themselves, the propagation of the species. The social organization under which the people of a particular historical epoch and a particular country live is determined by both kinds of production: by the stage of

development of labour on the one hand, and of family on the other. (Engels
1972 [1884]: 71–2)

Here Engels renders in a nutshell some of the basic ontological and
methodological assumptions concerning the study of society and history,
developed jointly with Marx in *The German Ideology* (hereafter *GI*) in
1845–46. More precisely, this paragraph summarises the longer sections in
the 'First Premises of Materialist Method' (*GI* in Arthur 1970: 42–52).
Engels's formulation of the premises of historical materialism could well
serve as a starting point, were it not for the fact that feminist uses of this
passage suffer from a chronic misinterpretation. In so far as a misleading
reading of Engels marks the feminist entry into the research tradition of
historical materialism, the common understanding among feminists
regarding this tradition has been flawed. I will dwell at some length on the
citation in order to explain what I mean by 'misinterpretation'. From
there, I will clarify how my point of entry into the materialist method
differs. I then discuss some of Marx's texts on method.
    The usual feminist reading of the above passage misleadingly rephrases
the key concept of 'twofold' production: from two 'kinds of production'
into 'production' on the one hand and 'reproduction' on the other. This
rephrasing is not only incorrect, it also has influenced the 'materialist
conception' among feminists. As I read this passage, the 'materialist conception' of history includes assumptions about human life as basically
dependent on two sorts of productive activity through which human
beings maintain and create themselves. By two sorts I mean that these productive activities *differ in kind*. In this sense the foundation of human life
is 'twofold' or *dual*. Of course, and this point needs to be strongly under-
lined,[7] this is not to say that the materialist conception should thereby be
seen as *dualist*, in the sense that Marx rejects programmatically and with
great emphasis in the critique of 'the economists' and their 'common
sense' approach.[8] What the passage says is that 'the determining factor in
history is . . . the production and reproduction of immediate life', and that
this 'production and reproduction' is 'twofold'. It does not say that the
'determining factor in history' is production on the one hand and reproduction on the other. It assumes that social production – which always also
implies reproduction – comprises a duality; that the foundation of human
social life, of society and history, *is*, in a sense, two different *kinds of vital
production processes*, each of which has its own reproduction aspects (on
a daily basis, and in changing forms over time). On the one hand, there
is the production (and reproduction) of the *means* of life/existence; on the
other hand, the production (and reproduction) of *life* itself, of *human
existence*.

My point of entry into the materialist method has been through Marx's dialectical conception of production, and not through reproduction *per se*. What difference does this make? The production point of entry is a precondition for the possibility of constructing an analytically distinctive theoretical domain for the study of society as a sociosexual system or context. Marx's production approach suggests guidelines for the selection of conceptual elements needed to make the study of sociosexual relations plausible within a realist framework within which specific explanatory theories of sociosexual power relations in various forms of societies can be developed. Central among the elements in Marx's production approach is *'practical*, human-sensuous activity' or 'human practice' ('Theses on Feuerbach' in Arthur 1970: 122). His realist dialectical outlook also suggests a plural (rather than monistic) view of how social life, seen as a complex *whole* with constitutive *parts*, is produced and should be understood.

From the point of view of Marx's realist dialectical method the two kinds of production, distinguished in *Origin*, can and must be seen as two different 'parts', but parts that are not totally detached or separated from one another. Together they constitute a larger 'whole', the base of human social life, the foundation of society. According to this method, a necessary presupposition for the understanding of such a social whole is that the specific character of the parts that comprise the whole must be clarified. It is not enough to clarify the character of *one* part, and then draw logical conclusions (dialectical or rationalist) about the nature of the rest (the whole). In particular, this plural (as against monistic) view of social reality is crucial to keep in mind when the part which is at issue is thought to be strongly significant as a 'determining factor' for the context of the whole. How far does this short exercise in Marx's dialectics take us in a process of inquiry aiming to explain 'our oppression' or contemporary patriarchy? Not far; but it lends support (at the level of research tradition) to the hypothesis that in order to use this method to help answer radical feminist questions, the sexual part of social life must be distinguished and analysed in and of its own.

In what way, then, is the prevailing feminist interpretation of the 'materialistic conception' mistaken? By making *production* refer to the *one part* only (the 'production of the means of existence'), and *reproduction* to the *other part* only (the 'production of human beings themselves'), and at the same time by approaching reproduction through the activity of (women's) work or labour, two mistakes are made. First, the processes of production and reproduction are *separated*. Then, the latter is constructed in the image of the former in the sense that it (reproduction) is specified by the *same activity* that characterises the former, that is, by work or labour. Both

kinds of production (represented as production vs. reproduction) are
included in the theoretical domain of political economy, conceptualised
by Marx as related only to the production and reproduction of the means
of existence.[9] The more complex analytical view hinted at, though not
elaborated in Engels's book, has been closed off by such a reductionistic
reading.

There is also a flaw in the text itself which must be problematised. The
same flaw is in the corresponding sections in *GI*, as we will see below. At
the end of the passage cited above, when each kind of twofold production
is distinguished as to what is specifically 'determining' about it, one kind
is distinguished by its peculiar *activity*, i.e., 'labour'. The other is depicted
by the *institution*, which is considered to be the setting that socially organ-
ises this other kind of production, i.e., the 'family'. No specific kind of
activity, assumed to be peculiar for the 'production of human beings
themselves', is indicated here. With respect to the further use and development of the 'materialistic conception' of history, this discrepancy in the
use of central concepts is crucial. This flaw in the manner in which the two
kinds of production were conceptualised initially, has, to my knowledge,
nowhere been criticised, and the misreading has continued within contemporary feminist theory.

The feminist misreading of twofold production and the conceptual
discrepancy in the text itself seem to reinforce one another. The use of
'reproduction' as the main entry into an intended feminist rethinking of
materialism effectively insures that this kind of discrepancy will fail to be
seen or problematised. If production is taken to equal economic production, reproduction becomes the maintenance (in largely the same *or*
developed form) of that kind of production and the power structure
belonging to it. Of course much of what takes place in the family and in
relations between the sexes is directly or indirectly attached to economic
production, perhaps increasingly so, today. But, from the twofold production point of view, nothing in the unitary, or quasi-unitary notion of
production/reproduction necessarily raises *theoretically radical* questions
concerning a fundamental specificity in the production of human beings
themselves. In particular, no incentive arises to identify a specific kind of
creative activity that mediates between man and nature (a common way of
characterising labour) in this particular production. What might be made
of the fact that the author(s) of the materialist method actually included
this kind of production as a 'first premise' and a historical 'circumstance'
of its own is a question that never comes up (Marx and Engels 1970: 42).

What, then, are the general assumptions that Marx selected out
(together with Engels) in *The German Ideology*, and stated as being 'fundamental conditions' in history?

## First premises of the materialist method and fundamental conditions of history

Consider the following excerpt from *The German Ideology*, which outlines the principles of Marxist methods:

> The premises from which we begin . . . are the real individuals, their activity and the material conditions under which they live, both those which they find already existing and those produced by their activity. These premises can thus be verified in a purely empirical way . . . the first premise of all human existence and, therefore, of all history . . . [is] . . . that men must be in a position to live in order to be able to 'make history'. But life involves before everything else eating and drinking, a habitation, clothing and many other things. The first historical act is thus the production of the means to satisfy these needs, the production of material life itself . . . The second point is that the satisfaction of the first need (the action of satisfying, and the instrument of satisfaction which has been acquired) leads to new needs . . . The third circumstance which, from the very outset, enters into historical development, is that men, who daily remake their own life, begin to make other men, to propagate their kind: the relation between man and woman, parents and children, the family . . . These three aspects of social activity are not of course to be taken as three different stages, but just as three aspects or three "moments", which have existed simultaneously since the dawn of history and the first men, and which still assert themselves in history today. The production of life, both of one's own in labour and of fresh life in procreation, now appears as a double relationship: on the one hand as a natural, on the other as a social relationship. By social we understand the co-operation of several individuals, no matter under what conditions, in what manner and to what end. It follows from this that . . . this mode of co-operation is itself a 'productive force'. (Marx and Engels 1970: 42, 48–50)

The ontological claims made here about human existence and history are established in two steps. The first expresses the realist variant of an activity/conditions (or agency/structure) approach which is Marx's standpoint as against the idealistic viewpoint: 'The premises from which [to] begin . . . are the *real individuals, their activity* and the *material conditions under which they live*' (Marx and Engels 1970: 42). Here the elements assumed to constitute human existence – individuals, activity, conditions – are stated in a general form, without differentiation or further qualification. The second step answers the question: What is it, more concretely, concerning the 'real individuals, their activity and the material conditions under which they live', that should be abstracted 'in the imagination' (Marx and Engels 1970: 42) in order to understand better human existence and the making of history? In other words: *which feature(s)* of individuals, _what kind(s)_ of activity, and _which setting(s) and context(s)_ shaping the conditions under which they live should be selected out? The answer comprises the list of four 'first premises' or 'four aspects of the primary historical relationships'. One more issue – language and consciousness – is added, which might be seen as a fifth premise (Warren 1988). 'Only now, after having considered four moments, four aspects of the primary historical relationship, do we find that man also possesses "consciousness", but, even so, not "pure" consciousness' (Marx and Engels 1970: 50). The kind of wary status given to language and consciousness does not trivialise the importance of these human faculties, but stresses the main point, namely, that individuals cannot sustain themselves by consciousness, nor do new individuals emerge from the signs or sounds of language. As Marx and Engels put it, 'language, like consciousness, only arises from the need, the necessity, of intercourse with other men' (1970: 51). In other words, the human potential of language and consciousness develops in and through the dual process of the production of life, as real individuals act practically in the 'primary historical relationships'. Of course, language and consciousness work back on, or, when seen concretely, are formative parts of both these production processes.

The key concept at the center of this whole mode of thinking is the concept of needs. Human beings, when understood as 'living human individuals' (Marx and Engels 1970: 42), have needs before anything else. People produce their life _because they need to_. Real individuals 'daily remake their own life' and make and remake the species ('make other men', 'propagate their kind') out of necessity. The production of life, 'both of one's own in labour and of fresh life in procreation', is need-driven. In this non-trivial sense, the two kinds of 'primary' needs stated as 'first premises' are constant. But since the human production of life is both natural _and_ social, these needs (as they are felt) and the manner or mode in which they are satisfied are neither immutable or always the same; they are historical and changing. Needs themselves, including the primary ones, are produced and are the results of historical processes, as the second premise – the 'production of new needs' makes clear.

Yet, the picture of historical materialism as need-centered must be qualified. Individuals do not simply have needs which are, or are not, fulfilled by Providence, or Fate. Most characteristic of Marx's version of materialism is the idea that primary needs are _connected_ with certain _human dispositions or potential capacities_ – not _only_ to act _rationally_ (as Hegel would have it, according to Marx's critique) but also to act _practically_ to satisfy these needs. The ability to employ the human potential – to practise the capacities, which enable people to satisfy their vital needs – is also a human need and necessity in itself. This need should be considered twofold. The actual practices of making tools and of making love, in short, are '*practical*, human-sensuous activities' (Marx and Engels 1970: 122) without which human life, humanity, would not exist.

As the excerpt on method illustrates, sexuality is explicitly included among the abstractions mentioned in *GI*, Marx's major text on method. It is assumed to be a 'circumstance which, from the very outset, enters into historical development' (Marx and Engels 1970: 49). Not only is it seen as being one of the 'four aspects of the primary historical relationships' (Marx and Engels 1970: 50), but it is also distinguished as one of the two kinds of relations that constitute the 'production of life'. Moreover, the sexual 'part' of the production of life is seen as *both* a natural *and* a social relationship; just as the economic 'part' is *both* natural *and* social. Both aspects, each in its own way, comprise such a 'double relationship'. The 'social' is, thereafter, defined simply as the antonym of one single individual's activity. Not restricted to economic or labour activity, the 'social' refers to the 'cooperation of several individuals, no matter under what conditions, in what manner and to what ends' (Marx and Engels 1970: 50). Cooperation, *alias* the social, the fourth of 'the four aspects of the primary historical relationships' is thereafter declared to be 'itself a "productive force"' (Marx and Engels 1970: 50). Here we may conclude that two kinds of human, natural/social intercourse (*Verkehr*) – two kinds of a necessarily interactive, or interc(o)ursive, 'double relationship' – constitute the foundation of society, and so are the dual source of 'historical development'. Both have 'existed simultaneously since the dawn of history and the first men, and . . . still assert themselves in history today' (Marx and Engels 1970: 50).

The 'four aspects of the primary historical relationships', can be divided into two pairs. The first and third premises comprise the '[twofold] production of life', while the second and fourth define this twofold production of activity process as the result of two different, yet similar, kinds of human relationships, which are historically changing and socially creative sources of human needs and modes of life.

Yet even if I claim that there is a fundamental dual aspect to Marx's production approach, and that the second aspect of production must be seen as a fit domain for social theorising, is not the whole effort made worthless empirically by Marx's claim that 'the family, which to begin with is the only social relationship, becomes later, when increased needs create new social relations and the increased population new needs, a subordinate one' (Marx and Engels 1970: 49)? But, for Marx, this statement was neither the end of family history nor the last word about it. An empirically oriented social scientist, Marx concluded the passage on the 'third circumstance' with the statement, that the family 'must then be treated and analysed according to the existing empirical data, not according to 'the concept of the family', as is the custom in Germany' (Marx and Engels 1970: 49). Even though Marx conceptualised the family in the context of the institutional setting of the capitalist economy when he depicted it as 'subordinate', because his economic view was empirically open, and not locked into Hegelian or post-Hegelian categories ('the concept of the family'), his method allowed for the possibility that the role (and the theoretical importance) of the family might change fundamentally. Other aspects of family relations included under the 'third circumstance' might become more significant – culturally or economically as the mode of production of economic needs shifted from a family-based system. Marx's economic view did not preclude the possibility that the set of social relationships he identified as a particular aspect of social being – 'the relation between man and woman, parents and children' – might later transform into a wholly new form, including the possibility of becoming a relatively 'superordinate' relationship.

Where does this take us? In the market societies of global capitalism family and the kinship structure have been threatened with economic and political marginalisation even more than in Marx's time (see Watson-Franke, chapter 5, this collection). Yet, this is not the whole story, particularly when we approach the study of political sexuality through 'existing empirical data' about the impact of 'increased needs' and 'new social relations', both within the family and in the economy. To do this, two intersecting lines of argument would need to be developed. First, as I emphasised in *WWAO*, the *family* alone should not be the focus when the aim is to understand the significance of sexuality and love in social life today. In particular, the 'relation between man and woman', as well as the relation between women or between men, and even that between 'parents and children' is neither conditioned mainly by a family system nor lived or 'acted out' solely in the family. The composite and complex set of activities that constitute individuals' sociosexual being, including modes of sexual intimacy, caretaking, and parenting, along with the material conditions shaping these activities form a social and political *setting*, a sphere of life which can and must be seen as a society-wide dimension. The family is only one historically changing locale in this wider setting. When I speak about the process of production of people in a sense that goes beyond biological procreation, this society-wide gendered setting of institutionalised power relations is the 'locus' of this production and the varying forms and modes of appropriation of love power.

Just as the study of individuals living and acting out the *economic* part of social life is analytically distinct, so also, in this perspective, is the mode of living and activities constituting human socio*sexual* life. In the concrete the production of sociosexual life is concurrent with, and connected to (intersected with) other dimensions of social life. Interactions among the various dimensions occur and changes take place between and among the different parts and their relationship to one another. As a method of investigation, the overall aim of dialectics is to solve the problem of grasping not only the external (such as the formally legal) but also the internal and ongoing interactions and changes in material reality. According to Marx's empirically demanding dialectical approach, the *internal relations* between the two main parts of the twofold production of human existence must be studied and analysed carefully. The mistake is to think that knowledge – particularly absolute knowledge – can be found in closed categories.

### How inclusive is the concept of 'activity' in Marx?

Let us now turn to the question of how inclusive Marx's notion of activity and human practice can be and consider whether the 'new materialist' or realist view he developed is flexible enough to support my theorisation of the concept of love power, and thus of love as a 'world-creating capacity' somehow comparable with labour. Despite the fact that Marx accounted for two different kinds of production, he did not specify clearly two kinds of productive *activity*; nor did he elaborate a kind of *creative capacity* belonging specifically to what I have called the sociosexual part of the production of life. In numerous places, though, he hints at such a notion. Generally, what he writes on human activity and human practice presupposes a wider and more complex notion than his own more frequent use of the economic concept of labour suggests.

Interpreters of Marx usually claim that in his view 'human practice' and 'labour' are one and the same thing. For example, Terence Ball writes about 'that peculiarly human mode of purposive action, viz., labor', arguing that 'it is the activity of laboring that provides the paradigm of causation central to [Marx's] *wirkliche Wissenschaft*' (Ball 1984: 247). Others take artistic practice as *the* paradigmatic human activity that might widen the concept of 'human practice' (Kosik 1976; Williams 1978: 10). Marx does often seem to collapse a wider or more general concept of human activity with a more narrow or economically specific concept of labour. Yet, I think it is fairer to read him on this point not as theoretically monistic on principle. His field of study was political economy. He occupied himself with economic questions (as he wrote in the 1859 Preface) as early as 1842 and for the rest of his life, his scholarly work concerned changing conditions of labour, changing forms of institutionalised economic power in property relations, and what the world of money, capital and markets does to human relations and the real life of individuals.

Therefore, in places where he applies or elaborates his general concept of human practical activity, the economic activity of work, or labour, is the *particular kind* that he privileged. However, his early writings, as well as *Grundrisse*, the notebooks he kept in preparation for *Capital*, provide a view of human activity that invites the interpretation I have offered here. Nor does anything in his later writings speak against it.

What did Marx write explicitly, that could be construed plausibly as an invitation to use his general historical materialist approach to occupy myself with sexual questions? At first sight, it may seem that Marx speaks in the plural about vital powers, dispositions, and capacities only when he describes man as 'a directly natural being', while when specifying man as 'a *human* [italics added] natural being' (Marx 1977: 104) the capacities for 'changing of circumstances and . . . self-changing' tend to take the singular form of labour (Marx 1977: 105). Yet he also speaks about the unique human 'powers to create' in the plural:

> The real, active relationship of man to himself as a species-being or the man-ifestation of himself as a real species-being, i.e. as a human being, is only possible if he uses *all his species powers* [italics added] to create (which is again only possible through the cooperation of man and as a result of history). (Marx 1977: 101)

When Marx (1977: 110) gives concrete examples of 'real human and natural faculties' he almost never limits these to labour; love is often the core example. For example, in the quite well-known passage in *MS* , 'On Money', he wrote: 'If you suppose man to be man and his relationship to the world to be a human one, then you can only exchange love for love, trust for trust, etc.' (111). Contrary to the inverted world of money in which reigns 'confusion and exchange of all natural and human qualities', in a truly human world:

> Each of your relationships, to man – and to nature – must be a definite expression of your real individual life that corresponds to the object of your will. If you love without arousing a reciprocal love, that is, if your love does not as such produce love in return, if through the manifestation of yourself as a loving person you do not succeed in making yourself a beloved person, then your love is impotent and a misfortune. (Marx 1977: 111)

In 'Private Property and Communism', Marx criticised the ideas of the French communists (the so-called utopian socialists) for being simply the most 'crude' inverted image of capitalist society. He wrote:

> In this theory the community merely means a community of work and equality of the wages that the communal capital, the community as general capitalist, pays out. Both sides of the relationship are raised to a sham

universality, labour being the defining characteristic applied to each man, while capital is the universality and power of society. (Marx 1977: 88)

This form of communalised capitalism and universalised wage labour was not what Marx dreamt of as a possible more fully human future. Marx presented ideas concerning the relationship between the sexes that have surprised those few who have commented on them seriously and not taken them only as a piquant illustration of the 'real thing', that is, the economic property relations he mainly discusses in this section. As Shlomo Avineri (1968: 91) put it, Marx here 'discovers [the] paradigm of the [fully human-ised] future in the relationship between the sexes'. Marx expressed it as follows:

> The immediate, natural, and necessary relationship of human being to human being is the relationship of man to woman. In this natural relation-ship of the sexes man's relationship to nature is immediately his relationship to man, and his relationship to man is immediately his relationship to nature, his own natural function . . . From the character of this relationship we can conclude how far man has become a species-being, a human being, and con-ceives of himself as such . . . Thus it shows how far the natural behaviour of man has become human or how far the human essence has become his natural essence, how far his human nature has become nature for him. This relationship also shows how far the need of man has become a human need, how far his fellow men as men have become a need, how far in his most indi-vidual existence he is at the same time a communal being. (Marx 1977: 88)[10]

'According to Marx', Avineri (1968: 91) argued, 'the unique pattern of these relations has a systematic significance which makes it possible to project them as a general model for the structure of human relations in socialist society'. Sexual relations are understood as 'at once necessary and spontaneous' and – a key point – 'other-oriented *par excellence*'. This is because 'Man's need for a partner in the sexual relationship makes his own satisfaction depend upon another person's satisfaction.' In other words, this particular relationship is assumed to generate needs for reciprocity and co-equality between human persons, as no other human relationship does. In fact, Marx used love as a metaphor for the egalitarian organisa-tion of labor as productive activity. Making a distinction between society and community, and using community to signal the organisation of the world in a human way, Marx argued that if we carried out production in a more fully human way, instead of limited by the social and economic laws of capital, the specific character of each person's activity would have been objectified and I would become 'the mediator between you and the species and therefore would be recognised and felt by you yourself as a completion of your own essential nature and a necessary part of yourself, and consequently would now know myself to be confirmed in your thoughts and your love' (Marx and Engels 1975: 228).

The problem here, as Avineri also emphasised, is to avoid romanticising what is being said. The point is not that the good society should, or could be constructed like a love relationship or a family. In so far as Marx's words here are taken as a vision, it is the 'basic structural principle of sexual relations', i.e. 'the possibility of other-oriented relations' between co-equal subjects, that should be made into a 'universal principle of social organization' (Avineri 1968: 91).

In *WWAO* (Jónasdóttir 1994: 210) I pointed out that socialist feminists seem to have ignored the places in Marx where he explicitly writes about sexuality and love. The only exception, known to me at the time, was philosopher Virginia Held's 1976 essay, 'Marx, Sex, and the Transformation of the Society', where she dealt positively with the section in the *MS* cited above. Held, however, recently changed her mind concerning the transformative significance of the man–woman relationship and sexual love, and now sees 'the relation between mothering person and child' as less 'remote and uncertain', and more 'illuminating as a model'. She now thinks that 'taking the relation between child and mothering person as the primary social relation [might remind us that] unequal power is ever present' (Held 1993: 212). The political-philosophical implications of this shift, from potentially co-equal relations between adult persons as a principle of social organisation to making the *necessarily unequal* relations of a 'child and mothering person' into a 'model', are worth pondering.

The fundamental difference between Held's view and mine is that her mode of reasoning is that of the philosopher raising moral questions and seeking models or visions for how to solve them, i.e. as issues of justice. For me, I read Marx's texts on method neither for moral visions nor for guiding threads concerning justice. Well aware of the floating boundaries between the empirically oriented and the normative theoretical enterprise, I insist on the adequacy and political importance, of maintaining such boundaries. And I think that this can be done in a fruitful manner by assuming the methodological principles of realism (see chapter 2, this collection). So when I read Marx I am not so much looking for solutions to normative problems of power, or seeking suggestions for a better social order. Rather, my question is whether, or in what way, Marx's general propositions, for instance about the character and significance of sexuality and love, are of interest *now* as assumptions from which we can generate issues to investigate in order to understand and explain the conditions under which people as sexual beings live at present. In other words: *how* do the specific features or relations of 'real individuals and their activity' that concern sexuality and love make themselves visible today?

The importance of marking the difference between a mainly philosophical and a mainly empirically oriented (social science) mode of reading and using Marx can be well illustrated by revisiting Marx's (1977: 101) claim that the 'real, active relationship of man to himself . . . as a human being, is possible only if he *uses all his species powers to create*' (italics added). These words can be read as a categorical philosophical statement, and as such treated as either true or false, or they can be taken as an assumption, not directly testable, but pointing toward the study of how people today actually use their powers, how they act and interact in order to create themselves and their conditions, and to what effect. We can see choices being made about the ends for which human powers have been appropriated when we realise that almost exactly the same ideas as Marx had have now become central ingredients of the dominant ideology in the advanced capitalist world. All human resources are now said to be necessary to create continuous and increasing economic growth. The most important capital is said to be 'human capital'. Moreover, *love* and *trust* are now at the centre of attention, not only in the management literature but also in the vocabulary of neoclassical economic theory, the tradition of thought most closely tied to the imperatives of capitalist growth itself. The competitive conditions under which capital itself lives today are such that it cannot really sustain itself by consuming ordinary (or even the most qualified) *labour power*. Capital seems to need *love power* too.[11]

### Labour and love as human activity: what is the difference?

To defend the plural in Marx's view of activity and human activity is not to say that he defined all sorts of human activity equally well. In fact, he left the notion of activity necessarily broad and vague. As I read Marx, he defines human activity in two different ways or from two different aspects. The first depicts human activity as genuinely lived capacities, contrasted with forms of power (like money, or violence) unable fully to realise human capacities. The second defines human activity by comparing it with animal behaviour, as exemplified in Marx's often cited distinction between the architect and the bee: 'what distinguishes the worst architect from the best of bees is this, that the architect raises his structure in imagination before he erects it in reality'. (Marx 1967 [1867]: 178) Animals may be said to labour in a sense, according to Marx; yet what makes labour human, is that: 'At the end of every labour-process, we get a result that already existed in the imagination of the labourer at its commencement' (Marx 1967: 178). According to this line of reasoning, what makes labour specifically *human* is consciousness of purpose. If these two aspects taken together are all there is to be said about what is *human* in human activity,

Marx could perhaps be taken and (ab)used as one of the best architects, providing capitalist ideologues with the means for constructing people 'in wax'. Perhaps. But I wish to add to this interpretation some final comments about love as an activity.

There is no crucial dividing line between labour and love, as I see it, in the first aspect of Marx's definition. Money cannot *substitute* for love, nor can it *substitute* for the quality of work in things. But there is a vital difference between what is human in the activity of labour, and what is human in the activity of love. The architect–bee paradigm does not work for capturing what is distinctive about love as a human activity as opposed to a biological activity. If love, trust (and other kinds of human activities) are practised primarily as purposive or instrumental activities, the genuinely human aspect of this lived activity tends to deteriorate. If individuals practise love and trust in relation to other persons, mainly as a result-oriented activity, in order to create or shape the other person into some imagined 'object', these activities become something else; they become 'impotent', as Marx (1977: 111) put it. For love to be a genuinely human activity its practitioner acts not in order to make the love object fit an 'already existing idea', but, rather, to enable the 'object' of love to confirm its own capacity to 'create' or 'shape' himself or herself and his or her own goals (Jónasdóttir 1994: 73). A key aspect of labour is the social relation between human beings, which mediates their relation to non-human matter. A key aspect of love is a relation between human beings, who are made of human matter.

Managers of capitalist economies today call for love. In a relatively short time, a whole new conceptual universe has emerged in the field of socioeconomic intercourse (and its discourses). An *idiom of love terms* intertwines with the prevailing terms of labor and capital in the workplace. 'Love', 'care', 'trust', and 'mutual empowerment' co-exist and mingle with 'work', 'result accounts', 'money' and 'competition'. This has mainly to do with two conditions: steadily increasing competitiveness in world markets, and the increasing proportion of production (in the advanced capitalist countries) in so-called service production (as against traditional industrial production. My reasoning is twofold. (1) As the production of value increasingly depends on people in social intercourse with other people, love will become more actualised as a factor of production *in* the economic work process, and not only as a precondition to be taken for granted and counted on (without counting the costs) within 'the family'. Increasing market competition demands continuous changes, more and more result oriented management of human resources, and more and more effective organisation. The call for management by love instead of fear, and the commingling of seemingly disparate activities and values comes from struggles to survive in that competition. (2) Given that struggle over the conditions of love and control over the use of love power continues, and that for various social, economic, political, and historical reasons, women are systematically under-balanced in that struggle compared to men the increasing need for human love in the production process of capital is a crucial new condition under which women and men live. Conversely the growth of capital also depends on how women and men live and lead their lives as sociosexual beings. As more love is needed in the production process of capital, we can expect to find increasing modes of struggle over love in our lives: person to person as sexes, and as gendered persons in a number of capacities including as lovers, as parents, as daughters and sons, as friends, and generally as co-existing humans. I conclude that it is plausible to think of material production as being fundamentally dual, and that the internal relation between the two main parts of twofold production – the economic and the sociosexual – is in a historically crucial phase of flux.

Neither Marx nor Engels ever distinguished a theoretical domain of what I have called *political sexuality*. Their substantial contribution to a feminist variant of historical materialism did not go much beyond the line of articulating assumptions (and none too precisely) on the level of 'first premises'. Still, these assumptions support the idea that such a research domain might be developed through a distinct materialist perspective or vantage point. Such a view implies that it is neither useful to be 'disappointed' over what they did not say, nor fruitful to ascribe to Marx and Engels 'good intentions', arguing that their economic determinism was the result of a 'distraction' (Humphries 1987: 16, 17). Instead, it is wholly up to us, contemporary feminist interpreters of the 'materialist method', to explore its usefulness *now* and apply it in historical analyses as well as contemporary studies.

## Notes

1 I coined the concept 'love power' (a parallel to 'labour power') in my *Why Women Are Oppressed* (1994), which was originally published as *Love Power and Political Interests* (1991).

2 I wrote this chapter in 1999 for a special volume on *Feminist Interpretations of Karl Marx*, a volume that will not now be published. A shorter version of this work was published in Swedish in the journal *Häften för kritiska studier*, 2–4, 2002.

3 I wish to underline that I do not think social being/existence and consciousness are two separate things. On the contrary, one point of assuming Marx's method is to take over a view – his realist variant of dialectics – that makes it possible to see these 'parts' or levels of human life in society as *both* related *and* distinct. The method demands that each part be conceptualised *in its*

*distinctiveness*, in order to understand and explain the relations between the parts, and the complex whole, which the parts comprise.

4  Elsewhere (Jónasdóttir 1984), I suggested approaching patriarchy as a theoretical problem by distinguishing among three different aspects or partial questions: (1) the *origin* aspect or the *anthropological question*: how did the social inequality between the sexes originate at the dawn of history?; (2) the *historical question*: how does patriarchy change historically, and how should its history be periodicised?; and (3) the *structural aspect*, or the *theoretical question*: what mechanisms produce and reproduce contemporary form(s) of patriarchy? The weight of my work is on the third question. However, since these three aspects are interconnected, it is necessary, when working with the third question to have relatively well developed standpoints on the other two questions. From this point of view, it is quite obvious that debates about whether attempts to develop system-level theories of patriarchy can be fruitful have been flawed because distinctions among these aspects have not been made. Frequently, theoretical questions concerning explanations of male dominance or patriarchy have been collapsed with the *origin question* of 'when it all started'. Maintaining distinctions among these questions also would help resist the onslaught of biologism in this field of study.

5  The only way to read Shulamith Firestone's technical 'solution' to the oppression of women in her *Dialectic of Sex* (1971) intelligibly, besides as a provocation, is to read it through Engels's method rather than Marx's.

6  Compare for instance, *Engels Revisited: New Feminist Essays*, eds Janet Sayers, Mary Evans and Nanneke Redclift (1987). Typical formulations can be found in the Introduction to that book, where the editors write that 'Engels' account in the 1884 Preface of the relation of production and reproduction constitutes the major unifying theme' of the papers in the book, i.e. 'the issue of the relation of reproduction and production, of patriarchy and capitalism, of sex and class'.

7  Surprisingly, Terrell Carver, a prominent interpreter of both Marx and Engels, speaks about 'Engels's dualism' as well as 'his theoretical dualism,' aiming at the phrase 'twofold character.' Carver argues that by this use of terms Engels brings in some strange element which was not at all included in 'the earlier, more complicated account in which Marx had a hand', that is in the 'formulation in *The German Ideology*' (Carver 1985: 481, 482). Yet, I argue, a closer more open-minded interpretation of both pieces would see that Engels's 'twofold character' is a short sum-up of the earlier text's longer formulation.

8  See, for instance, Marx's dialectical analysis of the concept of production in the 1857 Introduction, included in *Grundrisse* (1973).

9  A striking example of this kind of reductionistic view of sexuality is in Jaggar (1983: 135, 305). See my critical comments in *WWAO* (Jónasdóttir 1994: 207–8).

10  Although Marx represented the relationship between man and woman as 'immediate, natural, and necessary', evidently thinking of biological reproduction in the context of his time, everything in this passage points us past heterosexuality to a more universal theory of sexuality as intimacy between humans as a felt social need.

11 In an unfinished manuscript, with the working title 'Love, Economic Resources, and Power Discourses' (written in Swedish) I deal with these issues.

## References

Avineri, Shlomo. 1968. *The Social and Political Thought of Karl Marx.* Cambridge: Cambridge University Press.

Ball, Terence. 1984. 'Marxian Science and Positivist Politics', in Terence Ball and James Farr (eds) *After Marx*, pp. 235–60. Cambridge: Cambridge University Press.

Carver, Terrell. 1984. 'Marxism as method', in Terence Ball and James Farr (eds) *After Marx*, pp. 261–80. Cambridge: Cambridge University Press.

Carver, Terrell. 1985. 'Engels's Feminism', *History of Political Thought* 6 (3): 479–89.

Cohen, Gerald A. 1978. *Karl Marx's Theory of History: A Defence.* Princeton, NJ: Princeton University Press.

Elster, Jon. 1985. *Making Sense of Marx.* Cambridge: Cambridge University Press.

Engels, Friedrich. 1972 (1884). *The Origin of the Family, Private Property, and the State.* London: Lawrence & Wishart.

Firestone, Shulamith. 1971. *The Dialectic of Sex: The Case for Feminist Revolution.* New York: Bantam Books.

Habermas, Jürgen. 1978. 'Toward a Reconstruction of Historical Materialism', in Fred Dallmayr (ed.) *From Contract to Community: Political Theory at the Crossroads*, pp. 47–63. New York: Marcel Dekker.

Harding, Sandra. 1981. 'What Is the Real Material Base of Patriarchy and Capital?', in Lydia Sargent (ed.) *Women and Revolution: The Unhappy Marriage of Marxism and Feminism: A Debate on Class and Patriarchy*, pp. 135–63. London: Pluto Press.

Hartmann, Heidi. 1981. 'The Unhappy Marriage of Marxism and Feminism: Towards a More Progressive Union', in Lydia Sargent (ed.) *Women and Revolution: The Unhappy Marriage of Marxism and Feminism. A Debate on class and Patriarchy*, pp. 1–41. London: Pluto Press.

Hartsock, Nancy. 1983. *Money, Sex, and Power: Toward a Feminist Historical Materialism.* Boston, MA: Northeastern University Press.

Held, Virginia. 1976. 'Marx, Sex, and the Transformation of the Society', in Carol C. Gould and Marx W. Wartofsky (eds) *Women and Philosophy: Toward a Theory of Liberation*, pp. 168–84. New York: Capricorn Books.

Held, Virginia. 1993. *Feminist Morality: Transforming Culture, Society, and Politics.* Chicago, IL: University of Chicago Press.

Hobsbawm, Eric. 1984. 'Marx and History', *New Left Review* 143 (Jan.–Feb.): 39–50.

Humphries, Jane. 1987. 'The Origin of the Family: Born Out of Scarcity Not Wealth', in Janet Sayers, Mary Evans and Nanneke Redclift (eds) *Engels Revisited: New Feminist Essays*, pp. 11–36. London: Tavistock Publications.

Jaggar, Alison. 1983. *Feminist Politics and Human Nature*. Totowa, NJ: Rowman & Allanheld.

James, Susan. 1985. 'Louis Althusser', in Skinner, Quentin (ed.) *The Return of Grand Theory in the Human Sciences*, pp. 141–57. Cambridge: Cambridge University Press.

Jónasdóttir, Anna G. 1984. *Kvinnoteori*. Örebro University: Research Reports 32.

Jónasdóttir, Anna G. 1991. *Love Power and Political Interests: Towards a Theory of Patriarchy in Contemporary Western Societies*. Örebro University: Örebro Studies 7.

Jónasdóttir, Anna G. 1994. *Why Women Are Oppressed*. Philadelphia: Temple University Press.

Kosík, Karel. 1976. *Dialectics of the Concrete*. Trans. Karel Kovanda and James Schmidt. Boston Studies in the Philosophy of Science 52.

Laudan, Larry. 1977. *Progress and Its Problems: Towards a Theory of Scientific Growth*. Berkeley, CA: University of California Press.

Marx, Karl. [1867] 1967. *Capital: Volume I*. Ed. Frederick Engels. New York: International Publishers.

Marx, Karl. 1970. 'Theses on Feuerbach', in Karl Marx and Friedrich Engels, *The German Ideology: Part One. With selections from Parts Two and Three and Supplementary Texts*. Ed. with introduction by C. J. Arthur, pp. 121–3. New York: International Publishers.

Marx, Karl. 1973. *Grundrisse: Foundations of the Critique of Political Economy*. Trans. with a foreword by Martin Nicolaus. London: Penguin Books/New Left Review.

Marx, Karl. 1977. 'Economic and Philosophical Manuscripts', in David McLellan (ed.) *Karl Marx: Selected Writings*, pp. 121–23. Oxford: Oxford University Press.

Marx, Karl. [1859] 1977. 'Preface to A Critique of Political Economy', in David McLellan (ed.) *Karl Marx: Selected Writings*. Oxford: Oxford University Press.

Marx, Karl and Friedrich Engels. 1970. *The German Ideology: Part One*. Ed. with introduction by C. J. Arthur. New York: International Publishers.

Marx, Karl and Friedrich Engels. 1975. *Collected Works: Volume II*. London: Lawrence and Wishart.

Millet, Kate. 1970. *Sexual Politics*. New York: Doubleday.

Mitchell, Juliet. 1986 [1971]. *Women's Estate*. Harmondsworth: Penguin Books.

Roemer, John, E. 1988. *Free to Lose: An Introduction to Marxist Economic Philosophy*. Cambridge, MA: Harvard University Press.

Rowbotham, Sheila. 1974. *Woman's Consciousness, Man's World*. Harmondsworth: Penguin Books.

Sayers, Janet, Mary Evans and Nanneke Redclift (eds). 1987. *Engels Revisited: New Feminist Essays*. London and New York: Tavistock Publications.

Shapiro, Ian and Alexander Wendt. 1992. 'The Difference that Realism Make: Social Science and the Politics of Consent', *Politics & Society* 20 (2):197–223.

Smith, Anthony A. 1984. 'Two Theories of Historical Materialism', *Theory and Society* 13 (4): 513–40.

Smith, Dorothy. 1974. 'Women's Perspective as a Radical Critique of Sociology', *Sociological Inquiry* 44: 7–13.

Soper, Kate. 1979. 'Marxism, Materialism, and Biology', in John Mepham and D.-H. Ruben (eds) *Issues in Marxist Philosophy*, Vol. 2, pp. 61–99. Brighton: Harvester.

Warren, Mark. 1988. 'Marx and Methodological Individualism', *Philosophy of the Social Sciences* 18: 447–76.

Williams, Raymond. 1978. 'Problems of Historical Materialism', *New Left Review* 109: 3–17.

# 4

# Empowerment, development and women's liberation

*Ann Ferguson*

Empowerment of the oppressed, whether peasants, workers, racial minorities or women, has been taken as a goal by social movements since the 1960s. This has been true particularly with western-influenced women's movements and other grassroots movements in countries in Latin America and the South influenced by the theology of liberation, the radical pedagogy of Freire, and/or Marxism and struggles for national liberation. While consciousness-raising practices associated with empowerment as the means to challenge social oppression were initially used in radical ways by these movements, western women's movements and race/ethnic rights movements often subsequently developed an identity politics that ignored the real conflicts that intersections of gender, race, class, sexuality and nationality caused between members of these movements. This made these movements liable to co-optation or defeat.

In a further blow to radical movements for social justice, empowerment as a goal has been co-opted by the neo-liberal hegemonic development establishment, including the World Bank and various international funding agencies such as US AID. The concept and application of 'empowerment' is itself contested, as have been other normative political concepts such as freedom, democracy and rights. What consciousness-raising and collective self-organisation practices at the grassroots suggest, I argue, is that radical empowerment is only achieved when a participatory democratic culture is not accepted as a mere means to the ends of national development, but also one of the ends of the transformative process toward social justice.

My methodological assumptions stem from materialist feminism. I use a post-structuralist critique and historical genealogy of the ways in which empowerment has been used by contemporary global development discourses and projects to continue domination systems. Unlike some post-structuralists, however, my intent will be to give such a critique as a way to open the conceptual and political space for interpretations of empowerment and other relevant concepts (e.g. needs, interests and rights) from a feminist materialist perspective. I will give a brief survey of feminist contributors to the gender and development debate such as Molyneux, Moser, Jonásdóttir and Mohanty who have developed the above concepts. My own re-interpretation of Jonásdóttir and Mohanty's concept of women's interests denies there is a universal blueprint for women's liberation, and points us toward the formation of feminist coalitions in specific contexts which can make advances toward women's and human liberation.

### Empowerment, needs, interests and rights

The concept of empowerment was first developed in the context of modern social movements for human liberation that assumed a social justice critique of the existing order on behalf of certain oppressed groups. The national and international social order was seen to have dominant groups, whether economic ruling classes (Marx 1983), races (Mills 1997) and ethnicities, and/or the male gender (Pateman 1988), which maintained power through institutional domination, such as their control.

Modern movements for national and human liberation have assumed a social justice critique based on a theory of human rights and participatory democracy from below. Aspects of the classical liberal model of just government are assumed: just government is held to be a social contract between rulers and ruled. Hence government must be based on the democratic consent of the governed, and to be legitimate, it should protect the human rights of all their citizens, not just a privileged few.

In contrast to idealist reformers who have posited that social elites can reform the system from above, radical liberation movements have critiqued traditional and modern governments and other institutions (the church, the school, the legal system, the family) as exploitative and/or oppressive. Social movements' challenge to social injustice is not simply conceived of as a means to eliminate the injustice in the future, but as valuable for its own sake because it will also be a process of empowerment of individuals and groups who engage in the movement for social justice.

### Definitions of empowerment, power and interests

So what exactly is understood by 'empowerment' as a process and a goal, and how does this concept relate to the concepts of 'needs', 'interests' and 'rights'? The concept of empowerment of an individual or a social group presupposes that a state of social oppression exists which has disempowered those in the group, by denying them social power, opportunities and/or resources and by subjecting them to a set of social practices which has defined them as inferior humans, thus lowering their self-esteem. As a general goal, empowerment has been described as a political and a material process which increases individual and group power, self-reliance and strength. However, there is a key difference in the ways that empowerment is defined in the academic literature. Typical of the first camp of mostly feminist economists and sociologists is Paula England's treatment, which sees empowerment as a process that individuals engage in when they obtain both objective and subjective resources of power which allow them to use power to achieve outcomes in the actor's self-interest (see England 2000). On this definition, it would seem that economic, legal and personal changes would be sufficient for individuals to become empowered, and such a process does not require the political organisation of collectives in which such individuals are located.

The second camp, more influenced by empowerment as a goal of radical social movements, emphasises the increased material and personal power that comes about when groups of people organise themselves to challenge the status quo through some kind of self-organisation of the group. Jill Bystydzienski (1992) gives a typical definition:

> Empowerment is taken to mean a process by which oppressed persons gain some control over their lives by taking part with others in development of activities and structures that allow people increased involvement in matters which affect them directly. In its course people become enable to govern themselves effectively. This process involves the use of power, but not 'power over' others or power as dominance as is traditionally the case; rather, power is seen as 'power to' or power as competence which is generated and shared by the disenfranchised as they begin to shape the content and structure of their daily existence and so participate in a movement for social change. (Yuval-Davis 1997:78)

This political process of empowerment has been conceptualised as a process in which the personal becomes the political; as developed in the women's movements and New Left social movements of the 1960s in the west, it involves what has been called 'consciousness-raising', that is, a participatory process of individuals sharing their life experiences with others in a regular group process. This in turn aims to create the emotional space for individuals to challenge low self-esteem, fear, misplaced hostility, and other issues dealing with internalised oppression. In this process they can voice their own life experiences in a context where they learn to apply analytic tools and concepts to understand themselves as structured by oppressive structures and having a collective interest in challenging them.

In the 1980s in the US, the theory that social oppressions are intersectional and not merely additive, hence that feminists cannot detach gender identity from racial and class identity and interests, suggests the rejection of the idea that women have political interests in common as a group (Spelman 1988; Harris 1990; Collins 2000). But this conclusion seems to leave women's movements without any social base on which to unite across race, class and sexual differences. Gayatri Spivak suggests that we need to assume at least a 'strategic essentialism' of women as a social group (Spivak and Rooney 1997). But can we assume women as a social group have any common interests?

Jónasdóttir (1988, 1994) argues that the concept of 'interest' arose historically from the demand for participatory democracy in state and society. She argues that there are two components of this historical conception of 'interest': a formal and a content component. For members of a social group to have a common formal interest in X refers to the right of group autonomy and control over the conditions of choice to obtain a set of needed or wanted goods connected to X,[1] including the meeting of material needs.[2] For a group to share a content interest with regard to a particular content, X, implies that all members of the group have common needs and/or desires with respect to X, e.g. to obtain, do or achieve X. A group can have a common formal interest in X without a common content interest in X, that is, without having common needs or desires in X.

An example of a formal common interest that women share could be the interest in reproductive rights that are acknowledged and defended by the state in which they live. Claiming that women have a common formal interest in reproductive rights does not imply that they all need or desire to exercise reproductive rights: for example, pro-life women may desire to prohibit the reproductive right to abortion, both for themselves and others. It also does not imply that their social class or racial/ethnic position gives them the same material resources to achieve the goal of reproductive choice: for example, in the US, the Hyde Amendment creates a material limitation on poor women's access to abortions by denying funding for them through government welfare and health entitlements. What it does imply, however, is that all women have a minimally common social location as citizens of the nation states of the world, through legal differentiation by gender and other means, e.g. a structured sexual division of labor, so that, in spite of racial, ethnic, class, sexual and national differences, it would benefit all women to have access to reproductive choice because of this common social location.

Jónasdóttir's distinction between formal and content interests allows her to occupy a third position, a historical materialist feminist one, between those political theorists who conceptualise interests as merely subjective preferences or desires, on the one hand, and those who take them to be objective and ahistorically given as a part of an essentialist concept of human nature. She rejects the subjectivists who, by identifying interests with perceived needs and desires, give us no ground for critiquing the manipulation of the needs and desires of one group by another more powerful group, as with the creation of consumerism by advanced capitalist globalisation. She also rejects objectivist positions like conservatives who deny that women have interests as a group to challenge the existing order since their natural interests are confined to their familial role, and liberal humanists, who think women's interests are the same as men's interests, even though traditional gender roles have blinded us to our commonality as rational self-interested agents.

Her own position, that there are historically developed objective interests in individual freedom and democratic participation, is similar to those in the Marxist camp such as Paulo Freire (1972). Freire holds that human development in the capitalist age involves an interest in expanding individual freedom, but that this goal, as specified by the demand for participatory democracy, is unachievable for oppressed groups within capitalism, and thus we need a pedagogy of the oppressed to educate the oppressed to claim their rights. But I would claim, and Jonásdóttir would agree, Freire has failed to conceptualise the workings of the 'sex/gender system' so he does not see that there is another system besides capitalism, patriarchy, which has pitted men against women in terms of gender interest (Ferguson 1991).

I agree with Jonásdóttir that having an interest is not a permanent state but a historical one. A formal interest develops when a group, or an individual situated within a social group, comes to desire and to claim a right to participate in choosing which of its needs or perceived concerns (i.e. wants) it will meet with respect to a particular goal. Content interests, on the other hand, develop as groups in particular historically structured contexts have human needs, whether material or social, which come into conflict with other groups in achieving these needs because of structured relations of power. Interests are defined as objective relative to the historical context, and can be seen as involving the necessary conditions to meet material and social needs in that context. Many consumerist desires which have been created through manipulation would not count as interests on this way of understanding interests. Thus, the theory gives a way of critiquing desires as being 'false' in the sense of involving aims that will not achieve the satisfaction of the underlying relevant human need in the best or optimum way.

Further, this conception of interests defines them as always relational; that is, a person has an interest in deciding what to do regarding X, in opposition to other groups whose needs or perceived concerns regarding X may conflict. The relationality of the concept of 'interest' may be noted by connecting it to the concept of 'power over' which is also a relational concept. In Steven Lukes's terms, 'A exercises power over B when A affects B in a manner contrary to A's interests' (Lukes 1974: 34).[3] Individuals and groups only have interests in relation to particular other groups, in this formulation, and conceptions of who constitutes one's 'peers' (who has equal rights to negotiate) and who are not one's peers (children, social inferiors, foreigners, animals etc.) will determine whether individuals or groups desire to negotiate with, or to dominate (exercise power over), the other group in question, therefore, whether or not their interests are compatible.

## Needs vs. interests

What are the implications of Jonásdóttir's definition of interest with respect to the goals of development? First, let's look at how Maxine Molyneux uses her approach to make a distinction between practical and strategic gender interests, and then in turn how this distinction is used by Carolyn Moser to apply the concept of empowerment to gender and development discourse.

Molyneux's line of argument in her very influential 1985 article on the women's movement in Nicaragua aims to assess the claim of some feminists that the Nicaraguan revolutionary state did not promote 'women's interests' because of the control of the male-dominated Sandinista party, in which the interests of male leaders to preserve their patriarchal privilege was put above that of women's liberation. Rejecting universal 'women's interests', she does want to argue that there are relational 'gender interests' that women share because of their social positioning in relation to men, for example in the gendered/sexual division of labor. These relational interests are in turn of two sorts: practical gender interests and strategic gender interests. Practical gender interests are those which are defined by women acting to promote perceived practical needs that they have as a part of their given gender role in the sexual division of labor, while strategic gender interests are derived from a critique of male domination and a vision of an alternative set of gender arrangements that would eliminate it. In Latin America, 'feminine' vs. 'feminist' women's movements have been defined by Molyneux's distinctions: women's activism which promotes practical gender interests, since it does not challenge status quo gender domination, is feminine not feminist, while movements which explicitly act to promote social change toward a vision of gender equality can be called feminist.

If we re-interpret Molyneux's distinctions based on Jónasdóttir's definition of 'interest', we ought to reconsider the prioritisation of gender equality as a 'strategic interest', since 'strategic' is a concept relative to the assumed goal to be achieved. Women who are organised as women around meeting their practical gender needs, even though they may not be organ- ised around the demand for radically revising gender relations (strategic gender interests in Molyneux's sense), may be organised around critiquing and envisioning an alternative to their class situation, to promote their (visionary) class interests, and this puts them in potentially antagonistic relations with middle- and upper-class women's class interests. An example would be the demand for labour rights and the unionising of domestic maids in Latin America, something which if achieved would increase the maids' autonomy and control over their choices while weak- ening the control of their middle- and upper-class female employers over both the lives of their maids and their own lives.[4]

Thus, we should drop Molyneux's word 'strategic' and use instead the idea of visionary gender interests to describe goals that challenge male domination. A person may have different visionary content interests based on their social locations of race/ethnicity, class, gender, sexuality and national origin. When visionary interests conflict, as in the case of class vs. gender, only coalitions based on solidarity which shift one's politics from a politics of identity interest to a politics of social justice will solve the problem.[5]

Let us look now at Carolyn Moser's use of Molyneux's distinction between practical and strategic gender interests, and how she connects this to what she calls the empowerment paradigm for gender and develop- ment. Moser, a World Bank development planner, defines an interest as a 'prioritized concern', which she says 'translates into a need', which 'in turn is defined as the "means by which concerns are satisfied"' (1993: 37). Moser goes on to make the distinction that Maxine Molyneux (1985) makes between practical and strategic gender interests, although Moser redefines both 'practical and strategic gender interests' as 'practical and strategic gender needs' based on the definition of needs she has given above. Moser explicitly ties both practical and strategic gender needs to subjective claims of women, consciously identified, rather than ones defined outside of the context (see Moser 1993: 39). She does this because she wants to distinguish between what she calls 'top down' government approaches to development, such as that of welfare states who provide resources to less well off citizens, and 'bottom up' approaches which come from constituents organising in what they perceive to be their interests as the grassroots level. Moser contrasts what she describes as the bottom-up Empowerment approach to development, as initiated by a group called Development Alternatives for Women in a New Era (DAWN) at the 1985 Nairobi UN Women's conference, with other paradigms such as the top- down welfare and anti-poverty approaches, and the equity and efficiency approaches, in order to persuade planners to take the empowerment paradigm more seriously.

The equity approach, sometimes called the Women in Development, or WID approach, was the first to insist that women's equality with men needs to be an explicit goal of development, and not just assumed to be an effect that will automatically occur as a result of improving state welfare services, reducing poverty, or increasing the efficiency of development plans by including women's unpaid work in economic planning. The basic claim is that capitalist development and mainstream development discourse, as well as mainstream attempts to support development projects in the Third World, has marginalised women. They have done so by ignoring the central nature of women's productive, reproductive and community organising work to meet human material and nurturance needs, often in the subsistence and informal economies rather than in the capitalist labour market. Thus, women must be given equal opportunity with men, via education, health care and funding, to enter employed work and so develop some economic independence, and hence gain bargaining power with men in all important social sites, including the family/household, civil society and the state.

DAWN, a spokesgroup for the empowerment approach, is an example of a grassroots group which refuses reformist politics in favour of bottom-up organising by social movements and coalitions of poor, working-class and Third World women of colour who come to see their interests as allied. Unlike the equity approach, they refuse to target gender inequality rather than other social dominations in women's lives as the key issue to prioritise. They agree on the importance of a bottom-up emphasis on autonomous women's groups to improve women's capabilities of self-reliance, internal strength and self-esteem. As an 'integrative feminism' (see Miles 1996), it insists that the autonomous women's movement (1) be thought of not as just one but as many situated women's movements based on different race, class, sexual and national locations; and (2) ally its members to a broader social justice coalition seeking democratic control over crucial material and non-material resources for other dispossessed social subjects, including men.

### Empowerment, discourse and conflicts of interests

The discourse of interests as a base for politics and the discourse of empowerment have been co-opted by hegemonic funding agencies to serve the vested interests of wealthy elites. I shall argue that neither the interest nor the empowerment approach by itself can handle the intersectionality question of differences between women based on race/ethnicity, class, sexuality and national origin, but require supplementation by a integrative theory of human rights (Petchesky 2003), and what Rosemary Hennessy calls 'outlawed needs', such as the need for love and solidarity (Hennessy 2002). Secondly, empowerment discourse might be thought to presuppose a homogeneous community of the oppressed, either through an identity politics of gender or race, ethnicity/nationality or a Marxist structural analysis of class exploitation, and such a community or collectivity tends to suppress internal differences between its members in ways that ignores power and inequality relations (see Yuval-Davis 1997).

How does a gender interest approach handle the intersectionality question? It can be addressed by pointing out that a person or group A may have some interests in common with another person or group B with regard to X, and another set of interests which are in conflict with respect to another issue Y. So a white and an African-American woman may have a common interest in having their reproductive rights protected by a government law, but their interests may conflict with respect to an affirmative action policy for a job for which they are competing which gives preference to the African-American, even when they are similarly qualified for the position.[6] Similarly an upper-class woman and her domestic maid may have a common interest in legislation to make domestic violence against women illegal, yet may have divergent interests when it comes to living wage legislation that would force the upper-class woman to pay the maid a higher salary.

This example shows two problems with Jonásdóttir's important intervention concerning the historical nature of the concept of 'interest', which also relates to the concept of empowerment. First, if interests are not static effects of human nature but are goals developed historically, then they are defined by collectivities in struggle with each other as political priorities that connect to social identities. But the feminist empowerment theorists assume that these collectivities themselves are either naturally or structurally given, and downplay the fact that these collectivities are social constructs whose boundaries, structures and norms are the result of constant processes of struggles and negotiations (Yuval-Davis 1997: 80). Consider, for example, the following questions of identity boundaries: whether bisexuals are accepted as members of lesbian and gay communities engaged in identity politics of empowerment; whether male to female transsexuals are accepted as women; whether mixed race individuals in the US whose parents are white and Chicano are Chicano for the purposes of La Raza politics; and the question, subject to ideological debate, as to whether the 'popular classes' can be a unified community which includes native and immigrant workers, workers from different racial/ethnic backgrounds, peasant independent producers, salaried rural workers, market women and those in the informal economy, as well as regular working-class members who are employed for wages in factories or maquiladoras.

The point is that those advocating empowerment for a particular 'community's interests' will constantly have to deal with who counts as within the community and who is perceived as a hostile other, as well as differences of power of individuals within the community by gender, religion, sexuality, etc. As Nira Yuval-Davis (1997) points out: 'The automatic assumption of a progressive connotation of the "empowerment of the people" assumes a non-problematic transition from individual to collective power, as well as a pre-given, non-problematic definition of the boundaries of "the people"' (80).

The second problem has to do with conflicts of interests that may not be easily resolved by assuming a process of shared empowerment between homogenous individuals whose differences can be bracketed. So, for example, feminist explanations of the process of political empowerment differentiate between the individual 'power to' (enabling individuals), the 'power with' that a consciousness-raising group generates which increases the energy and capacity for self-organisation of the whole group, and the negative 'power over' that is typical of oppressive structures of racism, sexism and capitalist class relations. But since groups are not homogeneous, and individuals within each group may have power over other individuals based on class, race, national origin, etc., it may often happen that an empowerment process allows some people within the group to take more control over their lives at the expense of negative consequences to others. One case is that of the middle-class mother freed by the rise in her self-esteem from a feminist C-R group to seek a professional career, who uses an immigrant domestic servant to allow her this space, while the maid must sacrifice time with her own children (see Ehrenreich and Hochchild 2002).

### Empowerment discourse in development

Criticisms of a politics of empowerment can be raised from a post-structuralist perspective in the context where the discourse of empowerment is used by mainstream funding agencies to justify organising and funding groups to advance their development toward the goal of empowerment itself. For example, many community development projects in the Third World funded by the World Bank and other international donors, such as those promoting nutrition and health, literacy or sanitation, now attempt to enable women not only to acquire certain knowledges but to change their characters in such a way as to be able to continuously exercise power, hence demonstrate 'empowerment', in various venues, e.g. in the political and economic realms and in the family household.

From a Foucauldian analysis (1977, 1980), it can be argued that mainstream development institutions have appropriated the discourse of empowerment, along with self-disciplining practices, to create a new development rationality (see Escobar 1995). No longer is it acceptable to describe the Third World clients/recipients of the training or enabling practices called empowerment practices as 'illiterate', 'disenfranchised', 'backward' or 'exploited'. Rather, they are now to be described as 'rational economic agents', 'global citizens', potential 'entrepreneurs': they inherently think the way that producers and consumers of a globalised capitalist economy should think, but merely need some help honing specific skills to achieve their self-interests (see Sato 2003). Development education should both assume and advance such a mindset in its clients, as it will also encourage them to act as good entrepreneurs, wage earners, and consumers, that is, as proper 'subjects/objects' of development.

Foucault's work on the normalisation of various discourses and practices in new institutions claiming a scientific/rational base, such as the mainstream discourse of development, suggests that the new ways of thinking about and knowing such subjects involve power/knowledges. That is, researchers and practitioners teaching or applying these practices are creating what he calls a 'productive power' in which they gain power over the objects of research, their subjects, and their discourses about them change the subjects themselves. This happens through a process in which their subjects become 'subjectivated', i.e. internalise these new ways of thinking about themselves, even as they are also increasing their power to engage in various activities (e.g. self-scrutiny, for confessional purposes, or body exercises and comportment for increased military or socialisation efficiency, etc.) Typically, however, the positive side of this productive power, e.g. that the subjects are more disciplined, effective, efficient, or successful in certain tasks, is used as a justification of these new knowledges, while the negative side, that subjects are being increasingly exploited, or acclimated to a competitive individualism that may eventually undermine the very group cooperation that led to their empowerment, are ignored – these are, after all, in the vested interests of mainstream development agencies and the corporate capitalist world which funds them through the World Bank, the IMF and colluding wealthy capitalist nations, and not in the interests of the clients/subjects. Mary Hawkesworth (2002) argues convincingly that the use of empowerment discourse on behalf of women by governments, political parties and NGOs in the context of capitalist globalisation, although it aims to make women equal citizens by creating capitalist democracies around the world, in fact tends to make politics less democratic since it squashes the participatory democratic space of social movements in which women function as powerful collectives in solidarity with issues of social justice, and tends to substitute an individualistic entrepreneurial and male-identified interest group politics that both turns women off and discriminates against them.

A Foucauldian post-structuralist perspective is automatically suspicious of the positive discourse of power (power to, and power with) connected to identity politics. For such theorists, such group politics is another form of that 'productive power', the quintessentially modern form of power, which controls individuals through categorisation by experts (i.e. by Marxist, feminist, anti-racist theorists). Such a process makes invisible the way that the power over those so categorised by these experts is augmented and how it re-organises these targeted individuals' self-understandings. Individuals' feelings of increased capacities and abilities are manipulated to influence them to use identity discourses to monitor themselves so as to perform the norms expected of their social category (see Butler 1990; 1993; Brown 1995; Escobar 1995).

An example of this power/knowledge use of the concept of empowerment in a particular development project is discussed by Chizu Sato in a case study of a US AID funded project, the Women's Empowerment Programme, or WEP, designed to increase Nepalese women's empowerment by two projects in literacy and microfinance training. One NGO carried out six months training called 'Rights, Responsibilities and Advocacy' which taught participants their legal rights and responsibilities as Nepalese citizens as well as collective advocacy of social change to promote these rights. Another NGO ran a 'Women in Business' programme that taught women literary skills as well as how to be involved in micro-financing collectives which would operate somewhat like the Grameen bank model (but see the differences below).

The WEP project can be analysed as having created a set of group practices and a discourse (set of concepts) which allowed the participants to constitute themselves as subjects in different ways than they had traditionally done. The rule they were taught on which to run their micro-financing mandated that women must rely on mutual assurance for repayment of loans to individuals, and to think of this as group 'self-help', even though this rule and concept (what Foucault calls a 'technology of self') came from outside the group. Similarly the citizen and human rights they were taught were designed to create them as liberal pressure groups for government reform (but not revolution).

As Sato (2003) argues, coming to 'subjectivate', that is, think of themselves as agents (women) with common gender interests that connect to their individual self-interests, is connected to the idea of themselves as citizens with rights to promote these interests through collective political action. This created a 'constituency of becoming' (17) among the women that supported solidarity with other self-help groups. However, this solidarity presupposed the coming of participants to think of themselves as lacking certain skills (literacy) and resources (claimed to be rights) and hence, coming to desire empowerment on the terms of outside development experts who taught them this development rationality and desire; but with a modernist analysis of their problems that made invisible the vested interests of the outside powers (the US government, multinational corporations, etc.) that stood to gain by the success of such microfinance and political activist groups. For example, such groups, in learning networking skills among themselves (another technology of self) could come to displace traditional local patriarchal and feudal powers, and hence eventually 'modernise' their countries as terrains for the global penetration of capital.

The ideology of 'self-help' rationalised the lack of any initial seed money by the outside donors for the microfinance projects, hence ensuring that the poorest of poor women, those who had no initial capital at all, could not participate in the groups. This process created an excluded but invisible Other whose lack of class resources were ignored in the ideology of women's empowerment subjectivated by the group. Furthermore the development rationality of the discourse of women's empowerment as employed in the WEP projects made invisible ways in which male heads of households and other male elites could continue to appropriate the surplus labour of wives, daughters and other relatives involved in these projects by patriarchal practices in which women are expected to distribute their capital to other family members in ways not reciprocated by male members (Sato 2003: 22).

## Social movement empowerment vs. power/knowledge development empowerment

The objections that have been raised previously against a politics of empowerment used in various social movement identity politics suggest that empowering some in a social group may also inadvertently disempower individuals within that group or other social groups. Furthermore, the case study from Nepal presented above is an example of how dominant groups may co-opt empowerment discourses and processes by creating a productive power that gives individuals new powers but does so in a context which simply reorganises domination relations of patriarchy, racism, imperialism and class exploitation.

Nonetheless, movements for social justice require a discourse of liberation from those who have unjust power over them, and the language of empowerment is one that can continue to have a radical interpretation under the right circumstances. How then can we distinguish between the co-optive productive power enabled by mainstream development practice and the liberating sort of productive power found in grassroots women's movements and other left social movements?

The overall answer is simple, although discerning the difference in particular cases is much more difficult. Social movements which are mass movements are never simply engaged in identity politics, but are constantly negotiating for coalitions in solidarity with other oppressed groups. This means that there can be no one core of accepted 'experts' whose analysis of the relevant structures of oppression automatically gives them the best insight on the political strategy to change it, in part because that group of experts will have a social position with vested interests that may contribute to a new oppressive power/knowledge.[7] Thus, coming to agreement on what structural changes are necessary for empowerment or liberation cannot be achieved by fiat but must be the product of participatory democracy in coalitions. Such coalitions are never created by outside experts importing their own practices and discourses of identification or empowerment. This does not imply that outsiders may not come to be integral parts of social movements, however: the example of the Zapatistas demonstrates that an outsider, sub-commandante Marcos, can come to act in solidarity with a group in such a way as to become an insider, an 'organic intellectual' with leadership powers, in Gramsci's (1971) terms.

Secondly, understanding the intersectional nature of systems of social oppression leads one to the efficacy of using the discourse of human rights as the necessary historically developed supplement to the concept of empowerment. The concept of human rights, first explicitly formulated in western liberal thought, is now the dominant discourse there. Because of its global imperialism, western concepts dominate not only in western countries where they are used by political elites to justify their actions, but also have been used as a power/knowledge by those in power in formerly colonised countries and now through neo-colonialism, to advance their own agendas. This usual strategy for this is to claim that some rights, e.g. property rights, and civil and political rights, take priority over such material and economic rights as the right to life, health, food and water. Nonetheless, the general concept of human rights has affinities with similar concepts in non-western cultures, and has historically come to be used around the world as a common political language to make universalised demands to governments and other institutions with social and political power such as the United Nations, business corporations, churches and universities. For these reasons it is plausible to use some interpretation of it as an oppositional discourse to dominant development discourse. Social justice movements have demanded the re-conceptualisation of the goals of development not simply as economic growth, which may benefit those few with property but as the promotion of human rights for the many (Burns 2000; Fenster 1999). Fenster (1999) argues that such a re-conceptualisation of development puts equity (achieving majority rights) over growth, conceived merely as expansion of GNP.

In any case, since the exercising of certain human rights of some individuals may conflict with others exercising their human rights, which rights take priority in the case of a conflict will be different in different contexts. This means that there can be no blueprint which can resolve ethico-political conflicts. Rather, we must take what Petchesky (2003) calls an 'integrated rights' approach and reject the prioritising of political and civil rights, including the so-called right to property, over social and economic rights (the right to health and education, the right to a job). Thus, for example, liberal feminists who are busy defending women's rights as individuals to be a member of the military (freedom of association, freedom of job choice) tend to ignore the way that military engagements in war kill innocent civilians, thus depriving them of their right to life, or require the creation of an often exploited sex worker industry to service male soldiers stationed in foreign countries (Enloe 2000).

An empowerment-rights approach acknowledges the need to start with commonalities for political organising, that is, agreed-on, or consciously espoused, practical interests which may vary with the context. It will also require a common transformative vision of how the social order should change so as to guarantee more available rights to more people, not merely political rights but the economic and social rights necessary to exercise them. This implies the need to create a political process which promotes the rights of individuals within the group who face different oppressions than the majority or those with more institutionalised rights. Such has been the process of successful grassroots women's movements in both north and south, as can be seen by the adoption by many contemporary feminist thinkers of the intersectional and coalitional approach to understanding social justice rather than a simple identity politics. One way to conceptualise this is to hold that transnational feminist politics requires a solidarity social justice approach based on the creation of 'bridge identities' in those with greater privileges in hegemonic systems of domination (see Ferguson 1998).

But can transnational feminism find a way to uncover common interests and common rights between women in different national, class and race/ethnic contexts in spite of the conflict of rights demands their social differences inspire? Chandra Mohanty (1997) maintains that capitalist globalisation has relied on a ubiquitous sexual division of labor in creating the global assembly line; and that similarities between the ideology and exploitation of women workers whether they work for wages in Silicon Valley in the US or in the cottage lace industry in India have a common formal interest (note her use of Jónasdóttir's concept) in challenging these ideologies by obtaining the collective power to demand equality in status, wages and salaries with comparable men's work.

What is missing in Mohanty's account, which seems to focus on consciousness-raising as the solution to the lack of common social identities, needs and desires (i.e. content interests) between these two sets of workers, is an understanding that there may be an objective conflict of interests and rights, not just a conflict in consciousness, between two such groups. Such a conflict will have to be acknowledged and negotiated by any effective political process attempting to set up solidarity between these women. So, for example, as consumers both groups may want to have no tariffs placed on the other group's products in order to get them at lower consumer prices, but as workers they may be demanding a 'fair wage', not just a bottom-line market wage, and this may require tariffs of some sort in certain circumstances. Workers will have to negotiate these conflicts of content interests, and rights, not simply by overcoming the ideology of domesticity and gender and racial inferiority assigned to their work as Mohanty implies, but also by a direct, organisational education and negotiation with each other about how to resolve the conflict of rights and content interests they face as consumers and workers. In her recent book Mohanty (2003) does acknowledge the importance of understanding context and negotiation in wider coalitions of various grassroots women worker's groups, such as the Korean Women Workers' Organisation, the West Yorkshire Home working Group, and the South East Women's Association (SEWA) in India, but she still does not come to grips with the need for an understanding of how conflicts of rights may be at issue. For the resolution of such conflicts, we need solidarity and social justice ethics and politics that incorporate yet goes beyond the conception of interest politics as it has hitherto been understood (see Gould 2005).

## Conclusion

In this chapter I have argued that there are political disagreements as to the content and political application of the notion of 'empowerment' as a goal and strategy for women's liberation. I have contrasted mainstream development institutions' co-opted uses of the concept of empowerment with its more radical definition and applications by struggles for national liberation and movements for social justice. Identity politics by itself has not been successful in organising in heterogeneous communities, in which individuals and groups divided by gender, race, ethnicity, class, sexuality and nationality can only be empowered by a participatory democratic culture which strives for solidarity in a coalition of oppressed groups, espouses the goal of achieving human rights while acknowledging the possibility of conflicts of rights among its members, and sees a political group dialogue and decision-making to resolve the question as to which rights take priority in particular contexts as one of the ends of a developmental process toward social justice.

## Notes

1  In other words, it is the desire for what Étienne Balibar calls 'égaliberté' (Saleci 1994), i.e. the desire for participatory democracy – equal opportunity and freedom as a group to define and negotiate to achieve one's perceived needs with other individuals and groups. On Jonásdóttir's definition of 'interest', in a society structured in dominance, whether of gender, race, ethnicity, class, sexuality or other social grouping, social groups may have contradictory interests. With respect to formal interests, they are in conflict when structured social relations between them allow a dominating group to have greater conditions for overall autonomy in their lives based on the denial of another group or groups' reciprocal abilities to choose.

2  For Jonásdóttir, a need seems to be not simply a means to achieve a perceived concern, as it is defined by Moser (1989), but a material necessity, either to achieve physical survival or other basic good, which could then exist whether or not the individual who has the need actually has a perceived concern about it. (Imagine the anorexic who needs food to survive physically but does not have a perceived concern, or goal for, or want of, food.)

3  Paula England points out that a similar definition of power was maintained by Max Weber (1968) who claimed: 'Power is the probability that one actor within a social relationship will be in a position to carry out his own will despite resistance, regardless of the basis on which this probability rests' (quoted in England 1997: 38–9). She also cites the similar definition of Samuel Bowles (1998) among others: 'A has power over B to the extent that he can get B to do something that B would not otherwise do' (England 2000: 39, footnote 2).

4  So, women in a particular social class, ethnicity or nationality, imbued with the egalitarian ideals of democracy, may take themselves to be peers with men of their social class, ethnicity or nationality and hence believe their interest as women lies in achieving participatory democracy with men in the family, at work and in politics. Men in that same social group, who in a male-dominant society usually do not take themselves to be peers with women, may find it in their interest to deny claims addressed by women in their group to equal negotiation rights. (This is often summarised by the claim that the privileged will not find it in their interests to give up privileges.) But once we broaden the social

context, for example, comparing women of the upper social class or dominant race or ethnicity with women and men in all social classes and ethnicities, the former may not have an interest in allying with women of subordinate classes and ethnicities, since this may involve supporting social policies where they will have to give up their greater autonomy and control over choosing and meeting needs in comparison with lower classes and subordinated races and ethnicities.

5 Molyneux fails to note that feminists themselves may disagree on what constitute visionary gender interests, since, for example, socialist-feminists think class inequalities must be eliminated to empower women and give them more autonomy, while liberal feminists do not think this necessary. I prefer to frame this as a conflict between the interest politics of privileged women whose class and race/ethnic location does not incorporate a social justice politics based on promoting the economic and social rights of all, and those who adopt a coalition politics which must involve both interests and rights for all involved.

6 This claim is controversial, since it might be argued that the white woman's long-range interest involves making coalitions with women of colour to fight racism and sexism, and hence she should support an affirmative action policy that may not be in her short-term interest. Rather than make this distinction, I prefer to argue that we should distinguish between immediate interests and social justice visions. The white woman thus can be said to have a conflict of immediate interest with the African-American woman and affirmative action policies based on race, but can advocate out of solidarity a social justice vision which supports the elimination of racism, hence need not be in opposition with the social justice vision of the African-American woman.

7 The problems that Marxist-led national liberation movements have had because of the view that some group of experts (typically the party or front's central or governing committee) could best discern such strategies are well known, and suggest that factions must be tolerated in a process of participatory democracy and negotiation to avoid state power being used in repressive ways.

## References

Bowles, Samuel. 1998. 'Endogenous Preferences: The Cultural Consequences of Markets and other Economic Institutions', *Journal of Economic Literature* 36: 75–111.

Brown, Wendy.1995. *States of Injury: Power and Freedom in Late Modernity*. Princeton, NJ: Princeton University Press.

Burns, Shawn Meaghan. 2000. *Women's Rights as Human Rights, Women across Cultures: A Global Perspective*. San Francisco, CA: Mayfield.

Butler, Judith.1990. *Gender Trouble: Feminism and the Subversion of Identity*. New York: Routledge.

Butler, Judith. 1993. *Bodies that Matter: On the Discursive Limits of Sex*. New York: Routledge.

Bystydzienski, J. M. 1992. *Women Transforming Politics: Worldwide Strategies for Empowerment*. Bloomington, IN: Indiana University Press.

Collins, Patricia Hill. 2000. *Black Feminist Thought* (3ʳᵈ edn). New York: Routledge.

Ehrenreich, Barbara and Arlie Hochchild (eds). 2002. *Global Woman: Nannies, Maids and Sex Workers in the New Economy*. New York: Henry Holt and Company.

England, Paula. 2000. 'Conceptualizing Women's Empowerment in Countries of the North', in Harriet B. Presser and Gita Sen (eds) *Women's Empowerment and Demographic Processes: Moving beyond Cairo*, pp. 27–68. New York: Oxford University Press.

Enloe, Cynthia. 2000. *Maneuvers: The International Politics of Militarizing Women's Lives*. Berkeley, CA: University of California Press.

Escobar, Arturo. 1995. *Encountering Development: The Making and Unmaking of the Third World*. Princeton, NJ: Princeton University Press.

Fenster, Tovi. 1999. *Gender, Planning and Human Rights*. New York: Routledge.

Ferguson, Ann. 1991. *Sexual Democracy: Women, Oppression and Revolution*. Boulder, CO: Westview Press.

Ferguson, Ann. 1998. 'Resisting the Veil of Privilege: Building Bridge Identities as an Ethico-politics of Global Feminism', *Hypatia: Journal of Feminist Philosophy* (special issue): 95–113.

Foucault, Michel. 1977. *Discipline and Punish*. New York: Pantheon.

Foucault, Michel. 1980. *Power/Knowledge: Selected Interviews and Other Writings 1972–77*. Brighton: Harvester.

Freire, Paolo. 1972. *The Pedagogy of the Oppressed*. Harmondsworth: Penguin.

Gould, Carol. 2005. 'Conceptualizing the Role of Solidarity in Transnational Democracy'. Unpublished manuscript.

Gramsci, Antonio. 1971. *Selections from the Prison Notebooks of Antonio Gramsci*. Ed. and trans. Quintin Hoare and Geoffrey Nowell Smith. London: Lawrence & Wishart.

Harris, Angela P. 1990. 'Race and Essentialism in Feminist Legal Theory', *Stanford Law Review* 42 (581): 581–616.

Hawkesworth, Mary. 2002. 'Democratization: Reflections on Gendered Dislocations in the Public Sphere', in Nancy Holmstrom (ed.) *The Socialist Feminist Project: A Contemporary Reader in Theory and Politics*, pp. 298–312. New York: Monthly Review Press.

Hennessy, Rosemary. 2002. *Profit and Pleasure*. New York: Routledge.

Jónasdóttir, Anna. 1988. 'On the Concept of Interest, Women's Interests, and the Limitations of Interest Theory', in Kathleen Jones and Anna Jónasdóttir (eds) *The Political Interests of Gender*, pp. 33–65. London: Sage.

Jónasdóttir, Anna. 1994. *Why Women Are Oppressed*. Philadelphia: Temple University.

Lukes, Steven. 1974. *Power: A Radical View*. New York: Macmillan

Marx, Karl. 1983. *The Portable Karl Marx*. New York: Penguin.

Miles, Angela.1996. *Integrative Feminisms: Building Global Visions, 1960s–1990s*. New York: Routledge.

Mills, Charles. 1997. *The Racial Contract*. Ithaca, NY: Cornell University Press.

Mohanty, Chandra. 1997. 'Women Workers and Capitalist Scripts: Ideologies of Domination, Common Interests, and the Politics of Solidarity', in M. Jacqui Alexander and Chandra Talpade Mohanty (eds) *Feminist Genealogies, Colonial Legacies, Democratic Futures*, pp. 3–29. New York: Routledge.

Mohanty, Chandra. 2003. *Feminism without Borders*. Durham, NC: Duke University Press.

Molyneux, Maxine. 1985. 'Mobilization without Emancipation? Women's Interests, State and Revolution', *Feminist Studies* 11 (2): 227–54

Moser, Carolyn. 1989. *Gender Planning and Development: Theory, Practice and Training*. New York: Routledge.

Pateman, Carole. 1988. *The Sexual Contract*. Stanford, CA: Stanford University Press.

Petchesky, Rosalind. 2003. *Global Prescriptions: Gendering Health and Human Rights*. New York: Zed Books/Palgrave.

Saleci, Renata. 1994. *The Spoils of Freedom: Psychoanalysis and Feminism after the Fall of Socialism*. New York: Routledge.

Sato, Chizu. 2003. 'The Making of Global Citizens: A Nepalese Case of Women's Empowerment'. Unpublished manuscript, University of Massachusetts at Amherst.

Spelman, Elizabeth V. 1988. *Inessential Woman*. Boston, MA: Beacon.

Spivak, Gayatri Chakravorty and Ellen Rooney. 1997. 'In a Word: Interview', in Linda Nicholson (ed.) *The Second Wave: A Reader in Feminist Theory*, pp. 356–78. New York: Routledge.

Weber, Max. 1968. *Economy and Society*. New York: Bedminster.

Yuval-Davis, Nira. 1997. 'Women, Ethnicity and Empowerment', in Ann Oakley and Juliet Mitchell (eds) *Who's Afraid of Feminism?*, pp. 77–98. New York: New Press.

# 5

# To teach 'the correct procedure for love': matrilineal cultures and the nation state[1]

*Maria-Barbara Watson-Franke*

## Introduction

This chapter discusses ethnicity and gender as social relationships shaping the interaction between citizens and governments and thus peoples' daily lives. Analyses of the nation state often have overlooked how ethnicity and gender *interlock* in the process of state formation. In non-state society, ethnicity, anchored in kinship, determines largely the identity of community members. In the nation state, national identity based on citizenship becomes the focus. Historical processes as well as natural disruptions bring ethnic and national identity together, often under dramatic circumstances, such as war, revolution, persecution and natural catastrophes. Over the centuries millions of people have been displaced, replaced, separated or artificially united, each time creating new combinations and conditions defining the interaction between ethnic and national identity.

The modern nation state, anchored in the Western European experience, encompasses the notions of the people as a nation, the sovereignty of these people as a nation, and the state as the sum total of its individualised citizens. The state defines the meaning of citizenship and bestows citizenship according to its rules. And it is citizenship that defines identity (Joseph 1999: 162). Like the ethnic underpinnings of a community, i.e. a people's language, traditions, gender concepts or family structures, the nation state is a cultural creation and so are perceptions of it.

Feminist scholars have defined the nation state as a 'masculine construct' (Pettman 1996: 5) from which women are seemingly excluded (see Smith-Rosenberg 1999). Yet, mainstream debates about the state generally have excluded the network of human relationships stereotypically associated with women – kinship and the family – from consideration. Risseeuw, for example, has argued that without such a discussion the actual situation of people cannot be assessed:

> Social science inquiry continues as if state formation, large scale economic change or the effects of colonial rule are disconnected from changes in

gender, family and kin relations. This hinders an analysis attempting to pose questions not only in relation to changes in peoples' degree of wealth or poverty, employment or education, but also into the nature of their intimate life arrangements and support networks. (1996: 80)

Stevens (1999: 51) shares this view and calls for the evaluation of 'kinship practices', and an inquiry 'into the political processes that produce the family' (xv). She makes a convincing case that states define and manipulate the processes through which human communities are built beginning with birth: 'Of special interest to political societies is not that birth is natural, but that the very form of natality is intrinsically political' (267).

Yet, by situating her discussion essentially in the so-called western world, Stevens (1999: 223) assumes that the politics of birth are universally played out within a domain of male dominance. She contends that 'all kinship systems depend on the negation of mothers.'

Cross-cultural evidence, however, shows wide variation among kinship structures and practices and their accompanying gender dynamics. Accordingly, peoples' relationships to the state and vice versa are differently affected. The distinction between national and ethnic identity remains crucial because people bring their own, that is, ethnically defined, histories and cultures into this process (see Joseph 1999: 163). As the following discussion demonstrates, this has consequences for the ordering of daily life when kinship-based values, structures and ideologies clash with those presented and enforced by the state. This is particularly true in the case of kinship systems with a women-centred matrix.

This chapter discusses the significance of the social relationships of gender and ethnicity by looking at women-centred groups within their respective nation states, taking examples from matrilineal kinship systems characterised by high female autonomy and decision-making power. Although Stevens (1999: 224) does address the issue of matriliny, she defines it narrowly as a system of property transfer that does not affect male authority: 'The bare fact that wealth goes through the line of the mother does not speak to the relative power of women. The very fact that paternity exists for men already figures mothers as relational (to husbands) and not autonomous.'

Matrilineal realities challenge such a claim, suggesting instead that fathers become relational to wives. Women in these groups enjoy significant authority in the economic sector with the maternal role being defined by economic strength and control instead of dependency. Generally speaking, women play a structurally central role, which is acknowledged as such by the community at large and expressed by the rule that women determine a child's position in a matrilineal system. In state parlance this means that the mother bestows citizenship on the child, not the father. This fact among many others makes matrilineal systems an interesting case in discussions about women and the state.

Men in matrilineal groups do not exercise authority and control as husbands and fathers, that is, in their sexual persona, but as brothers and maternal uncles. This fact changes gender dynamics and alters the character of authority patterns because male heterosexual authority is diminished if not eliminated altogether (see Watson-Franke 2002). Matrilineal populations perceive power and authority patterns as related to gender differently than male-centred groups. Marriage does not give a man control over the next generation, a fact which is relevant to any debate on the nation state.

Throughout this discussion we must acknowledge the variance among matrilineal societies. Stivens's (1985) observation on matriliny in Malaysia is applicable to matrilineal systems in general. Matriliny, Stivens states, should be seen 'as a constantly reconstituted category of practices centering on descent ideology and property relations. These practices do not represent a persistent matrilineal "tradition", frozen by colonial process, but continuously developing relationships' (4). Awareness of such 'continuously developing relationships' is especially important to this discussion.

Today several million peoples worldwide follow various combinations of matrilineal principles. The difficulty of situating them within their respective nation states begins with naming them. They are included in categories which do not have universally valid meanings or interpretive consensus, such as 'ethnic minorities', or 'indigenous people' (see Knocke 2000: 141), these being, as Harrell (1995: 3) puts it, 'peripheral' because 'they are far from the centers of institutional and economic power and of dense population concentrations.'

Although Harrell's definition does not apply technically to all such groups, one could argue that, in an ideological and political sense, matrilineal groups are given such a place in western thinking. Like women, these groups are perceived as 'Other', or as being 'at the margins.' As such they have not been given special consideration nor deemed sufficiently significant to pose a threat to established institutions and processes. Stivens (1996: 30) suspects that she received permission from the Malaysian government to do fieldwork among a matrilineal population only because her project was seen 'as a relatively harmless exercise in antiquarian anthropological recovery.'

For decades numerous efforts have been made to guarantee minority or peripheral groups the right to self-representation as well as participation in their respective nation states. One example is some of the activities undertaken by the United Nations. The documents resulting from UN-based and -sponsored meetings and conferences have called for 'the right of indigenous populations to develop their own culture, traditions, language and way of life' (cited in Sverre 1985: 193), and 'to maintain and strengthen their distinct . . . social and cultural characteristics, as well as their legal systems' (Draft Declaration on the Rights of Indigenous People 1994: Article 4). The UN repeatedly has spelled out the responsibilities of the state in this respect. Among those of special interest in this discussion is the duty of the state 'to protect the cultural identity of minorities', and to guarantee peoples' right 'to enjoy their own culture' (Declaration on the Rights of Persons 1993: Articles 1 and 2). That this might evolve into a conflicted issue becomes apparent when the potential limits of these rights are spelled out: 'Persons belonging to minorities have the right to partici-pate effectively . . . in a manner not incompatible with national legislation' (Declaration on the Rights of Persons 1993: Article 2, section 3).

Discussing the relationship between Bushmen and the government of Botswana, Saugestad (2001: 48) notes the resulting need of democratic states 'to find a *balance* between the general ideals and equal rights and equal treatment, and the special needs of the minority for protection and affirmative action.' We might also wonder how far women's interests are being included in these documents when we are reminded as recently as 1998 that 'All persons . . . should act towards one another in a spirit of *brotherhood*' (italics added, Implementation Meeting 1998).

Again, questions of definition arise. What do terms like 'tradition', or 'way of life' actually mean? One reason there are no easy answers lies in the fact that the data tilt towards a one-sided view since the discourse, in stereotypical colonialist fashion, focuses on the state's attempts to deter-mine peoples' lives rather than the impact of these groups on the state. Keeping these constraints in mind, this chapter presents three examples of interaction between matrilineal groups and the nation state and how these processes show different levels and styles: The selected groups are:

1 the Asante from West Africa, who have faced intervention by colonial and post-colonial governments;
2 the Mosuo from Southwest China who have endured challenges to their culture by a communist state; and
3 the Minangkabau from Indonesia in the colonial and post-colonial era.

This chapter will discuss state intervention and these peoples' reactions as well as actions with a particular focus on kinship and family, especially women's position, maternal roles, and conjugal rights and responsibilities. Three aspects of this interaction process will be addressed:

1 the goals of the state with regard to a people's lifestyle and rights;
2 the strategies employed by the state to achieve these goals; and
3 the outcomes of this process, that is, the dialectic action and reaction between these populations and the state, and the emergent socio-political system that develops.

## Matrilineal people and the state

### The case of the Asante

The Asante are part of the matrilineal Akan people who constitute about half of the population of Ghana. In Asante society women play import-ant roles as mothers. Clark (2001: 106) has described the phenomenon of 'nursing mother work' which explains the important role of mother as provider: 'Without the capacity to take care of her children financially, a woman's biological power of childbearing cannot be fully realized.' Both, women and men 'confirm that they consider the economic imperative of motherhood much more absolute than the responsibility for physical child care, which can be delegated with comparative ease and confidence' (107).

While the Akan acknowledge that children affect women's resources they do not see a basic conflict between motherhood and work outside the home. Instead, they argue that the 'complex interpenetration of the finan-cial and the domestic responsibilities of motherhood . . . creates a positive identification of motherhood with work different from the conceptual opposition between the two that Eurocentric gender ideals continue to enshrine' (Clark 2001: 107).

According to their convictions, Akan people make certain provisions and require 'married men [to] pay twice the per capita contribution of women to lineage assessments for funerals or court cases' (Clark 2001: 108) because they spend less money on the children and thus have more chances for saving and end up with more money.

In the following we will look at interactions between Asante women and the colonial state in the 1920s and 1930s focusing on the issue of mother-ing. The colonial government ignored existing resources anchored in the Asante kinship system and in the political structure. One example is the oblivious stance towards the possibility of cooperating with the Queen Mothers, the powerful female leaders, concerning the solving of social problems. 'We have here', Rattray (1969 [1923]: 84) observed, 'a tremen-dous potential power for good in these old mothers of Africa.' But he was aware of the tensions between the state and the Akan and notes that the Queen Mothers did not remain passive but worked against the colonial government because these 'old women saw the whole weight of our power apparently used against them, breaking up their former pride of place in society and the state.'

The case of the Queen Mothers demonstrates that the government, representing the colonial state, was not at all interested in women as agents. But to say that it ignored women altogether would be incorrect because it was, indeed, very interested in shaping women's roles according to dominant western stereotypes at that time. Akan women were to become dependent mothers and subservient wives.[2] The result is a paradox typical of the patriarchal state: women are expected to bear and raise good citizens, while their own status as citizen remains in question. Allman and Tashjian (2000: 185) speak of the 'colonization of the maternal', a process that not only applies to the Asante but emerges as a *general* state project. Pettman (1996) makes this point when she says: 'Despite historical, cultural and national specificity, there are remarkable similarities in the construction of women as mothers and of motherhood as of political concern to states' (14).

The Gold Coast in the 1920s and 1930s was a telling example. In order to cement the colonial presence it was necessary to dismantle the matrilineal structure (see Rattray 1923: 84) and to change Asante women into 'real mothers.' This was to be accomplished by teaching them 'mothercraft' (Allman 1994; Allman and Tashjian 2000). Respective government programmes to achieve this goal were supplemented by missionary efforts which give support to Hastings's (1997) argument that the modern African nation state has been built on a Christian foundation by sharing a linguistic heritage through the translated Bible. In reality, of course, the programmes were to go far beyond the teachings of biblical texts and to imprint a 'Christian ethic' on Asante women. Allman's historical studies on the teachings of 'mothercraft' give us close insight into the details of this process, including the peoples' reactions to these interventions.

Two of the areas the government and the missions focused on were hygiene and nutrition. Targeting women and children, the government set up a health centre in Kumasi with the intention to provide prevention programmes. Yet, the women insisted on treatment of illness instead. Thus, in the end the government did not reach its goal because the women made their own specific demands on the provided structures and by doing so changed their intended functions. Other examples of shaping women's lives according to the government's ideas were the bathing and the pancake project: Convinced that 'poor mothering' was responsible for high infant mortality, white women in the service of the colonial government as well as the missions, visited Asante villages to teach Asante mothers how to bathe their babies and how to prepare pancakes. Asante women's reactions indicate that the goal of the programme to achieve cultural change was not reached. Some Asante women looked at these visits in a practical manner. There was a difference in bathing styles – the white women using a washbasin while Asante mothers pouring the water over the child – but the outcome seemed to them the same, a clean child. Some expressed amusement that white women would come to wash an African baby. They perceived it as a role reversal between coloniser and colonised, an interpretation that was definitely not intended by the government. Others saw it as welcome assistance rather than interference, an explanation, which makes perfect sense when we remember that Asante women were used to delegating childcare chores to others. To Asante women the economic angle of taking care of children was central, but flipping a pancake certainly would not measure up to their idea of economic resourcefulness and responsibility. One woman's comment on the pancake project shows its futility: 'They taught us how to make pancakes, but I knew how already' (Allman 1994: 42).

Parallel to these efforts to teach 'mothercraft' ran attempts to create 'new' wives in the image of the stereotypical European woman at the time. Through indirect rule and the tool of legislation the government tried to strengthen the spousal bond and with it paternal dominance. Inheritance rules now emphasised paternal rights and authority that were greatly limited before. However, the new system did not assure paternal accountability, which was typical of Asante life previously. The government's long-time goal was to create the nuclear family western style with a dominant father figure and a domesticated dependent mother (Manuh 1997; Mikell 1997).

The colonial government basically did not understand the matrilineal structure of the Asante and therefore was ignorant of the complex interplay between the sexes with regard to the upbringing of children. Officials did not realise that a matrilineal father had the duty of obligation but not the right to control. The government's unwillingness to acknowledge these realities of Akan kinship led to confusion in the legislation process and among the people.

Allman and Tashijan's analysis of Akan/state interaction does not address matriliny as a critical factor, which leads to some contradictions. In her discussion of Asante identity Allman writes:

> In the colonial world of Asante, the 'ethnic', the 'tribal', or the 'national' world are masculine worlds – despite (or perhaps because of?) the strong collective sentiments that were and are evoked by the powerful images of women like Asantehemaa Yaa Kyaa and Edwesohemaa Yaa Asantewa. (2000: 100)

The problem here lies with grouping together of 'ethnic' and 'national.' The Asante were, indeed, subjects of the colonised Gold Coast but they were also members of their respective kingroups. Allman (2000: 102) herself explains only a few paragraphs after the above statement that Asante citizenship was 'exclusively rested in and defined by membership of an abusua' lineage. However, she fails to spell out explicitly in this context that the abusua is the *matri*-lineage, which means that the mother bestows citizenship within the ethnic realm, independent from the colonial state. Keeping this in mind, the Queens do not represent conflicting images for the Asante with regard to their ethnic identity. But since the kinship system on the one hand and the state on the other use different structures and gender ideologies to order the world, ethnic and national identities are in conflict with each other. As demonstrated in Allman's study on mothercraft-teachings, Asante women had not given up on their world. They felt confirmed in their existence by their ethnic identity, which was their matrilineal reality.

In the postcolonial era the relationship between Akan mothers and the state remains problematic. As Afshar points out, the state remains highly focused on mothers:

> The state and its bureaucracy are increasingly important in the peoples' daily lives in the Third World. In particular, policies concerning population, the family and household are centred more and more on women, their sexuality and fertility. The part played by wives and mothers, both in terms of the survival of the nation and as unpaid or cheap sources of homebound labour is invaluable, but not recognized. Since many governments endorse the domesticity of women and the unwaged services they provide for the family, it is never easy to suggest and initiate measures that would provide alternative and more lucrative opportunities for them. As a result, much of the legislation concerning women has been directed at controlling them, their sexuality and fertility, and endorsing subordination. (1987: 1)

The problem remains the issue of agency.

Both the colonial and post-colonial state have not succeeded in destroying the traditional maternal image and role in Asante, as can be easily demonstrated with regard to women traders in contemporary Ghana (Clark 1994). These women have remained economically resourceful mothers who are supported by their matrilineal kin group in their daily efforts. At times this has been difficult, especially during periods when post-colonial governments followed the example of their colonial forebears in their attempts to control Akan mothers. The tensions that arose during the late 1970s between state and women traders due to the imposition or threat of price controls are a telling example. Traders were beaten, faced confiscation and destruction of goods, and endured demolitions of markets (Clark 1990). Yet, as Clark (1990) observed, in the end these efforts on part of the government have not been very effective.

### The case of the Mosuo

The Mosuo, also known as Moso, Na, Nazde, Nari, or Naxi, are an ethnic minority subsisting on farming. They live in Yunnan Province, a remote mountain region in the southwest of China. The Mosuo are seen as peripheral not only by location but also by their lifestyle.

The Mosuo's matrilineal social fabric, which has worked well for them for centuries, has created anxieties among many outsiders who seem to fear a tearing of the universe should Mosuo ideals be allowed to persist. What has caused the ire of communist Han officials and astonishment among travellers is their nearly complete rejection of paternal and spousal authority. They do not marry, nor identify fathers (Weng 1993; Knoedel 1997; Cai Hua 2001). Women are powerful central figures in this system. As Shih (1993: 95) states: 'The Moso gender system . . . disputes the view that universally males enjoy authority over females.'

They have lived for centuries in prosperous communities where crime is low and rape unknown (Knoedel 1997). The latter fact can probably be partially linked to Mosuo men's view of the vagina 'as the source of humanity' (Weng 1993: 218). Shih (1993: 58) quotes a communist party secretary from the region: 'I dare to say that the rate of sex related violence among the Moso is the very lowest in the whole world.' This is a significant admission considering the communist view of the Mosuo lifestyle as 'primitive' (see below) and therefore undesirable.

The interaction between Mosuo and Han, the latter being the dominant ethnic group in China, constitutes an especially fascinating chapter in the discussion of women's liberation. Communist governments generally have openly supported and encouraged women's equality. At the same time they have championed 'the family' with the exception of the very early phase of the first Soviet state when 'free love' and children without fathers were acceptable or tolerated out of necessity due to high death rates caused by revolution and war and their aftermath. The support for 'the family', of course, meant a challenge to women's freedom. The ensuing tension, according to communist philosophy, was to be resolved through appropriate legislation and programmes.[3] The Mosuo, however, did not embrace the communist concept of women's liberation but continued to follow their own model that gives sexual freedom to both sexes as experienced in the *acia* relationship and expects women to be the resourceful and reliable providers.

In the *acia* relationship women and men meet during furtive visits (Cai Hua, 2001: 185–236). Such a relationship, sometimes also referred to as 'walking marriage' can last one or several nights, but also weeks, months or even years. It is always set up in such a way that the man visits the woman. Both sexes will have many different sex partners over the course of their lives. As a consequence of this arrangement, the factors that characterise the marital union as legalised by the state, are absent: there is no expectation of a permanent attachment, the partners do not share a residence, paternity is not established, male authority based in heterosexual interaction is absent. This scenario contributes to increased female autonomy and power, a concept that is expressed in their creation myth. According to this account women are actually seen as superior to men:

> First of all, women are mentally more powerful and resourceful than men. Secondly, women are psychologically much stronger than men. Thirdly and most importantly, everything valuable to the human being in this world is from the woman rather than from the man. She was not only the source of wisdom, but also the actual founder of human society. It was she who brought about all the animals, plants, tools, and techniques that make up this world . . . For the Moso, although sexual production is imperative, the sperm provider in producing the first batch of human beings was only a monkey. In the last analysis, not only that the apical ancestor of human being was a woman and woman only, but also that this whole world was entirely reconstructed by a woman. (Shih 1993: 173ff.)

Men are dominant in the public arena, although the Mosuo give more weight to the domestic domain. 'The Naze society is domestic-oriented. [They] always tend to maximize the domestic domain while minimizing the public domain . . . the tendency to domesticate the public domain shows again the centrality of women in Naze society' (Weng 1993: 220). As an example of domestication of the public domain Weng mentions 'the fact that all commensal feasts are held within a household, whether they include kinsmen or all villagers . . . Contrarily, in public rituals . . . people are grouped in accordance with their household' (221).

The women-centred world of the Mosuo, therefore, does not conform to Han and, thus dominant Chinese gender ideals. Ethnographic scholarship in China (see Shih 1993: 19), generally speaking, has defined the Mosuo as primitive and backward barbarians who are still at an early stage of social evolution. Yan Ruxian (1982: 60, 73–4), for example, describes Mosuo family structure as an 'ancient' and 'unstable' one that has been blocking progress: 'It became clear that the unstable walking marriage could no longer meet the needs of the development of production.' According to Shih (1993: 21) this view of the Mosuo is also reflected in the government's refusal to grant them 'unitary nationality' status.

What the government wanted was to bring 'social progress' to the Mosuo so as to enable them to achieve the evolutionary level of the Han. The Han believed that the Mosuo would have to be moved from the (ethnic Mosuo) margins to the (national Han) centre, a goal the government tried to achieve by forcing the Mosuo into marriage and monogamy, with the nuclear family as the ultimate goal of the process. In five big campaigns between 1956 and 1974 pressure was put on the Mosuo to change their sexual practices and their gender dynamics. The state was intent on teaching the Mosuo 'the correct procedure for love' (Cai Hua 2001: 397). Part of these efforts was the 'One-Wife-One-Husband' campaign in the 1970s which made neo-local households mandatory (Shih 1993: 125). In this way, the state aimed directly to create marriage/family in its patriarchal image.

Harsh strategies, like fines and food rationing finally brought the Mosuo to their knees and they got married. But this worked only temporarily. As soon as the government eased up on its programme the Mosuo returned to the visit or pretended to adjust to a new lifestyle without actually doing so. Men, for example, who had married now moved out of their wives' homes and returned to their matrilineal kingroups. The Reform Programme had failed. However, a more recent strategy, that of schooling, is obviously making some inroads. By educating Mosuo to become teachers and by using textbooks that humiliate the student who does not know his or her father, the government seems to succeed somewhat (Cai Hua 2001: 400ff.). This situation is reminiscent of the schooling Native American children in the United States and Canada received that had the explicit goal of annihilating these children's cultural backgrounds. There was some success in those cases, but the US and Canadian governments and missions did not fully succeed and it remains to be seen how the Mosuo will fare in the end.

### The case of the Minangkabau

The Minangkabau, counting about four million people, are one of the many ethnic groups of Indonesia. Minangkabau life is guided by '*adat*, religion, and government' (Sanday 2002: 16). *Adat* in a general sense means 'customs', and refers in the context of Mingkabau culture to their matrilineal structure. But *adat* means much more than a socio-structural concept, as westerners might erroneously assume. *Adat* Minangkabau is a whole worldview, built on the central assumption that women are very important to society because they 'determine the continuation of generations' (Sanday 2002: 20).

Colonisation, migration and modernisation have not undone this system though numerous attempts to do so have occurred over the centuries. Colonial and post-colonial state programmes, Islamic teachings as well as the modern media have used their influence to create the nuclear family with the woman as dependent housewife and mother and the man as head of the family. In 1872, for example, the Dutch colonial government issued:

regulations controlling movement and *domestic behavior* for all *Non-European* residents of the colony . . . The law sets fines not only for unauthorized movement and residence but for what was deemed to be inappropriate behavior within the [traditional longhouse]: a woman sleeping with a man not her husband, or sleeping away from her house for more than one night without permission. (italics added, Hadler 2000: 157ff.)

In spite of all these efforts the matrilineal world has prevailed and Sanday (2002: x) refers to them as the 'most stable matrilineal society today.'

It is probably safe to say that *adat* has survived because Minangkabau society has accommodated change. Generational conflicts are a case in point (see Stivens 1996; 1998; Blackwood 1999; 2000; Sanday 2002). With regard to the mother–daughter relationship, a weakening of the mother's very strong central authority has been observed without any indication, however, that this has been replaced by paternal or male spousal control and dominance. Blackwood (1999: 43) found that 'daughters are vying for control with their mothers, not so much wives with their husbands'. Thus, the younger women actually reach for the state-supported goal of the nuclear family, but they find themselves at the same time in opposition to this very same goal when it comes to their embracing leadership roles in the family. State policy expects women to be *dependent* housewives and mothers and men to be head of the family (Stivens 1998; Whalley 1998: 240ff.; Blackwood 1999: 45). Different forces are at work to bring these ideas to the people, such as state programmes, the media, and Islamic teachings. Traditionally, a daughter will work for her mother and her siblings. To succeed her mother in her power position is not a right but a privilege to be earned.

The government-supported trend towards modernisation, i.e. creation of the nuclear family, becomes for some daughters a vehicle to escape the mother's dominance. But not surprisingly, the young women want to buy only half the package offered. They are not willing to exchange maternal dominance for spousal authority vested in the hands of the husband. 'These nuclear households', Blackwood (1999: 51) writes, 'remain firmly invested in matrilineal ideology . . . A wife has a right to her husband's income but the husband does not have the same right in his wife's income'. Husbands remain subordinate in spite of the state's efforts to increase male spousal authority because women use matrilineal ideology to their advantage (52). It becomes apparent at this point that this is not a simple move from the old and traditional world to a new modern stage. Stivens (1998: 72), indeed, warns of creating such 'a false duality' and speaks instead of 'shifting meanings'. Tradition, according to Stivens, does not disappear, but constitutes a highly complex, continuous development of discursive and social practices, constantly recreated in the 'present'.

Another important issue affecting gender dynamics in Minangkabau culture is the control of land. Women possess exclusive rights to ancestral land as guaranteed by *adat* Minangkabau. The more land a woman controls the easier it is for her to maintain her dominance also in these new single-family households with a husband present (Blackwood 1999: 51). But colonial and post-colonial government policies have created challenges to these rights. Dutch colonial policies supported a stronger role for men in the social structure and male control of land, both practices that have been continued in the post-colonial era under the national Indonesian government (Blackwood 2000: 75). Dutch and Indonesian laws signal to Minangkabau, Blackwood (2000: 76) states, 'that their land practices run "contrary" to others in the nation and the world. It therefore allows some men to feel justified in making claims to land despite family expectations about mutual cooperation and generosity'. Yet, these remain challenges rather than ultimate results, because especially elite women continue to be in control, as Blackwood (2000: 75) observed in the area where she carried out her field work. The state has not fully succeeded at subordinating women to men.

These controversies lead us to the final question: exactly how do these people feel about the laws and policies of the state, on the one hand, and *adat*, on the other? Sanday's (2002) observation of rural and urban life is instructive in this respect. Sanday remarks on various occasions how the Minangkabau accept the three-rope strand of *adat*, Islam and government. But when she discusses life in the villages and towns more specifically, the tensions emerge:

> When men speak *adat* proverbs on the Belubus [rural] ceremonial stage, they are clearly operating in a domain constructed by women. In Padang [urban], *adat* exists as a memory of the past revived in flowing speeches mixed with proverbs and maxims intoned by government officials on state occasions . . . The difference is palpable. (Sanday 2002: 22)

According to Sanday the government is sympathetic towards local *adat*, but 'the sympathy is only skin deep . . . Capitalism and national unity reduce *adat* to a thin veneer in keeping with the national ideology of unity in diversity' (66). In actuality the state perceives *adat* as a matter of the past and Indonesia, like many other developing nations, views the rural population as backward. 'By creating a dichotomy between rural ethnic groups and the "modern" state, the state established itself as the sole authority on progress while at the same time invalidating local practices and beliefs' (Blackwood 2000: 4). Migration, of course, has brought also Minangkabau in closer proximity to the so-called modern world as expressed through urbanisation and industrialisation. This has led to tensions, challenges and controversies coming to the forefront. Out of this, increased individualism has emerged, especially with regard to property, thus weakening the local *adat* structures (Stivens 1987: 97).

A different and surprising assessment of the impact of modernity on matriliny is made by Kato (1982), who studied male Minangkabau migrants. Like Sanday, he speaks of 'the remarkable resilience of Minangkabau matriliny' but he does not discuss rural dwellers as she does. He believes that migration facilitates the continuity of *adat* (241). Kato argues that for the male migrants in the new environment *adat* takes on a new function and meaning. They give up *adat* as a 'way of life' but it continues to exist as 'a means of assuring identity.' To these migrants it was important, Kato observed, that the people back in West Sumatra continued the tradition. In the migrants' experience, the chasm between structure and ideology becomes apparent. The latter lives on, a phenomenon that could be perceived as the residual strength of matriliny, while the former is being abandoned. But Kato speaks from the viewpoint of the male migrant while Stivens and Sanday discuss both rural and urban women.

### Conclusions

This chapter has presented three examples of a people's relationship with their respective nation state. In all three cases we see strong state intervention, lasting from decades to centuries. In each case the goal has been to regulate not only the people's public life but also their domestic and even intimate spheres and in each situation the government in power tried to define and control the circumstances under which children are conceived and raised and to introduce or increase paternal and male spousal authority. The examples show that the goal has been the same whether in Africa or Asia, or the shaping influences of Christianity, Communism or Islam. All attempted to establish the father-centred nuclear family with a dominant controlling husband and a subservient dependent wife. This applies to colonial as well as post-colonial situations. In the Akan case, secular and Christian western values have been used to create policy that will shape family composition and the upbringing of the next generation. Among the Mosuo a secular Communist government attempted to accomplish the same goal, though the male-centred nuclear family represented a contradiction within general communist discourse which claims to seek women's equality with men. The history of the Minangkabau reveals century-long efforts by various governments to weaken *adat*.

These examples illustrate that the state takes the ahistorical position that mothers and motherhood are to be perceived as resources rather than agents and agency. But matrilineal people think differently; they see mothers as resources who *are* agents with the consequence that gender dynamics are different. Tsing (1993: 27) has argued that the differences presented by so-called peripheral populations can actually be empowering: 'The cultural difference of the margin is a sign of exclusion from the center; it is also a tool for destabilizing central authority.' The cases presented in this chapter do not support the claim that these people, by adhering to matrilineal principles, have been able to destabilise the nation state, though it is apparent that the state has not fully succeeded in reaching its goal of moving these allegedly peripheral people into the center. The Mosuo have not created permanent nuclear families with dominant husbands and subservient wives; the same is true of the Akan and the Minangkabau. Thus, it seems kinship structures and gender dynamics present strong social forces that are not that easily changed in their entirety. Shifting meanings, to use Stivens's (1998: 72) concept, emerge that are not merely results but also are strategies that people use to manage challenges to their lifestyles. For the Mosuo this has meant that marriage was only an interlude and furtive visits continue openly as well as disguised under different names. Among the Akan women we saw, on the one side, their acceptance of white women bathing their children. Yet, they also insisted effectively on other services by redefining the function of the health centre in Kumasi, to cite one example. The new nuclear wife-centred families of the Minangkabau illustrate a shift from central maternal power to daughters and wives, which nonetheless left the matrilineal principle of husbands' marginality fully intact.

At the same time all three groups have faced decades, if not centuries, of challenges to the ordering of their daily lives. The 'imposition of state-endorsed order', Tsing (1993: 91) argues, 'can be one of the state's most terrifying threats.' The areas of kinship, family and marriage become means with which to create a new order of daily life. Because women in these groups represent the ordering structural principle due to the reckoning of descent, state-directed efforts to institute new forms of family life set matrilineal people in direct opposition to the state, whose goals has been to define and control women as mothers of new citizens. Kinship practices remain one of the very core issues in the debate on the nation state.

Matrilineal people are at the crossroads. The populations discussed here demonstrate the enduring power of both matrilineal structure and ideology. As the matrilineal debate makes clear, understanding the discourse and practices of the nation state requires the inclusion of kinship and gender dynamics as central issues.

## Notes

The author wishes to acknowledge the research assistance of Ms Anud Abbasi.

1 Cai Hua 2001: 397.
2 Ng and Mohamed (1990: 77), discussing rural women in Malaysia have called this process the 'housewifization' of women.
3 Relevant to this debate is the post-Soviet Russian Family Code from 1994, authored by the Communist Party, the Agrarian Party and Women of Russia, which, according to Tyurin (1995) creates matriarchal dominance in Russian families.

## References

Afshar, Haleh. 1987. 'Introduction', in Haleh Afshar (ed.) *Women, State and Ideology: Studies from Africa and Asia*, pp. 1–9. Albany, NY: State University of New York Press.

Allman, Jean. 1994. 'Making Mothers: Missionaries, Medical Officers and Women's Work in Colonial Asante, 1924–1945', *History Workshop Journal* 8: 23–47.

Allman, Jean. 2000. 'Be(com)ing Asante, Be(com)ing Akan: Thoughts on Gender, Identity and the Colonial Encounter', in Carola Lentz and Paul Nugent (eds) *Ethnicity in Ghan: The Limits of Invention*, pp. 97–118. New York: St Martin's Press.

Allman, Jean and Victoria Tashjian. 2000. *'I Will Not Eat Stone': A Women's History Of Colonial Asante*. Portsmouth, NH: Heinemann.

Blackwood, Evelyn. 1999. 'Big Houses and Small Houses: Doing Matriliny in West Sumatra', *Ethnos* 64 (1): 32–56.

Blackwood, Evelyn. 2000. *Webs of Power: Women, Kin, and Community in a Sumatran Village*. Lanham, MD: Rowman and Littlefield.

Cai Hua. 2001. *A Society without Fathers or Husbands: The Na of China*. New York: Zone Books.

Clark, Gracia. 1990. 'Class Alliance and Class Fractions in Ghanian Trading and State Formation', *Review of African Political Economy* 17 (49): 73–82.

Clark, Gracia. 1994. *Onions Are My Husband: Survival and Accumulation by West African Market Women*. Chicago, IL: Chicago University Press.

Clark, Gracia. 2001. ' "Nursing Mother-Work" in Ghana: Power and Frustration in Akan Market Women's Lives', in Linda J. Seligmann (ed.) *Women Traders in Cross-cultural Perspective: Mediating Identities, Marketing Wares*, pp. 103–26. Stanford, CA: Stanford University Press.

Declaration on the Rights of Persons Belonging to National or Ethnic or Religious Minorities. 1993. General Assembly Resolution 47/135, Annex, 47 UN GAOR Supp. (No. 49), at 210, UN Doc. A/47/49.

Draft Declaration on the Rights of Indigenous People. 1994. www.Uel.Ac.Uk/Law/Mr/Mrun10.Html.

Hadler, Jeffrey Alan. 2000. 'Places Like Home: Islam, Matriliny, and the History of the Family in Minangkabau'. Unpublished doctoral dissertation, Cornell University, Ithaca, New York.

Harrell, Stefan. 1995. 'Introduction: Civilizing Projects and the Reaction to Them', in Stefan Harrell (ed.) *Cultural Encounters on China's Ethnic Frontiers*, pp. 3–36. Seattle, WA: University of Washington Press.

Hastings, Adrian. 1997. *The Construction of Nationhood: Ethnicity, Religion and Nationalism*. Cambridge: Cambridge University Press.

Implementation Meeting on Human Dimension Issues. 1998. www.Minorityrights. Org/Istatement.Asp?Id=9

Joseph, Suad. 1999. 'Women between Nation and the State in Lebanon', in Cora Kaplan, Norma Alarcon and Minoo Moallem (eds) *Between Woman and Nation. Nationalism, Transnational Feminism, and the State*, pp. 162–81. Durham, NC: Duke University Press.

Kato, Tsuyoshi. 1982. *Matriliny and Migration: Evolving Minangkabau Traditions in Indonesia*. Ithaca, NY: Cornell University Press.

Knocke, Wuokko. 2000. 'Migrant and Ethnic Minority Women: The Effects of Gender-neutral Legislation in the European Tradition', in Barbara Hobson (ed.) *Gender and Citizenship in Transition*, pp. 139–55. New York: Routledge.

Knoedel, Susanne. 1997. Spaetere Heirat Unerwuenscht: Besuchsbeziehung Und Sociale Harmonie Bei Den Mosuo Suedwestchinas', in Gisela Voelger (ed.) *Sie Und Er. Frauenmacht Und Maennerherrschaft Im Kulturvergleich*, pp. 339–44. Cologne: Rautenstrauch–Joest Museum.

Manuh, Takyiwaa. 1997. 'Wives, Children and Intestate Succession in Ghana', in Gwendolyn Mikell (ed.) *African Feminism: The Politics of Survival in Sub-Saharan Africa*, pp. 77–95. Philadelphia, PA: University of Pennsylvania Press.

Mikell, Gwendolyn. 1997. 'Pleas for Domestic Relief: Akan Women and Family Courts', in Gwendolyn Mikell (ed.) *African Feminism: The Politics of Survival in Sub-Saharan Africa*, pp. 96–123. Philadelphia, PA: University of Pennsylvania Press.

Ng, Cecelia and Mazuah Mohamed. 1990 (1988). 'Primary But Subordinated: Changing Class and Gender Relations in Rural Malaysia', in Bina Agarwal (ed.) *Structures of Patriarch: The State, the Community and the Household*, pp. 53–82. London: Zed Books.

Pettman, Jan Jindy. 1996. *Worlding Women: A Feminist International Politics*. Sydney: Allen & Unwin.

Rattray, Robert Sutherland. 1969 (1923). *Ashanti*. Oxford: Clarendon Press.

Risseeuw, Carla. 1996. 'State Formation and Transformation in Gender Relations and Kinship in Colonial Sri Lanka', in Rajini Palriwala and Carla Risseeuw (eds) *Shifting Circles of Support: Contextualising Gender and Kinship in South Asia and Sub-Saharan Africa*, pp. 79–109. Walnut Creek, CA: Altamira Press.

Sanday, Peggy Reeves. 2002. *Women at the Center: Life in a Modern Matriarchy*. Ithaca, NY: Cornell University Press.

Saugestad, Sidel. 2001. *The Inconvenient Indigenous: Remote Area Development in Botswana, Donor Assistance, and the First People of the Kalahari*. Uppsala: Nordic Africa Institute.

Shih, Chuan-Kang. 1993. *The Yongning Moso: Sexual Union, Household Organization, Gender and Ethnicity in a Matrilineal Duolocal Society in Southwest China*. Unpublished doctoral dissertation, Stanford University, Palo Alto, CA.

Smith-Rosenberg, Carroll. 1999. 'Constituting Nations/Violently Excluding Women: The First Contract with America', in Mary Ann O'Farrell and Lynne Vallone (eds) *Virtual Gender: Fantasies of Subjectivity and Embodiment*, pp. 171–89. Ann Arbor, MI: University of Michigan Press.

Stevens, Jacqueline. 1999. *Reproducing the State*. Princeton, NJ: Princeton University Press.

Stivens, Maila. 1985. 'The Fate of Women's Land Rights: Gender, Matriliny, and Capitalism in Rembau, Negeri Sembilan, Malaysia', in Haleh Afshar (ed.) *Women, Work, and Ideology in the Third World*, pp. 3–36. London: Tavistock.

Stivens, Maila. 1987. 'Family and State in Malaysian Industrialization: The Case of Rembau, Negeri Sembilan, Malaysia', in Haleh Afshar (ed.) *Women, State, and Ideology: Studies from Africa and Asia*, pp. 89–110. Albany, NY: State University of New York Press.

Stivens, Maila. 1996. *Matriliny and Modernity: Sexual Politics and Social Change in Rural Malaysia*. Sydney: Allen & Unwin.

Stivens, Maila. 1998. 'Modernizing the Malay mother', in Kalpana Ram and Margaret Jolly (eds) *Maternities and Modernities. Colonial and Postcolonial Experiences in Asia and the Pacific*, pp. 50–80. Cambridge: Cambridge University Press.

Sverre, Knut. 1985. 'Indigenous Populations and Human Rights: The International Problem from a Nordic View Point', in Jens Brosted and Jens Dahl (eds) *Native Power: The Quest for Autonomy and Nationhood of Indigenous Peoples*, pp. 188–95. Bergen: Universitetsforlaget.

Tsing, Anna Lowenhaupt. 1993. *In the Realm of the Diamond Queen: Marginality in an Out-of-the-way Place*. Princeton, NJ: Princeton University Press.

Tyurin, Georgy. 1995. 'Code for Builders of a Matriarchy: (Russia's Family Code)', *The Current Digest of the Post-Soviet Press* 47 (45): 11–12.

United Nations. 1993. *Declaration on the Rights of Persons belonging to National or Ethnic or Religious Minorities* (General Assembly Resolution 47/135, Annex, 47 UN Gaor Supp. (No. 49), At 210, UN Doc. A/47/49).

Watson-Franke, Marie-Barbara. 2002. ' "A World in which Women Move Freely without Fear of Men": An Anthropological Perspective on Rape', *Women's Studies International Forum* 25 (6): 599–606.

Weng, Naiqun. 1993. 'The Mother House: The Symbolism and Practice of Gender among the Naze in Southwest China.' Unpublished doctoral dissertation, University Of Rochester, New York.

Whalley, Lucy A. 1998. 'Urban Minangkabau Muslim Women: Modern Choices, Traditional Concerns in Indonesia', in Herbert L. Bodman and Nayereh Tohidi (eds) *Women in Muslim Societies: Diversity within Unity*, pp. 229–49. Boulder, CO: Lynne Rienner Publishers.

Yan Ruxian. 1982. 'A Living Fossil of the Family: A Study of the Family Structure of the Naxi Nationality in the Lugu Lake Region', *Social Sciences in China* 4: 60–83.

# 6

# Confronting power and politics: a feminist theorising of gender in Commonwealth Caribbean societies

*Eudine Barriteau*

My conclusion is that there are currently efforts to de-politicize the field and the movement by removing the feminist political agenda. I see evidence of this in the co-option of feminist language (e.g. empowerment), feminist concepts (e.g. gender) and feminist visions (e.g. transformational leadership) and by the various bureaucratic devices such as gender main streaming, gender analysis, and the substitution of the word 'gender' for 'women' in so many programmes. (Antrobus 2000: 25)

## Introduction and overview

I write as a feminist and a political scientist negotiating the trenches of gender relations in the Commonwealth Caribbean. It is a ground-level vantage point that I use to reflect on and contribute to the ongoing dialogue on rethinking Caribbean culture from the perspective of investigating asymmetric relations of gender. From this position I argue that an understanding of the operations of the social relations of gender and gender systems should be pivotal to any assessment and critiquing of Caribbean societies. One of the first things I observe from this location is the inadequacy of state mechanisms in comprehending a fundamental issue that structures women's lives very differently to those of men. Living, working and simultaneously theorising this terrain, assists me in grasping that one of the core issues in women's lives is ongoing attempts by institutions and individuals to maintain conditions of inequality for women. I locate my analysis in the economic, political and social culture of the region as I attempt to examine how contradictory tensions within ideological and material relations of gender reproduce conflicting messages for women and men about their gender identities and civic relevance.

My analysis is concerned with the point where gender analysis meets or perhaps should meet public policy and everyday life. Governmental machineries such as women/gender bureaux should offer a tangible articulation on public policy on gender. The view from the trenches is dismal. These state mechanisms reflect lapses in policy and deep misunderstandings about the social relations of gender. A 1992 regional survey and assessment of gender training in the Caribbean defined four key concepts, none of which included the social relations of gender (Ellis 1992: 1; Barriteau 2001: 85). In 1999 the Gender Affairs Division of the Ministry of Culture and Gender Affairs, Government of Trinidad and Tobago, produced a 198-page manual, *Training and Sensitization in Gender Development* 'It managed to do this without using the word feminist or mentioning feminist contributions to theorizing the social relations of Gender' (Trinidad and Tobago 1999: 20; Barriteau 2001: 86).

Another report on gender main streaming in Jamaica, St Kitts, St Lucia, St Vincent and the Grenadines, and Montserrat concluded that all the countries display limitations in their understanding of the technical policy\planning requirements of both the Women in Development and the Gender and Development approaches (Harris 1999: 3; Barriteau 2001: 87). Harris goes on to describe four critical areas of confusion in women/gender bureaux in the region as to the correct interpretation of a gender focus and the legitimacy of continuing a focus on women. Bear in mind, Caribbean countries have one of the world's highest ratios of female headed households, with a regional average above 40 per cent.

Caribbean feminist scholars have established a solid record of research on women in the Commonwealth Caribbean, beginning with the seminal contributions of the Women in the Caribbean Project conducted between 1979 to 1982. Research contributions whether by university based academics or activists were more influential in shaping public policy during the 1980s. Now there is a disconnect between feminist analysis, popular understandings of gender as revealed in the work of women/gender bureaux, and the everyday life of women and men. A discourse on gender has developed and is in circulation, but seems uninformed by the existing diverse body of Caribbean feminist scholarship. One of the shortcomings of this existing discourse is our failure to confront the raw power dynamics impinging on our ongoing attempts to expose and alter the systemic character of women's multiple experiences of material and ideological subordination.

My use of the concept of gender refers to the social relations of gender as distilled from over seventy years of feminist and proto-feminist theorising. I do not pose the concept in opposition to the variations within Caribbean feminist scholarship. Rather, I oppose an understanding of gender as a social relation that is devoid of power relations and that is incompatible with Caribbean feminist thought. I want to distinguish this use from many of the conceptually confused renderings that now cloud the use of the concept and increasingly and deliberately seek to divorce it from its feminist roots (Barriteau 2003a).

Formulating extensive critiques of society, feminists investigated the public and private domains, the state and the economy, sexuality and sexual orientation, identity and ethnicity, mothering, fathering and other institutions and relations of society. Feminists created and applied analytical tools to every dimension of women and men's lives. The methodologies and concepts of gender analysis joined a long and distinguished stream of feminist explanatory tools that include, as a partial listing, biology is destiny, the personal is political, dual systems analysis, the sexual division of labour, capitalist patriarchy, sex/gender system, the public/private dichotomy, multiple consciousness, multiple jeopardies, africana womanism, the contours of a black feminist epistemology, and identity politics. The social relations of gender enabled many feminists 'to distinguish culturally specific characteristics associated with masculinity and femininity from biological features' (Hawkesworth 1997: 650).

From their investigations, feminists defined the social relations of gender to refer to a complex system of power played out in the different and often unequal experiences of women and men. I use gender and the social relations of gender interchangeably. I use both to refer to a feminist analytical category that brings to feminist epistemology its own set of conceptual tools and methodologies to yield additional insights into women's persistent but differing experiences of asymmetrical power relations in societies. In my critique of the abuse of the concept, I make distinctions between the sophisticated, feminist, analytical category indicated by the concept of the social relations of gender, and the pedestrian, but powerful, reductionist, rendering of the term to bleach it of its feminist roots and of having any relevance to ongoing feminist investigations (Barriteau 2003a).

My intent is to disrupt an all too facile accommodation and dilution of the analytical worth the concept brings to feminist and other social investigations (Barriteau 2003a). In its use, Caribbean feminists and feminists interested in the Caribbean should confront the politics and power relations inherent in creating new knowledges about women's lives. At this juncture in the genesis and maturation of Caribbean feminist thought we need to be aware of the power relations surrounding the generation of knowledge about women and the implications for the formulation of policy and the influencing of popular culture.

### Feminist scholarship in the region: knowledge without power?

Caribbean feminist scholars have expanded upon the earlier and necessary stock taking and data base the Women in the Caribbean Project (WICP) established. 'From 1979 to 1982 the WICP undertook the most extensive in depth study of women in the Caribbean. The research constitutes a powerful source of documentation and information on Caribbean women' (Barriteau 1992: 8). The cumulative WICP research produced visibility into areas then traditionally ignored by social science research and exposed the exclusion of Caribbean women from post-independence notions of economic and political development (Barriteau 1992: 8). More recently, feminist scholars have expanded upon and contributed to our understandings of the social relations of gender. Many have done so by exploring its intersectionality with other feminist or social analytical tools. They all subscribe to relations of power as a defining characteristic of gender. Somehow this never emerges in policy prescriptions on gender.

The 1998 special issue of *Feminist Review*, 'Rethinking Caribbean Difference', edited by Patricia Mohammed, offers a solid representative body of contemporary Caribbean feminist thought. Patricia Mohammed and RawwidaBaksh-Sooden are two of several Caribbean feminist scholars theorising the complexity of Caribbean gender relations and systems. Mohammed sets the tone of the collection by stating her project is a search, 'for a Caribbean feminist voice which defines feminism and feminist theory in the region, not as a linear narrative but one which has continually intersected with the politics of identity in the region' (Mohammed 1998b: 6). In a more recent work, Mohammed offers a sophisticated discussion on how feminists have 'troubled' the concept of gender. While noting that the twentieth-century feminist goal was to unearth the complexity of social and biological gender, she observes that, 'power in gender relations is not so easy to grasp except when it is physically demonstrated, as in the case of domestic violence or sexual abuse' (Mohammed 2002: xv).

Baksh-Sooden (1998: 74) locates the earlier feminist discourse as Afrocentric and continues the focus on identity politics by exploring the interaction of feminist theory and activism. She uses a standpoint perspective to argue, 'that second wave Caribbean feminism has been largely Afrocentric and simultaneously interlocked with the processes of independence and national identity struggles'. Hilary Beckles (1998: 34) traces, 'the evolution of a coherent genre in the written historical text during and after slavery and its relation to contemporary feminist writings in the West Indies'. Part of his conclusion speaks to my concern. Beckles cautions, 'ongoing projects of nation-state building that promote allegedly gender free notions of nationalist cohesion should be contested and unmasked as skilful projections of modernizing masculine political power' (53).

While not specifically interrogating the concept of gender, Rhoda Reddock (2001) underscores the inequalities and power relations governing how men interact with Indo and African Caribbean women in Trinidad. In an exploratory essay on conceptualising difference in Caribbean feminist theory, she notes that difference between African and Indian Caribbean women were both constructed and real. 'It served to maintain cultural spaces through which men could maintain control over "their" women and also alternate their behaviours towards women of different groups according to ethnic stereotypes' (207).

Linden Lewis contributes to the discourse on gender and masculinity through a literary lens. He examines a Caribbean novel to reveal the construction of both African and Indo Caribbean masculinity. Lewis (1998: 164) offers the literary text, 'as a critical site for further explorations of the illusive data on gender and especially that on masculinity'. These are welcome explorations. I share Patricia Mohammed's point that work on masculinity is necessary for the dialectic of feminist scholarship (Mohammed 1998a: 3). I add that it is necessary because we need to explore and understand the multiple subjectivities of Caribbean men freed from the traditional, worn interpretations (Barriteau 2001: 73). Keith Nurse's (2001) conversation on masculinity and the challenges it poses to men, feminists and feminist analysis is a particularly relevant and important dialogue. Nurse is the first male Caribbean scholar to state that men are gendered beings in addition to locating the analysis of masculinity in contemporary changes in Caribbean political economy.

The writings of these and other scholars working against the grain of a masculinity that is viewed as either wounded or victimised, or alternatively is positioned in a compensatory manner, have yet to penetrate the popular discourse on masculinity. As the popular discourse unfolds and articulated by some it is offered not to have a dialogue with feminist scholarship but to contain feminist voices.

Christine Barrow's (1998) edited volume, *Caribbean Portraits* makes another solid contribution to Caribbean feminist scholarship with a focus on interrogating gender ideologies and identities. The contemporary contribution continues. Feminist scholars are advancing ethnographic studies exploring the lives of women and men in the Caribbean and its diaspora (Bolles 2001; Thomas 2001). The work moves beyond confronting the fathers in the Caribbean literary canons and involves critiquing women writers and their treatment of female subjectivity (Boyce-Davies and Savoury 1990; Barnes 1999; Edmondson 1999). Elsa Leo-Rhynie, Barbara Bailey and others are proving that the process by which education as a public good is made available is gendered and deeply problematic (Leo-Rhynie, Bailey and Barrow 1997; Hamilton 1999). Kamala Kempadoo (1999) and Patricia Mohammed (2000) conducted exploratory studies on women's sexuality. Other feminists are crossing boundaries into studying, reflecting, ceasing to avoid creating a discourse on lesbian and homosexual sexual orientations (Silvera 1992; Cave and French 1995; Alexander 1997; Atluri 2001).

Carla Freeman (2000) and Daphne Jayasinghe (2001) dissect the global economy to expose women's continuous precarious insertions. Jacqui Alexander (1997), Eudine Barriteau (2001), and Hilary Beckles (1998) have taken on the state and exposed its patriarchal character. Tracy Robinson (2000; 2003) has moved beyond documenting how existing laws treat women and is using feminist legal theory to interrogate the law, revealing it as deeply problematic even as others theorise citizenship as a Caribbean feminist project. The record reveals that Caribbean feminist and other scholars have been creating knowledge. The concomitant challenge is twofold. This knowledge should confront patriarchal power and penetrate the policy formulation process. It should also influence daily experiences and expressions of gender relations. That partial sketch of the diverse and exciting body of recent feminist work points to new knowledges that should force a rethinking of Caribbean society and culture from the perspective of gender.

Yet, it is precisely at this stage feminists are being admonished, encouraged, cajoled, even seduced to abandoning investigations on the subjectivity of 'woman' the constructed being. Instead at the level of the academy feminists are being asked to concentrate our intellectual energies on investigating the competing manifestations of Caribbean masculinities.

Janet Brown and Barry Chevannes writing on their study of Caribbean masculinities state:

> We as project directors were reinforced in our belief that Caribbean men need their own 'gender agenda.' The word 'gender' In the minds of most of our informants has become equivalent with women's issues. Discussion of gender usually implies redress of women's experiences of patriarchy and subordination with men cast as the perpetrators by their direct action or by default. (1998: 3)

For at least three successive graduations in the late 1990s the Chancellor of the University of the West Indies (UWI) is on record commenting on the relatively higher enrolment ratio of women at the university and calling on the Centre for Gender and Development Studies (CGDS) to provide some answers for this. Pro-vice Chancellor Marlene Hamilton speaks to this dilemma in her analysis of women and higher education:

> That space is now being provided for more women does not mean that it is accompanied by any yielding of male power and privilege. What is particularly disconcerting is a point made to me on several occasions by the Professor of Gender and Development Studies at UWI, that men, having given

women more space, are now trying to use that space for their own concerns, in her words, 'to divert women's energies into men's anxieties'. She feels that the research on male underachievement is a case in point. Although this is legitimately sited in the Centre for Gender and Development, is it not further evidence of the research agenda being directed to a male, rather than a female, concern? (1999: 33)

At the level of activism, it is the same advice distilled differently. Women's organisations and the women's movement are asked to save our men from themselves even as the Men's Educational Support Association in Barbados warned that they will not allow women into their meetings, 'women who turn up at future "men only" forums will be cast out . . . They have even gone further and instructed all media houses that when they have meetings only male reporters will be admitted to cover them' (*Saturday Sun* 2001: 8). It is as if once the conceptual and methodological frame is gender then the subjectivity of women evaporates and women cannot legitimately constitute subjects for gender analysis. As Bridget Brereton (2002: 130) asserts in relation to gender history, the conceptual framework of gender should include studies on masculinity. She notes that a topic such as 'the construction of masculinity in the post-emancipation Caribbean would be a good example of a research topic in gender history'. What is problematic is that if femininity is substituted for masculinity in the topic, some would argue that this does not constitute gender history.

Feminists are told to do gender analysis means men and men's issues must be examined and questions around women's ontology and relevance seem to disappear. For example, the Men's Educational Support Association (MESA) criticised the programme of the renamed Bureau of Women's Affairs in Barbados and offers some policy doublespeak.

Obviously MESA supports the idea of following up matters related to women already begun by the Bureau of Gender Affairs. But with the coming into being of the Bureau of Gender Affairs, which replaced the Bureau of Women's Affairs, this follow up cannot continue without amendment if the new bureau is to fulfill its new mandate. (Men's Forum 2001: 20A).

This men's empowerment organization has set it self up as the arbiter of state sponsored programmes on women. It cleverly states it will support programmes already begun but simultaneously challenges these programmes if they were to continue without MESA's recommendations for amendment.

It is as if becoming engaged in interrogating masculinity would somehow negate, and should somehow negate, a feminist epistemological project. In the region we are told if you were really doing gender studies you would be looking at Caribbean men instead of continuing work on women. There are colleagues and members of the public who are either baffled or taken aback by what they interpret as the brazenness of having the Centre for Gender and Development Studies (CGDS) boldly, unapologetically, study women's lives. Is that due to a misunderstanding of the concept? Or is it a continuation of a belief in the irrelevance of women's subjectivity?

There is no common understanding in the region of what we mean by gender and currently there are at least ten competing meanings (Barriteau 2003a). These are not differing feminist conceptualisations of gender that I find problematic. For example, where Hilary Beckles (1998) speaks of a gender order I would say a gender system but the contents of the concepts have common currency and are vastly different from the usages of gender I critique. I cannot claim an omniscient stance and state which is the correct definition of gender. However, when I examine the uses to which these definitions are put, I identify one that I think come closest to serving the ideal of gender justice. With these competing definitions I ask, what purposes do they serve when they are deployed? How do women appear? How do men emerge? What relations are allowed to flourish and for what ends? How do they serve the development objectives of the state?

These popular understandings range from a more sophisticated concept for sex (*Voice of Barbados* 1996) to behavioural traits mapped onto biological differences or markers. It includes an understanding of the concept as a synonym for women and men, or even a process of benign socialisation that reproduces males and females as women and men. It may mean, as the Dominican Minister responsible for Gender Affairs wants it to mean, programmes and policies introduced to maintain a focus on men:

> Concerned about what it see as a deterioration in the lot of men in Dominican society, government plans changing the name of one ministry so it can look into the affairs of males. Minister of Community Development and Women's Affairs, Matthew Walters, said yesterday the term, 'women' will be struck off the name of his ministry and replaced with 'Gender' so it can accommodate men. 'Men over the years have been marginalised. They have been belittled, and also they have been abused. Literally men are emotionally abused, men are sexually abused, and men are even physically abused'. He said there are organisations like the women's bureau looking into the affairs of women and his ministry has to take the lead in catering to the needs of men. 'They are losing their sense of belonging, their sense of responsibility. As a result of that we have an escalation in social problems in Dominica. What I want to do is take men on board.' (*Trinidad Guardian* 2000: 7)

The minister does not connect the social problems in his country to changes in Caribbean political economy introduced by globalisation. And yes, gender is often used incorrectly to mean only women. Alternatively, it can be spoken of as new, slick strategies for dominating and emasculating men. The popular discourse on gender often appears as new, slick strategies for maintaining patriarchal dominance:

> Prime Minister Basdeo Panday [of Trinidad and Tobago] said yesterday that female graduates were gaining dominance in the better positions in Caribbean job markets. And, he noted, the social implications of this 'phenomenal gender development' poses a serious challenge to Caribbean societies. 'I cannot help remarking that it will also pose serious challenges to our political parties as well.' (Taitt 2000: 5)

What the social relations of gender never seems to mean is the conceptualisation I define as, 'complex systems of personal and social relations of power through which women and men are socially created and maintained and through which they gain access to, or are allocated status, power and material resources and which includes their capacity to exercise control over or benefit from these resources' (Barriteau 2000: 4; 1998a : 188; 1994). 'Gender relations constitute the continuous social, political, economic, cultural, and psychological expressions of the material and ideological dimensions of a gender system' (Barriteau 1998a: 189).

Although gender systems are isolated for investigation and analysis, I do not view them as separate or discrete subsystems but hold they are organically embedded in all subsystems making up the body and functioning of society (Barriteau: 1992). Gender is within race, within class, within economic activity, within sexualities and sexual orientations, within language. For example, I do not argue that any analysis of social movements should pay attention to class as well as race as well as gender. Instead, such an analysis should reveal gendered hierarchies within racial constructs and the daily practices of racism. It should expose gendered asymmetries in the antagonisms of class relations. As Hilbourne Watson emphasised, it should reveal the differing insertions of women and men into capitalist economic production (Watson 2001). It should decipher and disclose gendered hierarchies in sexualities and sexual orientations in society's tolerance-abhorrence of lesbianism-homosexuality. This approach seeks to move the analysis away from an additive approach to one that simultaneously incorporates what is known about the older and more researched social antagonisms of class and race and mediate these through a commingling with the relatively more recent social relations of gender.

Feminists are increasingly constrained in our attempts to examine and expose the multiple, contradictory and often harsh realities of women's lives. One of the reasons that this becomes more difficult to accomplish, government ministers aside, is that as feminists we have an ambivalent relationship with power and with acknowledging our need for it. Consequently, because we are not confronting power and the relations of power in the discourse on gender, we are not devising strategies of intellectual and activist engagements with the institutions and practices opposed to the ideals of gender justice. Both within the academy and the women's movement we should focus on feminist strategies that continue to develop a politics of epistemological and activist engagements with societal institutions and practices.

### Theorising 'a will to power' in Caribbean feminist discourse

I agree with Wendy Brown (1995) that feminist politics, or rather feminist activism, may have become too invested in a moral apparatus and the need to establish truth claims. I share her concern that this development will be, or is already, at the detriment of feminist politics being able to envision participatory, democratic, societies rather than mirroring the politics of the old. Drawing on her discussion of the Nietzschian 'will to power' we should deploy that concept to motivate feminist engagements in the pores of society and the academy.

The first step in theorising a will to power is to isolate the actions and outcomes implied by the term, will. What are the necessary actions feminists should undertake to work towards gender justice? How can that bring feminist influences closer to shaping the use of power in the public domains of the state, the economy and civic society? How should that access to power be used? Secondly, feminists should understand the significance of grappling with our own need to exercise power and of claiming it to inform political practices. We need to be up front and explicit that we are leaders or that we are seeking to be leaders both within feminist and wider social movements. Having identified the terrain in which we operate we should attempt to respond to a series of questions that should tease out a particular vision of society governed by a set of democratic practices, a principal one being a commitment to gender justice.

What do I mean by gender justice? A commitment to gender justice would mean working to end hierarchies embedded in the current gender ideologies that construct and maintain particular configurations of gender identities and the often punitive roles that flow from these for women and men. It includes working towards closing loopholes in the access, allocation or distribution of material and non material resources. Promoting the ideal of gender justice seeks to remove inequalities in the control over and the capacity to benefit from these resources (Barriteau 2000). To work towards gender justice not only means closing the gaps and removing the injustices exposed by gender analysis but actively promoting conditions in which women and men are not penalised or receive undue privilege for the gender identities with which they 'clothe' their biological, physiological selves or which they operationalise to negotiate life. Feminists need to use 'a will to power' to take us towards operationalising gender justice in Caribbean societies. Utilising this concept of a will to power, I map out some contours for feminist engagements in three principal sites. They are confronting power relations in the discipline, in the academy, and in everyday life.

### Moralism and power

While fundamentalist approaches to religion in the region are following the North American lead and increasingly taking on a politics of aggressive engagement with contemporary society, (Cuffie 2001) the feminist movement and its prescriptions are in danger of being seduced by and retreating into a doctrine of moralism. I define a doctrine of moralism as the pursuit and pronouncements of singular, essentialist, righteous truth claims about women's lives intended to convey the rightness of our positions and prescriptions. Whether as scholars or activists, a feminist mandate should not be to moralise. We should abandon and forcefully reject any attempts to force a mandate of moralism onto our academic and activist work. Instead we should pursue radical, democratic practices propelled by 'a will to power'.

What is the evidence that feminists are being seduced by a doctrine of moralism and the pursuit of truth claims? Ironically, too much intellectual effort is concentrated on how conditions continue to be bad for women (and they are) or in avoiding stating that. Currently two options are pursued. We either hope to persuade individuals and institutions to change through moral suasion. Alternatively, we pretend Caribbean states and societies have accepted women's ontology free of androcentric interpretations and disengage ourselves from women's subjectivity, while meandering off into esoteric inquiries.

There is a need to eschew a victim phase of the discourse and recognise that there will be even greater attempts to maintain and introduce new misogynous practices. It is not accidental that it is only in the last twenty-five years of the twentieth century, Caribbean states found the energy to address ingrained material conditions of inequality for women. This did not arise from a purely altruistic impulse but was, rather, the outcome of a combination of indigenous and international factors (Reddock 1998). On the part of the state a great deal of its motivation was located in the need to bring women into the labour force of modernising, restructuring, capitalist economies. Yet, in the last decade, just as the evidence started to come in that women were perhaps persons after all, most Caribbean states back-pedalled into a ready and willing acceptance of the yet unproven, wild assumptions of the male marginalisation thesis (Lindsay 1997; Barriteau 2000).

## Miller's male marginalisation thesis

Errol Miller was the first and only Caribbean scholar to theorise the idea of men at risk and the marginalisation of the black Caribbean male. Outside of his attempt to theorise the marginalisation of the black Caribbean male, no one else has done so. However, several public commentators and men's rights advocates have accepted his assumptions and premises as given and contributed analyses based on his foundational arguments (Barriteau 2003b). However, they have not tried to devise an explanatory framework for male marginalisation. In 1986 he published, *Marginalization of the Black Male: Insights from the Teaching Profession* which was revised within a more theoretical analysis and republished in 1994. He followed this with *Men at Risk* published in 1991. He offers the following as evidence of what is happening to men:

> The description of Caribbean societies points to lower-strata men's marginal positions in the family, role reversal in a small but increasing number of households, boys' declining participation and performance in the educational system, the greater prospect of men inheriting their fathers' position in the social structure, the decline in the proportions of men in the highest-paying and most prestigious occupations and the decrease in men's earning power relative to women's especially in white collar occupations. While some men, particularly in the highest social strata, have been able to maintain their traditional position in the family, educational system and labour force, the majority are being eclipsed by women rising in all these areas. (Miller 1991: 93)

In his 1986/1994 work, Miller states his purpose is to probe the situation of black men in America and the Caribbean and in particular to uncover the causes of the marginalisation of so many black males in the society (3). The work examines the teaching profession in Jamaica but offers generalisations for the entire region. He arrives at a number of conclusions in his case study of the marginalisation of the black male in Jamaica:

> Primary school teaching and teacher education shifted from being male dominated to female dominated because 'those holding central positions in the society' wanted to restrict black men to agricultural and industrial labour occupations.
> They wanted to loosen the hold of the church on the education system.

They wanted to limit the upward mobility of black men in the society.

They wanted to stifle the emergence of militant black educated men who could overthrow the power structure.

'In a real sense the black woman was used against the black man. In essence the logic seems to have been that if social advantage must be conceded to Blacks through teacher education and elementary school teaching, then allow black women such advancement instead of black men.' (Miller 1994: 125)

Miller concludes that the experience of black Jamaican men in being marginalised will become the experiences of all males of subordinate groups in patriarchal societies and goes on to list seven different groups of men regionally and internationally who can expect to share the fate of Jamaican black men. He attributes the creation of the women's lobby to the process that marginalises the black male rather than adverse conditions in women's lives forcing organisation and articulation. Miller's underlying thesis seems to be that men have an *a priori* right to the resources of the state and society over and above women and that attempts to correct for the explicit denial of women's political, economic and civic relevance are designed to punish men (Miller 1994: 124–31; Barriteau 2000: 11–12; 2001: 92–4). Miller spreads his conspiracy net to international waters. He also attributes blame to international development institutions, UN agencies and the World Bank for contributing to the marginalisation of black men in Jamaica:

Certainly UNESCO, the World Bank, US AID, and CIDA, which aided and assisted successive Jamaican governments since 1962 in expanding education, cannot stand aloof from the fact that their interventions have left black males in Jamaica more marginal in the Jamaican society than their grandfathers were. The full implications of this are still to be experienced. The recency of these interventions makes it still early to realize fully the entire extent of the social repercussions for family life, employment, religion, relations between the sexes, and the social structure. (Miller 1994: 124–31)

In 1997 Keisha Lindsay provided the first feminist response to this conspiracy theory of wilful destruction of the manhood of black Caribbean men. In her work, *Caribbean Male: An Endangered Species?*, Lindsay (1997: 1) offers a systematic, sustained critique of all of the arguments Miller posits in his theorisation of marginalisation. She declares that a reanalysis of the data surrounding women's participation in the family, the workplace and the classroom, casts doubts on both the extent and significance of women's participation in these arenas. Further, Lindsay maintains that male marginalisation stems not from any concrete material reality, but from a gender-biased methodological frame which recognises some data sources and ignores, or invalidates, others (1). Towards providing a methodology to investigate men's marginalisation, I offered a framework for assessing this. That is in determining whether gaps exist between a formal, juridical, gender equality and experiences that would indicate the relative disadvantages of men; then a theorisation of marginalisation should offer an analytical frame that seeks answers to the following:

> What are the policies, legislation, prejudices, practices that penalize or reward men?
> What are the deeply entrenched, policies of the state and its institutions that marginalize men?
> What are the contents and effects of the gender identities men subscribe to?
> What part do these play in expressions of masculinity that are viewed as problematic?
> What are the recommendations in the literature for dealing with marginality if it exists?
> And how do these address concerns for gender justice and equality?
> (Barriteau 2000: 6)

The unspoken underbelly of this set of ideas is of course, 'Caribbean women are taking over and must be reined in.' Instead of moralising about this, I believe we must acknowledge conditions are bad for women because deeply entrenched relations of power have recreated gender relations as they exist. Then we should continue to devise political strategies for changing these.

Rather than become immobilised by a doctrine of moralism we should develop a politics within our scholarship and activism that confronts and seeks to diffuse the raw power that feeds and fuels the manifestations and permutations of gender relations in our societies. The moralising approach will only take the discipline so far. It can take us to advocate for and seek to establish certain conditions of equality. Once the minimum requirements of these are in place it becomes very difficult to ensure what should have been a central political strategy – establishing the centrality of women's right of being, women's ontological right to occupy public and private spaces unencumbered by any notion of meeting some set of preconditions for participation.

### Site one: power relations in the discipline

How do these relations of power play out in the discipline? Feminist scholarship and activism in the Caribbean is in danger of buying into the redemption mission of saving men from themselves. I do believe that as gendered subjects men should be studied and support research, teaching and outreach on Caribbean masculinities. In 1998 the CGDS at Cave Hill was the first of any UWI department to develop two new courses on men and masculinities in the Caribbean and to begin teaching units of these. In fact, feminist analyses of the social relations of gender underscored the humanity and dignity of man the social being in spite of widespread and institutionalised violations of this to the detriment of women. The social relations of gender introduced two powerful ontological points of departure for men and women (Barriteau 2003a). Like women, the social relations of gender freed men from being imprisoned by biology. Gender analysis demonstrates that men, like women, are recreated by gendered power relations and practices in societies. These relations are asymmetric and privilege male behaviour and roles as more valuable and prized than that of females. This includes men who are less powerful in relation to men of other classes and races. In spite of this, the social relations of gender destabilised and reveal as foolish the arguments that men are intrinsically evil and exist to conquer women. Analytically the social relations of gender freed men from any genetic programming to be oppressors.

However, a sophisticated understanding of gender is not what motivates the impulse to redirect feminist scholarship even though the latter has made pivotal breakthroughs in comprehending masculinity. It is driven more by an intent to keep 'man' as the subject of intellectual inquiry even as it burdens feminism and women with the responsibility or blame for correcting aspects of masculine identity that may reproduce penalties for men, women, and societies.

The following are examples. An advertisement to support the purchase of groceries at a supermarket has been running on a popular Barbadian radio station since June 2000. It advises:

> Thank God for women, but mothers why do you allow your sons to walk around idling like non persons without any interest in themselves? Ladies how can you much up your boyfriends that believe being scruffy is the in thing? Thank God for women, they are the only ones who can bring our men to their senses. (*Voice of Barbados* 2000)

In Trinidad and Tobago, a Minister in the Ministry of Community Empowerment, Sports and Consumer Affairs, and former Minister of Culture and Gender Affairs, announced on International Women's Day 2001, that the state would establish an anti-horning unit to create jobs for men so that women would not have to horn them. This was the Minister's direct response to the Mighty Shadow Road March winning calypso, 'Yuh Looking for Horn':

> Paraphrasing Soca Monarch Shadow in his 2001 carnival hit 'Yuh Looking for Horn', Phillips said young men were 'looking for horn if [they] think they can take a wife without having the necessary training or employment or

income in order to support a relationship'. 'So what I intend to do in the Division of Gender Affairs, through our Male [Support] Programme is to create something of an 'anti-horn' programme for men' Phillips said. It will be similar to the Ministry's Second Chances Programme for women. (Andrews 2001: 1)

Working at the intersection of life and the law, Caribbean feminists such as Tracy Robinson (2000, 2003) will have to help us unravel the feminist and legal implications of a Trinidadian man having good, economic work and still getting horn, and deciding to do something about it. I hope if he acts at all, his actions would begin and end at suing the ministry for breach of promise, that is failing to protect his relationship, rather than the more macabre and violent outcomes that produce the following headlines in Trinidad and Tobago: 'Man kills himself after shooting girlfriend'; 'Confessions of a batterer'; 'Mother of four stabbed to death' and 'Woman chopped to death' (Barriteau 1998c). What type of woman would need the Ministry's second chances programme? A working-class woman without a man as economic provider? What has happened to the historical and contemporary evidence provided by Sidney Mintz (1981), Connie Sutton and Susan Makiesy-Barrow (1981), Joycelin Massiah (1982), Hilary Beckles (1989), Christine Barrow (1986) and Rhoda Reddock (1994) among others that Caribbean women have always worked, have always been inserted in the Caribbean economies irrespective of the latest fashionable, label stitched onto economic activity? Is one of the several gendered messages being sent, women should only work if they don't have a man? Does 'man' working automatically translate into 'man' providing? Should men alone bear the financial burden of running households? Have Caribbean men ever borne alone the burden of running households? What new ideological and material penalties are being added to both men and women in this over-simplistic but very dangerous thrust at creating policy based on the misunderstood dynamics of gender?

The redemption mission being demanded of Caribbean feminists extends to cleaning up the theorising of masculinity. In the field of masculinity studies, feminist scholars are being asked to do two things: (1) take on studies of masculinity at the expense of any ongoing work on women; (2) recognise that there are alternative masculinities and men are also subject to the power of other men. Robyn Wiegman's (2001:362) comment on Tania Modleski's (1991) study, *Feminism without Women* is relevant. She notes that Modleski 'casts the study of men and masculinity as a theoretically driven appropriation, if not displacement, of feminist political struggle' (Wiegman 2001: 362).

From the beginning of gender studies at UWI the discourse was carefully nuanced. CGDS recognised the role of men in women's studies and that gender studies was a better concept to capture the concerns and objectives of the Women and Development Studies Groups whose work created the CGDS (Leo-Rhynie 2002). There was an unstated desire to recognise that not all men practise hegemonic masculinity. But what else is new? Caribbean history reflects the power of elite men over other men and women. The functioning of the political economy of slavery seems a particularly relevant example of hegemonic and racist masculinity in full cry. Douglas Hall's (1999) study of the Thistlewood Diaries graphically underscores this. Wiegman also reminds us that:

> As feminists of color have routinely discussed, a monolithic understanding of man avoids the violent and discriminatory implications of white racial supremacy, displacing both white women's complicity with men of their own racial group and antiracist bonding across gender among the disenfranchised. (2001: 362)

Feminists are asked to note that hegemonic masculinity is heterosexist and actively seeks to suppress alternative masculinities, that it specifically seeks to repress and marginalise homosexual men. These qualifiers usually arise when feminists attempt to offer some generalisations about women's experiences with the continuing resilience of patriarchal power in the contemporary Caribbean. There is need for caution. While the dominant gender ideologies of Caribbean masculinity is predicated on virile, performative, heterosexuality, including displays of violence, there should be no automatic equation of the gender subordination women experience with the exclusionary practices targeted at homosexual men in attempts to deny that they are also masculine.

We should resist naming how homosexual men experience their lives, as alternative masculinities. This would suggest there is an accepted, standardised version of masculinity that is uncontested. This is in an area for research in masculinity studies in the region. Beyond knowing that the sexual orientation of homosexual men is different from heterosexual men, the evidence is not yet in that being homosexual makes men less patriarchal and less sexist in their relations with women. The evidence has not yet been presented that homosexual men are any less interested in subscribing to power relations associated with hegemonic masculinity. Wiegman (2001: 362) notes that Marilyn Frye (1978: 144) analyses 'gay male culture as congruent with and a logical extension of straight male-supremacist culture'.

Sexual relations form a critical dimension of gender relations but all relations of gender do not arise or end in sexuality. Economic, political and cultural institutions and practices reinforce gendered relations. We have grown so accustomed to thinking in hierarchical dichotomies that it

seems almost natural that if homosexual men are despised by a heterosexist culture then somehow these men automatically support feminist
visions. Homosexual men are not automatically less patriarchal and pro-
women than lesbian women are automatically pro-feminist or care about
issues that affect women.

One of the contributions of theorising gender was to break apart the
simplistic unity between biology and being. To prevent slippage in the
contributions that research in gender studies can make to understanding
Caribbean and other societies, scholars should avoid the tendency to elide
whole categories of analysis. Creative, analytical tensions should be maintained so that we can explore the continuum of gender relations across
configurations of race, sexuality and class. Homosexual men and lesbian
women who support the ideal of gender justice have developed a political
consciousness of how biological/anatomical differences are used to justify
conditions of inequality for the bodies 'marked' by societies as inferior.
That understanding does not arise automatically from one's sexual
orientation.

### Site two: power relations in the academy

In reviewing the establishment of the discipline of Women's Studies at the
UWI in the mid-1980s, Lucille Mair (1988) faces the emerging power relations and politics of knowledge creation inherent in studying women's
lives (Barriteau 2003a). She detected the coming struggle over feminist
knowledge as a source of power for Caribbean women. She recognised the
reservations and even resistance existing within the academy to efforts to
institutionalise women's studies lives (Barriteau 2003a). She states questions that were being asked included, 'should it be called women's studies
or gender studies? How feminist should such studies be?' (Mair 1988: 7).
Mair mentions that feminist academics were debating whether there is a
place for men in women's studies and if so, where?

The fact that feminists and other academics were debating whether
there should be a feminist content to these new studies exposes the first
stage of confusing the creation of feminist knowledge about women with
its applications. It also exposes the first attempts at the politics of con-
tainment. It is now reluctantly conceded that feminist studies may contribute to how we think about Caribbean society. There is an embryonic,
nascent, feminist intellectual thought that has to be excavated and reflected in what we understand as a Caribbean intellectual tradition. The
documentation and theorisation of a Caribbean intellectual tradition has
not yet fully discovered Caribbean feminist thought or women's subjectivity. Denis Benn's (1987) seemingly exhaustive study, *The Growth and*

*Development of Political Ideas in the Caribbean 1774–1983*, betrays no evidence that any women intellectuals in the Commonwealth Caribbean were capable of generating knowledge about Caribbean society, the work of Elsa Goveia (1980) and Mair (1974) to the contrary. CGDS has begun research, theorising the work of Mair as marking a point of departure in the development of Caribbean feminist thought.

Gordon K. Lewis's *Main Currents in Caribbean Thought 1492–1900* published in 1983 sets the stage for maintaining that exclusion which until recently remained closed to the ideas of feminists or female scholars. Slowly the academy is yielding. The journal *small axe* leads the way. Its editor, David Scott made a concerted attempt to have an article on Caribbean feminist thought included in a special issue published in 1998 on the theme, 'Caribbean Intellectual Traditions'. Still two articles within that issue, Paget Henry's piece, 'Philosophy and the Caribbean Intellectual Tradition', and Anthony Bogue's, 'Investigating the Radical Caribbean Intellectual Tradition' are aware that there must be engagements with class, race and gender formations in a project to create an inventory of Caribbean ideas as a necessary step to elaborating a critical Caribbean consciousness.

The latest volume in this field, *New Caribbean Thought: A Reader*, edited by Brian Meeks and Folke Lindahl (2001) also makes some amends with the inclusion of two chapters explicitly recognising feminist thought, while several others acknowledge it, albeit in passing. Fortunately Mohammed's (2002) volume, *Gendered Realities: Essays in Caribbean Feminist Thought*, constitutes a solid offering. As embryonic as this new field is, there has to be ongoing conversations among all those who produce knowledge about Caribbean society. Feminists have a political responsibility to critique the formation of new ideas that maintain old hegemonies.

### Site three: power relations in the pores of society

Several features emerge as evidence of the contested character of gender relations in everyday life. As much as Barbadian and other Caribbean governments are satisfied with their country's ranking on the United Nations Development Programme's (UNDP) indices to measure states' attempts to improve gender equality there are increasing levels of misogyny in these societies (Barriteau 1998b). In 1995 the UNDP constructed and published the Gender Development Index (GDI) and the Gender Empowerment Measure (GEM). The GDI concentrates on the same variables used to calculate the Human Development Index (HDI). It is intended to measure inequality between women and men as well as the average achievement of all people. The GEM assesses the extent to which women are empowered or enfranchised to take part in different aspects of public life (UNDP

**Table 6.1** Misogyny index: Caribbean countries, 1995–99

| Country | HDI rank, 1999 | World rank GDI, 1995 | World rank GDI, 1998 | Change in world rank GDI, 1995–98 | World rank GDI, 1999 | Misogyny points 1995–99 |
|---|---|---|---|---|---|---|
| Barbados | 29 | 11 | 16 | −5 | 27 | −16 |
| Bahamas | 31 | 26 | 21 | +5 | 29 | −3 |
| Trinidad & Tobago | 46 | 36 | 38 | −2 | 44 | −12 |
| Belize | – | – | 56 | – | – | – |
| Cuba | 58 | 47 | 69 | −22 | 53 | −8 |
| Jamaica | 82 | 52 | 65 | −13 | 69 | −17 |
| Suriname | 64 | 54 | 63 | −9 | – | – |
| Dominican Republic | 88 | 64 | 81 | −12 | 75 | – |
| Guyana | 99 | 70 | 95 | −25 | 83 | −13 |
| Haiti | 152 | 105 | 144 | −39 | 124 | −21 |

Notes: HDI: Human Development Index. GDI: Gender Development Index, introduced for the first time in 1995. The GDI concentrates on the same variables the UNDP used to create its HDI, but compares and takes note of differences in the achievement of women and men to determine a country's progress on efforts to attain gender equity.
Source: UNDP Reports 1995, 1998, 1999.

1995: 73). In 1995, Caribbean countries ranked within the first 70 of the 130 countries reporting on the GDI, with the exception of Haiti, which ranked at 105. Barbados was first in the Caribbean and 11th in the world. What is less known is that all of the Caribbean countries ranked in 1995, dropped in the world ranking by 1998 with the exception of the Bahamas which moved up by two places. Barbados fell by 5 places, Jamaica by 13 and Guyana by 25. In 1998 I constructed what I called a misogyny index in which I categorised the degree of slippage on these indices as evidence of declining commitment to promote gender equity on the part of Caribbean states (Barriteau 1998c). Table 6.1, depicting the latest index, reveals that all Caribbean countries reporting slipped significantly between 1995 and 1999, although a few improved between 1998 to 1999.

The widespread, uncritical acceptance and promotion of Miller's, 'Male Marginalisation Thesis' has caught the Caribbean women's movement by surprise and holds it in a state of suspended confusion. Women's organisations are unsure as to why their efforts to change adverse conditions in the lives of women and girls in very basic ways could so easily be misconstrued as a vested interest in emasculating boys and men.

The irony of this accusation is that Caribbean women have always made it very clear that working with and supporting men was very important to them (Anderson 1986). While there are Caribbean feminists, there is no radicalised feminist movement across the Commonwealth Caribbean (Baksh-Sooden 1998: 82). Most women's organisations are suspicious of feminists and have no intention of maintaining too close an association in case they catch whatever disease feminists suffer from. Caribbean women who are accused of coddling their sons and preventing them from being mature, responsible men, are now somehow collectively involved in a conspiracy to emasculate and effeminise boys and men. The state of uncertainty and doubt introduced by the rabid implications of the male marginalisation thesis has resulted in a certain degree of paralysis in women's activism. The uncertainty about whether women's social and economic activities hurt Caribbean men has forced women's organising into retreat – this of course is the intended effect.

To appease the male lobby, I have heard a female principal of a secondary school caution that the problem for boys is that there are too many women in teaching. A former female director of a national task force on crime introduced a mentoring programme for at-risk boys (a very good idea) but justified the exclusion of girls by stating boys are seeing too many powerful female role models. 'From the bus driver to the principal it is a woman. We want them to see men in a positive light' (*Barbados Advocate* 2000: 2).

The regional popularity, embrace, and articulation of the marginalisation thesis extends beyond any single argument Miller advances in his works on the subject. His arguments do provide a theoretical crutch for the deep resentments to women's overdue, comparatively greater labour force participation since it is evident that the deeply entrenched ideology of women's inherent inferiority as citizens has not changed. In a 1997 essay Miller seems to have revised some of his earlier positions. He states he does not hold the view that male under-achievement is caused by pedagogical approaches of female teachers in schools or the socialisation practices of single mothers in the homes. Rather, he views the feminisation of teaching, the matrifocal forms of an increasing number of households, the poor participation of boys in schools and the under-achievement of men at the workplace as symptoms of the intense conflict and competition among various groups that comprise society (Miller 1997: 44).

Miller uses the term 'gender' very liberally in his analysis but does not define it. As critical as the concept is to his arguments, his understanding is unfortunately limited to gender as a synonym for sex (Miller 1994: 127). By being incapable or unwilling to explore the power dynamics inherent in relations of gender, Miller misses an excellent opportunity to provide an analysis of Caribbean gender relations from the perspective of men. Instead, he offers the masculinist equivalent of some streams of feminist analysis that reify women as permanent victims of men (Barriteau 2001).

Caribbean states have also readily responded to arguments of the marginalisation thesis and are retreating from commitments on behalf of women. Several have assumed they have gone too far on behalf of women to the detriment of men (Harris 1999: 2). Their feelings of satisfaction surrounding the cumulative initiatives introduced in the post-independent, nation-building phase is not weighed against what has been introduced and whether these mechanisms were ever allowed to develop the capacity to tackle the deeply entrenched ideologies of 'woman', the second citizen. For example, Watson (2001) reminded us that the fact that Barbadian women constitute three majorities in Barbadian society has not translated into any social and political capital for women. They are the majority in the population, in membership of political parties, and of the electorate.

Ironically, institutional mechanisms for promoting gender equity within Caribbean states have historically been weak and ill defined. The Economic Commission for Latin America and the Caribbean (ECLAC) examined the efforts by Caribbean and Latin American states to promote gender equity and produced a schema that identified the structural framework for assessing these efforts. This includes: the legal mandate and position of the machinery within the state, staffing, source of funding, functions and sustainability of programmes (Economic Commission for Latin America and the Caribbean 1998: 7–13). When Caribbean mechanisms are held against this framework their fragility and inadequate capacity for promoting gender equity becomes very obvious, yet when the male marginalisation thesis coincided with changes in state and international development approaches to women, Caribbean states became convinced it was time to alter their focus on women, and many have (Harris 1999: 2).

But what really informed the earlier focus? Have Caribbean states ever conceived of women as enjoying full economic, political and cultural citizenship when these states had the opportunity to correct for the distortions introduced by colonialism? When Caribbean states announce they are shifting from a focus on women they are abandoning a project that has barely begun. Caribbean states introduced national mechanisms and policies to satisfy national and international demands that they pay more attention to women. The response was to provide mechanisms that recognised women's relevance to modernising state systems through their traditional roles as reproducers of the labour force and care givers in family and kinship groups. The original mandate has never been addressed. Caribbean states have not resolved whether women's full economic independence and political citizenship should engage public policy (Barriteau 2001: 75).

At this pivotal turning point in Caribbean gender systems, feminists have to accept the challenge of exposing the power relations of gender. We have to continuously devise political strategies informed by a commitment to working towards gender justice even as we continue to engage with socioeconomic and cultural contexts in which these relations of power are played out.

## Note

This chapter is a revised version of the article 'Confronting power and politics: a feminist theorising of gender in Commonwealth Caribbean societies', published in *Meridians* 3(2) 2003: 57–92. The publisher gratefully acknowledges the co-operation of Indiana University Press in granting permission to publish this revised version of the work.

## References

Alexander, Jacqui, M. 1997. 'Erotic Autonomy as a Politics of Decolonization: An Anatomy of Feminist and State Practice in the Bahamas Tourist Economy', in M. Jacqui Alexander and Chandra Talpade (eds) *Feminist Genealogies, Colonial Legacies, Democratic Futures*, pp. 63–100. New York: Routledge.

Anderson, Patricia. 1986. 'Conclusion: WICP', *Social and Economic Studies* 35 (1): 291–330.

Andrews, Arlene. 2001. 'International Women's Day: Daphne Sets Up Anti-horn Unit', *Trinidad Guardian*, 9 March: 1.

Antrobus, Peggy. 2000. 'The Rise and Fall of Feminist Politics in the Caribbean Women's Movement 1975 – 1995'. The Lucille Mathurin Mair Lecture at the Centre for Gender and Development Studies, University of the West Indies, Mona, Jamaica.

Atluri, Tara. 2001. *When the Closet is a Region: Homophobia, Heterosexism and Nationalism in the Commonwealth Caribbean*. Working Paper no. 5. University of the West Indies, Cave Hill: Centre for Gender and Development Studies.

Baksh-Sooden, Rawwida. 1998. 'Issues of Difference in Contemporary Caribbean Feminism', *Feminist Review* 59: 74–85.

*Barbados Advocate*. 2000. 'No Girls will get on Board: Forde Strictly for Boys' 2 March: 2.

Barnes, Natasha. 1999. 'Reluctant Matriarch: Sylvia Wynter and the Problematics of Caribbean Feminism', *small axe* 5: 34–47.

Barriteau, Eudine. 1992. 'The Construct of Postmodernist Feminist Theory for Caribbean Social Science Research', *Social and Economic Studies* 41 (2): 1–43.

Barriteau, Eudine. 1994. 'Gender and Development in the Postcolonial Caribbean: Female Entrepreneurs and the Barbadian State'. Unpublished doctoral dissertation Department of Political Science, Howard University.

Barriteau, Eudine. 1998a. 'Theorizing Gender Systems and the Project of Modernity in the Twentieth Century Caribbean', *Feminist Review* 59: 187–210.

Barriteau, Eudine. 1998b. 'Liberal Ideologies and Contradictions in Caribbean Gender Systems', in Christine Barrow (ed) *Caribbean Portraits: Essays on Gender Ideologies and Identities*, pp. 436–57. Kingston, Jamaica: Ian Randle Publishers.

Barriteau, Eudine. 1998c. ' "A Far Deeper Problem": Violence Against Women and Changes in Caribbean Gender Relations'. Keynote address at the Regional Conference on Sexual and Domestic Violence, Nassau, Bahamas.

Barriteau, Eudine. 2000. *Examining the Issues of Men, Male Marginalisation and Masculinity in the Caribbean: Policy Implications.* Working Paper no. 4. University of the West Indies, Cave Hill: Centre for Gender and Development Studies.

Barriteau, Eudine. 2001. *The Political Economy of Gender in the Twentieth Century Caribbean.* New York: Palgrave International.

Barriteau, Eudine. 2003a. 'Theorising the Shift from "Woman" to "Gender" in Caribbean Feminist Discourse: The Power Relations of Knowledge Creation', in Eudine Barriteau (ed) *Confronting Power Theorizing Gender: Interdisciplinary Perspectives in the Caribbean*, pp. 27–45. Kingston, Jamaica: University of the West Indies Press.

Barriteau, Eudine. 2003b. 'Requiem for the Male Marginalization Theory in the Caribbean: Death of a Non Theory', in Eudine Barriteau (ed) *Confronting Power Theorizing Gender: Interdisciplinary Perspectives in the Caribbean*, pp. 324–55. Kingston, Jamaica: University of the West Indies Press.

Barrow, Christine. 1986. 'Finding the Support: Strategies for Survival', *Social and Economic Studies* 35 (2): 131–76.

Barrow, Christine (ed.). 1998. *Caribbean Portraits: Essays on Gender Ideologies and Gender Identities*. Jamaica: Ian Randle Publishers.

Beckles, Hilary McD. 1989. *Natural Rebels: A Social History of Enslaved Black Women in Barbados.* London: Zed Books Ltd.

Beckles, Hilary McD. 1998. 'Historicizing Slavery in West Indian Feminisms', *Feminist Review* 59: 34–56.

Benn, Denis. 1987. *The Growth and Development of Political Ideas in the Caribbean 1774–1983.* University of the West Indies, Kingston: Institute for Social and Economic Research.

Bogues, Anthony. 1998. 'Investigating the Radical Caribbean Intellectual Tradition', *small axe* 4: 29–45.

Bolles, A. Lynn. 2001. 'Grassroots MBAs: Women Craft Vendors in Negril, Jamaica'. Paper presented to the 26th annual conference of the Caribbean Studies Association, St Maarten.

Boyce-Davies, Carole and Elaine Savoury Fido (eds). 1990. *Out of the Kumbla: Caribbean Women and Literature.* Trenton: Africa World Press.

Brereton, Bridget. 2002. 'Gender and the Historiography of the English-speaking Caribbean', in Patricia Mohammed (ed) *Gendered Realities Essays in Caribbean Feminist Thought*, pp. 129–44. Jamaica: University of the West Indies Press.

Brown, Janet and Barry Chevannes. 1998. *Why Man Stay So: An Examination of Gender Socialization in the Caribbean.* Mona: University of the West Indies.

Brown, Wendy. 1995. *States of Injury: Power and Freedom in Late Modernity*. Princeton, NJ: Princeton University Press.

Cave, Michelle and Joan French. 1995. 'Sexual Choice a Human Rights Issue: Women Loving Women'. Paper presented to the Caribbean Association for Feminists Research and Action Conference on Critical Perspectives on Human Rights Issues, Port of Spain, Trinidad.

Cuffie, Winston. 2001. 'Feminism, Motherhood and the Troubled Male Ego', *Newsday*, 12 May: 10.

Economic Commission for Latin America and the Caribbean. 1998. *The Institutionality of Gender Equity in the State: A Diagnosis for Latin America and the Caribbean*. Santiago.

Edmondson, Belinda. 1999. 'Jamaica Kincaid and the Genealogy of Exile', *small axe* 4: 72–9.

Ellis, Pat. 1992. *An Assessment of Gender Training in the Caribbean*. (Summary of Research Findings), Barbados.

Freeman, Carla. 2000. *High Tech and High Heels: Women, Work, and Pink Collar Identities in the Caribbean*. London: Duke University Press.

Frye, Marilyn. 1978. 'Lesbian Feminism and the Gay Rights Movement: Another View of Male Supremacy, Another Separation', in Marilyn Frye (ed) *The Politics of Reality: Essays in Feminist Theory*, pp. 128–51. Trumansburg, NY: Crossing.

Goveia, Elsa V. 1980. *A Study of the Historiography of the British West Indies to the End of the Nineteenth Century*. Washington, DC: Howard University Press.

Hall, Douglas. 1999 [1989]. *In Miserable Slavery: Thomas Thistlewood in Jamaica 1750–86*. Kingston: University of the West Indies Press.

Hamilton, Marlene. 1999. *Women and Higher Education in the Commonwealth Caribbean: UWI – A Progressive University for Women?* Working Paper no. 2. University of the West Indies, Cave Hill: Centre for Gender and Development Studies.

Harris, S. 1999. 'Study on Gender Main streaming in Caribbean Sub Regional Countries'. Paper presented at the ECLAC-CDCC Third Caribbean Ministerial Conference on Women, Port of Spain, Trinidad.

Hawksworth, Mary. 1997 'Confounding Gender', *Signs: Journal of Women in Culture and Society* 22(3): 649–86.

Henry, Paget. 1998. 'Philosophy and the Caribbean Radical Intellectual Tradition', *small axe* 4: 1–28.

Jayasinghe, Daphne. 2001. 'More and More Technology, Women Have to Go Home: Changing Skill Demands in Manufacturing and Caribbean Women's Access to Training', *Gender and Development* 9 (1): 70–81.

Kempadoo, Kamala (ed.). 1999. *Sun, Sex, and Gold: Tourism and Sex Work in the Caribbean*. London: Rowman and Littlefield Publishers.

Leo-Rhynie, Elsa. 2002. 'Women and Development Studies: Moving from the Periphery', in Patricia Mohammed (ed) *Gendered Realities Essays in Caribbean Feminist Thought*, pp. 147–63. Jamaica: University of the West Indies Press.

Leo-Rhynie, Elsa, Barbara Bailey and Christine Barrow (eds). 1997. *Gender: A Caribbean Multi-disciplinary Perspective.* Kingston: Ian Randle Publishers.

Lewis, Gordon K. 1983. *Main Currents in Caribbean Thought: The Historical Evolution of Caribbean Society in its Ideological Aspects, 1492–1900.* Kingston: Heinemann Educational Books.

Lewis, Linden. 1998. 'Masculinity and the Dance of the Dragon: Reading Lovelace Discursively', *Feminist Review* 59: 164–85.

Lindsay, Keisha. 1997. *Caribbean Male: An Endangered Species?.* Working Paper no. 1. University of the West Indies, Mona: Centre for Gender and Development Studies.

Mair, Lucille. 1974. 'A Historical Study of Women in Jamaica, 1655–1844'. Unpublished doctoral dissertation, University of the West Indies, Jamaica.

Mair, Lucille. 1988. 'Foreword', in Patricia Mohammed and Catherine Shepherd (eds) *Gender in Caribbean Development*, pp. x–xi. Mona, St Augustine: University of the West Indies.

Massiah, Joycelin. 1982. 'Women Who Head Households', in Joycelin Massiah (ed.) *Women and the Family*, pp. 62–121. Bridgetown: Institute of Social and Economic Research.

Meeks, Brian and Folke Lindhal (eds). 2001. *New Caribbean Thought: A Reader.* Kingston: University of the West Indies Press.

Men's Forum. 2001. 'Striking a Gender Balance', *Daily Nation*, 14 November: 20A.

Miller, Errol. 1991. *Men at Risk.* Kingston: Jamaica Publishing House.

Miller, Errol. 1994. *Marginalization of the Black Male Insights from the Development of the Teaching Profession.* Mona: Canoe Press, University of the West Indies.

Miller, Errol. 1997. 'The Caribbean Male in Perspective', in United Nations Economic Commission for Latin America and the Caribbean report, *Caribbean Social Structures and the Changing World of Men*, pp. 35–46. Port of Spain.

Mintz, Sidney M. 1981. 'Economic Role and Cultural Tradition', in F. C. Steady (ed.) *The Black Woman Cross Culturally*, pp. 515–34. Cambridge, MA: Shenkman Publishing.

Modleski, Tania. 1991. *Feminism without Women: Culture and Criticism in a Post-feminist Age.* New York: Routledge.

Mohammed, Patricia. 1998a. 'Editorial', *Feminist Review* 59: 1–4.

Mohammed, Patricia. 1998b. 'Towards Indigenous Feminist Theorizing in the Caribbean', *Feminist Review* 59: 6–33.

Mohammed, Patricia. 2000. 'But Most of All Mi Love Me Browning: The Emergence in the 18th and 19th Century Jamaica of the Mulatto Woman as Desired', *Feminist Review* 65: 22–48.

Mohammed, Patricia. 2002. 'Introduction: The Material of Gender', in Patricia Mohammed (ed) *Gendered Realities Essays in Caribbean Feminist Thought*, pp. xiv–xxiii. Jamaica: University of the West Indies Press.

Nurse, Keith. 2001. 'The Gendered Man', *Gender Dialogue An ECLAC\CDCC Publication* 5: 10–12.

Reddock, Rhoda. 1994. *Women, Labor and Politics in Trinidad and Tobago: A History*. London: Zed Books Ltd.

Reddock, Rhoda. 1998. 'Women's Organizations and the Movements in the Commonwealth Caribbean: The Response to Global Economic Crisis in the 1980s', *Feminist Review* 59: 57–73.

Reddock, Rhoda. 2001. 'Conceptualizing "Difference" in Caribbean Feminist Theory', in Brian Meeks and Folke Lindhal (eds) *New Caribbean Thought: A Reader*, pp. 196–209. Kingston: University of the West Indies Press.

Robinson, Tracy. 2000. 'Fictions of Citizenship, Bodies without Sex: The Production and Effacement of Gender in Law', *small axe* 7: 1–27.

Robinson, Tracy. 2003. 'Beyond the Bill of Rights: Sexing the Citizen', in Eudine Barriteau (ed.) *Confronting Power Theorizing Gender: Interdisciplinary Perspectives in the Caribbean*, pp. 231–61. Kingston, Jamaica: University of the West Indies Press.

*Saturday Sun*. 2001. 'Any Way to Treat a Lady?', 27 January: 8.

Silvera, Makeda. 1992. 'Man Royals and Sodomites: Some Thoughts on the Invisibility of Afro-Caribbean Lesbians', *Feminist Studies* 18 (3): 521–32.

Sutton, Connie and Susan Makiesky-Barrow. 1981. 'Social Inequality and Sexual Status in Barbados', in F. C. Steady (ed.) *The Black Woman Cross Culturally*, pp. 469–98. Cambridge: Schenkman Publishing Company.

Taitt, Ria. 2000. 'Women Dominance Posing Serious Challenge Says PM', *Trinidad Express*, 21 March: 5.

Thomas, Deborah. 2001. 'Seasonal Labor, Seasonal Leisure: The Gruntwork, Goals, and Gains of Jamaican Hotel Workers in the United States.' Paper presented to the 26th annual conference of the Caribbean Studies Association, St Maarten.

Trinidad and Tobago. 1999. *Training and Sensitization in Gender and Development: A Training Manual*. Division of Gender Affairs, Ministry of Culture and Gender Affairs, Port of Spain.

*Trinidad Guardian*. 2000. 'Men Belittled in Dominica – Minister' 18 March: 7.

United Nations Development Program, Human Development Report 1995. New York: Oxford University Press.

United Nations Development Program, Human Development Report 1998. New York: Oxford University Press.

United Nations Development Program, Human Development Report 1999. New York: Oxford University Press.

*Voice of Barbados*. 2000. Advertisement for Carlton A1 Supermarket, on VOB 92.9 FM Station, June.

Watson, Hilbourne. 2001. 'The Masses and the Classes: Anti-colonialism, Adult Suffrage and Social Transformation in Barbados'. National Heroes Lecture, Bridgetown, Barbados.

Wiegman, Robyn. 2001. 'Object Lessons: Men, Masculinity and the Sign Women', *Signs Journal of Women in Culture and Society* 26 (2): 355–88.

# 7

# Men, power and the problem of gender equality policy implementation

*Ingrid Pincus*

The history of men's opposition to women's emancipation is more interesting perhaps than the story of that emancipation itself.

(Woolf 1929: 55)

## Introduction

Since the late 1970s a number of different measures have been developed to put Swedish government gender equality policy into operation in local organisations – both public and private. Examples of such measures are the establishment in local political and administrative bodies of positions responsible for policy implementation, planning documents, gender statistics, various methods of gender mainstreaming, gender budgeting. The implementation of only one or two of these initiatives as intended would have resulted in a great deal of activity and work geared towards the implementation of government policy. This, for the most part, has not been the case. Progress has been slow when it has happened at all. The lack of impact can hardly only be attributed to limitations of the measures themselves. Feminist research has shown that, more often than not, different measures have lacked not only the resources needed to bring about change in the operations of local organisations but also the backing of those in leadership positions, most of whom have been men.

The problem of men actively or passively contributing to the meagre impact of this policy has been noted, but for the most part left undeveloped, in most of the existing feminist research in the field. The aim of this chapter is to shed light on the role of some of these men and the activities they engage in implementing government gender equality policy by focusing on men in leadership positions in three Swedish local authorities. More specifically, its aim is to present an analytical framework where policy implementation is conceptualised as a political process involving the activities of two sets of actors with asymmetrical access to power resources – those attempting to implement government policy and those acting in ways that prevent such implementation.

## Implementation research

After so many years, difficulties in putting government gender equality policy into operation in national as well as local level state organisations could be looked upon as a rather grave deficiency in the workings of our democratic systems. If democratic decisions are not implemented – if local actors instead decide which government policies to implement and which not to implement – this compromises the legitimacy of the democratic system. Implementation problems are hardly unique to gender equality policy. Yet mainstream implementation research has had little to say about gender equality policy. The slow and uneven progress in bringing about change and the difficulties encountered implementing this policy has, on the other hand, been widely documented in feminist empirical research from different countries. Some of the problems identified in this research are similar to those in other policy areas, while others can be interpreted as being more gender-related.

Feminist research about gender equality implementation, and more specifically the problems that arise when gender equality policy is to be institutionalised in local organisations (i.e. the establishment and work-ings of organisational steering instruments such as gender equality com-mittees, plans, civil servant positions), has shed light on a number of different factors inhibiting implementation (Stone 1990; Cockburn 1991; Lotherington and Flemmen 1991; Halford 1992; Halsaa 1995; van der Ros 1997a; 1997b).[1] Examples of these are

- *Structural factors* such as:
  – the weakness of state steering instruments;
  – bureaucratic inertia; and
  – marginalisation due to lack of legitimacy and resources.
- *Cultural / new institutional factors* such as:
  – prevailing organisational procedures and routines;
  – values and norms concerning gender relations.
- *Individual / group related factors* such as:
  – lack of interest and indifference on the part of personnel;
  – lack of knowledge and understanding on the part of personnel; and
  – lack of interest and passivity on the part of those in leadership positions.

In addition to the above, almost without exception, feminist researchers have noted two other factors: The first concerned the passivity and lack of interest in implementation on the part of men in the organisations investigated, and the second related to the peculiar political nature of gender equality policy. Gender equality policy goes to the heart of organisational life. Its purpose is to document and bring into focus inequalities built into the structures, processes and norms of organisations. In other words, such policies aim to make gender visible and to create both the space and means to bring about change in existing gender relations. Thus, these reforms are intended to bring about changes affecting both women and men in organisations – in favour of women.

Both conventional and feminist research has, for the most part, viewed the implementation of government policy as an administrative activity. However, given the problem of leadership and men's disinterest noted in feminist research, we seem to be dealing not simply with an administrative problem, but also with a political problem. How can we conceptualise this political dimension of the implementation process? More specifically, what analytical approach can make visible the activities of actors with different interests and asymmetrical powers who are engaged in and have a stake in whether or not gender equality policy is implemented?

### Implementation, politics and power

In *The Politics of Gender Equality Policy: A Study of Implementation and Non-Implementation in Three Swedish Municipalities* (2002) I developed an analytical framework to explain the implementation of government policy as a political process where conflicts and power relations are controlling. I drew, first, on the writings of Carl van Horn (van Horn 1979, 1983). Van Horn argued that analyses of the policy process should recognise not only that the establishment and formation of policy at the national level is a political process, but that the implementation of government policy in local organisations is also political. He noted that national policy decisions are frequently vague, since they are products of political struggles, negotiations and compromises at the national level. As a result, the translation of government policy vagueness and resolution of conflicting meanings is left to local-level actors. Local-level actors are individuals and groups not only responsible for policy implementation, but also are those most often affected concretely by these policies. Thus, van Horn argues, policies to be implemented in local organisations often become the focus of different, sometimes conflicting interpretations and interests. The outcome of such struggles can be the result of negotiations and compromises mediated by the power of the various actors.

But what kind of power is at play in the process of gender equality policy implementation? Although power has many dimensions, for the most part power has been conceptualised as the capacity to bring about particular results. Yet in the case of gender equality policy the problem at hand is the lack of particular results called for in policy. In other words, the question becomes why does the implementation of government policy not happen? To answer this question I adopted a concept of power developed in the 1950s by Peter Bachrach and Morton Baratz (1970) which Steven Lukes (1974: 16) referred to as the 'second face of power'.

The particular problem Bachrach and Baratz (1970) investigated was why the issue of poverty in the black community did not reach the political agenda in the city of Baltimore. They argued that the exercise of power reflects not only the capacities of individuals and groups to get things done, but can also be exercised to maintain the status quo. In other words power can be exercised to prevent demands or initiatives that threaten an existing order. Bachrach and Baratz developed a political process framework to document and analyse the activities of individuals and groups involved in preventing change. In their case they showed how the white establishment and white citizens, individuals and groups privileged by the existing order, prevented the issue of poverty in the black community from reaching the political agenda and becoming a problem to reform. They referred to this process as 'nondecision-making' (1970: 39). Bachrach and Baratz found that the methods used by individuals and groups to prevent change created barriers that, in effect, maintained the status quo and sustained existing privileges. An important aspect in the Bachrach and Baratz framework concerned the question of what role the motives of those involved in activities played in preventing change. The main concern of any policy process should be not 'whether the defenders of the status quo use their power consciously, but rather if and how they exercise it and what effects it has on the political process and other actors within the system' (1970: 50).

### Nondecision-making and non-implementation

The conceptual framework developed by Bachrach and Baratz to analyse nondecision-making in the policy process included the implementation stage. However, since this stage was not the focus of their investigation, they left analysis of it underdeveloped. In order to disclose the power relations and conflicts that take place in the implementation process in more detail I adapted and developed this aspect of their model. In addition, rather than using the term nondecision-making to describe the politics of this process, I referred to it as *non-implementation*. I argue that this term more accurately reflects the political problem at this stage of the policy process. To be more explicit, important distinctions must be made between the *policy access stage* – getting a policy onto the political agenda – and the *policy implementation stage*.

When it comes to implementation, political struggles involved in putting an issue onto the agenda have already ended; the problem has gained political legitimacy as a social problem in need of reform. In addition the government has developed policy, legislation and measures with which to bring about change. At this stage, the political process shifts to arenas in the state bureaucracy, the 'locale' of policy implementation. This is true for all government policy decisions. But in the case of the implementation of government gender equality policy the situation is further complicated by particular dimensions of this policy, which may thwart its implementation.

The purpose of gender equality policy is to change the power relationship between women and men to the advantage of women. Yet, those who hold most of the political and administrative power positions in local organisations and who are, in the end, responsible for implementing the political decisions aimed to promote and sustain this change are, in fact, men. To put it more starkly, gender equality policy aims to redistribute power between men and women. Yet, because men are the key administrators, implementation of that redistribution has fallen to those who have the most to lose. In the following, I look at how these political dynamics played out in three Swedish municipalities.

### Non-implementation: a political process framework

The political process model presented in the figure below is the analytical framework developed for the investigation and analysis of the implementation process. I investigated three Swedish municipalities over a period of 15 years and in one case 20 years (1980–1995/2000) and have drawn examples from this research to illustrate how power is exercised to prevent implementation. I used this model to investigate the institutionalisation of gender equality policy, including the establishment of different forms of steering instruments with which to put gender equality policy into operation, such as committees, plans, official positions, projects etc. I was interested not only in the creation of these implementation measures but equally in the allocation of, or failure to allocate, necessary resources with which to put these reforms into operation and effectively changing the routines and procedures of these organisations.

In Figure 7.1 the political interaction between two categories of actors involved in the policy implementation stage is the focus. One category is comprised of actors referred to as *change-seekers*, while the other includes *status-quo keepers*. I argue that access to power on the part of these groups is pivotal in determining the implementation outcome. Although the distribution of power is for the most part asymmetrical, and to the advantage of the *status-quo keepers*, neither category lacks resources. In addition,

**Figure 7.1** Political process of implementation

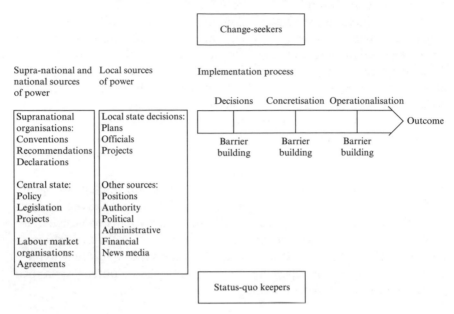

access is not static but changes over time. Barriers, viewed as the exercise
of power, can be constructed at any or all of the three implementation
stages: (1) decisions, (2) institutionalisation and (3) operationalisation.

## Change-seekers

Bachrach and Baratz (1970: 53) defined *change-seekers* as those 'persons
and groups seeking the reallocation of values', who have 'some capacity
to exercise power and its correlates in order to achieve their objectives'. In
my study this group included individuals and groups in politics and
administration. For the most part, they were women. These persons and
groups were openly interested and involved in implementing the policy,
aiming for change in the operations of the local authorities.

## Status-quo keepers

*Status-quo keepers* are those 'persons and groups committed to existing
values' (Barach and Baratz 1970: 56). In my study this group was made up
of men in positions of political and administrative authority, who, as
holders of these offices, were responsible for implementing government
policy. Individually and collectively they, intentionally or unintentionally,

engaged in activities, which prevented or obstructed the implementation of initiatives that threatened to bring about changes in the existing operations of the local authorities. *Status-quo keepers*, Bachrach and Baratz maintain further, start from a comparative advantage in relation to the *change-seekers*. This advantage is founded on the particular organisation of the political system, referred to by Elmer Schattschneider (1960: 71) as 'the mobilization of bias', which not only deters change but also buttresses the position of those opposed to change (see Davies in Bachrach and Baratz 1970: 120).

In Sweden, inequality in opportunity structure between *status-quo keepers* and *change-seekers* is not extreme in the policy access stages, but is exacerbated in the implementation process. At this stage social problems or concerns already have passed through all the formal political decision-making stages of the democratic system. Whether the *status-quo keepers* or the *change-seekers* have a comparative advantage in the political implementation process varies more than in the policy access stage, depending on policy area or the actual issue. Yet in the case of gender equality policy, the opportunity structure, or system-embedded power, needed either to implement effectively or prevent the implementation of democratically processed political decisions, is implicated directly. The policy aim is to change the power relationship between women and men to the advantage of women. Yet, those who hold most of the administrative power positions responsible for implementing the political decisions to promote this change and sustain it are those who have the most to lose. The *change-seekers* are mainly women.

It is important to note that not all men in leadership positions are *status-quo keepers*. In my study a chief administrator in one of the local authorities joined the ranks of the *change-seekers* during three years of the period studied. Yet the central issue here is how to conceptualise and deal with the problems involved in implementing government policy and the role of men in leadership positions in this process.

There are several reasons to focus on men in leadership positions, rather than concentrating on individuals or groups in general who oppose gender equality initiatives in organisations (Lotherington and Flemmen 1991; Halford 1992) or conceptualising resistance as the outcome of relations between men (Cockburn 1991). Most of the research in this field points to men's resistance as a key element in the restraining of gender equality policy implementation. In local authorities men comprise a large majority of those who hold political and administrative offices with particular obligations and responsibilities regarding government policy directives. They have at their disposal substantial resources because of the positions they hold. What they do or do not do has considerable influence in the organisation and on subordinates because of their status in these organisations. Nevertheless, their role in the implementation of gender equality policies in these organisations rarely has been considered as a political problem in mainstream policy analysis literature. Even in feminist policy analysis, although men's resistance has been observed, it has neither been problematised nor investigated further. My contention is that it is plausible that men's noted indifference toward the implementation of gender equality is related to their sex.

## Power

Access to and utilisation of power, authority and influence is pivotal to efforts to bring about or restrict change. In my study power, authority and influence available to *change-seekers* and *status-quo keepers* come from two sources. One source was linked to authoritative decisions concerning gender equality taken in supra-national organisations and in the central government, as well as in labour market organisations. The second source was linked to local level factors, which included local state decisions as well as power sources related to organisational positions in the hierarchical structure of local authority politics and administration, and other forms of political, administrative and financial resources. An additional local level resource available to both *status-quo keepers* and *change-seekers* was access to and utilisation of the local news media.

The use of power to obstruct the implementation of government policy can take place at *different stages of the implementation process*. These are the local decision-making stage, the institutionalisation stage and the operation stage. I use these stages or phases of the implementation process primarily for analytical purposes. In reality, these stages often overlap. Developments within them tend to flow back and forth, which means that what takes place at one stage is often difficult to keep separate and distinct from the other stages. Decisions concerning a given policy may include both long- and short-term concrete formulations about policy goals as well as instructions for how these are to be put into operation. For the most part, however, this is not the case. Local policy decisions made in the representative or executive bodies usually are turned over to other political or administrative bodies, where policy is turned into more concrete, operational terms and then returned to decision-making bodies for further consideration.

## Barriers

Bachrach and Baratz use the term 'barriers' to refer to the different means that *status-quo keepers* use to render challenges to the status quo ineffective. They distinguish between indirect and direct barriers, or forms of

**Figure 7.2** Barriers in the implementation process

## BARRIERS

**Power exercised to prevent change**
**Power exercised to maintain the status quo**

| BARRIERS | METHODS |
| --- | --- |
| *Indirect* | |
| Activities that serve to maintain existing values, norms, procedures and routines (bias). | Inactivity/passivity<br>Sham-decisions<br>Co-optation<br>Denial and withdrawal of resources |
| *Direct* | |
| Activities directed against persons working for change. | Branding<br>Discrediting<br>Harassment |

exercising power to prevent or limit change. Indirect barriers consist of the *ideological and procedural mechanisms* that maintain the existing order in an organisation. Ideological barriers consist of the dominant values, beliefs, and myths. *Status-quo keepers* use these to suppress or render illegitimate those issues or measures that conflict or are at odds with prevailing norms (Bachrach and Baratz 1970: 58). Procedural barriers, in turn, consist of those political and administrative procedures, customs and institutions used to block initiatives from being put into operation and bring about change (Bachrach and Baratz 1970: 57). Direct barriers are status-quo keeper actions and activities aimed directly against individuals or groups who call or work for change. Power exercised by status-quo keepers in more *direct forms* is, according to Bachrach and Baratz, predominantly used against persons or groups engaged in activities to bring about change. Figure 7.2 indicates the different barrier forms and the various methods of non-implementation used by status-quo keepers in the three local authorities investigated.

### Indirect forms of obstruction

My investigation of the implementation process in three Swedish local authorities found indirect barrier forms to be the most prevalent methods used by *status-quo keepers* to prevent change. This is, of course, hardly surprising. Given the current status and legitimacy of this issue in Swedish politics one does not expect to find public displays of resistance to gender equality measures by those in positions of political and administrative authority. It is even less probable that public administration leaders, whose task and responsibility it is to implement public policy, would declare that they neither care nor wish to do their job when it comes to gender equality issues. Indirect barriers were the methods used by status-quo keepers to deny legitimacy to government policy and local initiatives or otherwise render them ineffective on organisation operations.

A particularly common form of obstruction was the widespread *passivity and indifference* exhibited by men in upper-level politics and administration regarding both the policy itself and the initiatives and work of those engaged in implementation. In one local authority, for example, inactivity on the part of these actors maintained the status quo by keeping gender equality policy off the organisation's agenda despite government policy and legislation and the local authority's participation in a five-year government gender equality project (Pincus 2002: 172).[2] Inactivity and lack of interest on the part of leadership in the two other local authorities also hindered progress in gender equality implementation though executive political bodies in both had responded positively to proposals to establish gender equality institutions, such as political committees, plans, project leader positions, as well as to participate in a government gender equality project (Pincus 2002: 88–92, 102, 119).

Passivity on the part of men in upper level political positions – for the most part expressed in the form of silence – prevents the policy from acquiring status and legitimacy in the organisation (Pincus 2002:101–4). It also lowers the status of those working to implement this policy and prevents them from acquiring political and professional legitimacy in the eyes of their peers and superiors. In addition, leadership passivity and indifference concerning the work allocated to and performed by gender equality workers undermines the personal and professional self-confidence of those working to implement this policy. This is thus an effective form of control and an effective method used in non-implementation of gender equality policy at all stages of the implementation process (Pincus 2002: 136–43, 162, 167–9).

*Sham-decision-making* was another method of obstruction used by status-quo keepers in all three local authorities. Sham-decisions are decisions made by those in political and administrative leadership, which appear to promote gender equality work in an organisation but, in fact, are made for other reasons. In my study examples of sham-decisions include decisions to draw up gender equality plans to keep up an appearance of activity or to avoid being fined, a decision to apply to a government gender equality project to placate an already marginalised gender equality committee, a decision to apply to the government gender equality project to give publicity to this rural municipality and put it 'on the map', a decision to include vague and noncommittal gender equality related formulations in the local authority's personnel policy to ward off accusations of inactivity (Pincus 2002: 89–92, 118–20, 159–60, 172–5).

Other indirect means of maintaining the status quo, such as activities to co-opt gender equality measures, undermine ongoing gender equality operations and discredit gender equality initiatives, involve a more active engagement in the implementation process on the part of men in leadership positions. This applies to direct forms of obstruction as well, which are activities directed against persons rather than gender equality initiatives and measures and discussed below. These indirect and direct forms of obstruction take place, for the most part, when elites anticipate that gender equality initiatives will acquire the resources needed to have an impact on organisational routines and activities, or when these resources are already in place.

*Co-optation* refers to activities, which aim to move the responsibility for gender equality matters from individuals or groups with competence or interest in the field to persons or units lacking interest and competence. In one local authority, for example, the chair of the personnel board and the head of the personnel department had the responsibility for gender equality policy implementation moved from the newly established gender equality committee to the personnel department. When the gender equality committee presented its plan for gender equality policy operations to the local authority executive board these actors claimed that, given their responsibility for personnel matters and the importance of gender equality issues, they had already planned to include gender equality measures in the new personnel policy they were developing at the time. Following their arguments the local authority executive board did not grant the newly established gender equality committee the mandate or necessary administrative and financial resources to pursue gender equality work in the organisation. With this, the personnel department became responsible for putting gender equality initiatives into operation, which it did not do. Nor did the executive board, of which the chair of the personnel board was a member, follow up the claims of these actors regarding their alleged plans to include and pursue gender equality issues in personnel operations. It became evident ten years later, when the local authority was chosen to participate in a government gender equality project that no gender equality work was in operation in the organisation (Pincus 2002: 88–92). Interestingly the same chair of the personnel board once again engaged in co-optation activities, this time to render the gender equality project ineffective by moving the responsibility for the project from the gender equality committee to the personnel department, which had previously shown no interest in pursuing gender equality policy implementation (Pincus 2002: 92–8).

In another of the local authorities the chief administrator managed, after several years of *discrediting* the ongoing and rather successful operations of the gender equality committee, to co-opt the administrative responsibility for gender equality policy implementation. The chief administrator argued that gender equality operations, as they were organised, were old fashioned and out of line with the new public management type of planning and budget system he was implementing at the time. He argued that a political committee should not be running gender equality policy implementation. The implementation of this policy was, he claimed, an administrative matter and to be effective should be integrated into the local authority's regular planning and budget system. He noted when interviewed that: 'Perhaps gender equality work is looked down on. This might have to do with the fact that it isn't run according to the modern forms that are required' (Pincus 2002: 128–32). The gender equality committee was later dismantled and responsibility for gender equality policy implementation moved to his office. With this move, and an increasing disregard for gender equality operations among middle-level leadership in large part nurtured by the chief administrator, the implementation of gender equality policy came more or less to a halt. Several years later, in the late 1990s, an auditing firm was engaged to examine the implementation of gender equality policy in this local authority. The auditors found that there was little evidence to suggest that gender equality issues had been integrated into the planning and budget process. They were particularly critical of local authority leadership and its disregard for the Equal Opportunities Act as well as its own gender equality policy (Pincus 2002:127–49). As this local authority moved into the 2000s, gender equality operations had returned mostly to where they began in the late 1970s!

Co-optation, when successful, means that *change-seekers* are left with responsibilities and tasks of rather negligible importance in terms of organisational impact, making it an effective means of maintaining the status quo. *Denial and withdrawal of political, administrative and financial resources* required for effective operations is another form of obstruction with similar effect. For example, in two of the local authorities gender equality committees were established and gender equality plans drawn up yet these measures were rendered ineffective because they were provided neither with the formal directives nor the resources with which to change organisational routines and procedures. Lacking both directives and resources undermined the legitimacy of these institutions in these local authorities as well (Pincus 2002: 88–92, 118–20).

The gender equality committee in one of the local authorities, after a number of proposals, did acquire the authorisation of the municipal council to establish a gender equality officer post. This form of administrative resource is a minimum requirement for the effective functioning of any political board. A woman was appointed to this position, which, a couple of years later, became vacant when she became project leader of the local authority's gender equality project. The gender equality officer post was left vacant for some time and the project leader, who was trying to do both jobs, asked about the procedure for appointing someone to fill this post. She was told that the chief administrator had decided to dismantle this position. The project leader informed the chair of the gender equality committee, who knew nothing of the chief administrator's intentions. The chair of the gender equality committee, a woman who was also one of the local authority's full-time politicians with both influence and power, called the chief administrator to a meeting. She questioned him on his intentions to dismantle the gender equality officer post. After discussing this issue she directed him to recruit and appoint a person to fill this post, which he did. The woman he recruited lacked both knowledge and experience of gender equality policy matters, and, initially, had no interest in these issues. She was later removed from this post and the chief administrator, once again, attempted to dismantle it. Again, the chair of the gender equality committee prevented him from doing that. Yet, eventually, this man was able to dismantle the gender equality committee, move the position of gender equality officer to his department, and reduce the time allocated to this post from 20 hours per week to 11 hours per week (Pincus 2002: 120–1, 132–6).

Appointing persons without competence or experience in gender equality work to positions established to promote gender equality work, as described above, was a method used by *status-quo keepers* in all three local authorities to prevent gender equality initiatives from acquiring adequate resources. The head of the personnel committee in another local authority employed a woman without competence and experience in gender equality to lead its five-year government gender equality project. He did this against the recommendation of the chair of the gender equality committee and the majority of the recruitment committee, who both strongly recommended the appointment of a candidate with such qualifications. The only dissenter in the recruitment committee was the head of the personnel department. His choice of candidate was also a woman without competence or experience in gender equality, although a different candidate from the one employed by the chair of the personnel committee. This strategy, however, turned out to be rather short-lived. The woman he employed signed up for a university course in the women's studies department called 'Gender and Power' shortly after she started working in the local authority, and began to change her strategy (Pincus 2002: 93–8, 101).

## Direct forms of obstruction

Bachrach and Baratz categorise, as mentioned, the activities described above as indirect methods of maintaining the status quo. Other forms of obstruction employed by men in politics and the administration were more direct and were aimed at those individuals and groups working to implement gender equality policy. One such activity was *branding* or labelling women with knowledge in and experience of gender equality work as 'red-stockings' or 'feminists'.[3] Applying terms commonly loaded with derogatory meaning to these women was a way to challenge their professional competence and undermine their legitimacy in the eyes of other organisational members. For example, in one local authority the chair of the gender equality committee invited a candidate to the post of project leader to join him and the chair of the personnel board for lunch to discuss the development of the local authority's gender equality project. The chair of the gender equality committee was impressed by her qualifications, which included both training in and experience of gender equality work. When the lunch was over the chair of the personnel committee commented to the chair of the gender equality committee that this woman was hardly appropriate for the job since, in his opinion, she was too much of a 'red-stocking' (Bylund 1989; Pincus 2002: 93–4).

Another direct form of obstruction, found in the local authorities, was leadership *discrediting* of the measures adopted and the work done by gender equality workers to promote the implementation of this policy. In one local authority the project leader initiated a study group for women interested in politics and a luncheon network for women in the community. Both of these initiatives gathered a fair amount of women over a number of years. The local authority's executive councillor stated, in an interview with the local press, that he considered these two initiatives to be 'ludicrous' and that he was opposed to all forms of separate organising for women (Rygaard 1991; Pincus 2002: 162–3). It is not unusual for individuals to have different opinions concerning the form, content and direction of initiatives and work. Yet, in these cases criticism was not preceded by expressions of interest or support on the part of these men, nor was it followed up with discussions or suggestions on how to improve the work being done. Instead gender equality workers were, for the most part, left alone to interpret and respond to their superiors' negative views of their work. Like passivity and neglect, levelling criticism against gender equality initiatives and workers by men in leadership positions undermined the legitimacy and status of gender equality work in these organisations, and in a more direct way decreased the professional self-confidence of gender equality workers.

A third direct method of obstruction exhibited by men in leadership positions took the form of *harassment*. In one local authority the head of the personnel department remarked to the woman employed to lead the local authority's five year gender equality project that she had not been the candidate of his choice and then went on to tell her that she was, in his view, no more than a 'glorified clerical worker' (Pincus 2002: 101). In one of the other local authorities, harassment took the form of a number of particularly aggressive reprimands directed by the chief administrator against the gender equality project leader. Together with other persons the project leader had criticised the head of one of the departments who had attended a gender equality committee meeting, claiming that he had conducted himself unprofessionally at the meeting. The chief administrator overheard this conversation and later called the project leader to his office. He then notified her angrily that she was under no circumstances to talk about one of her superiors in such a critical fashion (Pincus 2002: 137–8). The project leader had had a similar experience of this kind of aggressive behaviour on the part of this man, when she had informed the chair of the gender equality committee that the chief administrator did not intend to fill the gender equality officer position after her departure. On that occasion, the administrator had reproached her and informed her angrily that she had no business, as part of the administration, going to the politicians with that kind of information. On both of these occasions the project leader was quite upset at being subjected to this kind of behaviour by the local authority's chief administrator, and insulted both by his questioning her loyalties and his attempts to regulate her behaviour toward her superiors no matter what their conduct (Pincus 2002: 133).

## Summary and discussion

In this chapter a framework has been presented with which to document and analyse the implementation of government policy as a political process and to illustrate how power is exercised by those in leadership positions to prevent or inhibit implementation. This approach to power, developed by Peter Bachrach and Morton Baratz, and referred to by them as *nondecision-making*, is in this chapter referred to as *non-implementation*. Illustrations of the exercise of this form of power are taken from my dissertation, in which the role of men in leadership positions in three Swedish local authorities in the implementation of gender equality policy was investigated.

The Swedish government's stance on gender equality policy and its adoption at the national level of different gender equality reforms have over the years gained international recognition and are seen as being particularly far reaching and progressive even in the Nordic context (Borchorst 1999: 206). There is indeed substantial evidence that the government's intention is that this policy is to be put into operation, even though one could hardly claim that it is one of the government's primary concerns. The choice of steering instruments on the part of the state is of course an important factor in determining level of commitment as well as in terms of realising policy. It is, however, also important to note that the state is dependent on local political and administrative actors for the implementation and realisation of its reforms. The sluggishness with which gender equality policy is implemented at these levels in Sweden does not seem to differ from most other countries.

Feminist researchers have exposed a number of different factors contributing to the meagre outcome of gender equality policy in local organisations in different countries, including the problem of men as actively or passively contributing to the sluggishness in bringing about change. In this research those working to implement gender equality policy (femocrats, gender equality workers etc.) are perceived, documented and analysed as actors actively engaged in bringing about change. However, very little has been done to explore what it is that men do, or do not do, in various organisations to prevent or to promote implementation. Instead gender equality workers and femocrats are conceptualised as interacting with structures, cultures, institutions, norms, etc., whereas the living and gendered beings with real stakes in this struggle are left both undocumented and unanalysed. The importance of understanding norms, structures and practices of institutions as determinants and constrictions of human behaviour, including those of men, is not in question here. However, what also needs to be recognised is that the implementation of gender equality policy is not only about focusing the norms, structures and practices in these organisations – the aim of this policy is to change them – to the advantage of women. As van Horn notes, it is at the local level that the redistribution of values is most keenly experienced by those involved. In the case of gender equality policy implementation those with most to lose are men and it is the changing of existing norms, structures and practices that the power struggles are all about – in Sweden as elsewhere. There is a need, as Anna Jónasdóttir (1994: 208ff., 235ff.) points out, for more empirical research of the concrete workings of men in various settings and to take men theoretically seriously as an active party in producing and reproducing the various existing forms of patriarchy. The aim of this chapter has been to move some of these concretely situated men onto front stage and to shed some light on their activities as counterparts in the struggle to bring about change in gender relations – in a country where gender inequality is regarded as a pressing social and political problem.

## Notes

1 See Verloo 2004 'Understanding Gender Mainstreaming in Terms of Power'. Paper presented at the Athena project's Working Group 3B seminar 'Strategies of Equal Opportunities in Europe', Antwerp, 20 and 21 February 2004 for overview and discussion of research dealing with the implementation of mainstreaming initiatives. According to Verloo so far, these policies have not been better implemented than gender equality policy. Verloo notes that power is a neglected factor in this research and argues for the importance of acknowledging and conceptualising this aspect in the implementation of various gender equality initiatives.

2 The following analysis draws from my doctoral dissertation Pincus, 2002, The Politics of Gender Equality Policy: A Study of Implementation and Non-Implementation in Three Swedish Municipalities, Örebro University, Sweden: Örebro Studies in Political Science 5, especially from chapter 5, 6 and 7.

3 'Red stocking' – the name given to the different groups that comprised the new women's movement in Denmark from the 1970s and onward (Clayhills 1991; 1992: 433).

## References

Bachrach, Peter and Morton S. Baratz. 1970. *Power and Poverty: Theory and Practice*. New York: Oxford University Press.

Bäckström, Sylvia. 1994. 'Pampkursen', *FeMedia* 2: 74–6.

Borchorst, Annette. 1999. 'Equal status institutions', in Christina Bergqvist (eds) *Equal Democracies? Gender and Politics in the Nordic Countries*, pp. 167–89. Oslo: Scandinavian University Press.

Bylund, Berit. 1989. 'Evert Gustavsson uteslöt sökande med 'fel' åsikter', *Västerbottens-Kuriren*, 15 June, 17.

Clayhills, Harriet. 1991–92. *Kvinnohistorisk Uppslagsbok*. Vänersborg: Rabén and Sjögren.

Cockburn, Cynthia. 1991. *In the Way of Women: Men's Resistance to Sex Equality in Organisations*. London: Macmillan.

Halford, Susan. 1992. 'Feminist Change in a Patriarchal Organisation: The Experience of Women's Initiatives in Local Government and Implications for Feminist Perspectives on State Institutions', in Mike, Savage and Anna Witz (ed.) *Gender and Bureaucracy*, pp. 155–85. Oxford: Blackwell.

Halsaa, Beatrice. 1995. *Forsøk til nytte? Erfaringer med likestillingsarbeid lokalt.*

Forskningsrapport i prosjektet 'Organisering av kommunal likestillnings-politikk i 90-årene'. Research report no. 1. Lillehammer: University of Lillehammer.

Jónasdóttir, Anna. 1994. *Why Women are Oppressed*. Philadelphia: Temple University Press.

Lotherington, Ann Therese and Ann Britt Flemmen. 1991. 'Negotiating Gender: The Case of the International Labour Organisation, ILO', in Kristi Anne Stølen and Mariken Vaa (eds) *Gender and Change in Developing Countries*, pp. 273–307. Oslo: Oxford University Press.

Lukes, Steven. 1974. *Power: A Radical View*. London: Macmillan.

Pincus, Ingrid. 2002. 'The Politics of Gender Equality Policy: A Study of Implementation and Non-implementation in Three Swedish Municipalities'. Örebro University, Sweden: Örebro Studies in Political Science 5.

Rygaard, Maria. 1991. 'Kvinnoföreningar hämmar jämställdhe', *Nya Wermland-stidningen*, 19 April: 25.

Schattschneider, Elmer E. 1960. *The Semisovereign People: A Realist's View of Democracy in America*. New York: Holt, Rinehardt and Winston.

Stone, Isabelle. 1990. 'Institutionalising Feminism: A Contradiction in Terms? Paper presented to the Friedrich-Ebert-Stiftung, Anglo-German Conference on Equality Policies for Women in Local Government, Bonn, April.

van der Ros, Janneke. 1997a. 'The Organisation of Equality Policies at the Local Level: The Case of Norway', in Frances Gardiner (ed.) *Sex Equality Policy in Western Europe*, pp. 142–58. London and New York: Routledge.

van der Ros, Janneke. 1997b. *Et femokratisk prosjekt: organisering av likestilling*. Sluttrapport av forskningsprosjektet: 'Organisering av kommunal likestilling i 1990-årene'. Research report no. 28/1997. Lillehammer: University of Lillehammer.

van Horn, Carl E. 1979. *Policy Implementation in the Federal System: National Goals and Local Implementors*. Toronto: Lexington Books.

van Horn, Carl E. 1983. 'Policy, Implementation and Politics', in Ian Masser (ed.) *Evaluating Urban Planning Efforts: Approaches to Policy Analysis*, pp. 57–69. Aldershot: Gower.

Verloo, Mieke. 2004. 'Understanding Gender Mainstreaming in Terms of Power'. Paper presented at the Athena project's Working Group 3B seminar ,'Strategies of Equal Opportunities in Europe', Antwerp, 20–21 February.

Woolf, Virgina. 1989 [1929]. *A Room of One's Own*. Orlando, FL: Harcourt Brace Jovanovich, Publishers.

# 8

# Explanations of internal sex segregation in a male dominated profession: the police force

*Berit Åberg*

## Introduction

Why is there a gender division of work even in professions with conditions of formal equality for female and male employees? In order to explain sex segregation in working life, I studied two professions where women and men worked together and initially had the same positions and training–emergency ward nurses (female dominated) and police patrol officers (male dominated) (Åberg 2001). This chapter discusses sex segregation in working life, confining itself to explaining internal sex segregation in male-dominated professions, using the police force as an example.

My explanation for internal sex segregation at work depends upon a multi-level analysis of gender identity processes.[1] This kind of explanation has grown out of and is developed from three research fields, gender and working life (Holter and Hem 1982, 1985; Sørensen 1982; Fürst 1985, 1986, 1987, 1988; Lindgren 1985, 1992, 1996, 1999; Acker 1990; Adkins 1995), gender and social theory (Hartmann 1981; Jónasdóttir 1991; Walby 1986, 1990) and theories of social science (Sayer 1984; Layder 1990, 1993, 1998; Danermark *et al.* 1998). My aim is to elaborate a new mode of explanation to understand the social process of gender production in the workplace that produces sex segregation at work. In this way, I hope to develop further the field of labour market/workplace based approaches to gender. I discuss how women and men are produced as gendered workers through their interaction within social and organisational gender power structures. Understanding these processes as a structural and agency relationship I first clarify my perspective on these relationships, which is influenced by feminist theory, Marxist theory, and the realist tradition in social science. Then, I explain the internal sex segregation in a male-dominated police force based upon a developed structure – agency concept.

My explanation is not only inspired and dependent on research on gender and working life, but also on a concept of structure as found within the realist tradition of scholarship (Sayer 1984; Layder 1990, 1993, 1998; Danemark *et al.* 1998) and Jónasdóttir's (1991) social theory of gender. Realism underlines the relational conditions between structures and agency and stresses the need for structural analyses at different levels of abstraction: societal, organisation and individual. This specific concept of structure allows us to theorise how women and men produce and reproduce gender identity at their workplace in connection to society. Within an organisational system, gender practices interact with societal and work structures to produce women and men's gender identity in specific ways.

Until now research on sex segregation has focused too much on women and men as individual workers in professions and at workplaces as opposed to gendered actors. This 'individual worker' perspective explains the gendered division of work by differences between women's and men's qualifications and competencies. Yet, research on gender systems and work has demonstrated that concentrating on women's and men's qualifications and competencies alone cannot explain the persistence of sex segregation in working life (Fürst 1985, 1986, 1987, 1988; Lindgren 1985; Göransson 1988; Wikander 1988; Dahlerup 1989; Hagberg *et al.* 1995).

The following case study of the police in Sweden illustrates how societal and work-based systems of gender relations operate to maintain sex segregation in the workforce despite legal and formal equality in the labour market. I will show how certain apparently neutral organisational conditions within the police, such as the bureaucratic nature of the organisation and its mode of professionalisation, support or obstruct particular gender practices. The bureaucratic nature of the organisation supports, for instance, masculinised gender practices to a greater extent than feminised gender practices. The interaction between organisational conditions and gender practices constitutes an organisational gender power structure, which strongly influences women and men at work and therefore leads to internal sex segregation.

### A historically variable social system of gender and its practices

Anna G. Jónasdóttir (1991), sought to explain the persistence of women's subordination in formally equal societies. She argued that women's subordination as women cannot be explained fully by women's economic dependence on men. Instead, in formally equal societies, the reasons for women's subordination are to be found in a particular social organisation of women's and men's physical and emotional socio-sexual needs, that is to say as socio-sexual beings. She contended that humans have an absolute need to create and affirm socio-sexual identity, the historical organisation of which produces people as gendered subjects. Jónasdóttir describes this essential feature as follows:

Women and men, in their total intercourse in pairs and groups, also create each other. And the needs and capacities that generate this creative process have our bodies-and-minds as their intertwined living sources. These needs and capacities must be satisfied and developed for the human species to survive, and for us as individuals to lead a good and dignified life. Our bodies and souls are both means of production and producers in the life process, and herein lies the core of the power struggle between the sexes. (1991: 33)

What Jónasdóttir claimed is that women and men exist not only as workers and citizens, but also as gendered human beings. Gender relations are, according to Jónasdóttir, fundamental, that is, they are not inter-changeable with other relations such as class. Women and men are pro-duced as gendered beings through the social organisation of a particular activity – the appropriation of love or love power. In patriarchal, or male-dominated, societies, men's appropriation of love power creates and affirms a particular pattern of gender identity and gender practices. The social organisation of love produces gender or women and men as socio-sexual beings and structures relations between them.[2] The production of gender thus creates opportunities and limitations for women and men in both the private and the public spheres.

For Jónasdóttir, love is a concept analogous to labour in Marx's theory of capitalism; both concepts refer to specific social activities organised under particular conditions. Jónasdóttir defines love first and foremost as relational love practices, and not primarily as feelings existing in the minds of women and men. Feelings of love can be understood instead as the portal to love practices: a society's time- and place-specific way of organising love as a feeling. Love practices create and recreate people as women and men in particular ways in a specific society. Perhaps one can say that the organisa-tion of love practices affirms peoples gender identities in the name of love.

Jónasdóttir further claims that men's exploitation of women's love power is at the nucleus of patriarchy in formally equal western societies. She writes:

By 'exploitation' I refer to the appropriation of certain human/natural powers or capacities which are indispensable to people. Appropriation refers to the situation where a person or a group of people extract these powers from others without exchanging them, or returning them, equivalently and where those who are exploited do not have control over the situation, i.e. they have no real alternative to the exploitative relationship. (1991: 91)

The appropriation of love power produces culturally and historically specific gender processes. Love power as opposed to labour power is exploited when women and men in a particular society think and act in accord with certain hierarchical, non-reciprocal love practices. They are described in Jónasdóttir's theory as the affirmer (women) and the empowered (men). The affirmer's position involves being the person expected to give love to the other person and be sexually available for that person. The empowered person's position entails the right to receive love and be allowed to give full expression to one's sexual needs.

Men who exercise these love practices achieve a higher social status in society than women. These men can, through the creation and affirmation of their gender identity, gain authority and status. In this way they take – and are given – social status on account of their gender. Women, however, do not achieve status or acquire authority as gendered beings by exercising love practices. Women can, on the other hand, exercise influence. [3] Jónasdóttir's theory identifies a gender structure in contemporary society operating both at workplaces and in occupations as well as in private life.[4]

## Dominant gender practices

Empirically oriented gender research in Scandinavia has developed concepts that portray gender identity processes on a more concrete analytical level, illustrating Jónasdóttir's two social positions, the *affirmer* and the *empowered*. These concepts are the practice of responsible rationality and caring practice as instances of the affirmer position, and the practice of subject neutrality and appropriation practice as instances of the empowered position respectively. These concepts portray what I subsequently term *dominant gender practices*. They are the gender practices, or to put it less formally, the typically female and male practices in contemporary western society. They do not include all women and men. Some women and men resist the dominant female and male gender practices. They try in one way or another to influence and change them (Ethelberg 1980; Fergusson 1980; Bengtsson and Frykman 1987; Åberg 2001).

## Responsible rationality and subject neutrality

The term responsible rationality was coined by Bjørg Aase Sørensen (1982), who used it to demonstrate that women's actions were to a high degree rational, and not just emotional. She considered responsible rationality to be based on women's social practices in the private sphere, but made visible in a study of working life, where it was contrasted with instrumental rationality. Subsequently, several researchers worked with the concept, including Harriet Holter (see Holter 1984; Gunnarsson 1994). Holter defined responsible rationality in the following way:

This rationality contains three, sometimes four, elements: an identification with the wellbeing of another/others, attention to the consequences of one's activities for another/others, and taking responsibility for the consequences, changing one's behavior accordingly. The fourth element is acceptance of non-reciprocity, which implies, among other things, that women are responsible to a large extent also for their self-care. (1984:15)

Holter's definition of responsible rationality is often understood to originate in women's work in the home, that is, housework and care work. Responsible rationality entails understanding and satisfying other people's needs on the basis of their conditions. With this approach it follows that it is not right to reduce another person to a means, or to hurt her or him. Responsible rationality also includes being aware of what consequences your own actions have for the other person. This awareness means that responsible rationality actors also take responsibility for the consequences of their actions towards the other person. Lastly, responsible rationality means that women do not make demands on the other person concerning the gratification of needs, but must in the main take care of themselves.

Responsible rationality can be summarised as seeing and understanding other people regarding their circumstances and needs, and also taking practical responsibility for that insight. This responsibility can be expected to be a long-term commitment, for instance a parent–child relationship. Many women are socialised into thinking and acting in a responsible-rationality way, making it one of the most commonly occurring patterns of thought and action for women in our present-day western society. This practice gives women opportunities to be formed and recognised in social contexts.[5] Most women relate to this socially dominant gender practice in one way or another, whether affirming it or resisting it.

In research on gender, men are often attributed with instrumental rationality in working life and in private life. The question remains, however, how one behaves with the other person apart from instrumental rationality. In my research I found the concept *subject neutrality*, developed by Øystein Gullvåg Holter and Helene Aarseth (1993) to be most useful. The concept refers to men and how they behave with other men, and seems to be an equivalent to responsible rationality in women.

Subject neutrality concerns men's relations with men and starts out from the father–son relationship. In a qualitative study, Holter and Aarseth have described and problemised men's relational activity as a combination of dissociation and advances at a distance from the other person. The other person is not permitted to come too close physically, psychologically or emotionally, apart from under certain conditions when distance can be maintained. An example of this is the football field, where the men can act freely towards each other and yet still be together. Such a place is called the integrated room, and ensures that the encounter with another man is not too close.

The concept subject neutrality thus includes men's relations vis-à-vis men both in the public and the private spheres. Subject neutrality is not about caring for the other person, but recognising rights for me and for the other person. The rights consist of being able to meet and be met by another man, while expecting to manage things yourself, making your own decisions. This partly involves treating the other man with respect for his integrity. The relation involves an acceptance that there is something inviolable about the other man that cannot always be understood, but which should be respected. Subject neutrality can therefore imply an acceptance of the authority of the other man.

Subject neutrality involves a high level of freedom in relation to the other person. You are allowed to do your own thing and at the same time you show respect for the other person by not taking too much care of him in a practical way. When subject neutrality results in neglecting the other person's need for practical care, there can be problems. The other person is then viewed too much from a distance and not as someone who occasionally might need some care and attention. There are thus advantages and disadvantages with this approach, just as there are with the dominant female gender practice.

This subject-neutral approach includes patterns of thoughts and actions that many men are socialised into, and it can also be understood as an existential possibility for men in a specific society. In parallel with this, women are socialised into responsible rationality. Both subject neutrality and responsible rationality describes what I call dominant gender practices. They entail certain approaches to the other person.

### Caring practices and appropriation practices

Liselotte Jakobsen and Jan Ch. Karlsson (1993) developed the concepts caring practices and appropriation practices and explicitly argue that they are associated with Jónasdóttir's two social gender practices in society, the affirmer and the empowered.[6] They have illuminated how caring practices and appropriation practices are performed in everyday life between a man and a woman with a description of the couple Annika and Anders. It is in this context primarily about who adjusts to whose working life, and accordingly who takes the overall responsibility for work in the home. These approaches have important consequences for how one engages in an occupation, for instance the police force.

During the four years of Annika and Anders' everyday life portrayed by Jakobsen and Karlsson, Annika worked as an assistant nurse,

**Table 8.1** Connections between gender structure and gender practices

| Social gender structure | Dominant gender practices |
| --- | --- |
| Empowered | Subject neutrality<br>Appropriation practices |
| Affirmer | Responsible rationality<br>Caring practices |

employed at the same workplace. Anders changed work assignments five times. His last job was his own company selling computer software. During this period, Anders invested time and energy in his own career and saw that as natural. In the way that he leads his everyday life, he expresses a responsibility for supporting his family that is a part of appropriation practice, but this responsibility is not the same as caring practice. Responsibility for support is primarily about labour and wages, while caring practice is first and foremost about love power and love. Anders is created and affirmed in his masculinity when Annika does not expect him to take overall responsibility for care and the housework. Annika's femininity is created and affirmed when she is expected to take overall responsibility for work in their home, and when she is expected and allowed to adapt to her partner's working life.

Annika is gainfully employed and also does the work in their home. Annika is the person who has taken the overall everyday responsibility for the children and the work in their home. This does not mean that Annika does all the work in their home and that Anders does nothing. They help each other a lot with the work in their home. But Annika thinks she has to take a major part of the responsibility for care and the housework when Anders spends a lot of time doing his job, for example during intense periods of work and business trips. From his perspective, Anders takes it for granted that he can spend time on his work and following his career. In this mutual process, Anders benefits to a greater degree from Annika's care than she is repaid by him.

Connections between Jónasdóttir's theory of love power and the gender practices in society, and the illustrations of these in empirical studies that I have accounted for as dominant gender practices above can be clarified in table 8.1.

## The regular police force

The workplace for the patrol officers in this study was situated in a medium-sized Swedish town. The police force was regarded as a typical male occupation on account of its male traditions and male dominance. Police patrol officer occupation connotes on intermediate position as a public servant in the public sector, characterised by collaborating in the performance of work. I considered this aspect, compared to individual work, to reinforce the possibility of studying identity processes.

In the police authority of the town, I selected a work group (turn group) consisting of four women and ten men, and carried out a total of seven observations and ten interviews with patrol officers.[7] There was no formal division of labour in the turn group, and the general understanding was all of the police did all of the tasks. Women and men were assumed to be professional, regardless of gender. The formal division of work between women and men in the Swedish police force was removed in 1971. Women and men now have the same training and equal standing, conditions that have made them formally of equal status.

### Four conditions in the police force

Within the police force there are four apparently gender neutral conditions. They are the bureaucratic organisation, the professionalisation of the occupational role, the coordination, and the timetable.

A first condition is that the police authorities carry out their assignment through a bureaucratic organisation. According to Weber, formal rationality permeates the modern rational form of organisation, with centrally steered goals (Brubaker 1984: 13). The exercise of bureaucratic power in particular is based upon formal rationality (Kalberg 1980: 1158). The bureaucratic organisation is typified by hierarchical order and authority is legitimised on rational grounds. The hierarchical positions consist of delineated roles with corresponding qualifications and assignments. The holders of the positions are expected to make decisions to a large extent based upon written procedures. When employees carry out their assignments, they are guided by the rules and goals of the organisation. From these, they are expected to take a formal and impersonal interest in their work, that is, it is assumed that they are not influenced in their work by self-interest or emotions.

Formal rationality can cause a lack of sensitivity when carrying out the work. The intention is to avoid arbitrariness in the handling of assignments and protect the legal rights of the customer/citizen/client/patient. The formal rationality inherent in positions in a bureaucratic organisation steers social interactions. The other party may be regarded as a means by the formally rational actor. She/he is not expected to put her/himself in the other's life situation. In a bureaucratic organisation decisions can also be made without taking an individual's life situation into consideration.[8]

Formal rationality is a precondition for the patrol officer to be able to exercise her/his authority. As the holder of a specific position in the bureaucratic organisation, he/she is expected to apply formal rationality.

The second condition in the police force that will be discussed here is the professionalisation of the occupational role. A profession means, among other things, that an occupation has a professional monopoly, a knowledge monopoly and acknowledgement as a service to society (Karlsson 1983). The police profession fulfils all three of these require-ments. There is a knowledge monopoly in a special sense, that is, police training gives the police cadets specific professional knowledge. However, this knowledge comes from different academic disciplines and not from one special field of knowledge which is their own, as is the case with social work for social workers or nursing for nurses, for example.

The police profession has traditionally been built up by men who have used historically specific gender practices. It was considered sufficient to have 'white teeth and big hands', as one of the officers put it, referring to the lack of theoretical and practical training. This basis is still predomi-nant in an informal way in the profession, even if that is not formally the case (see Martin 1990: 154). Professionalisation of police work has meant that these officers now receive training in both theoretical and practical knowledge. The demand for theoretical knowledge in the exercise of an occupation is what I term professionalisation.[9] Here it includes the need for theoretical knowledge, and thus cognitive and emotional distancing, in the work of a professional police officer. Professionalisation means that it is no longer sufficient, to as great an extent as before, just to be a man and use traditional male gender practices to be competent in the police pro-fession. The police profession is now characterised by, among other things, competence in civil and criminal law, social studies, psychology, social and criminal policies, the use of force and the use of weapons, self-defence and emergency treatment.

Professionalisation also involves a certain approach to colleagues and clients. It is expected to entail, what one might call a 'distanced engage-ment'. Having a position in a hierarchical structure and a profession does not primarily lead to personal responsibility and care for clients and col-leagues. It can also be described as involving formal rationality, but in a context other than the bureaucratic. Celia Davies writes (1995: 57): 'The professional encounter, at first sight so particular and contextualized, also turns out to encompass, though not in identical form, the features of impar-tiality and impersonality previously discussed in relation to bureaucracy.'

The third condition is what the police officers call *coordination*, or an informal division of labour among patrol officers. One of the officers described coordination as follows:[10]

In that case, they are the only times when there is a difference between the genders. Really, I think the co-ordination we have works bloody well. The only time you still think about all that with women and men actually is if you are going to send a patrol. And we talk about that in here, the officer in charge, me and the radio operator . . . If we know we're going to an address and there's some big guy there, because there sometimes is. We know that it'll take at least two men to get him. We've got four girls in our group. That means that they are often out together, two girls. And it does happen that we send a girls' patrol, as we call them, and then some other patrol as backup, or we don't send the girls, but send the others instead. And word has got round once or twice – and the girls get to hear – that we sent the others first, and then they get a bit upset. But we do that a bit because you can't always say that you can talk your way out of a situation. Of course, the girls . . . They must do that quite a lot really, because if there was a fight they would- n't have much chance – that's just the way it is.

Uniformed police perform their duties through this coordination system, even though the general view is that 'if you are a police officer, you are a police officer', regardless of gender. In this system the officer in charge and the patrol officers expect most of the male patrol officers to carry out their work using physical force if necessary, and the female patrol officers carry out theirs using social competence. Men are often sent instead of women to be officers who can work using physical force to solve the problem about making arrests. When two men work together, it is assumed they use an approach where physical strength is decisive for how they carry out their tasks (see also Sørensen and Hetle 1985: 73–4). Some policemen think that by using this approach they get their work done more quickly. If they are not available, another patrol (often a 'girl' patrol) is sent and it is assumed the women will use a different approach and must be 'covered' by a man's patrol as reinforcement. In this way, they assume, it is only under exceptional circumstances that the police cannot manage or get injured, that is, that they fail to protect and give security to each other and the general public.

To work with social competence means, among other things, being able to deal with people, being able to read them, joke, and make use of specific knowledge about human behaviour. Both women and men work use social competence at work. Yet, the expectation is that women will utilise this approach, while it will be an exception for men. A female patrol officer relates how she often restores order in public:

By talking and . . . It's even happened when I've been out on patrol with male colleagues – they'll say to me – You talk to him – to this gigantic bloke – because they know that, as a rule, they don't hit girls. If you're just going to separate some people having a row, well . . . Most people have a thing about not hitting girls, and many are the same about not hitting the police. But if a beefy policeman turns up, I think he can be more provoking in the heat of the moment than if it's little me who arrives.

This female gender practice is used particularly in certain areas of work, gathering information, writing tasks, in situations involving children or domestic violence.[11]

The timetable is a fourth condition in the collaboration between women and men in the police force. In the group I followed, the working hours meant that the officers in charge and the other patrol officers worked in 'turns'. A turn consisted of working three shifts followed by three days off. The first shift is from 22.00 to 07.00. The next shift starts the following afternoon at 15.00 and goes on until 22.00. The last shift in the turn begins the next morning at 07.00 and ends at 16.00. This is generally followed by three days leave. These shifts can be demanding, both physically and mentally. There are only eight hours rest between the shifts, compared to fourteen to fifteen hours between shifts in ordinary day or night work. The timetable also means that the people in the watch group always work together, including those in charge. The arrangement of the working hours and the organisation of the work means that the police in the turn group are obliged to be very close to each other, physically, emotionally and cognitively. Sørensen and Hetle (1985) describe these working conditions as a 24-hour community always on full alert.

### Gender identity affirmation processes in the police force

Two sets of factors structure the gender distribution of police work. The first concerns the macro-social gender structure and its empirically illustrated dominant gender practices described in previous sections. The second relates to the four seemingly gender neutral organisational conditions within the police force. These social and organisational conditions affect work strategies used by patrol officers, simultaneously positioning them as workers and as gendered women and men. Sometimes these strategies harmonise and sometimes they conflict with dominant gender practices. To the degree they harmonise, gender identity is affirmed at work; to the degree they conflict, gender identity affirmation is impaired at work. In other words the four organisational conditions provide both opportunities and limitations on gender identity processes and dominant gender practices in the organisation. I analyse these gender identity processes in the police force below.

The first condition in social organisation of police work that structures gender identity affirmation is its formal rationality. Formal rationality

harmonises with subject neutrality, and works against responsible rationality. In other words, it favours dominant male gender practices and conflicts with dominant female practices. It is less difficult for the holder of an
organisational position to carry out his tasks in an impersonal and formal
way if he can also use subject neutrality. The responsibility for practical
care for colleagues and clients can then, to a certain extent, be dismissed
on formal and subject-neutral grounds.

Consequently, the formal rationality of the bureaucratic organisation
of police work does not support gender identity affirmation for women (or
men) who use responsible rationality. The prevalence of formal rationality can be said to hinder the creation and affirmation of gender identity
for the women. In gender research, the bureaucratic organisational form
has been discussed in terms of its favouring and supporting men's experiences, attitudes, sexuality and rationality to a greater degree than women's
(Ferguson 1984; Ressner 1985; Kvande and Rasmussen 1991; Davies 1995;
Wahl, Holgersson and Höök 1998). Men can therefore get a 'feeling that
they "own" the organisation, that they are natural inhabitants of the
organisation, and therefore have the right to determine the conditions'
(Wahl *et al.* 1998: 46). Women's experiences, approaches, sexuality and
logic are not regarded as being favoured to the same extent in a bureaucratic organisation. In this research tradition, the form of the organisation
has been described as authoritatively hierarchical, in contrast to humanist and participative (Ressner 1985). It has also been described as simply
bureaucratic, in contrast to an organisation that is designated as a network
or ad hoc (Kvande and Rasmusson 1991; Blomqvist 1994). The bureaucratic form of organisation can therefore be seen not only as a means to
further the work of the police authority, but can also be a means for
supporting men and their interests.[12]

The weaker congruence between responsible rationality and formal
rationality than between subject neutrality and formal rationality has gendered consequences. The affirmation of a gender identity associated with
responsible rationality is made more difficult, while gender identity associated with subject neutrality is supported. To put it differently, to the
extent that men are more likely to exhibit subject neutrality, there is greater
congruence between their affirmation as police and as men. For women
who exhibit responsible rationality, a conflict exists between their gender
identity and their work.

The second condition in the police force important for gender identity
processes is the professionalisation of the occupational role. Formal
rationality reflected in the professionalisation of the police occupational
role also is more compatible with subject neutrality, with similarly
gendered consequences. Celia Davies (1995: 57) even maintains that the

professionalisation process is shaped through condescension about and repression of empathy and caring in personal relations. Consequently, women (or men) who use responsible rationality can experience conflicts in professionalised occupations between their professional role and gender identity (see Davies 1995: 60).

The third condition relevant to gender identity processes in the police force is the coordination system. According to the coordination system the patrol officers utilise two different strategies in their profession: social competence and physical strength (see Martin 1980: 17, 18ff.). The coordination system leads to gender-bound patterns based on these two approaches. Interviews revealed that women are not expected to use physical strength to the same extent as men, even if they are physically strong. This may be so because, both according to the male colleagues and those in command, women are not used to using force. Military service and primary socialisation are held to be of importance in preparing men to be able to build strength and use physical force. Coordination implies that the male police officer, to a greater extent than the female, takes responsibility for physically demanding work. Men believe that in this way they are supporting their female colleagues, even though in a longer perspective it can be a disservice.

Women keep to the informal division of labour reflected in the coordination system. They ascribe physical superiority to the men, while they emphasise their own importance as women and police in situations where physical strength is not required. One of the women says:

> It's only in a small percentage of all the work that you need this male strength that we girls don't have. But it's something that, as a girl, you have to be aware of when you have a job like this, that just physically you can't match them. That's what I think, anyway, that maybe we girls have to bear that in mind. You can't blow your own trumpet and think you're just as strong, because you aren't, no matter how hard you train.

Even though women and men state that the former are less physically strong, they do not see that as a problem in their daily work. The reason is that it is almost always possible to call in reinforcements. They express no palpable concerns that women and men will not be able to manage their work tasks together; any fears are confined to extreme circumstances (see Hejsedal 1996: 20).

Women's anticipated lack of physical strength is the Achilles' heel of their occupational role, and something that they always need to take into account and also defend (Cedermark-Hedberg 1985: 12; Jones 1986: 134–5; Hesjedal 1996: 22). In fact, it is not possible for the women to demonstrate whether they have the same physical strength and skills requisite for their profession as the men. The coordination system hinders them from training their self-confidence by using physical strength. This makes women's professional careers more difficult because physical strength is so strongly associated with being a good police officer (Martin 1980: 130; Cedermark-Hedberg 1985: 12; Jones 1986: 65, 69, 73; Lord 1986; Boëtius 1995: 10; Hesjedal 1996: 65).

The physical strength approach favours dominant male gender practices, and the social competence approach supports dominant female gender practices. The former is associated to a great extent with male patrol officers and the latter with female officers. The social competence approach coincides with the concept of the relation to the other described above as responsible rationality. Social competence in police work includes, amongst other things, giving of one's best and using insight and empathy to understand how a client might feel in a given situation. Subject neutrality can be compared with working using physical force. The client can be kept at a distance and communication may be limited. Patrol officers using this strategy rely more on doing their work through the threat of physical force. This means that the officer does not necessarily make contact in a cognitive or emotional way.

The professional role strategies demonstrate that there is a relatively rigid dichotomy between the professional role of the police and gender identity, particularly for female police. The strategy that coordination circumscribes for men means controlling clients through the use or threat of physical force. Male patrol officers who use subject neutrality can thus create and affirm their gender identity at work. This does not mean that all men use this strategy, even if it is assumed that most men can. At the same time, female patrol officers are not expected to use the physical force strategy, but are expected to use the social competence strategy, providing women officers an opportunity to affirm their gender identity through responsible rationality. Female patrol officers do not see themselves as being typically female. Yet, the general expectation in the organisation is that they should behave in traditionally female ways.

The system of coordination steers women into specific kinds of assignments. These coincide with those formerly allotted to the police matrons, in the days when there was a formal division of labour between the genders. This division of labour prevents women's affirmation in their profession as 'real police officers', that is to say, as officers who keep order by using physical strength. By contrast, the coordination system creates and affirms dominant male gender practices in connection with professional police intervention strategies. In the coordination system, masculinity is associated with being a competent police officer, and femininity with being less than competent. At the same time, her colleagues recognise her contributions to police work in certain gender-specific ways. According to her male colleagues, she is fully competent in those fields, though not on the basis of her profession but because of her gender. The following statement made by a male patrol officer illustrates this informal division of labour: 'I never open my mouth if it's a child case, if there's trouble in a flat and there are kids there. That's her job. I can do it too, but I think she's better at it than me, so she gets to.' In this way, the women get affirmed as policewomen and the men as police officers, reproducing an internal division of labour in an otherwise formally equal system.[13]

The challenge to men's gender identity is reduced to a certain extent by the coordination system, since only men are expected to use physical strength to keep order. Men can thus continue to be police officers in a distinct way, maintaining congruence between their gender identity processes and professional roles. But the coordination system makes a male patrol officer fully competent at the expense of a female officer. This system of coordination reveals how certain gender practices are created and re-created in the professional role approach, leading to internal sex segregation. The police become gendered actors when, in their daily work, they create and affirm gender identity, even under conditions of formal equality.

The timetable is a fourth condition affecting gender identity affirmation in the police force. There are some young patrol officers in the turn group, who have small children. The patrol officers can apply for part-time positions if they wish to reduce their working hours to take responsibility in their private lives. In that case, they are put on a special list. This applies both to women and to men.

One of the officers in charge is strongly against part-time work for regular police duties. He thinks that it causes interruptions if an officer does not work one hundred per cent and follows the turn exactly; he even regards it as being disloyal to the turn group. According to this officer in charge, reduced working hours, such as parental leave, are not a natural feature of the timetable arrangement: 'There is somebody here working seventy per cent, and that really does upset the planning. You never know when they're going to turn up. No, it's not accepted as natural.'

Cedermark-Hedberg (1985: 53, 143) argues that many in the police force think that absence and part-time work show a lack of loyalty to the police. The attitude of the officer in charge is that police work is correctly done when the family, children, or care of the elderly do not encroach on working life. The private lives of patrol officers should be arranged to not disturb their working lives. Cedermark-Hedberg also demonstrates that care work in private life is regarded as a hindrance to the demands made by the police profession, especially for women: 'Having families and babies involves special problems for female policemen' (1985: 53). However, even men are affected by the attitude that taking leave of absence shows disloyalty to the police force. Some men in the turn group work part-time and have to put up with being ridiculed by their colleagues – even including female colleagues. That someone is absent 'caring for their child' is talked about in a negative way.

The timetable arrangement gives greater opportunity to use appropriation practices than to exercise caring practices. Despite parental leave policies, men are not expected to have commitments in their private lives, for instance child or elderly care. A 'real' policeman can work according to the timetable because he is not expected to have any practical responsibilities outside his working life, even though he has financial responsibilities. By contrast, women are expected to have practical responsibilities outside working life, which disturbs the planning at the station. A good and competent patrol officer who, on the other hand, uses caring practices regarding children, spouse, partner/friend or an elderly person in private life gets no support from the arrangement of the timetable or the attitude of the officer in charge.

The arrangement of the timetable means that the patrol officers who use appropriation practices are those who find it easiest to meet the demands that the working hours make on them in the turn group. The arrangement of the timetable supports appropriation practices. On the other hand, working hours make it difficult for women and men who want to be both good and loyal police and at the same time get identity affirmation through caring practices. The planning of working hours thus supports typical masculinity, but works against dominant femininity in the profession.

### An organisational gender power structure

The organisational gender structure, like the gender structure in society previously described, is also a historically variable system of gender relations among gender practices. The organisational gender structure comprises not only dominant gender practices in society; it is also a result of the support and/or obstruction of dominant gender practices in the organisation.

This study has demonstrated that dominant female gender practices were not entirely compatible with the formal rationality of the bureaucratic organisation and professionalisation of police work. Responsible rationality was not congruent with the strategy to keep order through the use or threat of physical force, which was the assumed ideal approach in interventions and arrests. The timetable did not support responsible rationality and caring practices in the concept of a competent police patrol

**Table 8.2** An organisational gender power structure: conditions important for the creation and affirmation of dominant gender practices

| Conditions and basic approaches | Dominant female practices | Dominant male practices |
|---|---|---|
| A bureaucratic organisation | obstructs | supports |
| Professionalisation of the occupational role | obstructs | supports |
| The coordination | obstructs & supports | supports |
| Timetable | obstructs | supports |
| *Organisational structure* | *obstructs* | *supports* |

officer. Table 8.2 illustrates the organisational gender structure and its gender practices.

All the bureaucratic and professional conditions in the police force result in an almost entirely one-sided obstruction of gender identity affirmation for women in connection with competence and authority as a patrol officer. This particularly applies to keeping order, where interventions and arrests are involved. In contrast, the same conditions support men, which makes them appear to be authoritative and competent police officers.

The gender structure in society and the organisational gender structure and practices both contribute to formation of the internal sex segregation known as the coordination system for police officers. An idealised image of a 'real' police officer becomes one who, above all, is *physically strong*, but who also uses *straight communication*, and who plays *floorball*. One could say that a small group of men with dominant gender practices legitimise and overdetermine these things. Such stereotyping is not called into question by, for instance, more senior officers. As a result women face difficulties being accepted as authoritative and competent police officers who can keep order and make arrests. They become police*women*.

## Notes

1 In this chapter I concentrate on gender identity processes taking place in the regular police force in order to describe these in full detail. Gender identity processes at the emergency ward are described in detail in Åberg (2001).

2 Jónasdóttir (1991: 41, note 2) sometimes uses the concepts 'sociosexual' and 'sociosexual system' instead of gender beings. The former is to be understood as the gender aspect of humankind. The latter is the many relationships that people as sociosexual beings enter into. They refer not only to the relation between woman and man, but also to relations within the same gender.

Jónasdóttir also uses the concept 'sociosexual relational practices'. The concepts are open empirically, that is, their content is variable.

3  Jónasdóttir makes a distinction here between authority and influence that I do not go into in greater detail in this context. The distinction is significant in the establishment of her political theory.

4  Jónasdóttir has nevertheless been criticised for her patriarchal theory. Hanne Marlene Dahl (1994) argues that women's acquiescence to subordination is problematised too little by Jónasdóttir, even though she considers that women do also get something out of the exploitative sociosexual relationship. Øystein Gullvåg Holter (1992) has criticised Jónasdóttir's methodological approach. Jónasdóttir's and others' attempts to find reasons for women's subordination have been criticised by above all the postmodernist school of thought (Fraser and Nicholson 1990). Jónasdóttir's theory about men's exploitation of women's love power has previously been used by other researchers, including Nordlander (1992); Holmberg (1993) and Jakobsen and Karlsson (1993).

5  The concept responsible rationality touches a moral-philosophical discussion about the ethics of care and of fairness respectively. An example of this discussion is known as 'the Gilligan-Kohlberg controversy' (Benhabib 1987; 1994; Michaeli 1995).

6  To date, empirical studies of these practices are rare, so occasionally fiction must serve as an example. Jónasdóttir argues, for instance that Virginia Woolf's novel *To the Lighthouse* can be seen as an illustration of the structural love practices (see Woolf 1982, especially pp. 43–6 and 93–5).

7  This was the optimal gender ratio that could be achieved in the police force.

8  Research shows that formal rationality is used less strictly in the lowest positions in a bureaucratic organisation. These so-called grass-roots bureaucrats are characterised by a considerable amount of freedom of action in their assignments because of their direct contact with the client (Lipsky 1980 in Johansson 1992:41). So, when they are dealing with a case, it is feasible that they are able to see the other party as a complete person with specific life conditions. However, according to more recent research, their freedom of action has considerable organisational limitations (Johansson 1992). The surrounding organisation in which she/he works has rules, principles and practices that do in fact restrict what grassroots bureaucrats can do in their encounters with the other party. There are thus restrictions on their freedom of action. So, instead of characterising them as having freedom of action, we should speak about their having room for action.

9  The usual definition of the concept professionalisation as the striving by professional groups to delimit or close an occupational field, that is, to organise and protect an activity, is included but not stressed in my use of the term (see for example its customary use in Silius 1992).

10  All of the quotations are taken from interviews conducted during the year of 1995.

11  For similar views expressed by police in the USA and the UK, see Jones 1986; Lord 1986; Balkin 1988; Heidensohn 1992.

12 Even though the above research gives considerable information about what significance organisations can have for women and men, it does not utilise the detailed patterns of thoughts and actions that my approach demands. Weber's discussion about formal rationality seems therefore to be more fruitful than the above research about how women and men are favoured or disadvantaged in organisations. See Jones 1993.

13 In her study, Susan E. Martin (1980: 185) has identified two extreme categories in a continuum: *police*women and police*women*. The former strive to be accepted as professionals in the police force. They also expect the same recognition as the men. The latter use a strategy of above all being personally accepted, but not necessarily being generally accepted as a member of the category professional policewomen. They work to a larger extent with social work in keeping order, and they want to be respected as women in their occupational role.

## References

Åberg, Berit. 2001. *Samarbete på könsblandade arbetsplatser. En könsteoretisk analys av arbetsdelning mellan kvinnor och män i två yrken: akutsjuksköterskor och ordningspoliser*. Örebro: Örebro Studies in Sociology 1.

Acker, Joan. 1990. 'Hierarchies, Jobs, Bodies: A Theory of Gendered Organizations', *Gender & Society* 4(2): 139–58.

Adkins, Lisa. 1995. *Gendered Work: Sexuality, Family and the Labour Market*. Philadelphia, PA: Open University Press.

Balkin, Joseph. 1988. 'Why Policemen Don't Like Policewomen', *Journal of Police Science and Administration* 16(1): 29–38.

Bengtsson, Margot och Jonas Frykman. 1987. *Om Maskulinitet: Mannen som forskningsprojekt*. Delegationen för Jämställdhetsforskning (JÄMFO): Rapport nr 11.

Benhabib, Seyla. 1987. 'The Generalized and the Concrete Other: The Kohlberg–Gilligan Controversey and Moral Theory', in Eva Feder Kittay and Diana T. Meyers (eds) *Women and Moral Theory*, pp. 154–77. Otowa, NJ: Rowman & Littlefield Publishers, Inc.

Benhabib, Seyla. 1994. *Autonomi och gemenskap*. Göteborg: Daidalos.

Blomqvist, Martha. 1994. *Könshierarkier i gungning. Kvinnor i kunskapsföretag*. Uppsala: Uppsala Universitet, Studia Sociologica Upsaliensia nr 39.

Boëthius, Monica. 1995. *Patriarkatets sista skansar*. Stockholm: Arbetslivsfonden.

Brubaker, Roger. 1984. *The Limits of Rationality*. London: George Allen & Unwin.

Cedermark-Hedberg, Gunilla. 1985. *Kvinnor och män i polisutbildningen. Polissystemets reaktioner på en ökad andel kvinnor i polisyrket*. Stockholm: Stockholms universitet, Pedagogiska institutionen.

Dahl, Hanne Marlene. 1994. 'Nyere patriarkatsteori – Som en fugl uden vinger? Magt, mening og køn i reproduktion af patriarkatet.' i Anna G. Jónasdóttir och

Gunnela Björk (red) *Teorier om patriarkatet – Betydelser, begränsningar och utvecklingslinjer.* s.123–44. Örebro: Örebro Universitet, Kvinnovetenskapligt forums skriftserie nr 2.

Dahlerup, Drude (ed.). 1989. *Køn sorterer. Kønsopdelning på arbejdspladsen.* Nord 1989:1 Det nordiske BRYT-projekt 7/1989. Köpenhamn: Nordiska ministerrådet.

Danermark, Berth, Mats Ekström, Liselotte Jakobsen and Jan Ch. Karlsson. 1998. *Att förklara samhället.* Lund: Studentlitteratur.

Davies, Celia. 1995. *Gender and the Professional Predicament in Nursing.* Philadelphia, PA: Open University Press.

Ethelberg, Eva. 1980. *Kvindelighedens modsigelse – om kvinders person-lighedsstrategier overfor mandlig dominans.* Köpenhamn: Antropos.

Ferguson, Kathy 1980. *Self, Society and Womenkind.* Connecticut: Greenwood Press.

Ferguson, Kathy. 1984. *The Feminist Case against Bureaucracy.* Philadelphia: Temple University Press.

Fraser, Nancy and Linda J. Nicholson 1990. 'Social Criticism without Philosophy: An Encounter between Feminism and Postmodernism', in Linda J. Nicholson (ed.) *Feminism/Postmodernism,* pp. 19–38. New York: Routledge.

Fürst, Gunilla. 1985. *Reträtten från mansjobben: En studie av industriarbetande kvinnor och arbetsdelningen mellan könen på en intern arbetsmarknad.* Göteborg: Göteborgs universitet, Sociologiska institutionen.

Fürst, Gunilla. 1986. *Från försök till vedertagen ordning – om kvinnors integration i traditionellt manligt arbete.* Göteborg: Göteborgs universitet, Sociologiska institutionen.

Fürst, Gunilla. 1987. 'Arbetsmarknadskrafter och könssegregation.'I Ulla Björn-berg och Inga Hellberg (red) *Sociologer ser på arbete,* s. 73–94. Stockholm: Arbetslivscentrum.

Fürst, Gunilla. 1988. *I reserv och reservat – Om villkoren för kvinnors arbete på mansdomi-nerade verkstadsgolv.* Göteborg: Göteborgs universitet, Sociologiska institutionen.

Göransson, Anita. 1988. *Från familj till fabrik: Teknik, arbetsdelning och skiktning i svenska fabriker 1830–1877.* Stockholm: Arkiv.

Gunnarsson, Ewa. 1994. *Att våga väga jämt. Om kvalifikationer och kvinnliga förhållningssätt i ett tekniskt industriarbete.* Luleå: Tekniska högskolan i Luleå.

Hagberg, Jan-Erik, Anita Nyberg and Elisabeth Sundin 1995. *Att göra landet jäm-ställt. En utvärdering av kvinnor och män i samverkan – Sveriges största satsning av jämställdhet på arbetsmarknaden.* Stockholm: Nerenius & Santérus.

Hartmann, Heidi. 1981. 'Kapitalismen, patriarkatet och könssegregationen i arbetet', *Kvinnovetenskaplig tidskrift* 1(2): 7–30.

Heidensohn, Frances. 1992. *Women in Control? The Role of Women in Law Enforcement.* Oxford: Oxford University Press.

Hesjedal, Jorunn. 1996. *Kvinner i Politiet – en studie av internasjonal forskning.* Oslo: Politihøgskolens forsknings- og utviklingsavdeling. PHS Forskning 1996:1.

Holmberg, Carin. 1993. *Det kallas kärlek.* Göteborg: Anamma.

Holter, Harriet. 1984. 'Women's Research and Social Theory', in Harriet Holter (ed.) *Patriarchy in a Welfare Society*, pp. 9–25. Oslo: Universitetsforlaget.

Holter, Harriet and Hem, Lars 1982, 1985. 'Om relasjonslogikk. Inledning', in Harriet Holter (ed.) *Kvinner i Fellesskap*, s. 371–7. Oslo: Universitetsforlaget.

Holter, Øystein Gullvåg. 1992. 'Recension av Anna Jónasdóttirs Love Power and Political Interests. Acta sociologica', *Journal of the Scandinavian Sociological Association* 35 (1): 71–4.

Holter, Øystein Gullvåg och Helene Aarseth. 1993. *Mäns Livssammanhang*. Stockholm: Bonnier Utbildning.

Jakobsen, Liselotte och Jan Ch. Karlsson. 1993. *Arbete och Kärlek*. Lund: Arkiv.

Johansson, Roine. 1992. *Vid byråkratins gränser. Om handlingsfrihetens organisatoriska begränsningar*. Lund: Arkiv.

Jónasdóttir, Anna G. 1991. *Love Power and Political Interests*. Örebro: Örebro Studies 7.

Jones, Kathleen. 1993. *Compassionate Authority: Democracy and the Representation of Women*. New York: Routledge.

Jones, Sandra. 1986. *Policewomen and Equality: Formal Policy v Informal Practice?* London: Macmillan.

Kalberg, Stephen. 1980. 'Max Weber's Types of Rationality', *American Journal of Sociology* 85(5): 1145–79.

Karlsson, Jan Ch. 1983. 'Yrken', in Jan Ch. Karlsson (ed.) *Om lönearbete – en bok i arbetssociologi*, s. 168–88. Stockholm: Norstedts.

Kvande, Elin och Bente Rasmussen. 1991. *Nye kvinneliv. Kvinner i menns organisajoner*. Oslo: Ad Notam.

Layder, Derek. 1990. *The Realist Image in Social Science*. London: Macmillan.

Layder, Derek. 1993. *New Strategies in Social Research*. Cambridge: Polity Press.

Layder, Derek. 1998. *Sociological Practice: Linking Theory and Social Research*. London: Sage.

Lindgren, Gerd. 1985. *Kamrater, Kollegor och Kvinnor – en studie av könssegregeringsprocessen i två mansdominerade organisationer*. Umeå: Institutionen för sociologi, Umeå universitet.

Lindgren, Gerd. 1992. *Doktorer, systrar och flickor*. Stockholm: Carlssons.

Lindgren, Gerd. 1996. 'Broderskapets logik', *Kvinnovetenskaplig tidskrift* 1: 4–14.

Lindgren, Gerd. 1999. *Klass, kön och kirurgi – relationer bland vårdpersonal i organisationsförändringarnas spår*. Malmö: Liber.

Lord, Leslie K.1986. 'Comparison of Male and Female Peace Officer's: Stereotypic Perception of Women and Women Peace Officers', *Journal of Police Science and Administration* 14(2): 83–97.

Martin, Susan E. 1980. *Breaking and Entering: Policewomen on Patrol*. Berkeley, CA: University of California Press.

Martin, Susan E. 1990. *On the Move: The Status of Women in Policing*. Washington: Police Foundation.

Michaeli, Inga.1995. *Omsorg och rättvisa – ett dilemma*. Gävle: Meyers.

Nordlander, Kerstin. 1992. 'Att vara kvinnlig kapitalist', *Historisk tidskrift* 4: 446–67.

Ressner, Ulla. 1985. *Den dolda hierarkin*. Stockholm: Raben & Sjögren.

Sayer, Andrew. 1984. *Method in Social Science*. London: Hutchinson.

Silius, Harriet. 1992. *Den kringgärdade kvinnligheten*. Att vara kvinnlig jurist i Finland. Åbo: Åbo Akademis förlag.

Sørensen, Bjørg Aase. 1982. 'Ansvarsrasjonalitet: Om mål- middeltenkning blant kvinner', in Harriet Holter (ed.) *Kvinner i Fellesskap*, s. 392–402. Oslo: Universitetsforlaget.

Sørensen, Bjørg Aase och Aslaug Hetle 1985. *Oppgavemestring og Arbeidsorganisasjon i politi- og Lensmannsarbeid*. Oslo: Arbeidsforskningsinstituttene.

Wahl, Anna, Charlotte Holgersson and Pia Höök. 1998. *Ironi & Sexualitet – om ledarskap och kön*. Stockholm: Carlsson.

Walby, Sylvia. 1986. *Patriarchy at Work: Patriarchal and Capitalist Relations in Employment*. Minneapolis: Polity Press.

Walby, Sylvia. 1990. *Theorizing Patriarchy*. Oxford: Basil Blackwell.

Wikander, Ulla. 1988. *Kvinnors och mäns arbeten: Gustavsberg 1880–1980. Genusarbets-delning och arbetets degradering vid en porslinsfabrik*. Lund: Arkiv.

Woolf, Virginia. [1927] 1982. *Mot fyren*. Stockholm: Forum.

# 9

# Queer citizenship/queer representation: politics out of bounds?

*Kathleen B. Jones and Sue Dunlap*

It's only by being shameless in risking the obvious that we happen into the vicinity of the transformative. (Sedgwick 1990: 22)

## Mise-en-scène: *Sail to Victory*, the hosting of the RNC in San Diego

The cast of characters was unimpeachable: a Mayor from a city wanting to trumpet itself as the bridge over the Pacific Rim who had her sights on higher state, or even national, public office; a Governor who had once been Mayor of that same city, and who had more immediate aspirations to the Presidency; and a seasoned actor who may as well have won an Oscar for his performance as President. The screenplay? – to sell San Diego as the site for the Republican National Convention (RNC) in 1996. 'Take it from someone who has surfed the California beaches long before Annette Funicello and Frankie Avalon, San Diego has a lot to offer, and I urge you to come to California' (*San Diego Union Tribune* 1994, 13 July: B-1; see also 1995, 21 April: B-1; 1994, 14 December: B-6). Thus spake Ronald Reagan to the site-selection committee of the GOP ('Grand Old Party': Republican Party) in *Sail to Victory*, the City of San Diego's video produced to persuade that same group that 'America's Finest City' was Republican country. Whether it was Reagan's legerdemain, the city's sweet offer of a $16–20 million funding package, mostly from private sources, or the appeal of the much touted natural beauty and fabulous weather of the region, the Republicans were coming to San Diego in 1996. What were queers to do?

This chapter explores queer politics in a local context, but within the horizon of the RNC's presence in San Diego, a spectacular horizon that opens out into a global arena constituted not only by San Diego's existence as a border land, but also by the worldwide attention guaranteed to be focused on San Diego as host city to the GOP. By 'queer politics' we mean to invoke both a complex, multiple set of practices of political resistance that have been mobilised before, in, and around the site of the RNC, as well as the strategic challenges to traditional practices of politics which are represented by the efforts of different marginalised groups to gain access to public space, or, at least, to gain media attention within and around this same site. These practices include not only the obvious counter-discourses about sexuality and identity that have characterised gay and lesbian politics' contestation of the exclusionary dynamics of mainstream US politics. They also include other discourses about how positions of marginality in American politics such as discourse of race, ethnicity and gender have framed contemporary debates about rights, citizenship and representation, such as those about immigration and citizenship, about affirmative action, and about women's reproductive rights.

We consider the shifting tides of responses to the RNC's efforts to contain protest and resistance to its presence in San Diego on the part of gays and lesbians, anti-Prop 187 (immigrant restrictions) and anti-Prop 209 (anti-gay marriage) coalitions, and pro-choice activists as an occasion to observe the constantly mobilised tension between 'inside' and 'outside' strategies of different groups to represent themselves, or to be present, in public space. By considering the linkages between and among contestations about whether these 'different' groups – of gays and lesbians, immigrants and women – should have full membership in the American polity, we intend to contribute to the democratising disruption of the category 'queer' itself. We want to open up the categories of citizenship, representation, and queer politics to the question of what it means to 'queer' these categories, that is, to make them signify 'in ways that none of us can predict in advance' (Butler 1993: 29). Without such an opening up, queer politics fails to realise its own radical potential, remaining mired in what Cathy Cohen (1997: 441) has called the 'disjuncture between an articulated commitment to promoting an understanding of sexuality that rejects the idea of static, monolithic, bounded categories and political practices structured around binary conceptions of sexuality and power'.

## Queer categories?

Citizenship has been one of the most contested categories of political analysis. The stakes surrounding the debate about citizenship – what it is and who can claim it – have always been high. Citizenship signals membership in a political community. Within the modern liberal state, citizenship constitutes an array of rights and responsibilities assigned to any individual who is deemed to belong, or to be a full member of, the political community. Citizenship also represents a specific type of social bond between members of a community which symbolises material connections of culture and often of geography. Within modern states, these connections most often constitute a shared national identity that aims to transcend other socio-demographic divisions of region, ethnicity, sexuality, class or of gender, and separate one group of citizens from another.

T. H. Marshall (1964: 91) called citizenship a 'direct sense of community membership based on loyalty to a civilization which is a common possession'. In Marshall's language, citizenship is about the boundaries between one civilisation and another. Yet, what constitutes a 'civilisation' to which citizens feel 'loyal'? What are its rituals, its traditions, its ceremonies of belonging? How far can they be expanded to include not only many more, but many more unusual folks before these rituals, traditions and ceremonies lose their purgative powers? What happens to those rituals and mechanisms for certifying membership, such as marriage, family and kin networks, and electoral participation, when they become expropriated by those who had been traditionally deemed unfit, marginal? If citizenship is about loyalty to a civilisation, in what sense can there be 'queer citizenship'?

The oxymoron, 'queer citizenship', invites the construction of a paradox. Once queers are citizens they are no longer 'queer', since citizenship is a process of normalisation; yet, if citizenship is 'queered' through the incorporation of the identities, actions, and locales represented by the previously marginalised, then, by definition, its process of normalisation has been disrupted. Paraphrasing Eve Sedgwick (1990: 10), a reversal of the rhetorical opposition between the dominant and the dependent, between the normal and the marginal enables the identification of these oppositions 'as sites that are peculiarly densely charged with lasting potentials for powerful manipulation'. Nothing, of course, guarantees that the reversal itself, or the recognition of it as a moment of disruptive potentiality, will lead to democratic expansion or transformation of political membership.

In this chapter, we explore several contemporary cases of, or occasions for, such disruption within the context of the Republican National Convention, or, at least, the preparation for it made by various groups in protest and in support of the Republican agenda. Each of these cases or moments represents a 'queering' of citizenship and representation in different ways. Each differently pushes at the limits of exclusion that citizenship and representation construct. Each differently represents a desire forbidden to its subject(s). Each differently risks normalisation. And, especially important, each is not necessarily about the politics of gay and lesbian sexuality in the ordinary sense or at all. And that is our point.

If citizenship and representation are 'queered', then they can no longer be limited either to the territory of sexuality that they have occupied in queer theory or to the territory of the nation state and nationalism that they have occupied in modern political theory. If citizenship and representation are queered, then they cannot limit their scope to membership, presence and action in a new, fluid, yet still nationally bordered and bounded, community. Queer citizenship and queer representation each become an ironic juxtaposition of terms whose uneasy coupling suggests the need to call into question the discourse and practices of citizenship and representation themselves.

Yet, the discourse and practices of citizenship and representation have not been seriously enough acknowledged as limits to the project of queer theory itself. Queer politics and queer representation have announced themselves as the radical democratic heirs to liberationist politics in general, and lesbian and gay activism in particular (Seidman 1993: 10). Ester Kaplan's 'Queer Manifesto', first appearing in the streets of New York in April 1990, and circulated widely throughout that summer, rhetorically highlighted the distance between straights and queers, between 'them' and 'us' with an explosive, angry call to turn the tables on the dominant culture: 'Let yourself feel angry that THERE IS NO PLACE IN THIS COUNTRY WHERE WE ARE SAFE, no place where we are not targeted for hatred and attack, the self-hatred, the suicide – of the closet' (cited in Trebay 1990: 36).

By citing homophobia as the root of the problem and by naming the 'country'/nation as an unsafe place, this manifesto meant to go beyond the gay/lesbian and white/of color divisions within the movement which had plagued many of the organisations that had emerged around the politics of sexuality in the US since the late 1960s. Its demand that 'queers read this' rhetorically constituted a group that was both part of and yet radically separate from the heterosexual mainstream. Its announcement of a 'nation of queers' appropriated the language of anti-colonialism, black nationalism, radical lesbianism and feminism in an effort to refocus questions of liberation onto the project of reclaiming and reforging the public space of the modern state.

Refocusing questions of liberation onto access to and reformulations of public space marked one of the positive connections imagined by *Queer Nationalism*. Safety came to mean not just safe at the borders of the public realm, but safe within its dominant parameters. 'To be safe in the national sense mean[t] not just safe from bashing, not just safe from discrimination, but safe *for* demonstration' (Berlant and Freeman 1993: 198).

Yet, the demand for queer access to dominant spaces of power and presence was also one of *Queer Nationalism's* limiting features, as Frank Browning (1994: 46–7) notes in his interpretation of *Queer Nation* of San Francisco's intervention into certain public spaces representing themselves 'not as a part of a moral call for civil rights . . . [but as a] "threatening and perhaps unpredictable social force" '. Cathy Cohen (1997) has extended this criticism by observing that mall invasions sponsored by groups such as *Queer Shopping Network* of New York or the *Suburban Homosexual Outreach Program* of San Francisco failed to address adequately 'the different social locations in which queers exist' (448). She writes:

> The activity of entering or 'invading' the shopping mall on the part of queer nationals is clearly one of subversion . . . However, left unchallenged in such an action are the myriad ways, other than through the enforcement of normative sexuality, in which some queers feel alienated and excluded from the space of the mall . . . If you are a queer of color your exclusion from the mall may, in part, be rooted in racial norms and racial stereotypes which construct you as threatening every time you enter this economic institution. (449)

From these perspectives, the category 'queer', taken up by activists since the early 1990s, and defended by a number of theorists of culture and politics as an anti-identity marker, has become a privileged, nationalised, academic term.

Can a claim to 'queerness' and, even more, a declaration of 'queer citizenship' signal a radical politics? Does the insistence on 'queer' as a political position risk reaffirming the very power of heterosexism as a necessary and singular oppositional moment? Is this a risk worth taking? If queerness has been the basis on which full citizenship has been denied to anyone in this country – indeed, in many countries – who actively and openly resists the conforming regimes of sexuality or who is suspected of resisting them, then how can 'queer' be recuperated to unsettle the exclusionary terms of such citizenship? If citizenship is always based on exclusions, on statuses and divisions between the native and the naturalised, then how can citizenship be made queer? What critiques of the term queer citizenship will necessarily have to be initiated in order to open up 'new possibilities for coalitional alliance that do not presume that . . . constituencies [of feminist, anti-racist mobilization within and around lesbian and gay politics] are radically distinct from one another' (Butler 1993: 229)? More than this, what critiques of queer citizenship will necessarily have to be initiated to dislodge queerness from its increasingly comfortable terrain of sexualised, Americanised counterpolitics (see Cohen 1997)?

Reading the discourse and practices of citizenship and representation through the lens of queerness and reading the discourse and practices of queerness through the lens of the language of citizenship and representation enables an exploration of the pleasures and danger provoked on either side of the terms 'queer citizen' or 'queer representative' by its strangely desired and rejected companion. Such readings prompt the insight that 'queer citizenship' and 'queer representation' are important moments in the history of gay and lesbian politics, but ones that cannot and should not be contained within the geographic or discursive boundaries of their 'native soil' of sexual politics in the US.

## Who is out, where and how?

The history of modern citizenship is the history of various social groups' demands to be included and counted among those considered full members of the political community. In western liberal democracies throughout the nineteenth and twentieth centuries, these groups have included the working class, women nationals, former colonists, former slaves, and other previously excluded groups, such as the disabled, youth groups, and gays and lesbians. Each of these groups' demands for representation and citizenship – that is, for recognition from the state of their right to have access to and participate in public spaces, including the institutional arenas of power, and access to other state guaranteed civil, social, and political rights and benefits – has been formally equivalent.

Yet, the challenge that the demands of such particular groups represent not only has been to determine how to accommodate so many *additional* 'places at the table', or slips in the marina, but whether and how to incorporate fully the *specific sorts of claims* against the state, and reconstitutions of public and social life, that such groups have made, or are understood to be making. Thus, from the perspective of those who are already citizens, already represented, already at the table, and at the yacht club, the demands of 'outsiders' for inclusion represent not only the expansion of the community, but also signal the effort of those who have been marked as 'different', as 'other', as 'alien', or as 'queer', to belong and live fully among those within the bounded community that citizenship constitutes. Whether such groups intend to be disruptive of the social order or not, all excluded groups who seek to participate in the mainstream always also represent, to those who are inside, threats to established mores and institutions. Thus, whether or not they are 'seeking participation as a means of articulating their group identity, or as a means of transcending it; whether they assert a demand to be heard as a group, or a demand to cease being categorized as such' (Squires 1993: 10), the participatory effects of inclusion exceed the intentions of their actors, and, by definition, constitute a transforming disruption.

From those who oppose such expansive integration we hear perhaps the most pronounced, even panic-stricken, recognition of the potentially transformative effects of even liberal acts of inclusion. For example, after an April 1992 White House meeting, where people such as Christian fundamentalist Bob Jones III, Beverly LeHaye of Concerned Women of

America, and Gary Bauer of the Family Research Council met to express their concerns about the increasing visibility of the 'gay agenda', these same leaders emerged to announce that President George Bush (senior) 'had convinced them that he shares their belief that gays and lesbians pose the greatest threat to traditional American values' (Burrington 1993: 7).

Response to President Bill Clinton's initial announcement of his intent to lift the ban on gays in the military reflected similar fears. Right-wing groups became increasingly mobilised to defeat that prospect at almost any cost. Jerry Falwell's Liberty Alliance produced a video with accompanying text, *Gays in the Military*, in order 'to educate and alert thousands of concerned Americans' about the gay threat to American values 'to insure that the United States maintains its superior and unparalleled military force and to protect our culture from sweeping revolutionary upheaval' (Dunham 1993). Although much more mild in its rhetorical flourish, Secretary of Defense, Les Aspin, testifying before the Senate Armed Services Committee Hearings on Gays in the Military offered the insight that 'all of the members of the Joint Chiefs would also ascribe to . . . a general rule that homosexuality is incompatible with military service' (cited in Federal News Service 1993).

As a final example of the recognition of the social disruption represented by claims for juridical rights by excluded groups, Justice Scalia's dissent in *Romer v. Evans* (1996: 15) to the striking down of Colorado's Amendment 2 defended that amendment on the grounds that it was a 'rather modest attempt by seemingly tolerant Coloradans to preserve traditional sexual mores against the efforts of a politically powerful minority to revise those mores through use of the laws'. He concluded that 'Amendment 2 is designed to prevent piecemeal deterioration of the sexual morality favored by a majority of Coloradans, and is not only an appropriate means to that legitimate end, but a means that Americans have employed before' (20).

Those who oppose such transformative disruptions are separated from those who support them not so much by differences in the degree of acknowledged effects as in the narratives that they tell about their kind of impact. Progressives have interpreted transgressions of public space by the excluded in more positive ways. To paraphrase Judith Butler (1993: 137), the issue of the visibility of the excluded within the legitimate, public arenas of what has always been marked as the space for the dominant represents a resignification of the very terms that have effected our 'exclusion and abjection', and, through the appropriation of the 'terms of domination . . . turns them toward a more enabling future'.

Excluded groups have demanded not only to be present in public space, but also to occupy that space on our own terms. This has led to divisions among such groups over which strategies of inclusion and modes of visibility have the most liberatory effects. Using several instances of disagreement about resistant presence in public space in and around the RNC, we will observe that the question of choosing between inside or outside tactics becomes an impossible one to resolve. Ironically, as we will show, the 'terms of our own making' with which most groups choose to install our presence become terms that, in one way or another, engage the engines of traditional politics as mechanisms with which to legitimate resistant practices. Effecting representation in terms of state-legitimated modes of access can work excessively to delegitimate the state itself as an adequate or 'privileged location of political address' (McClure 1992: 112).

There is a long history of debate about whether or not representation begins or ends with the right to have standing in public space. Most advocates of what Benjamin Barber has called 'strong democracy' have contended that 'formal equality is a precondition, but not a sufficient condition for the adequate participation of all groups within society' (cited in Squires 1993: 11). Strong democracy requires institutions of participation and arenas of activism to supplement legal access and formal equality. A similar distinction between having standing in terms of one's group affiliation and acting out of that group affiliation, or in terms of that group affiliation, is to be found in feminist assessments of the difference that women's election to public office has made to enhancing the representation of women's interests (see Gelb 1989; Darcy *et al.* 1994). Finally, efforts at mobilising the gay and lesbian community and encouraging them to participate in mainstream politics as voters and as candidates reflect similar themes.

Although some theorists have recognised that the distinction between formal and substantive conceptions of representation and public space is overdrawn, we want to push this insight further. As the examples we investigate will show, especially through the reactions of those opposed to excluded groups' mere presence in certain spaces, if the 'difference' marking what has been excluded from public space is the delimiting device whereby that space is constituted as 'public' in the first place – because it is defined as space for 'us' and not for 'them' – then excluded groups' demand for recognition and the right to representation itself constitutes a 'disruptive return of the excluded' (McClure 1992: 112; Butler 1993: 11–12).

### 'As normal as anyone else in Mid-City'[1]: queer contests

Representing a disruptive return of the excluded, the candidacy of Chris Kehoe for city council captured the attention of voters in San Diego in

1993. In anticipation of voter resistance to any campaign launched by an open lesbian, yet wanting to run for public office, and being an open lesbian, Chris Kehoe constructed a strategy for her first campaign for San Diego City Council's Third District seat that would accommodate each of these aspects of her political equation. Before she even committed herself to the endeavour, she conducted a poll that indicated that the tide of voter resistance to a gay candidate was low enough to be managed. Next, she invited potential supporters to a campaign kick-off party at a local park in a part of town that intersects the gay and straight communities of District 3. Finally, Kehoe represented her campaign as a community partnership. 'All of us make up District 3. Young people and seniors, Asian, Latino, black and white, lesbian and gay, homeowners and renters, those of affluence and those with little money, mothers and fathers raising their children – we have common problems. We must work in partnership to be problem-solvers' (*San Diego Union Tribune* 1993, 11 April: D-1).

Developing a partnership approach to problem-solving was the rhetoric of choice with which Kehoe hoped to maintain a focus on the issues that she considered germane to the politics of the 3rd District, a district characterised by political consultant Tom Shepard as the 'only truly liberal council district in the city' (*San Diego Union Tribune* 1993, 24 October: B-1). This characterisation was the result, in part, of the fact that the area comprising the 3rd District consists of a 'patchwork of communities, with high-crime war zones spliced between some of the city's most attractive, close-knit urban neighborhoods' (1993).

Kehoe's partnership approach was also a subtle way to capitalise on her ironic 'insider' status as a politician. Having served as aide to retiring 3rd District Councilor John Hartley for two and a half years, and having worked as a community development specialist for the city of San Diego, Kehoe was no stranger to City Hall. Combining her focus on the issues with local political expertise Kehoe struck a balance between her recognition by local and national gay and lesbian political organisations as a trend-setter in gay politics, and her perception among voters as politically mainstream. Perhaps best representative of this effort to achieve balance was the statement by William Waybourn, executive director for the Victory Fund, a gay and lesbian political action committee: Kehoe's 'not a lesbian candidate. She's a candidate who happens to be a lesbian' (1993).

To complicate matters, Kehoe was being opposed by a strong candidate, Evonne Schulze, who had worked as a San Diego community college trustee and, before that, had been an aide to 78th Assembly district representative Mike Gotch. Schulze's familiarity with and experience in San Diego local politics had won her the endorsements of several critical community leaders and the reputation of someone who had a record of supporting gay and lesbian issues. Yet, because she had lived most of her life in a neighbouring district, renting a condominium in the 3rd District in order to establish her residency, Kehoe was able to characterise Schulze's campaign as 'opportunistic', contending that Schulze 'emigrated' to the 3rd District in order to seek office. (1993).

What's queer about this contest? The alliances and strategy deployed by each of these candidates depended upon each side marking the other as 'outside' in order to appear as the candidate experienced enough to represent District 3. Kehoe was an 'out' lesbian; but her own survey had disclosed that almost one-third of the constituents of District 3 said they would be less likely to vote for a candidate running openly as gay or lesbian. For Kehoe's campaign to succeed, she needed to position herself as an 'insider' – inside City Hall and inside the communities of District 3 – without undermining her strong support within the gay and lesbian community. Schulze wanted to magnify the fact of Kehoe's sexual identity into the complete definition of her candidacy, and thus to exploit Kehoe's potential vulnerability at the polls. At the same time, Schulze needed to maintain her own alliances within the gay and lesbian community. Since the mid-1980s gay and lesbian activists had been recognized as a considerable political force in San Diego city politics. In District 3, estimates of the size of the gay and lesbian voting bloc ran as high as 25 to 30 per cent of voters (*San Diego Union Tribune* 1991, 23 August: A-1).

Kehoe's strategy queered the meaning of being a lesbian by acknowledging her identity, yet expanding its significance to the horizon of 'normality'. Chris Kehoe became the lesbian candidate who focused on issues that seemed to have nothing to do with sexual orientation: crime, jobs and neighborhoods. She promised supporters that she would 'get the abandoned cars towed and get the trees trimmed' (*San Diego Union Tribune* 1993, 24 October: B-1). She took the same message to every venue in which she sought votes. A voter registration drive was designed to target gay and lesbian voters, including those who were most alienated from the political system. This strategy included trips to gay and lesbian bars several nights a week, regular appearances at the gay bowling league, the occasional Saturday morning spot at the gay softball league, and even a fund-raiser with the San Diego Leather Society. Yet, at each of these venues, as well as in more 'mainstream' locations, the message was that Kehoe was a lesbian candidate for all constituents.

As a result of the apparent success of Kehoe's strategy, Schulze was confronted with an ironic dilemma – how to appear as a mainstream candidate without calling attention to her own sexuality. While being a lesbian candidate had become a non-issue for Kehoe, the question of Schulze's sexuality haunted her campaign like the heterosexualised political equiv-alent to the military's 'Don't Ask, Don't Tell' policy. 'Normal' became the most difficult position to maintain once everybody was talking about sex.

Schulze chose to respond to this dilemma directly. When a Kehoe cam-paign flier characterised Schulze as a perpetual candidate – or, as one reporter put it, as a 'political bridesmaid' – Schulze returned with a flier that called attention to Kehoe's sexuality within the terms of the 'family values' debate. Schulze's campaign produced a resume-style flier listing both candidates' birthdays, occupations, education, residence and family status. Schulze listed her 'family' assets as 'Two sons: Mark, Mid-City business owner; Eric, physician'. Yet, under the Kehoe column the data on 'family' was left blank (1993).

The gay and lesbian community responded to Schulze's flier with outrage: 'I was shocked when I saw it. The message is that Chris Kehoe is not normal', Waybourn recounted (1993). On election eve, the only leader in San Diego's organised queer community to continue to endorse Schulze's candidacy was Imperial Court Empress Nicole Ramirez-Murray, a man known for his exquisite taste in gowns.

Butler (1993: 113) has argued that the occupation of certain subject-positions within the existing dominant discourse by those who have been excluded from its cultural terrain represents a 'political opportunity to work the weakness in heterosexual subjectivation, and to refute the logic of mutual exclusion by which heterosexism proceeds'. Rather than require 'seamless coherence' Butler contended that 'it may be only by risking the "incoherence" of identity that connection is possible'. Kehoe's strategy to portray herself as a 'normal lesbian' who supported a beefed-up police force and cleaned up neighborhoods represented such a strategy of risked incoherence. As a consequence of setting in motion discussions of sexual-ity, but making an effort not to reduce those discussions to an oppositional dialogue between gays and straights, Kehoe pushed the issue of her sexu-ality into the arena of the normal. By contrast, Schulze's insistence on the clarity and coherence of her heteronormative family status – her prized 'two sons' – both depended upon and disavowed its appeal to representa-tions of desire and desirability in the gay community.

### 'If "Normalcy" Were Required for Political Office Our Ship of State Would Be Rudderless'[2]

'As we meet this week to nominate our candidate, all eyes will be focused on sunny San Diego by the sea, a perfect launching point for us to set sail for the White House in November '96'. These words of welcome by Haley Barbour, Chairman of the Republican National Committee, printed in the

*Official Delegate and Media Guide* for the 1996 RNC greeted visitors to San Diego that summer. The sentiments behind them were shared by local gay and lesbian rights activists who saw the convention's presence in San Diego as a perfect launching point for different political approaches to promoting gay and lesbian rights and as an opportunity to contribute to the further democratisation of American politics.

One approach involved an 'unprecedented public relations campaign created by Gay and Lesbian Families of America (GLFA)' to 'promot[e] gays and lesbians as contributing members [of] mainstream society' (GLFA Press Release 1996, 12 July). The ad campaign featured three images scheduled to appear on billboards and bus shelters around the city. The first image depicted four generations of one family at a backyard barbecue, with the tagline, 'Someone You Know and Love is Gay.' The second image featured photos of San Diegans from various walks of life under the heading 'Gay. Not Gay. Does It Really Matter?' The third asserted: 'Millions Can't Share in the American Dream, Just Because They're Gay.'

Because this campaign depended on the use of family metaphors to construct positive images, several other groups in San Diego criticised its approach. Among these was LGBT VOICES '96 ('Lesbian, Gay, Bisexual and Transgendered' Voices Organized in Coalition for the Elections). LGBT VOICES '96 wanted to avoid limiting its agenda to gay and lesbian rights narrowly defined or made legitimate by depending upon mainstream values and tactics. Consequently, it specifically called for 'envision[ing] a society free from discrimination regardless of race, ethnicity, gender, disability, class, national origin, religious affiliation, sexual orientation, citizenship status, or any other category of difference' (VOICES '96 brochure).

Such an inclusive platform aimed to broaden the framework of political causes that the group supported beyond the scope of sexual identity to include defence of affirmative action, federal assistance entitlement programmes, immigrant rights, women's rights and secularism in American politics among its specified goals. This broadening also applied to the organisation's self-proclaimed political tactics: to 'converge in San Diego to make their voices heard and challenge attacks from religious political extremists threatening to dominate the convention' by 'organizing rallies, town hall meetings, cultural events, and a progressive calendar of activities to inform and motivate activists into action' (1996). VOICES '96 intended to be outside the mainstream, to resist co-optation, and to retain the critical edge over groups such as GLFA, which it saw as more comfortably conformist.

An impressive array of organisations supported VOICES '96 including the National Gay and Lesbian Task Force, the Human Rights Campaign, the Gay and Lesbian Alliance Against Defamation (GLAAD) National Chapter, Los Angeles Lesbian and Gay Community Services Center, and the National Latino/a Lesbian and Gay Organization (LLGO). Locally, they were endorsed by the Rainbow Congress, the San Diego Democratic Club, the San Diego Log Cabin Republican Club, Trans-Action, the First Unitarian Universalist Church, San Diego Parents and Friends of Lesbians and Gays (PFLAG), Gay and Lesbian Latinos, Lesbian Avengers, Imperial Court, Daraja, Bi-Pole, San Diego GLAAD, the Gay Men's Chorus of San Diego, the Tom Homman Law Association, and Woman-Care: A Feminist Health Center. Some of these same organisations supported GLFA's billboards campaign.

On the face of it, VOICES '96 appeared to be taking the more radically democratic stance. By resisting the legitimacy supposedly conferred on GLFA by the latter's embrace of 'family values', VOICES '96 represented an implied critique of GLFA's apparent conformism. Such a critique had been expressed before by activists who were concerned that gays and lesbians pushing a 'family agenda' were abandoning the ship of the sexual revolution ('We Are Family', 1996, 16 June: 30). Yet, denying a radical edge to a queer family agenda had elicited the response from lesbians and gays interested in being recognised as parents or as caretakers that short-sightedness on this issue within the community effectively policed the borders of community and denied lesbians and gays important human and civil rights.

Nevertheless, even VOICES '96 depended upon the pre-existent privileging of electoral politics in general, and the convention in particular, as notorious sites of power without which the effectiveness of its own strategy would have run aground. As its printed literature declared, but did not question, 'no event [would] capture the controversy [around LGBT issues] more than the Republican National Convention this August' (VOICES '96 brochure). VOICES '96 co-chair Brenda Schumacher would proclaim victory while waiting in line to seek a reserved spot in the Republican convention protest area: 'We think we have a good shot at getting a permit with the city. It's a fair process, and we're first in line' (*San Diego Union Tribune* 1996, 19 June: B-3).

Such a declaration left unchallenged the power of political conventionality to continue to set the terms of debate with which oppositional strategies contend. Ironically, GLFA's apparently more traditional incursion onto the dominant terrain through its billboard campaign, and its refusal to concede conventional family values to the logic of the GOP's platform opened up the streets of San Diego while the demonstrators were fenced into a police-designated protest zone in a parking lot across from the convention centre, albeit a visible one.

As a further irony, the Republicans for Choice, in coalition with the bipartisan National Women's Political Caucus, chose the San Diego Harbor as its designated protest space. Organising a 'Boat ProChoice' flotilla headed for the Convention Center, Republican women queered the space of Republican politics by demanding the attention of those inside the convention center to the positions of those within the party who had been forced outside by its abortion plank. These protesters were not the ubiquitous members of the NOW legal defence fund, but well-heeled Republican ladies urging their colleagues to 'Yank the Plank'.

In an effort to take the wind out of their sails, Senator Dole planned to be ferried to the convention site, leading amused (perhaps bored) journalists to speculate about potential Monday morning headlines: 'Dole Boat Rams Abortion Rights Flotilla' (*San Diego Union Tribune* 1996, 6 August). It is beyond the scope of this chapter to speculate about the offspring of Dole's ferry ramming the women's boats and what this would have meant in a world without choice. Nevertheless, this was certainly a queer San Diego encounter of the close kind.

## Conclusion

In moments of critical exchange in public space between previously excluded 'out groups' and foundational 'in groups', the tension between equality and freedom, between the sameness of the status of citizens and the difference and uniqueness of living citizens, becomes exacerbated. When we who have been excluded, or who have passed, or who have assimilated come out in public space, the 'range and variety of bounded spaces' upon which heterosexism, racism, sexism, classism, able-bodiedism and a host of other supremacist-isms, have depended become exposed (Berlant and Freeman 1993: 205). When we demand inclusion in these forbidden spaces we force open those spaces to the identities and actions of those whose exclusion has defined that space itself as public space.[3]

The exposure and opening of public space, as well as the disturbance of the apparent stability of 'private' institutions constructed by public means, such as marriage, accomplished by queer transgression can generate as much intensified hostility and panic as it can welcoming good neighborliness. The increasing use of homosexual panic defence (Sedgwick 1990: 19), condemnation of gays in the military for weakening national defence, and fears that gay marriage will lead to the desiccation of the moral fibre of the country are only some of the indicators of the depths of the New Right's perception that 'gays and lesbians pose the greatest threat to traditional American values' (Bull 1992: 45).

There is much truth in that perception. Moments of critical exchange enact what we call *Queer Citizenship*. These moments include not only Queer Nation Kiss-Ins, but demands for political rights for 'guest workers', for political asylum for gays and lesbians fleeing persecution based on 'sexual orientation', for political asylum for women seeking refuge from domestic violence, for equal employment benefits for gays and lesbians on college campuses demanding the same rights accorded their 'straight' colleagues, and for all those who 'queer' the category of citizenship by refusing to limit what counts as normative civic action to armed intervention in defence of the state.

Queer citizenship confounds citizenship's national, sexual, racial, gendered, and class parameters in the name of a different citizenship. This different citizenship has as its purpose the building of a different kind of democratic community that would be genuinely constitutive of the plurality, and hence, the 'queerness', of the concerns raised by new social movements. Queer citizenship refuses to cede the territory even of established definitions of intimacy and embrace, and of kin and network to the hegemony of 'straight' society. (We define 'straight' society as consisting of intra- not inter-national networks of intra- not inter-racial constellations of intra- not inter-class coalitions of inter- not intra-sexual relations of intra- not inter-species affinities understood to operate in limited public spaces.) Queer citizenship represents multiply excluded alien partnerships between strangers and friends.

In *Bodies That Matter*, Judith Butler (1993: 224) asks 'how is it that the abjected come to make their claim [for recognition] through and against the discourses that have sought their repudiation?' In other words, how is it that those who have been kept outside the nation come to call themselves nationals, naming their nationality and announcing their citizenship with the same term that has been used to name them as aliens, as outsiders? How is it that those who have been kept outside the family come to call themselves families, naming their families in the same language that has been used to name them as outsiders: 'We're here. We're Queer. Get used to it.'

There are multiple, contested, ambiguous, and even contradictory relationships to nationalism and to the idea of citizenship and the benefits that it confers that figure in the concept of *Queer Citizenship*. 'Queer' has been a name whose power has been derived from the power to insult, to shame, to isolate, and to stigmatise. Now the insulted, the shamed, the isolated, and the stigmatised have reclaimed and reversed this slur-name in an attempt to make it mean something different. Queer has moved out of the closeted boundaries of a small, privatised space and into the public arenas of the house-next-door, the courtroom, the shopping mall, the television station, the community centre, the stock exchange, the academy, the publishing house, and the PTA. Its insistent, often theatrical, presence has refused the silence that equals death, the quiet assimilation that is tantamount to disappearance, and the politeness that represents conformity with the status quo.

The more fully democratic impulse behind queer politics-out-of-bounds depends upon the tolerated exceeding the boundaries of their allotted sphere, transforming the ethos and norms of public space. No more bantustans, homelands, ghettos: 'We are Everywhere.' This is the fundamental dilemma of queer citizenship: If citizenship is truly to be 'queered' it must lose its anchor in identity markers, yet we cannot know if it has been fully queered without these markers. Hence, the doubts voiced by women about whether they were being fully welcomed as queer nationals if they could not speak loudly and in imitation of a macho 'bash back' style ('Women as Queer Nationals' 1991: 23), and the complaints from activists of colour about their gay subjectivity not simply being defined by sole opposition to a heterosexual category (Fernandez in Seidman 1993) represent some of the necessary critiques of the queer citizen 'crucial to the continuing democratization of queer politics' (Butler 1993: 227). Indeed, the very undoing of *Queer Nation* as an (ironically) organised movement was triggered by the insistent return of class, race, sex, and gender as boundary markers that the concept 'queer' necessarily, but only temporarily, could have suspended.

### Postscript: the queer case of Sgt Danny Lightfoot, 'Illegal alien'/ US Marine

'Should I have to make the ultimate sacrifice one day, I would willingly die defending America. My only regret would be that I would not die as an American.' With these words, Sgt Danny Lightfoot, Marine of 11 years, and a native of the Bahamas, turned himself in to the Naval Investigative Services. Lightfoot had entered the country under a student visa but stayed beyond its expiration, enlisting in the Marines in 1983 by using fraudulent papers 'that he contend[ed] were supplied by a recruiter' (*Los Angeles Times* 1994, 6 April: A1). His appeal to stay any efforts at deportation were supported uniformly (all puns intended) by his superiors. 'Sgt. Lightfoot is deserving of special consideration because he has demonstrated his commitment to America by his willingness to defend it with his life', wrote Lt.Col. F. L. Kebelman III (1994).

Lightfoot's claim both queers and contains the discourse of citizenship. The illicitness of his desire for America as an 'illegal' is counterbalanced by the licit nature of his expression of that desire – 'willing to defend it with his life'. His desire for the nation becomes legitimated by the militarisation of this desire. All illegal immigrants in the military have to meet residency requirements of only two years to apply for suspension of deportation proceedings compared with the seven years required of all other applicants.

Yet the legitimisation of desire for the nation worked in Lightfoot's case not only because of his military service, which was never a sufficient condition to suspend deportation, but also because of his marital and parental status. Married to a Bahamian, who also was not a legal resident, and father of three children, one of whom was born in the US, Lightfoot's desire was to have his 'family privileged with everything that the average American has' (1994). On 13 December 1994, only eight months after his initial appeal to stay his deportation, Danny Lightfoot became a legal resident of the US and immediately filed for citizenship.

What if the demilitarisation of desire for a country that harbours queer pleasures joins forces with a denationalised desire for public spaces? Resisting the conflation of sexual and political spectacle, as well as the identification of sexual with political identity, remains imperative to the mooring of coalitions, or affinities, whose proliferation is essential to the transfiguration of nationality and of citizenship itself. Then, queer citizenship might disrupt the national boundaries of citizenship. Rather than taking the fact of national identity for granted, 'our greatest challenge rests in finding a language, a way of communicating across our subjectivities, across differences, a way of navigating the cultural borders between and *within* us so that we do not replicate the chauvinism and reductive mythologies of the past' (Riggs 1991: 19). Perhaps we should all apply for refugee status on the grounds that we are aliens in the nation *and* that the nation is a false unity masking the privileged identities of sex, sexuality, class, and race upon which it is founded.

## Notes

1 *San Diego Union Tribune.* 1993, 14 November. p. D-1.
2 *Ibid.*
3 Perhaps in recognition of this, queer theorist John D'Emilio has assumed the identity of Director of the Policy Institute of the National Gay and Lesbian Task Force. One of the central components of the task force's political strategy for 1996 has been to produce *Power at the Polls: The Gay, Lesbian, and Bisexual Vote.* This study was touted as the 'first statistically reliable picture of self-identified gay, lesbian, and bisexual voters' and functioned to document their constitution as an official voting bloc.

## References

Berlant, Lauren and Elizabeth Freeman. 1993. 'Queer Nationality', in Michael Warner (ed.) *Fear of a Queer Planet: Queer Politics and Social Theory*, pp. 193–229. Minneapolis, MN: University of Minnesota Press.

Browning, Frank. 1994. *The Culture of Desire: Paradox and Perversity in Gay Lives Today*. New York: Vintage Books.

Bull. 1992. *The Advocate*, 20 October: 45.

Burrington, Debra. 1993. 'Competing Visions of Community: The Religious Right and Gay Rights'. Paper presented at the Annual Meeting of the American Political Science Association, Washington, DC.

Butler, Judith. 1993. *Bodies That Matter: On the Discursive Limits of 'Sex'*. London: Routledge.

Cohen, Cathy. 1997. 'Punks, Bulldaggers, and Welfare Queens: The Radical Potential of Queer Politics', *Gay and lesbian Quarterly: A Journal of Lesbian and Gay Studies* 3(4): 437–65.

Darcy, Robert, Susan Welch and Janet Clark. 1994. *Women, Elections, and Representation*. Lincoln, NE: University of Nebraska Press.

Dunham, David. 1993. *Gays in the Military: The Moral and Strategic Crisis* (video). Franklin, TN: Legacy Communications.

Federal News Service. 1993. *Hearing of the Senate Armed Service Committee*, 20 July.

Gay and Lesbian Families of America (GLFA). 1996. Press release, 12 July.

Gelb, Joyce. 1989. *Feminism and Politics*. Berkeley, CA: University of California Press.

*Los Angeles Times*. 1994. 6 April. p. A1.

McClure, Kirstie. 1992. 'On the Subject of Rights: Pluralism, Plurality, and Political Identity', in Chantal Mouffe (ed.) *Dimensions of Radical Democracy*. London: Verso.

Marshall, Thomas Humphrey. 1964. *Class, Citizenship, and Social Development*. Chicago, IL: University of Chicago Press.

Riggs, Marlon. 1991. 'Ruminations of a Snap Queer', *OUT/LOOK*, Spring: 12–19.

*Romer v. Evans*. 1996. 517 US 620.

*San Diego Union Tribune*. 1991. 23 August. p. A-1.

*San Diego Union Tribune*. 1993. 11 April. p. B-2.

*San Diego Union Tribune*. 1993. 24 October. p. B-1.

*San Diego Union Tribune*. 1993. 14 November. p. D-1.

*San Diego Union Tribune*. 1994, 13 July. p. B-1.

*San Diego Union Tribune*. 1994. 14 December. p. B-6.

*San Diego Union Tribune*. 1995. 21 April. p. B-1.

*San Diego Union Tribune*. 1996. 19 June. p. B-3.

*San Diego Union Tribune*. 1996. 6 August. p. B-1.

Sedgwick, Eve. 1990. *Epistemology of the Closet*. Berkeley: University of California Press.

Seidman, Steven. 1993. 'Identity and Politics in a "Postmodern" Gay Culture', in Michael Warner (ed.) *Fear of a Queer Planet: Queer Politics and Social Theory*, pp. 105–42. Minneapolis MN: University of Minnesota Press.

Squires, Judith. 1993. 'Recognizing Group Difference: Representation and a Politics of Identification'. Paper presented at the Workshop 'Citizenship and Plurality,' Joint Sessions of the European Consortium on Political Research, Leiden, The Netherlands.

Trebay, Guy. 1990. 'In Your Face', *Village Voice*, 14 August: 35–9.

We Are Family. 1996. *San Francisco Bay Guardian*, 16 June: p. 30.

Women as Queer Nationals. 1991. *OUT/LOOK*, Winter: 23.

# 10

# Injecting a woman's voice: conservative women's organisations, gender consciousness and the expression of women's policy preferences

*Ronnee Schreiber*

## Introduction

A question that has consistently motivated women and politics research is: which women support the 'women's movement' and its policy goals?[1] Explorations of this question have come from scholars examining 'gender consciousness' (Klein 1984; Gurin 1985; Conover 1988; Miller *et al.* 1988; Tolleson-Rinehart 1992; Hildreth and Dran 1994; Rhodebeck 1996). Their analyses suggest that gender conscious women, that is, those who identify with women as a group and feel affected by the social conditions under which that group lives (Tolleson-Rinehart 1992), are the ones who support the women's movement and will express a 'woman's perspective' on policy issues (Conover 1988). Because this literature frequently conflates *women*'s activism and policy issues with *feminism*, however, it fails to explain the behaviour of conservative women. As such, it not only forecloses understanding of conservative women's activism, but leads to mistaken conclusions and assumptions in feminist explanations of women's policy preferences and activism.

In this chapter I examine two US national conservative women's organizations – Concerned Women for America (CWA) and Independent Women's Forum (IWF) – to show how conservative women leaders link gender identity and policy preferences. I describe these organisations below. Like feminists, these women, through their organisations, not only act collectively as women, but also bring a 'woman's perspective' to policy issues. Although some scholars have not denied the impact of right-wing movements on feminist goals and activities (Conover and Gray 1983; Klatch 1987; Marshall 1995), others characterise conservative women as victims of false consciousness, pawns of conservative men or right-wing funders (Dworkin 1983; Hammer 2002) or 'women's auxiliar[ies] of the conservative elite' (Kaminer 1996), diminishing the attention and serious consideration appropriate to such a political force. While we get some sense of the relationship between gender identity, political activism and policy preferences among feminist women from gender consciousness research, there is little beyond the small number of studies of women's activism on abortion and the Equal Rights Amendment (ERA) (Brady and Tedin 1976; Luker 1984; Mansbridge 1986; Ginsburg 1989) to explain the link between gender identity and policy preferences among conservative women (see Klatch 2001, for a discussion of the formation of gender consciousness among conservative women). And, in studies of women's organisations, and women's collective policy activism (Freeman 1976; Gelb and Palley 1987; Boneparth and Stoper 1988; Bookman and Morgen 1988; Costain 1988; Ferree and Martin 1995), almost no research exists on how conservative women's organisations act in the policy-making process (for an exception see Marshall 1995; 1996). As the CWA and IWF are prominent national organisations, these omissions are significant ones.

With its 500,000 members,[2] CWA is one of the largest grassroots women's organisations in the country and has been described as 'a key Christian-Right organization of the post-Reagan era' (Moen 1992: 53). Now some years old, it actively participates in national debates on a range of significant political issues. Since the recent weakening of the Christian Coalition, the organisation is well positioned, and likely to become, an even stronger leader in the conservative movement (Wilcox 2007). For its part, the high-profile IWF was featured in a *Washington Post* story that emphasised its keen ability to get its leaders on the public airwaves and detailed the number of its associates who have positions in, or strong ties to, the current Republican Administration (Morin and Deane 2001). These political powerhouses include 'Second Lady' Lynne Cheney and US Secretary of Labor Elaine Chao. And, in the spring of 2002, the IWF's President, Nancy Pfotenhauer, was appointed by US President George W. Bush to be a delegate to the United Nations Commission on the Status of Women. She has also been selected to sit on the US Secretary of Energy's Advisory Board.

CWA and IWF are not 'just' conservative organisations, however, they are national conservative *women*'s organisations. Their status as such shapes policy debates and influences political outcomes. They are well positioned to exert influence as countermovement organisations – to take on the feminist movement, mobilise women and vie for the right to make claims about women's policy preferences and goals. In the following section I discuss in more depth how the gender consciousness literature portrays the relationship between gender consciousness and policy preferences, and indicate how it fails to account for, or explain, the actions of conservative women leaders and organisations.

## Gender consciousness and policy preferences

Although a survey of the gender consciousness literature shows some lack of consistency across the studies (Jenkins 2002), generally scholars argue that gender consciousness is an important link between gender identity, political action and policy preferences (Klein 1984; Gurin 1985; Conover 1988; Miller *et al.* 1988; Tolleson-Rinehart 1992). Measures of gender consciousness include some sense of discontentment with women's social and political status, such as views about gender roles, feelings of relative deprivation, and/or support for the women's movement. In this context, gender identity is politicised and, mostly, feminist. It is the basis for gender consciousness and guides women's political ideologies and policy goals. It appears from this body of work, therefore that only feminist policy preferences are motivated by gender consciousness. This finding is incongruent with the fact that these same researchers note an increase in the number of women who do identify with their gender, and do not support feminist goals (Miller *et al.* 1988; Tolleson-Rinehart 1992). Consequently, conservative women's unique, but gendered, perspectives on public policies are never fully evaluated. Indeed, one often gets the impression from these studies that conservative women are either motivated by something other than gender consciousness, or, are not really considered to be 'acting as women' in the political process.

To their credit, gender consciousness scholars do indicate that identifying with women as a group is not a sufficient condition for collective action among women. Ideological differences preclude such unity (Tolleson-Rinehart 1992; Hildreth and Dran 1994). It has been argued, however, that feminist consciousness and/or politicisation[3] can be a bridge between gender identity and collective action (Conover 1988; Tolleson-Rinehart 1992; Hildreth and Dran 1994). And, in terms of collective policy preferences, feminist consciousness, coupled with liberal ideological values, is found to create gender gaps between men and women (Conover 1988). I do not dispute these findings. They come from the relatively few, but important studies that examine the connections between gender identity, ideological perspectives and policy preferences (Klein 1984; Conover 1988; Tolleson-Rinehart 1992; Hildreth and Dran 1994; Rhodebeck 1996). As such, the data help explain why some women are more likely than others to support feminist policy goals. For feminist activists, this is a critical, and often vexing question.

The link between identity and ideology, however, needs to be pursued even further. My concern with the gender consciousness literature is not only its lack of attention to conservative women but its conflation of feminist interests with women's interests.[4] Conover (1998: 1005), for example, argues that the 'expression of a *woman's* perspective' with regard to policy preferences is facilitated, in part, by a *'feminist* identity' (italics added). Additionally, Tolleson-Rinehart asserts that gender conscious women are the ones who create gender gaps, even though conservative women, many of whom are gender conscious, do not align themselves with the women who sway public opinion and voting outcomes in more liberal and feminist directions. In effect, for Tolleson-Rinehart, gender consciousness is a proxy for feminist ideology, as evidenced by the following statement:

> Consciousness, beyond stimulating women's beliefs about their own political roles, also reorganizes orientations toward other issues by motivating women to believe that they have unique perspectives on public problems and can offer unique solutions. Gender conscious women, in short, are the women who create gender gaps. (1992: 154)

Finally, while Rhodebeck (1996: 390) does distinguish between feminist and nonfeminist women in her terminology, her measure of 'feminist opinion' includes support for women's equal roles with men in business and government, a belief that many conservative women hold as well. (See Sapiro and Conover 2001, for more discussion about the problematic uses of an 'equal roles' measure.)

In these studies, gender consciousness research, therefore, is more revelatory of feminist beliefs than it is of women's self-awareness as a demographic cohort (Jenkins 2002). The end result is a clustering of conservative women with men, erasing the potential for, and thus the understanding of, the distinctively gender-conscious policy preferences among conservative women. And, even when scholars are attentive to the differences between feminist and nonfeminist women, conservative women are eventually left out of analyses because they are not feminist and presumably act like men. But conservative women are changing public discourse about women's interests; indeed one of the main goals of the IWF is to transform debates about 'women's' issues by offering the viewpoints of conservative women. Similarly, CWA refers to itself as the 'nation's largest public policy women's organization'. As these interest groups lay claim to representing women, they also have the potential to mobilise women and link them to conservative causes (Marshall 1996; Schreiber 2000). In addition, when conservative women leaders act as women to make claims for women, they undermine feminist claims to knowing and representing women's interests.

My corrective to the omission of conservative women from the gender consciousness literature is to study conservative women collectively organised – that is, in women's organisations. Although the gender consciousness literature mostly focuses on women at the mass level, it can also be used to explain women active at the elite level and those organised into interest groups. We know, for example, that feminist women's organisations can be gender-conscious in that they have organised collectively as women and speak for women from a woman's perspective (Gelb and Palley 1987; Costain 1988; Ferree and Martin 1995). Building on the knowledge we have about feminist organisations and their policy advocacy, but using concepts from the gender consciousness literature, I show that conservative women collectively organised are gender conscious in their expression of women's policy interests. That is, I apply insights about the relationship between gender consciousness and policy preferences among women at the mass level to women organised at the elite institutional level. In so doing, I not only add to knowledge of women's organisations, but show how the gender consciousness literature needs to account better for politically active conservative women. Although I do not examine the 'grassroots', it is my intention that observations gleaned from this analysis can be used to better understand gender consciousness among conservative women at the mass level as well. (For studies of conservative women activists at the mass level see Klatch 1987; Blee 1998; Bacchetta and Power 2002.) The potential for applying my findings to this larger population is detailed in the conclusion.

The CWA and IWF are clearly gender-conscious in one sense: They are women's organisations and identify themselves as such (Schreiber 2002). But, without seeing or understanding the relationship between gender consciousness and policy preferences for conservative women, we cannot adequately explain the terrain of political debates on a range of important political issues. Thus, I ask if and how collectively organised conservative women are gender conscious in their expression of public policies. That is, do they, like feminist activists and organisations, articulate a 'woman's perspective' on policy issues?

## Data and methods

Data analysed for this study were originally collected for another research project designed to explain how national conservative women's organisations represent women's interests (Schreiber 2000). Because that project explored how conservative women make political claims as and for women, I chose to examine two organisations that specifically identify as 'women's' organisations – the CWA and IWF. Data came from interviews with organisational leaders of the CWA and IWF, content analysis and participant observation. As my research concerned organisational policy goals and strategies, I pursued and completed interviews with those most likely to be responsible for such duties: the organisations' presidents, executive directors, lobbyists, public relations directors and editors. In addition, I analysed organisational periodicals and other relevant publications.[5] Since I also pursued questions about the significance of gender identity to the CWA and IWF, and examined their policy goals in the original project, data gathered for it are also relevant to my analysis here.

## The organizations

Both the CWA and IWF represent conservative women; each speaks for a slightly different constituency. Like feminists, conservative women are not monolithic. Klatch (1987) categorizes them as either 'social conservatives' or 'laissez-faire conservatives', with each expressing a different worldview about gender, religion, economics, and the role of government. 'Social conservatives' are deeply religious, see the traditional heterosexual family as the core of society and root social problems in the moral realm. 'Laissez-faire' conservatives point to the economic realm as the source of problems, and emphasise individuality and the desire for freedom from government intrusion. Klatch also argues that socially conservative women tend to be gender identified, while laissez-faire conservative women do not recognise their 'collective interests as women' and are not necessarily antifeminist (10). While the organisations I study generally conform to Klatch's distinctions, with the CWA being comprised of socially conservative women and the IWF of laissez-faire conservatives, the laissez-faire conservatives of the IWF also express the need to act collectively as women and thus have formed into a women's organisation. Unlike the laissez-faire women that Klatch interviews, this group of laissez-faire conservatives does believe that feminism is, at least, partly to blame for many social and economic problems. Thus, both organisations are explicitly antifeminist and both believe that feminists have undervalued the need for attention to gender differences between women and men. Despite these variations from Klatch's ideal types, these two organisations nicely represent the range of conservative women in the US.

## Concerned Women for America (CWA)

CWA was founded in 1979 by Beverly LaHaye. Its formation and subsequent growth coincided with the politicisation of the Christian Right in the late 1970s and early 1980s (Green, Guth, Smidt and Kellstedt 1996).[6] Originally located in San Diego, California, CWA began with local prayer chapters that mobilised women around issues like opposition to the Equal Rights Amendment (ERA) and legalised abortion. In 1987,

CWA relocated to Washington, DC, establishing a national office and a national presence. Today CWA has a professionally staffed office in Washington, DC, and members in all fifty states, and claims to be the largest women's organisation in the United States.[7] Through e-mail, a monthly magazine, a website and phone calls, its national staff work closely with local members to update them on legislative affairs and train them to be effective activists. CWA's socially conservative mission, according to its website, is to 'protect and promote Biblical values among all citizens – first through prayer, then education and finally by influenc-ing our society – thereby reversing the decline in moral values in our nation' (www.cwfa.org/about). Its multi-issue policy agenda includes opposition to homosexuality, abortion, pornography, and funding the United Nations. Through advocacy on its issues, CWA works in coali-tion with such conservative organisations as the Christian Coalition, the American Family Association, the Family Research Council, and several anti-abortion groups.

### Independent Women's Forum (IWF)

In comparison to CWA, IWF is a much younger and smaller organisation. While it only claims about 1,600 paid subscribers to its publications, this media-savvy group has garnered considerable attention and clout since its founding. Established in 1992, it grew out of a group of women who worked for President George H. W. Bush's administration and who met regularly to hear speakers and network. These conservative women leaders are well-connected to, or are in themselves, key policy and opinion makers (Morin and Deane 2001). Resembling more of a think tank than a grass-roots organisation, it was founded to take on the 'old feminist establish-ment' (Independent Women's Forum 1996). As a group of 'laissez-faire' conservatives (Klatch 1987), it describes itself as an organization that promotes 'common sense' and provides 'voice for American women who believe in individual freedom and personal responsibility . . . the voice of reasonable women with important ideas who embrace common sense over divisive ideology' (Independent Women's Forum 1996). Unlike the CWA, it does not have a grassroots membership, but like the CWA, it employs professional staff.

The IWF delights in caricaturing feminists[8] and 'debunking' supposed myths about issues such as the need for an Equal Rights Amendment and pay equity policies. To advocate for its issues, the IWF has collaborated with other conservative organisations such as the American Enterprise Institute, the Center for Equal Opportunity, and the Foundation for Academic Standards and Tradition.

## The CWA and IWF as gender-conscious policy advocates

The CWA's and IWF's expression of a 'woman's perspective' on policy issues reflects a complex interplay between ideology and strategy. First, both groups believe that women bring gendered and unique perspectives to policy concerns. In this sense, their gender consciousness has ideological roots emanating from the belief systems of the women who lead the organisations. But, as countermovement organisations, vying with feminists over who legitimately represents women, the CWA and IWF also recognise the value of having conservative women as policy advocates. It is more difficult for conservatives to be attacked as 'anti-woman' if women are making political claims as and for women (Schreiber 2002). Thus, the framing of policy goals from a 'woman's perspective' both reflects their conservative ideology about gender differences and stems from a desire to establish credibility as women's organisations. In this latter sense, it is a strategic choice – one that exemplifies the power and salience of identity politics in the United States (Schreiber 2002). The purpose of this study is not to disentangle the ideological effects from the strategic ones, but rather to show the results of both.

In the sections below I discuss one of the primary missions of the CWA and IWF – to offer women's, but not feminist, voices in debates on a range of public policies. Second, I provide in-depth analyses of two policy issues that have been central to the feminist movement for decades – reproductive health and Title IX – to show how the CWA and IWF, like feminists, articulate 'women's perspectives' in these cases. Here I offer evidence that challenges the prevailing notion that only feminist women express women's perspectives on policy issues.

## Just 'mainstream' women speaking out

The CWA and IWF chastise feminists for making universalist claims on behalf of women. Nonetheless, both CWA and IWF also make broad-based claims for women. In much of its publicity information, IWF (1996) proclaims itself to be the 'voice of *reasonable* women with important ideas who embrace common sense over divisive ideology' (italics added). Here the phrase 'reasonable' is loose and unspecific, suggesting that its constituency of women can be construed quite broadly. In addition, showing that it thinks of itself as speaking to and for a majority of women, IWF declares on its website: 'Who represents the *real* interests of American women? The IWF does, and here's how' (www.iwf.org). CWA offers analogous reasoning about its representation of women. Although the organization clearly talks about being comprised of, and speaking for,

'Christian'[9] women, it also frequently asserts that it is 'mainstream' (Barbara Franceski, personal communication, 29 October 1998). Indeed, in speaking of which women the CWA's goals appeal to, group founder LaHaye (1993: 138) claims that 'the *vast majority* of women, thank God, want to raise children with integrity and strong character' (italics added).

Interviews with organisational leaders also produced narratives about the organisations' perception of the relationship between gender identity and policy preferences. Respondents expressed strong commitments to helping women and examining issues as they affect women. And, according to these organisations, women's interests are not just those associated with traditional women's issues, but also those that arise in the context of dealing with a range of public policies. Although IWF Board member Wendy Gramm (personal communication, 20 January 1999) initially qualified that 'the main mission [of IWF] is simply . . . to educate others about how *this* group of women thinks', she emphatically added that 'the IWF also seeks to show how issues affect women, what is the impact on women of different policy issues. So it really is an educational role, injecting *a woman's* voice into the policy debate' (italics added).

Her colleague Kimberly Schuld also expressed how the organisation is gender conscious in its expression of women's policy interests:

> We talk about the impact on women, not women's issues. That is the way I see it. For instance, we could take a tax issue and say 'how does this impact women' and 'where are you missing that in your communications to women'. (Kimberly Schuld, personal communication, 24 November 1998)

IWF's rationale for sponsoring a conference on what it calls 'junk science' also shows that the organization sees a relationship between gender and political interests. 'Junk science', according IWF, is research motivated by politics and lacking in solid empirical findings. An example of this is the case of silicone breast implants, in which women were awarded damages by breast implant manufacturers based on claims that these implants caused connective tissue diseases and a host of other ailments. IWF argues that there is little evidence to back up these claims, and that politics, not facts, led to women being awarded damages by the courts. In speaking about the organisation's decision to address the issue of 'junk science', the IWF's Sally Satel related why she felt the issue was considered to be in the interest of women:

> Those of us who follow the junk science debate know that scientific illiteracy is certainly not gender-specific. But survey data . . . do show that *women, as a group*, tend to be more risk-averse. That's why the IWF has chosen to explore the relationship between unjustified fears and health and science policy. (Sally Satel, personal communication, 17 February 1999)

Similarly, CWA's former president Carmen Pate noted how the organisation seeks to speak for women:

> With every issue, we can bring in why it should be of concern to women, and that is what we try to do: why mom should be concerned, why wives should be concerned, why you should be concerned about your daughters. That is the connection that we try to make. How will this impact women long term? (Carmen Pate, personal communication, 18 August 1998)

Although these organisations are critical of feminists for making universal interest claims as and for 'women', both groups link their identities as women's organisations with their stances on public policies. CWA and IWF also incorporate narratives about men's, children's and familial interests into their rhetoric. This enables them to link women's interests with conservative rhetoric about families, and to build bridges between women and the broader conservative movement (see Marshall 1996 for a related argument). From the standpoint of the CWA and IWF, it also helps to mark them as different from feminist organisations, since both the CWA and IWF contend that feminists care little about the interests of men and families. For example, the IWF's Anita Blair told me:

> We don't simply look at what is good for women, because that obviously puts you in opposition to men and children. So our principles are to try and get the facts to use common sense, and then to make public policy decisions based on what's best for everybody, for a society, as a whole, not just women. (Anita Blair, personal communication, 30 October 1998)

She added that 'I believe that men and children are just as important in the world as women are'.

The CWA makes similar claims about men and children, but, consistent with many socially conservative organisations, emphasises the word 'family' to do so. For example, in contrasting the CWA's policy agenda with that of its feminist counterparts, Seriah Rein noted that the CWA's issues were 'family issues . . . women impacting family issues. They are not all women's issues' (personal communication, 6 August 1998). Finally, the CWA's LaHaye critiques feminists for not recognising that women's lives are intertwined with men. LaHaye considers this to be a result of feminists' self-centredness and an affront to 'family values'. On this issue LaHaye (1993: 186) writes: 'The pitfall of the feminist is the belief that the interests of men and women can be severed; that what brings suffering to the one can leave the other unscathed.'

Although these organisations formed because they were critical of feminists for claiming to represent the majority of women, both groups talk about their missions in ways similar to those of feminists. These conservative organisations speak on behalf of women, demonstrating that the expression of a woman's perspective with regard to public policies may not necessarily be feminist. In addition, the CWA and IWF have the potential to transform the meaning of women's interests to be more consistent with conservative values about gender roles and families. In so doing, they effectively compete with feminists over the construction of women's interests.

### CWA's opposition to abortion: it's a woman thing

CWA challenges the feminist assertion that when it comes to abortion rights, it is in the interest of women to be pro-choice. For the socially conservative CWA, opposition to abortion and most forms of birth control is central to its agenda.[10] The organisation lobbies for legislation to limit and/or make abortion illegal, and opposes federal funding of most domestic and international family planning programmes. While its position on reproductive health issues is consistent with many other socially conservative organisations that oppose abortion because of beliefs about the 'sanctity of life' (e.g. the Christian Coalition, the National Right to Life Committee), CWA also strongly holds that support for abortion and family planning programmes hurts women. That is, it is gender conscious in its explication of why it opposes abortion. Women are, according to CWA, 'abortion's second victim' (Wadkins 1999: 2). Talking as women, about women's interests in this case, not only reflects the CWA's gendered perspective on the issue, but also enables it to tackle pro-choice advocates who have long argued for attention to women's bodies and lives in reproductive health care debates.

Another example of how CWA articulates a 'woman's perspective' about abortion policy is found in its discussions about 'Post Abortion Syndrome' (PAS). In effect, PAS is shorthand for what the organisation believes are negative consequences women face after having abortions. The CWA argues that:

> Post-abortive women may: require psychological treatment/therapy, suffer post-traumatic stress disorder, experience sexual dysfunction, engage in suicidal thoughts or attempt suicide, become heavy or habitual smokers, abuse alcohol and illegal drugs, acquire eating disorders, neglect or abuse other children, have relationship problems, have repeat abortions, re-experience the abortion through flashbacks, be preoccupied with becoming pregnant to replace the aborted child [and] experience anxiety and guilt. (Wadkins 1999: 6–7)

In linking specific women's health concerns to its anti-abortion platform, CWA also claims that 'abortion can significantly increase a woman's risk of getting breast cancer'; [11] therefore, 'abortion is deadly – not only for unborn children, but also for the women who abort them' (Wallace 1997: 11). The group urges lawmakers to require reproductive health professionals to inform women of this link and touted the case of a woman who sued a North Dakota clinic for false advertising when it claimed in a pamphlet that no correlation has been found between abortion and breast cancer (Green 2002). Much to the dismay of CWA, a judge found for the clinic. At the time this article went to print, the case was being appealed.

CWA also condemns international family planning programmes that provide women with Norplant, a form of birth control that can have adverse side-effects on women. It refers to women in the US and abroad who use Norplant as 'human guinea pigs' (MacLeod 1997: 18) and worries that 'today, the US government is using our money to bruise and batter women and children around the world' (MacLeod 1997: 20). Thus, CWA lobbies for abolition of federal funds to support domestic and international family planning programmes, especially those that counsel for, or perform abortions and those that provide Norplant and other 'abortifacients'. Indeed, here CWA's arguments, or at least its gender consciousness policy stance, is reminiscent of feminist critiques of sterilisation abuse.

CWA also raises similar concerns about the abortifacient RU-486, 'partial birth (PBA)' abortion,[12] unlicensed abortion clinics and the contraceptive pill. For example, in a *Family Voice* article entitled 'RU-486: Killer Pills' one author warns women of the 'dangerous' side effects of RU-486:

> Women who took RU-486 in clinical trials experienced firsthand just how 'easy' the abortion pill is. Common side effects included: painful contractions, nausea, vomiting, diarrhea, pelvic pain and spasms, and headaches – as well as the trauma of seeing their aborted baby . . . Chemical abortions like RU-486 will *not* advance women's health. (Wallace 1997: 6)

And, on the subject of 'partial birth abortions', the CWA writes that not only is the end result of a 'purely elective' abortion a 'dead child', but:

> Few people realize the *danger to the mother*. Dr. Joseph DeCook of the American College of Obstretics and Gynecology declares *PBA is riskier for the mother than any other type of abortion*: the opening of the cervix for a prolonged time involves a greater risk of infection. (Wallace 1997: 6)

Finally, in a pamphlet detailing the negative side effects of most forms of birth control, the CWA cautions women that: 'In the past 30 years, various chemicals and devices that manipulate women's reproductive systems have come on the medical scene. Women need to know precisely what they do and what risks they present.'

Clearly, these reproductive health narratives promote the CWA's socially conservative anti-abortion stance. Of course, this is not without intention on the part of the CWA. Since feminists have long argued for redirecting attention from fetal rights to women's health concerns in abortion debates (Daniels 1993), using gender conscious arguments enables CWA to counter feminist claims about women's interests. In doing so, CWA demonstrates how a group of 'gender conscious' women can be anti-abortion and do so from a 'woman's perspective'. While its position on abortion is hardly consistent with that of most feminist organisations, its speaking as and for women indicates coherence between identity and policy preferences for these conservative political actors.

### IWF on Title IX: demeaning to women

Through a programme entitled 'Play Fair', IWF takes on a prominent feminist policy achievement – Title IX. Title IX, part of a 1972 law that outlaws gender discrimination in federally funded educational institutions, has been used successfully to increase attention to, and funding for, women's sports in colleges and universities. The Office for Civil Rights (OCR), a division of the US Department of Education, is the agency in charge of enforcing Title IX. To do so, the OCR developed a three-prong test to determine if schools were in compliance. Schools could show: that the ratio of male and female athletes closely parallels the ratio of male and female students – this is sometimes known as 'proportionality'; a history of expanding opportunities for athletes of the under-represented sex; or that the interests of the under-represented sex had been fully and effectively accommodated. A school only needs to meet one of these three criteria, but in 1996, the OCR issued a clarification stating that the first option, or 'proportionality', was the surest way for schools to demonstrate that they were in compliance. IWF likens this 'proportionality' option to a quota system and is therefore highly critical of Title IX. It claims that too many schools opt for this, thereby strangling men's sports and demeaning women's athletic accomplishments.

From the point of view of IWF, Title IX regulations are akin to affirmative action, a policy the IWF opposes and contends hurts women. Speaking from a 'woman's perspective', the organisation argues that it is women's relative lack of interest in sports, not discrimination, that creates discrepancies in the numbers of female and male college athletes. IWF charges that feminists have misinterpreted the meaning of gender differences and women's interests in this case, because feminists are prone to anti-male biases. Feminists, it argues, are quick to blame men for women's relative lack of involvement in collegiate athletics and are eager to cut resources for men's sports.[13] As IWF founder Anita Blair says about the enforcement of Title IX through proportionality:

This is mean-spirited, dog-in-the-manger feminism at its worst. Why deny men sports opportunities just because relatively fewer women are interested in athletics? (Independent Women's Forum 1997: 15)

Noting that women should be concerned about Title IX enforcement, and anticipating the queries about its position, the IWF published a document entitled 'Why Would a Women's Group Complain About Title IX?' (Schuld 1998). In this text, the IWF declares that Title IX 'demeans the legitimate athletic accomplishments of women' (1998: 1). It also proclaims Title IX to be a woman's issue because, as the organisation sees it, Title IX reinforces misguided ideas about the origins and meanings of gender differences. From the point of view of the IWF:

Most women know that men and women are different, and that women are different from each other. Not all of us want to be scholars, not all of us want to be athletes. We look to ourselves, not the government to know the difference. (Schuld 1998: 5)

Its expression of a 'woman's perspective' on the issue is also evidenced in the organization's statement of support for Brown University in a highly publicized, landmark Title IX lawsuit. In 1995, IWF filed a brief in *Cohen et al. v. Brown University*. In the case, Brown University appealed a lower court ruling that upheld the argument of plaintiffs who alleged that Brown discriminated against women athletes and violated Title IX. Ultimately, the United States Supreme Court refused to hear the case and let the ruling, in favour of the women, stand. In its brief, IWF maintained that student interest, not quotas, should determine spending on sports programmes. In not doing so, IWF argues, female students' interests are determined by feminists and policy-makers. As such, the organisation argues, women are deemed helpless bystanders unable to decide what types of activities best suit them. And, because of the federal oversight necessary to monitor compliance with the law, IWF charges that Title IX encourages governmental bureaucracies to 'run amok' (Schuld 1998) and interfere with how gender differences play themselves out in terms of interest in sports.

Finally, IWF also suggests that enforcing Title IX through 'proportionality' damages women's sports. It contends that is has a responsibility as a woman's organisation to care about the issue and inform women about the dangers of implementing Title IX in this way. In an extensive, thirty-five page policy brief the IWF alleges:

By allowing, and even encouraging, schools to set high minimums for women's teams, coaches are finding themselves taking on some sub-standard players to beef up the roster. This affects the competitiveness of women's teams, as well as their morale. It cannot be good for women's sports markets in the long term to field non-competitive teams. (Schuld 2000: 21)

Title IX is one of the most profound legislative achievements of the feminist movement since the 1970s. Certainly it is a 'women's issue' from the standpoint of those who fought for it and have benefited from it. But IWF, critical of how the law has been interpreted and enforced over the years, sees it as an affront to women's abilities to make decisions about their interests free of government involvement and ideological persuasion. And, like the CWA, the IWF articulates its concerns from a woman's perspective, indicating that these organisations are indeed gender conscious as they make policy claims.

## Conclusions

My foray into conservative women's organisations' framing of policy goals does not only highlight the limitations of current research on gender consciousness. It also elucidates the very real and significant consequences of having conservative women's voices reverberating through legislatures and in the media. The presence of the CWA and IWF means clashes will occur among women about the meaning of women's status in politics and the family, the nature and origins of gender differences and the role of government in women's lives. As gender conscious political institutions, both feminist and conservative women's organisations battle over whose stories about women are most representative. And, given that their narratives about women's lives have concrete policy implications, this battle over authenticity is meaningful. Shane Phelan (1993: 773) suggests that 'rather than arguing with one another about which story is true, [we] must look instead at what is at stake in our different stories; we must examine the consequences of our stories in terms of power and change'. Following this thinking, the next step in this line of inquiry would be to examine the relative impact feminist and conservative women have had on policy debates and outcomes. How have differences in the expression of 'women's perspectives' influenced policy-makers' ideas about women's interests? Which policies have been shaped by the public debates and lobbying efforts of conflicting groups of women? Is there any room for coalition or compromise among women on certain issues?

In terms of the gender consciousness literature specifically, I propose exploring the intersection of gender and ideology more closely. Gender consciousness can compel women to act as women, for women, across the political spectrum. Through gender conscious arguments, conservative women's organisations articulate and legitimate their perspectives on a range of important public policies. Thus, understanding the actions and relevance of these ideologically conservative organisations requires using gender as an analytic category. In so doing, we also see how different women construct the meaning of gender roles and differences, and what gender identity means to different women in the context of political participation.

While this study examines conservative women's organisations, it also suggests ways to expand our thinking about gender consciousness among conservative women at the mass level of politics. For example, measures of gender identity and consciousness need to be better attuned to ideological differences among women. As noted in this chapter, 'support for equal roles' is not the most useful way to determine differences among women (see Conover and Sapiro 2001). Demographic measures, such as education and professional status, may also not be the best measure of women's affinity for liberal or conservative goals. As Wuthnow (1998) has shown, the educational and professional achievements of Evangelicals and Catholics, many of whom are politically conservative, have become more like those of everyone else in the population. Thus, neither education nor professional status alone can stand as an adequate proxy for political ideology. Finally, even if some women support the Republican party and vote more like men as a group, researchers should ask why this is so. That is, why do *conservative* women vote as they do? It is necessary to get beyond the idea that conservative women have no agency and instead explore their reasons for joining conservative organisations and forming alliances with groups that disapprove of feminist and liberal values and beliefs.

The meaning of gender identity and its relationship to policy preferences can vary depending on the ideological beliefs of women. Here, I have argued that these differences require more detailed analyses. Conservative women, after all, speak as women. This may not necessarily be a new insight to those familiar with women's activism, but it is one that remains almost entirely unexplored and perhaps intentionally dismissed or distorted because it challenges feminist claims about women's interests. But Marshall (1995) argues, and I agree, that feminists should take heart in, or at least heed that, conservative women's engagement with 'women's issues' reflects the careful and tireless work of feminists to render women, and women's policy concerns, relevant to lawmakers, the media and the public.

## Notes

This chapter is a revised version of the article 'Injecting a woman's voice: conservative women's organisations, gender consciousness and the expression of women's policy preferences', published in *Sex Roles* 47 (7/8) October 2002: 331–342. The publisher gratefully acknowledges the co-operation of Springer in granting permission to publish this revised version of the work.

For invaluable feedback on various incarnations of this work, I thank MaryAnne Borrelli, Sue Carroll, Cyndi Daniels, John Evans and Debra Liebowitz. Research for this project was supported in part by the American Association of University Women (AAUW) Educational Fund and the Center for American Women and Politics (CAWP), Rutgers University.

1 Here I use the phrase 'women's movement' to mean the *feminist* women's movement as it reflects how the gender consciousness scholars cited in this article have defined and measured the term.

2 According to CWA, this figure represents the number of people who have contributed money to the organisation within the 24-month period preceding the count.

3 Hildreth and Dran (1994: 36) define 'politicization' by linking 'identification with women as a group' with 'perceived status deprivation and the necessity of political redress'.

4 There are several other aspects of the gender consciousness literature that fail to explain conservative women's activism. For example, one study asserts such a narrow interpretation of 'politicization' that it suggests 'traditional women' are not likely to seek government assistance in dealing with 'privatized' women's issues (Hildreth and Dran 1994). Others use an 'equal roles' measure as one proxy for feminism (Tolleson-Rinehart 1992). But as Sapiro and Conover note, an 'equal roles' measure may not be an accurate indicator of feminism. As they argue, 'the majority of men and women believe that men and women can have different roles and still be equal' (2001: 10). This is certainly the case for both the CWA and IWF, organisations that believe gender differences are natural, but should not be the basis for gender discrimination. For a broader critique of the gender consciousness literature, see Jenkins 2002.

5 I conducted 20 semi-structured, open-ended, in-depth interviews with leaders and professional staff of the CWA and IWF between August 1998 and January 2002. All but two of the women with whom I requested interviews were willing to speak with me. As for organisational literature, both the CWA and IWF publish their own periodicals. The CWA puts out the monthly *Family Voice* and the IWF publishes a journal entitled *The Women's Quarterly* and a newsletter called *Ex Femina*. I analysed articles from the 1996–2001 editions of these publications, as well as relevant policy papers, press releases and website pages, for this project. For participant observation, I attended two national CWA conventions – 19–21 September 1996 at the Sheraton Washington Hotel in Washington, DC, and 24–7 September 1998 at the Radisson Plaza Hotel in Alexandria, VA. I also participated in a day-long IWF conference entitled 'Scared Sick?' at the National Press Club in Washington, DC on 17 February 1999; observed a meeting organised by the CWA entitled 'Reproductive Rights of the Girl Child' at the United Nations Special Session on Children in New York City on 9 May 2002; and was an invited participant at the 'Core Connections: Women, Religion and Public Policy' symposium, held 8–9 October 1999 at the John F. Kennedy School of Government at Harvard University; associates from both organisations were present and participated in this conference.

6 Most of the members of the CWA identify as Evangelical or fundamentalist Protestants (Guth, *et al.* 1995).

7 On its website, www.now.org, the National Organization for Women (NOW) also claims to have 500,000 members, but the CWA contends that NOW really has less than 100,000.

8 The feminist movement in the United States is diverse and includes national organisations, community groups, direct service providers, campus-based groups, websites and list servers (Katzenstein and Mueller 1987; Bookman and Morgen 1988; Echols 1989; Martin 1990; Ferree and Martin 1995; Cohen *et al.* 1997; Blee 1998; Brownmiller 1999). When the CWA and IWF talk about the feminist movement, however, they are mostly referring to nationally organised interest groups, especially the National Organization for Women (NOW), the National Abortion and Reproductive Rights Action League (NARAL), the Planned Parenthood Federation of American (PPFA), the American Association of University Women (AAUW) and the Feminist Majority Foundation (FMF). CWA and IWF name these feminist groups as proxies for the entire feminist movement.

9 While the CWA just uses the term 'Christians,' it is specifically referring to Evangelical Protestant and fundamentalist Christians, the religious group that comprises most of its membership (Guth *et al.* 1995).

10 CWA refers to the Intra-uterine Device (IUD), Norplant, Depo-Provera, and the 'Pill' as 'abortifacients' on the grounds that each of these forms of birth control can prevent a fertilised egg, or embryo, from becoming implanted in a woman's uterus. Since, the CWA recognises the term 'human embryo' to be the same as 'unborn child', intentionally making the uterus 'hostile' to the embryo is considered equivalent to having an abortion (Concerned Women for America 1998).

11 Its argument is based on a meta-analysis conducted by Brind, Chinchilli, Severs and Summy-Long (1996). As summarised by the CWA, Brind *et al.* argue that 'early in her pregnancy, a woman experiences a major surge of estrogen that causes immature breast cells to multiply. These cells are allegedly more susceptible to carcinogens, but are protected when a woman begins to lactate. If her pregnancy is aborted, however, the women's breast cells are left in the vulnerable state, because they do not receive the benefit of lactation that comes from full-term pregnancies' (Wallace 1997: 10). The pro-choice Planned Parenthood Federation of America (PPFA) notes, however, that in an analysis of the approximately 25 studies examining the link between breast cancer and abortion, cancer researchers at the National Cancer Institute and the American Cancer Society found no conclusive relationship. It also asserts that Brind and his colleagues analysed studies that contained faulty methods and inconclusive findings (Planned Parenthood Federation of America 2000b).

12 This refers to an abortion procedure known as a 'D and X' or dilation and extraction in which a foetus is removed whole from a woman. The procedure is most common in second and third trimester abortions (after 24 weeks)

and usually performed when the fetus or woman's life is endangered. According to the Planned Parenthood Federation of America (who cites the Centers for Disease Control), in the US 1.5 per cent of abortions are performed after 20 weeks of pregnancy (Planned Parenthood Federation of America 2000a).

13 For detailed arguments against IWF's position on Title IX see the websites of the Women's Sports Foundation, www.womenssportsfoundation.org, and the Feminist Majority Foundation, www.feminist.org.

## References

Bacchetta, Paola and Margaret Power. 2002. *Right-wing Women: From Conservatives to Extremists Around the World*. New York: Routledge.

Blee, Kathleen. 1998. *No Middle Ground: Women and Radical Protest*. New York: New York University Press.

Boneparth, Ellen and Emily Stoper. 1988. *Women, Power and Policy: Toward the Year 2000*. New York: Pergamon Press.

Bookman, Ann and Sandra Morgen (eds). 1988. *Women and the Politics of Empowerment*. Philadelphia, PA: Temple University Press.

Brady, David W. and Kent L. Tedin. 1976, March. 'Ladies in Pink: Religion and Political Ideology in the Anti-ERA Movement', *Social Science Quarterly* 56: 564–75.

Brind, Joel, Vernon M. Chinchilli, Walter B. Severs and Joan Summy-Long. 1996, October. 'Induced Abortion as an Independent Risk Factor for Breast Cancer: A Comprehensive Review and Meta-analysis', *Journal of Epidemiology and Community Health* 50: 481–96.

Brownmiller, Susan. 1999. *In Our Time: A Memoir of a Revolution*. New York: Dial Press.

Cohen, Cathy, Kathleen B. Jones and Joan Tronto (eds). 1997. *Women Transforming Politics: An Alternative Reader*. New York: New York University Press.

Concerned Women for America. 1998, July. Glossary of Abortifacients. In library (online), www.cwfa.org/library/life/1998–07_pp_glossary.shtml, accessed 21 July 2000.

Concerned Women for America. nd. *High-Tech 'Birth Control': Health Care or Health Risk?* (pamphlet). Washington, DC: Author.

Concerned Women for America website. www.cwfa.org, accessed 5 September 2002.

Conover, Pamela. 1988. 'Feminists and the Gender Gap', *Journal of Politics* 50(4): 985–1009.

Conover, Pamela J. and Virginia Gray. 1983. *Feminism and the New Right: Conflict over the American Family*. New York: Praeger.

Conover, Pamela and Virginia Sapiro. 2001. 'Gender Equality in the Public's Mind', *Women and Politics* 22: 1–36.

Costain, Anne N. 1988. 'Representing Women: The Transition from Social Movement to Interest Group', in Ellen Boneparth and Emily Stoper (eds)

*Women, Power and Policy: Toward the Year 2000*, pp. 26–47. New York: Pergamon Press.

Daniels, Cynthia. 1993. *At Women's Expense: State Power and the Politics of Fetal Rights*. Cambridge, MA: Harvard University Press.

Dworkin, Andrea. 1983. *Right-wing Women*. New York: Perigree Books.

Echols, Alice. 1989. *Daring to Be Bad: Radical Feminism in America 1967–1975*. Minneapolis, MN: University of Minnesota Press.

Feminist Majority Foundation website. www.feminist.org, accessed 5 June 2002.

Ferree, Myra Marx and Patricia Yancey Martin. 1995. *Feminist Organizations: Harvest of the New Women's Movement*. Philadelphia, PA: Temple University Press.

Freeman, Jo. 1976. *The Politics of Women's Liberation*. New York: David McKay Company.

Gelb, Joyce and Marion Lee Palley (eds). 1987. *Women and Public Policies*. Princeton, NJ: Princeton University Press.

Ginsburg, Faye. 1989. *Contested Lives: The Abortion Debate in an American Community*. Berkeley, CA: University of California Press.

Green, John C., James L. Guth, Corwin E. Smidt and Lyman A. Kellstedt. 1996. *Religion and the Culture Wars: Dispatches From the Front*. Lanham, MD: Rowman and Littlefield.

Green, Tanya. L. 2002, 1 April. 'Bad Day for Pro-Lifers in North Dakota', http//cwfa.org/library/life (online), http://cwfa.org/library/life/2002–04–01_abc-link.shtml, accessed 5 May 2002.

Gurin, Patricia. 1985. 'Women's Gender Consciousness', *Public Opinion Quarterly* 49: 143–63.

Guth, James L., John C. Green, Lyman A. Kellstedt and Corwin E. Smidt. 1995. 'Onward Christian Soldiers: Religious Activist Groups in American Politics', in A. J. Cigler and B. A. Loomis (eds) *Interest Group Politics*, pp. 55–76. Washington, DC: Congressional Quarterly Press.

Hammer, Rhonda. 2002. *Antifeminism and Family Terrorism*. Lanham, MD: Rowman and Littlefield Publishers, Inc.

Hildreth, Anne and Ellen M. Dran. 1994. 'Explaining Women's Differences in Abortion Opinion: The Role of Gender Consciousnessness', *Women and Politics* 14(1): 35–51.

Independent Women's Forum. 1996. *Who Are We? The Future* (recruitment pamphlet). Washington, DC.

Independent Women's Forum. 1997, June. 'Bad Sports: The Quota Team Scores a Touchdown', *Ex Femina* June (1): 15.

Independent Women's Forum website. www.iwf.org, accessed 5 September 2002.

Jenkins, Krista. 2002. 'The Paradox of Feminist Consciousness and Political Participation'. Paper presented at the annual meeting of the American Political Science Association, Boston, MA.

Kaminer, Wendy. 1996. 'Will Class Trump Gender?', *American Prospect* Nov–Dec.: 44–52.

Katzenstein, Mary Fainsod and Carol McClurg Mueller. 1987. *The Women's Movement of the United States and Western Europe: Consciousness, Political Opportunity and Public Policy*. Philadelphia, PA: Temple University Press.

Klatch, Rebecca. 1987. *Women of the New Right*. Philadelphia: Temple University Press.

Klatch, Rebecca. 2001. 'The Formation of Feminist Consciousness among Left- and Right-wing Activists of the 1960s', *Gender and Society* 15(6): 791–815.

Klein, Ethel. 1984. *Gender Politics: From Consciousness to Mass Politics*. Cambridge, MA: Harvard University Press.

LaHaye, Beverly. 1993. *The Desires of a Woman's Heart*. Wheaton, IL: Tyndale House Publishers.

Luker, Kristen. 1984. *Abortion and the Politics of Motherhood*. Berkeley, CA: University of California Press.

MacLeod, Laurel A. 1997. 'Mexico City Revisited', *Family Voice October*: 16–20.

Mansbridge, Jane. 1986. *Why We Lost the ERA*. Chicago, IL: University of Chicago Press.

Marshall, Susan E. 1995. 'Confrontation and Cooptation in Antifeminist Organizations', in M. M. Ferree and P. Y. Martin (eds) *Feminist Organizations*, pp. 323–38. Philadelphia, PA: Temple University Press.

Marshall, Susan E. 1996. '*Marilyn vs. Hillary*: Women's Place in New Right Politics', *Women and Politics* 16(1): 55–75.

Martin, Patricia Yancey. 1990. 'Rethinking Feminist Organizations', *Gender and Society* 4(2): 182–206.

Miller, Arthur H., Anne Hildreth and Grace L. Simmons. 1988. 'The Mobilization of Gender Group Consciousness', in Kathleen B. Jones and Anna. G. Jonasdottir (eds) *The Political Interests of Gender*, pp. 106–34. London: Sage Publications.

Moen, Matthew. 1992. *The Transformation of the Christian Right*. Tuscaloosa, AL: University of Alabama Press.

Morin, Richard and Claudia Deane. 2001. Women's Forum Challenges Feminists, Gains Influence. *Washington Post*, 1/2001. p. A06.

National Organization for Women website. www.now.org, accessed 5 September 2002.

Phelan, Shane. 1993, '(Be)Coming Out: Lesbian Identity and Politics', *Signs: Journal of Women in Culture and Society* 18(4): 765–90.

Planned Parenthood Federation of America. 2000a. 'Abortions after the First Trimester', in Fact Sheets (Online), www.plannedparenthood.org/library/facts/abotaft1st_010600.html, accessed 27 April.

Planned Parenthood Federation of America. 2000b. 'Anti-choice Claims about abortion and Breast Cancer', in Fact Sheets (Online), www.plannedparenthood.org/library/facts/fact_cancer_022800.html, accessed 26 April 2000.

Rhodebeck, Laurie A. 1996. 'The Structure of Men's and Women's Feminist Orientations', *Gender and Society* 10(4): 386–403.

Sapiro, Virginia and Pamela Conover. 2001. 'Gender Equality in the Public Mind', *Women and Politics* 22(1): 1–36.

Schreiber, Ronnee. 2000. ' "But Perhaps We Speak for You": Antifeminist Women's Organizations and the Representation of Political Interests Dissertation'. Dissertation New Brunswick, NJ: Rutgers University.

Schreiber, Ronnee. 2002. 'Playing "Femball": Conservative Women's Organizations and Political Representation in the United States', in P. Bacchetta and Power Margaret (eds) *Right-wing Women: From Conservatives to Extremists Around the World*, pp. 211–23. New York, NY: Routledge.

Schuld, Kimberly. 1998. *Why Would A Woman's Group Complain about Title IX?* Washington, DC: Independent Women's Forum.

Schuld, Kimberly. 2000. 'National Girls and Women in Sport Day', in News (Online), www.iwf.org/news/000209.shtml accessed 2 April.

Tolleson-Rinehart, Sue. 1992. *Gender Consciousness and Politics*. New York: Routledge.

Wadkins, Jessica. 1999. 'Reaching Abortion's Second Victims', *Family Voice* January: 3–8.

Wallace, Marian. 1997. 'The Hidden Link: Abortion and Breast Cancer', *Family Voice* January: 10–11.

Wilcox, Clyde. 2007. 'Of Movements and Metaphors: The Co-evolution of the Christian Right and the GOP'. Paper presented at the Christian Conservative Movement and American Democracy conference, Russell Sage Foundation, New York.

Women's Sports and Fitness Foundation website. http//:womensportsfoundation. org, accessed 5 June 2002.

Wuthnow, Robert. 1998. *The Restructuring of American Religion*. Princeton, NJ: Princeton University Press.

# 11

# Women in movement: transformations in African political landscapes

*Aili Mari Tripp*

Women's organisations have increased exponentially throughout Africa since the early 1990s as have the arenas in which women have been able to assert their varied concerns. Today women are organising locally and nationally and are networking across the continent on an unprecedented scale. They have been aggressively using the media to demand their rights in a way not as evident in the early 1980s. In some countries they are taking their claims to land, inheritance and associational autonomy to court in ways not seen in the past. Women are challenging laws and constitutions that do not uphold gender equality. In addition, they are moving into government, legislative, party, NGO and other leadership positions previously the exclusive domain of men. They are fighting for a female presence in areas where women were previously marginalised, such as the leadership of religious institutions, sports clubs and boards of private and public institutions.

In these and other ways women have taken advantage of the new political openings that occurred in the 1990s, even if the openings were limited and precarious. The expansion of women's organisations and associational life more generally accompanied the move away from the older single-party systems toward multi-party politics and the demise of military regimes in favour of civilian rule. The expansion of freedom of speech and of association, although usually constrained, also increased possibilities for new forms of mobilisation. The international women's movement and, in particular, the 1985 and 1995 UN Women's conferences in Nairobi and Beijing respectively, gave added impetus to women's mobilisation. Moreover, shifting donor strategies gave greater emphasis to non-governmental organisations in the 1990s, and women's organisations were among the main beneficiaries of the new funding orientations. The expansion of the use of the cell phone, e-mail and the Internet in the late 1990s, although primarily among the urban organisations, enhanced networking exponentially, not only Africa-wide and internationally but also domestically. These new conditions, coupled with a significant increase in secondary and university educated women since independence, set the stage for new forms of women's mobilisation.

This chapter first summarises the patterns of women's mobilisation in the period after independence in the early 1960s up to the late 1980s, when new forms of women's mobilisation began to emerge. It then explores some of the main factors that account for these changes. In the next section it looks at some of the characteristics of women's new mobilisation strategies, including the diversity in the types of organisations created, the autonomy of these new associations from the regime and/or ruling party in terms of leadership, financing and agendas. The chapter examines the ways in which autonomy was challenged by the authorities and defended by women's organisations. It shows how in this period women's associations expanded their focus from developmental issues to the inclusion of more explicitly political concerns through legislative and constitutional changes, advocacy and demands for female leadership and representation. The chapter then identifies ways in which women's collective action is distinct from that of other interest groups. These differences lie not only in its goals, but also in the size of the movements, their inclusiveness, the unique ways they link the personal and political and the use of motherhood as a political resource. Finally, the chapter examines the diversity of debates within the women's movements and concludes with reasons for the transformations in women's mobilisation after the late 1980s.

The chapter outlines some of the main changes that have occurred in sub-Saharan Africa. It recognises that even though Africa is a continent of enormous diversity based on culture, language, colonial legacy, history, political orientation and other dimensions, some general patterns and trends have emerged in women's mobilisation in the context of political liberalisation. This chapter is thus one of the first attempts to begin to identify a set of commonalities shared by a growing number of women's movements in Africa. Because of this intended focus, it does not explore many of the differences that will need to be further interrogated. The chapter is, however, limited by the lack of country-specific literature in several parts of Africa, especially in several of the francophone and lusophone countries. As more research is published on these parts of Africa, the conclusions will no doubt become more nuanced.

## Women's mobilisation after independence

In the earlier post-independence period, women's organisations tended to be focused around religious, welfare and domestic concerns. Local handicrafts, savings, farming, income generating, religious and cultural clubs dominated the associational landscape of women. The discourse was primarily one of 'developmentalism' (Ngugi 2001: 6). Women's organisations adopted a *women in development* approach, which was generally divorced from political concerns. They did focus on research into discriminatory practices and laws and on consciousness raising, referred to in English-speaking Africa as 'gender sensitization' or 'conscientization' (Geisler 1995: 546). However, in general they were reluctant to engage in advocacy and push for changes in laws, if it put them at odds with the government authorities.

For example, Maendeleo Ya Wanawake (MYW), which has had the largest membership of any organisation in Kenya, was confined to improving childcare, domestic care, handicrafts, agricultural techniques, literacy and engaging in sports (Wipper 1975: 100). The conservative stance of this organisation, which persists to this day, is reflected in the thinking of its president at the time, Jane Kiano, who claimed in 1972 that 'women in this country do not need a liberation movement because all doors are open to us' (Sahle 1998: 178). Hussaina Abdullah (1993: 27) argued that the key state-sponsored women's institutions in Nigeria, i.e. Better Life Programme, National Commission for Women and National Council of Women's Societies, were primarily concerned with keeping women in their roles as mothers. Ngugi (2001: 6) says of the Nigerian National Council of Women's Societies, which was formed in 1959: 'Unlike the human rights organisations like FIDA [Women Lawyers], it has not ruffled the feathers of the male dominated state by taking up issues on women's rights vis-à-vis men, such as equality and equal representation.'

At the national level, the mass women's organisations had been tied to the single party or regime. Some were formed after 1975 in response to the calls for the establishment of institutional mechanisms to promote women's advancement made at the first United Nations World Conference on Women held in Mexico City in 1975. These objectives were incorporated into the UN International Decade for Woman (1976–1985), so that by 1985, 127 countries had created some type of national machinery. In Africa, some countries set up ministries of women (Côte d'Ivoire), others established women's bureaus, departments or divisions within a ministry of community development or some other non-gender-specific rubric (Kenya). Yet others established commissions, committees or councils like the National Council on Women and Development formed by the ruling National Redemption Council in Ghana or the National Council of Women in Uganda formed by Idi Amin that was situated inside the Prime Minister's office. In creating the Council, Amin simultaneously banned all other women's organisations. By 1985 almost all African countries had set up a national machinery of some kind and the mass organisations were generally under the auspices of these machineries. The success of the machineries was limited by the extent to which their respective governments funded them (Tsikata 1989: 81; Mama 1995: 40).

Where the national machineries were not in and of themselves an umbrella organisation for local women's groups, umbrella organisations were sometimes formed by the ruling authorities, like the Nigerian National Council of Women Societies (NCWS). Other such politically inspired organisations catered to particular constituencies like the Better Life for Rural Women in Nigeria. Still others were aimed at mobilising all women under one mass organisation, for example, the 31st December Women's Movement in Ghana, Umoja wa Wanawake wa Tanzania, Women's League in Zambia and Association des Femmes de Niger (AFN). These organisations were generally run along patronage lines by wives, daughters and relatives of male leaders in the regime. For example, in Nigeria until the 1990s, wives of prominent state officials dominated the leadership of NCWS.

First ladies frequently headed up the larger national women's organisations: Nana Ageman Rawlings chaired the 31st December Women's Movement in Ghana; Maryam Babangida headed the Better Life Programme for Rural Women in Nigeria; while Betty Kaunda was affiliated with Women's League in Zambia. In the 1990s first ladies started becoming patrons of the new independent NGOs as the large mass organisations lost their appeal. For example, Janet Museveni, wife of Uganda's President Yoweri Museveni, is patron of the popular Uganda Women's Effort to Save Orphans (UWESO). However, even these NGOs have been used politically as in the Zambian case, where the former president's wife, Vera Chiluba, used her Hope Foundation to attack the political opposition.

In the past, as in the case of mass party-affiliated organisations like Maendeleo Ya Wanawake (MYW) in Kenya, nominees for leadership elections typically had to be approved by the ruling party. Their funding generally came from the party or government. Their party-dictated agendas were limited and basically did not challenge the status quo when it came to pushing for women's advancement. This is not to say there were no instances of political mobilisation for women. However, generally it was limited. For example, NCWS in Nigeria lobbied the government to amend its discriminatory population control policies that targeted only women and not men. It also got the state commission for women upgraded into a full-fledged Ministry of Women Affairs and Social Development. But for the most part, these structures did not tackle the difficult laws, policies and practices that discriminated against women.

Another case in point is Ghana under Jerry Rawlings, who came to power through a military takeover and headed up a populist government under the Provisional National Defence Council (PNDC) from 1981 to 2000. The PNDC reformed laws affecting women, including inheritance laws and the banning of degrading widowhood rites. The national machinery charged with coordinating women's activities, the National Council for Women and Development (NCWD), was active in promoting such legislation. However, during these years, Ghana's women's movement was constrained by the Government both in terms of growth, vitality, breadth of its agenda and capacity to bring about major changes in the status of women. By trying to subsume the entire women's movement within the PNDC by creating the 31st December Women's Movement (31DWM) in 1981 as one of its 'revolutionary organisations', the regime crippled the women's movement and limited it to publicising and promoting government policies. As Tsikata (1989: 89) put it: the relationship between women's groups and the regime 'has been maintained at the expense of the women's struggle . . . In so doing women's issues have been shelved; or at best, they have received very casual attention'. The close ties between the 31DWM and the government/ruling party have basically kept the organisation from exerting pressure on the government to adopt policies that would promote the welfare and interests of women (Mikell 1984; Dei 1994: 140). As 31DWM absorbed many independent women's organisations at the grassroots level, women were left with muted representation.

Even though these organisations claimed to represent the interests of all women in their respective countries, especially rural women, they often served as mechanisms for generating votes and support for the country's single party, getting women to attend party rallies and meetings, and sing, dance and cook for visiting dignitaries. Beyond these functions they were kept apolitical. They were, in fact, used to contain women's political activity within these designated women's organisations, which meant that few women ever worked outside the bounds of these organisations to involve themselves in the actual parties (Geisler 1995: 553). This further reinforced women's political marginalisation. In a multi-party context, these state affiliated mass unions, leagues, women's wings of parties and umbrella organisations decreased in importance as a plurality of new independent associations emerged. In some cases, women's organisations like Maendeleo ya Wanawake, which had thousands of affiliates throughout the country, remained until 2002 linked to the dominant party in Kenya, the Kenya African National Union, but was officially an independent organisation.

There are still countries where this old model persists that have not embraced new autonomous organisations. For example in Eritrea today, there is basically only one national women's organisation, the National

Union of Eritrea Women (NUEW), which was founded by the Eritrean People's Liberation Front in 1979, when it was fighting for Eritrean independence from Ethiopia. After independence was achieved in 1991, the 200,000-member organisation became semi-autonomous and shifted to educate women for involvement in service provision and project management, but did little in the way of advocacy. It did succeed in making a few modest changes in the old Ethiopian civil code. For example, marriage contracts had to be made with the full consent of both parties; the eligible age for marriage for girls was raised from 15 years old to 18 years old to match that of men; and the sentence for rape was extended to 15 years. But NUEW did little to concretely address the backlash against women that occurred after independence from Ethiopia. Many felt that there was a need for a multiplicity of organisations to work on the most pressing issues, but the few organisations that attempted to work as autonomous organisations were closed down by the government on various pretexts (Connell 1998).

### Reasons for the transformations in mobilisation

What then gave rise to these new women's movements in the 1980s and especially in the 1990s? There is no one explanation but some of the most important reasons for women's heightened activism in Africa would include the following: as mentioned earlier, the move toward multi-partyism in most African countries in the 1990s diminished the need for mass organisations linked and directed by the single ruling party. Where the state opened up to women's independent mobilisation, the new organisations flourished. Thus, the opening of political space that occurred in the early 1990s allowed for the formation of many new autonomous organisations. In addition to these changing opportunity structures, women also found that they had new resources at their disposal. Much of formal politics in Africa is underwritten and controlled by informal patronage politics. Economic crisis forced many women into formal and informal economic associations and into heightened entrepreneurial activity, giving them the resources with which to operate autonomously of state leaders. Increased donor funding of women's associations also helped break the ties with patronage networks. In addition, with the increase in educational opportunities for girls and women in Africa, a larger pool of capable women who were in a position to lead organisations emerged, especially at the national level.

Women in many countries frequently had longer experiences than men in creating and sustaining associations, having been involved in church-related activities, savings clubs, income-generating groups, self-help associations, community improvement groups and many other informal and local organisations and networks. Thus, they often found it easier to take advantage of new political spaces afforded by liberalising regimes. Women in Mali, for example, brought to NGOs their well-developed organisational skills, drawing on a long history of maintaining social and economic networks. As a result, women claimed a strong presence in the NGO movement both in terms of making sure development associations include programmes that address women's issues, but also in their own organisations that range from legal to health, education, credit and enterprise development associations (Kante and Hobgood 1994). Similarly, in Tanzania, it is no accident that the main NGO networking body, Tanzania Association of Non-Governmental Organizations (TANGO), was started by women's organisations and has had strong female representation in its leadership.

Donors placed greater emphasis on funding NGO activities in the 1990s. For example, by the late 1990s, almost 40 per cent of USAID programme funds in Africa were going to Private Voluntary Organisations and NGOs. Part of this aid was directed at NGOs because it was easier to ensure accountability from them than from the state, but also, as Owiti (2000) has pointed out, because of the role they could play as counterweights to the state, as monitors of the state and as sources of reform and pressure for social justice and democratisation.

For women's organisations and movements, the 1990s saw a shift in donor strategies from a sole emphasis on funding activities related to economic development, education, health and welfare concerns to an added interest in advocacy around women's rights, and promoting women's political leadership and political participation. In Africa, parties were generally weak and did not play much of a role in advocacy, leaving associations to carry out many of the interest aggregation functions often associated with parties. Donors began to fund organisations involved in advocacy around equality clauses in constitutions undergoing revision. They supported non-partisan activities around legislation regarding women's land ownership, marriage and inheritance, female genital cutting, rape, domestic violence and many other such issues. Other donors helped support women's caucuses of parliamentarians or members of constituent assemblies. As the decade progressed, funding for national and regional networking also increased.

Although the driving forces for these changes were internal, international pressures and norms gave added impetus to these new demands. The international women's movement played a significant role in influencing women's mobilisation and encouraging women in Africa to think how their struggles related to an emerging globalisation of women's concern for equality (Mbire-Barungi 1999: 435). The UN Beijing Conference on Women in 1995, for example, encouraged women's organisations to hold their governments accountable to their various commitments to improving women's status. Women's organisations also learned considerably from sharing experiences and strategies with activists from other parts of Africa and the world. As in Latin America, the Beijing conference legitimised key elements of feminist discourse in African NGOs, parties, states, international development agencies and other for a (Alvarez 1998: 295).

Networking carried out domestically, throughout Africa and internationally, was greatly facilitated by the use of the Internet and e-mail. Many regionally based organisations focused on making information available to activists and policy-makers on women's experiences, realities and organisational strategies. The use of cell phones, especially starting in the late 1990s, exponentially increased the level of communications both within urban areas but also between rural and urban areas. This had a dramatic impact on the ability of groups to mount campaigns and build political support around various issues. New organisations like Gender in Africa Information Network and Sangonet became involved in promoting the use of information and communication technologies.

Finally, the expansion of media coverage of women's issues, especially promoted by members of new women's media associations in various parts of Africa, provided the mainstream media outlets and women's own media houses an alternate coverage of women to counter the often demeaning and sexist portrayal of women in the media. Information on the activities of women's organisations and their leaders has also helped publicise and give further impetus to the movements (Ojiambo Ochieng 1998: 33).

### Characteristics of new women's mobilisation

A new generation of autonomous organisations emerged primarily after the 1985 UN Nairobi women's conference, although a few had started earlier. The earliest of the new generation of organisations included Women in Nigeria, formed in 1982, Uganda's Action for Development, formed in 1986 and Tanzania Media Women's Association, formed in 1987. These associations became pioneers in the new push to advance women's rights. They were characterised by their autonomy from the state, which meant that they were heterogeneous in the kinds of issues they took up.

#### *Heterogeneity of organisations*
In the new context, the heterogeneity of organisations was striking. At the national level women formed myriad organisations, including professional

associations of women doctors, engineers, bankers, lawyers, accountants, market traders, entrepreneurs and media workers. There were national women's rights groups; organisations focusing on specific issues like reproductive rights, violence against women and rape; groups catering to particular sections of the population, including disabled women and widows. Some provided services to women in areas of health, transportation, banking, protection, legal aid, publishing and education to respond to the neglect of women in the mainstream institutions (Olojede 1999: 33). New forms of developmentally oriented organisations became especially popular in the 1990s such as women's credit and finance associations as well as hometown and development associations. Women also formed social and cultural organisations. Some occupational and political institutions like trade unions and parties often had a wing devoted to women.

Most organisations, both at the local and national level, were in some way concerned with advancing women's political, economic, legal or social status. Women's advancement was being pushed on many perhaps unexpected fronts. The Uganda Women Football Association successfully worked to introduce women's soccer throughout the country. They sought corporate and government sponsorship for games, equipment, training and uniforms, all of which have been difficult to come by (Zziwa 1996: 15). Second wives in polygamous relationships have been mobilising in Uganda, Kenya and Tanzania and have been meeting on both a national and regional basis. Women parliamentarians have national caucuses and are also meeting regionally, for example, the Union of Women Parliamentarians in East Africa.

Women even began to claim leadership of organisations that had primarily a male-membership base, allowing them to introduce women's concerns into new arenas. There were many firsts: a woman, Constantia Pandeni, was elected for the first time to head the Mineworkers Union of Namibia in 2001; Olive Zaitun Kigongo was the first woman elected president of Uganda National Chamber of Commerce and Industry in 2002; and Solomy Balungi Bossa was the first woman to head the Uganda Law Society in 1993.

In war torn areas, women organised across 'enemy' lines (ethnic, clan, religious, regional) to find bases for peace. We saw bold efforts of this kind in Congo, Somalia, Liberia, Sierra Leone, Nigeria, Sudan, Rwanda and other countries. Often they formed coalitions and networks for peace and/or collaborated in joint, mutually beneficial activities to help build new bases for solidarity.

At the local level there were numerous multi-purpose clubs that engaged in savings, farming, income-generating projects, handicrafts, sports, cultural events and other functions, depending on the needs and priorities of members (Strobel 1979; Feldman 1983: 68; Mwaniki 1986: 215).

Even many older organisational forms were revived or modified, including location-based development associations and dual-sex organisations. One type of organisation tied to a cultural gender division was the dual-sex societies. There has been a revival of the dual-sex governance structures in Igbo as well as other West African societies. A dual-sex political system is one in which representatives of each gender govern their own members through a Council. In much of former Eastern Nigeria most communities had a broad-based Women's Governing Council that had sole jurisdiction over wide ranging political, economic and cultural affairs of women, from market issues, to relations with men, and to morality. These organisations, according to Nzegwu (1995), were autonomous of the state, yet their decisions were binding regardless of social status, education or income level. Moreover, the local councils could represent women living as far apart as Lagos, Kano or New York. Their leaders served a wide range of associations and therefore were multifaceted in their approach, since they were concerned with social, cultural, religious, economic and political issues simultaneously (Nzegwu 1995).

Some organisations had branches throughout Africa, including the Forum for African Women's Educationalists (FAWE) that worked on issues having to do with girls' education; Women in Law and Development (WILDAF); Society for Women and AIDS in Africa; Akina Mama wa Africa; and many others. Others were regionally based, including Women and Law in East Africa and Southern Africa and Association de Lutte Contre les Violences Faites aux Femmes. Still others were part of international associations, for example, the International Federation of Women Lawyers (FIDA), Young Women's Christian Association (YWCA), Girl Guides, and Zonta International. Most organisations in which women have involved themselves were gender specific, partly as an outgrowth of cultural divisions of labour and a historic preference for gender specific organisation. Women have often shared an implicit understanding based on past experiences that by cooperating with men in mixed organisations, they run the risk that men might hijack the organisations and their finances.

### Autonomy

The new generation of organisations tended to be independent of the regime and of ruling political parties both in terms of their leadership and agendas. Perhaps in reaction to the dominance of single women's organisations and umbrella organisations under authoritarian rule, there was little interest in creating large overarching organisations and no attempt to create organisations that could speak for all women's interests, as there had been in the past. Instead, the new organisations represented a diversity of interests and political leanings. They came together in coalitions and networked around land issues, violence against women, women's political participation, constitutional reform and other such concerns, rather than attempting to form all-encompassing structures.

The new autonomous organisations were also financially independent of the state or ruling party. Women in Nigeria (WIN), one of the earliest of these new organisations, had primarily funded its activities through membership fees, sale of publications, T-shirts, levies, grants and donations from individuals, organisations and agencies with similar objectives. Members also provided skills free of charge or parts of their houses for office space. Changing donor strategies to assist organisations were evident as WIN gained external donor support for specific projects after 1991 (Olojede 1999).

Financial independence meant that the new organisations were outside the patronage networks that the ruling party and/or state used to build loyalty. Their very existence challenged the legitimacy of state patronage, which had been on the decline throughout the 1990s. This made these autonomous associations potentially threatening to the state, especially if they involved large numbers of rural women, as was the case with the tree planting Green Belt Movement in Kenya, that had been increasingly repressed by the government. The ruling party's (Kenya African National Union (KANU)) fight for the political loyalty of autonomous rural women's groups was particularly fierce as their numbers increased and economic resources grew. KANU politicians courted and manipulated local women's groups and made promises of patronage in order to win their votes (Sahle 1998: 175, 182–4). Some male politicians even formed women's groups through their female relatives in order to garner votes (Kabira and Nzioki 1993: 70). Thus, many have concluded, as Kabira and Nzioki did in Kenya, that the 'first and most important issue to resolve is the question of autonomy' (73).

Associational autonomy was critical to the success and legitimacy of this new generation of organisations. When the 12 June 1993 Nigerian presidential elections were annulled, this led to a serious human rights crisis. WIN and other human rights and pro-democracy activists launched a media campaign and demonstrated against the human rights abuses under the military administration, including the planting of explosives; disappearances of opposition politicians as well as human rights and pro-democracy activists; and destruction of public property (Olojede 1999). These efforts and others eventually culminated in the restoration of an elected civilian government in May 1999, after which the most blatant human rights violations diminished considerably (Obiorah 2001). But clearly the organisations tied to the regime did not respond to the annulment of the elections in the same way that the autonomous ones did. As the National Council of Women Societies (NCWS) benefited from government largesse, it was 'very unlikely for NCWS to pursue autonomous positions or present strong opposition to government on significant political issues such as political accountability and human rights', Olojede (1999: 33) argues.

More than at any time in Africa's post-independence period, women's organisations found themselves challenging the governments' gender policies, pushing for changes in legislation and policy regarding inheritance and property ownership, land ownership, women's political leadership and many other issues. But in Africa, where the majority of regimes today are semi-authoritarian, power is still thought of in zero-sum terms, even in a multi-party context. Any manifestation of opposition to government policy, even basic advocacy around a policy change, could be interpreted by the authorities as a sign of adopting an anti-governmental position. NGO mobilisation, especially where it is active, is seen frequently as 'political', hence 'anti-governmental' and threatening. As a result, some organisations came under attack by their governments, which tried to revoke their registration, co-opt their leadership, buy off the organisations and harass and manipulate their leaders.

A case in point is a struggle that erupted after the 1995 formation of the Tanzanian Women's Council (BAWATA), which had been launched by the ruling party's women's wing, Umoja wa Wanawake wa Tanzania (UWT). Initially, elements within the leadership of the UWT had wanted to make the wing independent of the party, but the top party and the UWT leadership opposed this strategy. Instead, they decided to form an 'independent' nongovernmental umbrella organisation that could access donor funds yet remain under UWT's thumb. One top official in the ministry explained that women's NGOs did not feel 'comfortable with the Ministry' and so the thinking was that the Ministry would find it easier to 'monitor, regulate and collabourate' with women's groups through a separate council.

BAWATA's leadership envisioned a broad-based autonomous organisation that was to push for women's advancement on a number of fronts, including strengthening women's political leadership, pushing for legislative change and conducting civic education. It claimed a membership of 150,000 in 3,000 groups, although its actual strength at the grassroots level is disputed. BAWATA became involved in policy advocacy on issues such as violence against women, sexual abuse of children, improved social services delivery, inheritance laws, land ownership and girls' access to education. BAWATA drew up a document evaluating each of the presidential candidates and their parties in the 1995 elections regarding women. In doing so, they had overstepped their bounds in a society where the female electorate was critical to the ruling party's continued success.

As Chris Peter explained:

> Every sensible State knows that women are faithful voters. They normally register and actually go to vote. Unlike men who talk a lot and do little. They might even register only to forget to vote on the elections day. Thus women are regarded as a safe and sure constituency and whoever controls them is guaranteed victory. By touching this sensitive area – BAWATA was seen as a mischievous lot. (1999: 11)

The Ministry of Home Affairs banned BAWATA on the grounds that it was operating as a political party and was not holding meetings or submitting annual financial accounts to the Registrar of Societies. The Minister of Home Affairs warned in July 1997 that NGOs engaging in hostile exchanges of words with the government would risk losing their registration as would NGOs that confronted the government through forums that created confusion and insecurity. An NGO policy drafted by the Office of the Vice President (1997: 5) stated that 'NGOs as legal entities are restricted from engaging in any activity that will be construed to be political in nature', but are allowed to 'engage in debate on development issues'. The charges against BAWATA, which by all accounts were fabricated, indicated that the party and the government were not interested in permitting the formation of independent organisations with a bold agenda that might diverge from the party's interests. One top UWT leader, who was also the Minister of Local Government, ordered women District Commissioners to discourage women from participating in BAWATA because it was being managed by women who were allegedly too 'independent-minded.'

BAWATA took the matter to the High Court on the grounds that the government action was unconstitutional and in violation of international human rights conventions, to which Tanzania is a signatory. The Court issued an injunction against the government prohibiting it from deregistering BAWATA. In the meantime, members of BAWATA faced death threats, harassment and intimidation, sometimes even from security officers. Husbands of BAWATA leaders were demoted or lost their government jobs, while members of the organisation's branches faced intimidation from local authorities. Local chapters found themselves unable to meet and run their nursery schools and day care centers. Although BAWATA eventually won its case against the government, in the process the organisation was destroyed and the intimidation of its leadership left local chapters in disarray.

The deregistration of BAWATA was widely condemned by other NGOs who were disturbed and demoralised by the implications of this action on the freedom of association. As one lawyer and journalist, Robert Rweyemamu put it:

> Can an NGO geared to the development of the people be completely cut off from political life? It [the deregistration of BAWATA] is a test for those who claim to be devoted to uplifting the social, economic and cultural standards of Tanzanians. (1997: 9)

In Tanzania, which has been a multi-party state since 1992, the BAWATA case illustrates the limits of freedom of association and speech, even in a fairly tolerant country. The fate of BAWATA is indicative of the prevalent view that equates autonomous non-governmental activities with an anti-governmental stance, making any kind of advocacy difficult.

In Tanzania and elsewhere in Africa the most active women's organisations with the most far-reaching agendas often had difficulty registering, or had their registration delayed indefinitely. They faced external manipulations and pressures to keep opposition party members from leadership of the organisations, even though their activities were non-partisan in the context of the association. In the late 1980s and especially in the 1990s, NGOs found themselves opposing governmental legislative efforts to create an agency for the monitoring and control of NGO activities in Tanzania, Botswana, Ghana, Kenya, Zimbabwe, Malawi and Uganda. Uganda has some of the best NGO–government relations in Africa, but in 2001 even Ugandan NGOs were forced to protest, which stepped up government efforts to increase scrutiny of NGOs and threaten their autonomy. In particular they rejected government efforts to create a board that would be based in the Ministry of Internal Affairs, giving the board a focus on security rather than developmental concerns. All these examples of repression or efforts to control and monitor NGOs exposed the limits of freedom of association even in liberalising countries.

### Emphasis on political strategies

Although the older welfare and domestic agendas persisted into the 1990s in women's organisations, a new emphasis on political participation emerged. New women's organisations formed to improve leadership skills, encourage women's political involvement on a non-partisan basis, lobby for women's political leadership, press for legislative changes and conduct civic education. Groups mobilised around issues like domestic violence, rape, reproductive rights, sex education in the school curriculum, female genital cutting, sexual harassment, disparaging representation of women in the media, corruption and other concerns that had rarely been addressed by the women's movements in the past and often were considered taboo by the government.

Kabira and Nzioki underscored the need for women to assert themselves politically in a 1993 statement that was indicative of the change in thinking that had occurred in the early 1990s, that is, a shift from a previous emphasis strictly on developmental approaches to a new adoption of political strategies. As they explained:

> The state may criticize women's organisations as being elitist, ineffective, politically motivated, misguided or foreign. But women have to go where power and resources are by being powerful and resourceful themselves. Since groups know and express this desire, we suggest that women's organisations and political leaders focus their attention on long term changes that touch on the root causes of women's inequality and subordination in society. This approach will advance the women's cause towards meaningful transformation as opposed to individual advancement. (Kabira and Nzioki 1993: 73)

### Distinctiveness of women's collective action

Women's mobilization, while sharing much in common with other interest groups, also stood apart from them in important ways. They often represented the largest organised group within society. Their new organisations were not only pluralistic in the kinds of issues they took up, they were also internally pluralistic in their makeup. The demise of the single party and its affiliated women's organisation often meant a decline in ethnically based mobilisation in which the ethnic group in political power dominated women's associations. Similarly expanded educational opportunities also helped break the past dominance of specific ethnic or religious groups in the leadership of women's groups, who had come from regions where missionary education had first been concentrated. Women's mobilisation also drew in particular ways on women's identification with motherhood and the private sphere to make claims on participation in the public sphere. But it also worked the other way around as women saw that participation in the public sphere gave them entitlements to make claims for greater decision-making within the home.

### *Largest organised sector*

Women's associations often constituted the largest organised sector in many countries. They made up the majority of NGOs in countries like Tanzania and Mali. In Kenya they were the fastest growing sector of civil society (Ngugi 2001). Other sectors may have even ended up numerically dominated by women's organisations. The largest proportion of human rights organisations in Africa, for example, were women's rights organisations. In Kenya 40 per cent of all human rights groups operating in 1992–7 were women's organisations. The majority of lay organisations in both Protestant and Catholic churches were women's groups and women in general were more active than men in church activities. Although men participated in savings and credit associations, by far the majority of participants in such organisations in most African countries were women. In Uganda, it was widely acknowledged that no other societal group was as organised and cohesive as women's organisations when it came to making a concerted effort to influence the constitution-writing process. Women's organisations wrote more memoranda submitted to the Constitutional Commission than any other sector of society (Bainomugisha 1999: 93).

The number of women's networks, coalitions and ad hoc issue-oriented alliances was multiplying throughout Africa, also suggesting a strengthening of the non-governmental sector. Given the weakness of existing political parties, women's NGO coalitions and networks represented a more stable coalescing of interests. In a country like Uganda, coalitions of NGOs formed in the 1990s around national debt, domestic violence, the common property clause within the Land Act, the domestic relations bill and to change the way in which women politicians were elected through an electoral college that was susceptible to manipulation. Also more ad hoc and short-term coalitions formed around particular incidents. Such coalitions formed, for example, when a male member of parliament almost slapped a female member of parliament. They formed to abolish the customary practice in which the Buganda king was to have had sexual relations with a virgin prior to his wedding ceremony in 1998; to protest the Italian court's ruling in 1999 that a woman wearing jeans could not be raped; and to protest racist statements of a top US Agency for Development officer in 2001.

### Building cross-cutting ties

A related characteristic of women's mobilisation that set it apart from other forms of mobilisation was the keen interest in building ties across ethnic, clan and religious lines, especially where relations in the broader society had been conflictual. As women's organisations were trying to influence opinion, practice and policy affecting over half of society, the movements generally sought to be as broad as possible and saw their goal as influencing society at large. Unlike other movements, women who identified with aspects of the women's movement could be found in government, in the media, in trade unions, in environmental and human rights groups, in their own organisations, in grassroots organisations and throughout society. In other words, the movement permeated society in a way that other societal interests did not. Even environmental and human rights activists hardly claimed the kind of popular support the women's movements enjoyed in many countries. Other societal organisations were focused around catering to the interests of their particular constituencies such as labour, cooperatives, vendors and therefore did not aspire to build a popular base.

For example, in South Africa, no other group united as broad a spectrum of individuals as the Women's National Coalition (WNC), which was formed in 1991. It brought together eighty-one organisational affiliates and thirteen regional alliances of women's organisations, including organisations affiliated with the African National Congress, the Inkatha Freedom Party, the National Party, Pan Africanist Congress, Azanian Peoples Organization and the Democratic Party. WNC also brought together interests as diverse as the Rural Women's Movement, Union of Jewish Women and the South African Domestic Workers Union. Over three million women participated in focus groups organised by WNC to voice their opinions on women's concerns. Regional and national conferences were held and a Woman's Charter was drafted and endorsed by the national parliament and all nine regional parliaments in 1994. The Charter addressed a broad range of concerns, including equality, legal rights, economic issues, education, health, politics and violence against women (Kemp *et al.* 1995: 151). The new constitution allows for the Charter to be used as a basis for reforming government policy regarding gender concerns.

The inclusiveness could be found along many dimensions. Women's organisations, unlike most civil society actors (with some important exceptions like hometown and development associations), were usually also very concerned with how to build rural–urban linkages and bridge some of the gaps that divided better educated women involved in national organisations from rural women in local groups.

Due to the limited resources of NGOs and the monetary weakness of their constituent base, they relied heavily on donors to fund their activities. This has resulted in what some might call the 'NGO-isation' of feminism, which refers to the evolution of a feminist movement of professionals that since the 1995 UN Beijing conference has come to rely heavily on urban educated women. In the Latin American context these professionals were divorced from grassroots women's organisations (Alvarez 1998: 306–8). NGOs were important to the women's movements in Africa and were very much a part of them, but they were not the only arena of women's mobilisation. There did not exist in Africa the same kind of rift between women's NGOs and the 'movement.'

Although there were gaps between the rural and urban groups and between educated and poorer women's organisations, the aim was always explicitly to bridge those gaps and cooperate as much as resources and time permitted. It was not just national organisations that sought these linkages. In Uganda, even educated women in rural towns sought to share their income-generating skills and know-how regarding nutrition, child-rearing, prenatal care and preventative health measures with poorer rural women. Others encouraged rural women to get into business or to save money. For example, A Stitch in Time Women's Association was formed in Kabale in 1989 for women involved in tailoring, crocheting and making carpets. But it also had as an objective to help poorer less educated women's groups get involved in income-generating activities and savings clubs with the understanding that women's economic clout was a key to their empowerment. I found many such examples of rural–urban linkages in my study of the political impact of women's associations in Uganda 1992–2000 (Tripp 2000).

## Making the political personal

One of the reasons women have prioritised political action has to do with the indignities and difficulties they face on the domestic front. Unlike other sectors of society, there is no way to address women's advancement in the public realm without also tackling their obstacles on the domestic front and vice versa. In African movements, women have not only made the personal political, but they have also sought political power and influence in order to make the political personal (Geiger 1998). The battle in the two spheres is inseparable. For example, in the 2001 Ugandan presidential elections, women's organisations, including the Uganda Women's Network (UWONET), made appeals to the Electoral Commission and the media to warn against intimidation and harassment by husbands of wives over differing political opinions. In the 1996 elections there were numerous reports of women killed, beaten, thrown out of homes and some had their voters' cards grabbed from them or destroyed as a result of these differing views. As a result of official and media warnings, there were no reported incidents of politically related domestic violence in the 2001 elections.

### *Motherhood as a basis of political authority*

The public and private spheres are connected in other ways as well. Women have different resources from men with which to fight for change in the context of political movements. Due to the historically cultural separation between women's and men's mobilisation, women have often used their position as 'mothers' as a basis of moral authority from which to argue for their inclusion in politics. They have used it as a resource with which to demand political changes not only in practice, but also in political culture, demanding that the values of nurturing, caring and justice be included in political practice and that corruption be rejected. As Winnie Byanyima, Ugandan Member of Parliament and leader of the women's rights group Forum for Women in Development, explained in a reference to 'eating' (a metaphor with multiple meanings but often connoting personal appropriation of state resources):

> Values which we women care about such as caring, serving, building, reconciling, healing and sheer decency are becoming absent from our political culture. This eating is crude, self-centered, egoistic, shallow, narrow and ignorant. We should ban eating from our political language. Madam Chairman . . . it is a culture which we must denounce and do away with if we are to start a new nation. (Proceedings of the Constituent Assembly 1994: 1490)

The use of motherhood is not the only basis for women's authority, nor is it the only resource used by women, but neither is it considered controversial nor problematic in the way that it is regarded by many western feminist academics and activists. Judith Van Allen (2000) has shown that the public/private divide in Tswana society, but even more generally in Africa, does not correspond to western perceptions, which draw a sharp divide between domestic/household/child-rearing activities and work/politics/warfare. In Africa, women's labor, whether it is in the fields, in a factory or as a professional is generally seen as an extension of her reproductive activities, as part of caring for her children, and feeding and clothing them. In politics, as in other 'public spaces', women generally want equality but they do not aspire to be considered in the same way as men. As Van Allen explains:

> Women's rights discourse itself reflects the continuing construction of 'woman' as 'mother,' and the assertion of the nurturing, provisioning, suckling mother as a model of female leadership, both in its goals and in its language . . . In campaign slogans and campaign discourse in general, this assumption is carried into a positive statement about women: they are better fitted than men to be in government because it is in their 'nature' to be caretakers. (2000: 8)

One women's rights organization, Emang Basadi, even has had as its slogan: 'Vote a Woman! Suckle the Nation!' Women sometimes draw on their domestic experiences to create a new kind of political imagery that defies the paternal one that evolved with the colonial state and has remained in the post-colonial context. For example, in Kenya during the 1992 elections, one delegate argued at a meeting of the National Committee on the Status of Women that since women carry the responsibility for the security and stability of the family and community, 'let it be under-stood that women are already minister of culture in their own homes' and now they want to take charge of key portfolios (International Press Service online 1992).

Alexandra Tibbetts (1994) shows how elderly rural mothers of pro-democracy political prisoners in Kenya drew on their position of being mothers in 1992 to claim a public political identity in protesting the imprisonment of their sons, who had been incarcerated since October 1990 for demanding multi-partyism and who were still imprisoned long after multi-partyism had been adopted in December 1991. The moral authority of older mothers made their protest a particularly powerful one in demanding justice, especially when they stripped themselves naked in a confrontation with police, who were trying to end their hunger strike in Uhuru Park in the center of Nairobi. They drew on the prevalent cultural imagery and symbolism to give added potency to their protest, drawing attention to the maternal body, which in Kenyan society is a symbol of the life-generating potential of women. In the Kenyan context, and also more generally in Africa, the public nakedness of women, especially older women, is the ultimate curse, in this particular case, aimed at the govern-ment. The women, who had never been involved in politics, launched their protest in February 1992. As one of the women, Gladys Thiitu wa Kariuki, put it: 'The pain of bearing a child does not allow me to let my son continue suffering in prison.' Not only did the women speak bravely against the injustices of the government, but hundreds of Kenyans came to where the women were staging their hunger strike and set up micro-phones for anyone who wished to speak.

Although the maternal symbolism is still powerful, Van Allen argues that in Botswana and other parts of Africa, there is a gradual shift taking place as a result of the expansion of market forces from the system of authority based on kinship to a gender-based system as in the West. In other words, people had been relating to each other primarily in the context of the kin categories such as 'father', 'mother', 'son' and 'daugh-ter.' Increasingly, however, they are adopting a gender system based on the categories, male and female, in which social relations are not defined by custom but are being negotiated within the context of changing urban capitalist societies (Van Allen 2000).

## Debates within women's movements

Given the pluralism seen in types of organisations found in African women's movements and given the inclusiveness of their memberships, it comes as no surprise that women's movements encompass a plurality of views regarding how women's interests should best be conceived, prioritised and pursued. The debates have varied depending on the country and organisation. I will highlight a few issues that have been evident in multiple contexts.

In some countries, there were debates over the utility of reserved seats and quotas for women in legislatures (e.g. Cameroon, Tanzania, Nigeria, Kenya) and how women occupying those seats should be selected (Uganda) (Koda and Shayo 1994: 11; Killian 2000). Others have disagreed over which women's interests should be prioritised. The South African Commission on Gender Equality, formed in 1996, found itself by 2000 embroiled in internal conflicts over how feminist concerns ought to be raised in the context of addressing racial and economic inequalities. Some wanted to privilege the interests of poor rural women, for whom issues like child support, job creation and access to water were paramount. Others, mindful of their urban educated feminist constituency, thought that the commission should be a site for 'theoretically informed feminist challenges to gender hierarchy' and should not shy away from taking up important yet controversial issues (Seidman 2001: 18).

There have been debates over the utility of women's ministries in ensuring the adoption of feminist demands in government (South Africa) given that so many ministries were underfunded, understaffed and focused on women's domestic roles (Seidman 1999). Others have debated the utility of working within political parties, given their weakness and lack of interest in women's concerns. In some movements, there were debates over how to regard sex workers and whether to incorporate their demands into the women's movement. The spread of AIDS made these debates all the more contentious. Some have discussed the extent to which NGOs should be primarily accountable to the people they work with or to donors (Tsikata 1995: 11). Poor and educated professional women have differed over the need to tax women, the latter seeing tax payment as an obligation of equal citizenship, while poorer women resent the additional burden. Women's right to land inheritance has also divided women. For some, their loyalties lay with their clan and the customary patrilineal practice in which properties of the deceased husband are claimed by his kin. Others see the right to own and inherit property as one that needs to be extended to women.

The expansion of educational opportunities since independence meant that there was a larger pool of university educated professional women in the new organisations. It was not uncommon to find tensions between the new professional women and the women in the women's wing of the ruling party, who tended to be less educated. Professional women often felt that the ruling party women did little to advance women's equality, while the leaders of the party organisations feared competition posed by the NGOs run by professional women, which manifested itself in conflicts over access to donor funds as well as other issues. Even among the professional women, there appeared to be emerging differences between an older generation of activists and the younger more radical activists who, while mindful and respectful of the older activists, would have liked to see a faster pace of change in the new organisations and were not afraid to embrace issues that had been virtually taboo among the older generations such as abortion and lesbian rights. All these debates nevertheless fell along many lines based on levels of education, class, generation and urban vs. rural residence. Many of the debates reflected the transitions societies were undergoing with respect to gender relations.

## Conclusion

The most important change that occurred in the late 1980s and 1990s was the creation of autonomous organisations that began to challenge the stranglehold clientelism and state patronage had on women's mobilisation in the post-independence period. The new autonomy allowed women to create organisations and forge alliances across ethnic, religious, clan, racial, rural–urban, generational and other divides. Associational autonomy made it possible for women's organisations to challenge corruption, injustice and their roots in clientelistic and patronage practices. It meant that they could freely select their own leaders, create their own agendas and pursue their own sources of funding. It helped women's organisations to expand their agendas from a focus on income-generating and welfare concerns to a more politicised agenda. It allowed women to broaden their demands to challenge the fundamental laws, structures, and practices that constrained them. Many for the first time took on issues like domestic violence, female genital cutting and rape that had been considered taboo in the past. Nevertheless, the cultural and political challenges are far from over, and associational autonomy is constantly under threat. The lack of civil and political liberties and the ever-present threat that political space will close in the semi-authoritarian African states pose serious constraints on women's movements. Yet, women are in movement in Africa and they have set in motion important and unprecedented societal transformations.

## Note

This chapter is a revised version of the article 'Women in movement: transformations in African political landscapes', published in *The International Feminist Journal of Politics* 5(2) October 2002: 233–255. The publisher gratefully acknowledges the co-operation of Taylor & Francis in granting permission to publish this revised version of the work.

# References

Abdullah, Hussaina. 1993. ' "Transition Politics" and the Challenge of Gender in Nigeria', *Review of African Political Economy* 56: 27–41.

Alvarez, Sonia. 1998. 'Latin American Feminisms "Go Global" ', in S. E. Alvarez, E. Dagnino and A. Escobar (eds) *Cultures of Politics/Politics of Cultures: Revisioning Latin American Social Movements*, pp. 293–324. Boulder, CO: Westview Press.

Bainomugisha, A. 1999. 'The Empowerment of Women', in J. Mugaju (ed.) *Uganda's Age of Reforms: A Critical Overview*, pp. 89–102. Kampala: Fountain Publishers.

Connell, Dan. 1998. 'Strategies for Change: Women and Politics in Eritrea and South Africa', *Review of African Political Economy* 25 (76): 189–206.

Dei, George J. S. 1994. 'The Women of a Ghanaian Village: A Study of Social Change', *African Studies Review* 37 (2): 121–45.

Feldman, Rayah. 1983. 'Women's Groups and Women's Subordination: An Analysis of Politics towards Rural Women in Kenya', *Review of African Political Economy* 27/8: 67–85.

Geiger, Susan. 1998. 'Exploring Feminist Epistemologies and Methodologies through the Life Histories of Tanzanian Women'. Presentation at the International Gender Studies Circle, University of Wisconsin-Madison, WI.

Geisler, Gisela. 1995. 'Troubled Sisterhood: Women and Politics in Southern Africa', *African Affairs* 94 (377): 545–78.

Kabira, Wanijiku Mukabi and Elizabeth Akinyii Nzioki. 1993. *Celebrating Women's Resistance*. Nairobi: African Women's Perspective.

Kante, M. and H. Hobgood. 1994. *Governance in Democratic Mali: An Assessment of Transition and Consolidation and Guidelines for Near-term Action.* Washington, DC: Associates in Rural Development.

Kemp, Amanda, Nozizwe Madlala, Asha Moodley and Elaine Salo. 1995. 'The Dawn of a New Day: Redefining South African Feminism', in Amrita Basu (ed.) *Challenge of Local Feminisms*, pp. 131–62. Boulder, CO: Westview Press.

Killian, Bernadetta. 2000. 'A Policy of Parliamentary "Special Seats" for Women in Tanzania: Its Effectiveness', *Ufahamu* 24 (1–2): 21–31.

Koda, Bertha and Rose Shayo. 1994. *Women and Politics in Tanzania: Empowerment of Women in the Process of Democratisation – Experiences of Kenya, Uganda and Tanzania*. Dar es Salaam: Friedrich Ebert Stiftung, pp. 5–23.

Mama, Amina. 1995. 'Feminism or Femocracy? State Feminism and Democratisation in Nigeria', *Africa Development* 20 (1): 37–58.

Mbire-Barungi, Barbara. 1999. 'Ugandan Feminism: Political Rhetoric or Reality?', *Women's Studies Forum International* 22 (4): 435–9.

Mikell, Gwendolyn. 1984. 'Filiation, Economic Crisis and the Status of Women in Rural Ghana', *Canadian Journal of African Studies* 18 (1): 195–218.

Mwaniki, Nyaga. 1986. 'Against Many Odds: The Dilemmas of Women's Self-help Groups in Mbeere, Kenya', *Africa* 56 (2): 210–28.

Ngugi, Mumbi. c. 2001. 'The Women's Rights Movement and Democratization in

Kenya: A Preliminary Inquiry into the Green Formations of Civil Society', series on Alternative Research in East Africa (SAREAT), Nairobi. Unpublished paper.

Nzegwu, Nkiru. 1995. 'Recovering Igbo Traditions: A Case for Indigenous Women's Organisations', in M. Nussbaum and J. Glover (eds) *Women, Culture and Development: A Study of Human Capabilities*, pp. 444–65. Oxford: Clarendon Press.

Obiorah, Ndubisi. 2001. 'To the Barricades or the Soapbox: Civil Society and Democratization in Nigeria'. Paper presented at Berkeley–Stanford Joint Center for African Studies conference, Stanford University, Palo Alto, CA.

Office of the Vice President, Steering Committee for NGO Policy Formulation (Tanzania). 1997. *The National Policy on Non-governmental Organisations in Tanzania*. Dar es Salaam: Office of the Vice President.

Ojiambo Ochieng, Ruth. 1998. 'Information Services: Tools for Politicians and Policy Makers', *Impact* 1 (1): 33.

Olojede, Iyabo. 1999. *Women Interest Organisations: Encounters with the State on Issues of Good Governance*. Kano, Nigeria: Centre for Research and Documentation.

Owiti, Jeremiah. 2000. 'Political Aid and the Making and Re-making of Civil Society', Civil Society and Governance Programme, Ford Foundation Project, Institute of Development Studies, University of Sussex, Brighton.

Peter, Chris Maina. 1999. 'The State and Independent Civil Organisations: The Case of Tanzania Women Council (BAWATA)', Civil Society and Governance in East Africa Project (Tanzania side), Ford Foundation Project.

Proceedings of the Constituent Assembly (Uganda). 1994. *Official Report* 3 August: 1490.

Rweyemamu, Robert. 1997. 'The Women Who Scared the Men of Power', *East African*. Nairobi, 11 June.

Sahle, Eunice Njeri. 1998. 'Women and Political Participation in Kenya: Evaluating the Interplay of Gender, Ethnicity, Class and State', in J. M. Mbaku and J. O. Ihonvebere (eds) *Multiparty Democracy and Political Change: Constraints to Democratization in Africa*, pp. 171–93. Brookfield (USA), Singapore and Sydney: Ashgate.

Seidman, Gay W. 1999. 'Gendered Citizenship: South Africa's Democratic Transition and the Construction of a Gendered State', *Gender and Society* 13 (3): 287–307.

Seidman, Gay W. 2001. *Institutional Dilemmas: Representation versus Mobilization in the South African Gender Commission*. Madison, WI: University of Wisconsin-Madison.

Strobel, Margaret. 1979. *Muslim Women in Mombasa, 1890–1975*. New Haven, CT: Yale University Press.

Tibbetts, Alexandra. 1994. 'Mamas Fighting for Freedom in Kenya', *Africa Today* 41 (4): 27–48.

Tripp, Aili Mari. 2000. *Women and Politics in Uganda*. Wisconsin: University of Wisconsin Press, James Currey & Fountain Press.

Tsikata, Dzodzi. 1995. 'NGO Forum Showed Growth, Strength', *African Agenda* 1 (7): 10–12.

Tsikata, Edzodzinam. 1989. 'Women's Political Organisations 1951–1987', in E. Hanson and K. Ninsin (eds) *The State, Development and Politics in Ghana*, pp. 73–93. London: Codesria.

United Nations International Research and Training Institute for the Advancement of Women. http://www.un-instraw.org/en/index.php, accessed 27 May, 2007.

Van Allen, Judith. 2000. 'Must a Woman (Politician) Be More Like a Man? Constructing Female Political Power and Agency in Botswana.' Paper presented to the 43rd Annual Meeting of the African Studies Association, Nashville, Tennessee.

Wipper, Audrey. 1975. 'The Maendeleo ya Wanawake Movement: Some Paradoxes and Contradictions', *African Studies Review* 18 (3): 99–120.

Zziwa, Hassan Badru. 1996. 'Women Soccer Should be Supported', *Monitor*. Kampala, 29 April: 15.

# 12

# European Central Bank, monetary policy and the 'social Europe'

*Brigitte Young*

## A dilemma: the European Economic and Monetary Union and the defence of the 'social Europe'

In response to the Danish referendum on 28 September 2000 to join the European Economic and Monetary Union (EMU), the German daily newspaper, *Frankfurter Rundschau*, (2000a: 2) signalled with the headline 'Courting the sceptical women' that all was not well with the EMU. That the majority of Danish voters declined to join the EMU with a margin of 53 to 46 per cent is largely the result of the scepticism of Danish women. One of the many opinion polls two days before the referendum suggested that the support for the EMU among men was 51 per cent in comparison to only 30 per cent of women. Many women worry about the danger to the social welfare state, as the Danish political scientist, Anette Borchorst, describes the uneasiness women feel toward joining the EMU. More women than men see the European Union (EU) and the introduction of the Euro as a threat to the universal social system. It is feared that the impending drive toward European tax harmonisation would replace the tax-financed social system with the more common European insurance-financed social system. European tax harmonisation, according to Drude Dahlerup, speaker of the anti-European 'June Movement', would imply a redistribution away from the universal welfare system and the loss of women's employment opportunities.[1] Thus the fear of losing jobs and 'people's pension' is the driving force behind the scepticism of many Danish women about joining the EMU.

It is thus not surprising that Sweden confronting an equally EU-sceptical fraction of women voters is taking the female 'exit' threat serious. Sweden for the first time since joining the EU chaired the presidency in January 2001. A country notoriously sceptical about the idea of European integration, it has also refused to join the EMU. This was all the more interesting, since Sweden, holding the EU presidency in the first six months of 2001, had an important role in the preparations for the intro-duction of the Euro in January 2002.[2] Realising the high stakes in terms of its domestic and foreign reputation, Sweden went on the offensive and presented a clear outline of the goals it wanted to pursue during its first presidency.[3] Prime Minister Persson announced that the symbol 'e' marks Sweden's presidency. 'E' not only for Europe, but also for 'enlargement', 'environment' and 'employment'. Sweden wanted to build on its successful domestic strategy in the labour market and emphasise 'education' and 'equality' to improve the European employment situation (*Frankfurter Rundschau* 2000b: 6). Sweden thus became the first country presiding over the EU to stress specifically equality between women and men as a goal to pursue while at the helm of the Presidency.

Nordic scepticism among the female population and their power to use the 'exit' option seems to bear fruit. If Sweden and Denmark want to join the EMU, a goal Prime Minister Göran Persson strongly pursues for his country, then both Sweden and Denmark have first to overcome the scepticism of many of their women voters. Sweden courts its women with the promise not to sacrifice the existing achievement in gender equality and is ready to confront the other fourteen members of the European Union with a solidaristic gender regime that is unique to Sweden. In the same vein, the Danish Minister of the Interior, Karen Jesperson, appeals to the sceptical female voters that only by joining the EMU are the conditions for a stable welfare system guaranteed. A 'no-vote' could lead to isolation and endanger the Danish economy. Another strategy of the Danish 'yes-faction' is to shift the debate to issues of human rights and culture away from economic issues such as the convergence criteria agreed upon in the Maastricht Treaty to usher in the European Monetary Union, and foreign exchange rates (*Frankfurter Rundschau* 2000a: 2).

What makes this 'puzzle' of Nordic recalcitrance so interesting is that for the first time a large section of women voters hold the key to joining the EMU. The question I want to pursue in this paper is whether the discrepancy between the present construction of the EMU with its aim to maintain rigid price stability and the Nordic promise to preserve the present level of social programmes can be reconciled.[4] This chapter differs from many other feminist approaches to the EMU and equal opportunity policy in that it combines a constructivist understanding of the EMU with feminist political economy. There is an extensive literature on the equal opportunity policies in the EU and their impact on women in member states (Ostner and Lewis 1995; Hoskyns 1996; Rubery 1998; Walby 1999; Young 2000). Much of the published works interpret European employment and equal opportunity policies within a narrow policy focus. Only a few feminist scholars situate employment policies within the larger context of economic globalisation with its emphasis on deregulation and political disengagement from the economy.

Instead of a policy approach, the intent of this chapter is to focus on the macroeconomic environment of the EU and analyse the effects of the institutionalisation of the EMU on reconstituting a new 'ordering rationality' (Rosamond 1999: 658) that regulates and constrains actors' behaviour and limits policy options. Most economic accounts have privileged a rational choice or neo-institutional account of the EMU. Much less attention has been paid to the interest- and identity-forming roles of institutions. This chapter stresses the active role of institutions in creating systems of beliefs and norms (Christiansen *et al.* 1999; Checkel 1999). A constructivist approach is particularly well suited to pursue the question how the European Monetary Union is involved in constructing identities and interests of member states and groups within them (Checkel 1999; Rosamond 1999).

The first part of the chapter gives a short overview of the present debate on EU gender and equal opportunity policies. It concludes that the present policy studies are too narrow in focus and suggests that the macroeconomic environment of the EMU is essential to understanding both the limits and opportunities of labour market policies for women. However, the argument does not stop here as it goes on to interpret the EU as a strategic site of centrality in the global economy. Investigating the discursive construction of globalisation and European integration, it will argue that the EMU constitutes a new governance framework to make member state governments more responsive to the discipline of market forces and correspondingly less responsive to social democratic forces and gender-friendly processes. Next, we focus on the 'content' of the new disciplinary governance framework by highlighting the effects of the EMU's monetary policy on the creation of new norms and systems of beliefs that are much more commensurate with neo-liberal practice and discourse. Essentially the question will be asked what interests are legitimized by the EMU's unilateral focus on price stability. We then return to the question of gender and equal employment politics. Utilising the tools from feminist economics, three forms of bias are discussed that need to be avoided if macroeconomic policies are to promote equal opportunities for women and men in the European Union. Failing to consider the social content of macroeconomic policy will make it difficult, if not impossible, to live up to the promise the Danish and Swedish pro-EMU factions have made to their female constituency to maintain the Nordic model.

## EU employment policies and gender politics

Much of the feminist analysis on EU employment and equal opportunity policies has paid little attention to the EMU and its institutional effects on social construction. Scholars have mainly stayed within the confines of particular policy studies. As a result, we have scholars who focus on EU labour market policies (Cook 1998; Walby 1999) and others who study the welfare state (Ostner and Lewis 1995; Elman 1996; Hoskyns 1996; Rossilli 1997). Only some feminist economists have taken the macroeconomic environment and macroeconomic policy framework into account that provide the context in which the policy programmes are implemented (Rubery, Smith, Fagan and Grimshaw 1998). As a result, the dominance of the Maastricht convergence and stability criteria over issues that deal with employment targets and the resulting supply-side-oriented measures contained in the employment guidelines are largely disregarded in policy studies.

The Maastricht criteria (signed 1992) were established for individual member countries to enter into the European Economic and Monetary Union by 1999 at the latest. Qualifying countries had to meet the following criteria:

1  General government deficits to be no more than 3% of GDP
2  Gross Public Sector Debt to be no more than 60% of GDP
3  Long term interest rates to be no more than 2% higher than the average of the three member states with the lowest inflation
4  Inflation to be no more than 1.5% higher than that of the average of the three member states with lowest inflation. (Teague 1998: 119)

Fearing a 'soft' Euro currency, Germany insisted on the additional 'Stability and Growth Pacts' signed at the 1996 Dublin summit. The intent of the Stability Pact is to secure fiscal prudence in a future Euro-zone by levying automatic penalties against members running excessive deficits. Governments with budget deficits greater than 3 per cent of GDP will be immediately fined.[5] As a result of the Maastricht Criteria and the Stability Pact, the European Economic and Monetary Union has largely removed the scope for flexibility. In particular, countries experiencing a recession cannot run higher budget deficits in order to stimulate the economy. Insisting on the 2 per cent upper limit for inflation, countries are thereby locked into restrictive fiscal policies regardless of the capabilities and needs of member countries. In order words, the pact removes the capacity to pursue an independent counter-cyclical fiscal strategy in case of an economic downturn in economic activity (Soskice 1999). The European Central Bank (ECB) is only charged to guarantee price stability and not to ensure employment and foster economic growth (Huffschmid 2001).

The Amsterdam Treaty, signed in 1997 and amending the EC and EU Treaties, did subsequently include provisions for a coordinated approach to employment policy. While the Maastricht Treaty committed member states to follow agreed economic guidelines, this new Treaty places obligations on every member state also to consider and act on the issue of employment in line with agreed common guidelines, although the commitments are looser and less tied to quantitative targets than the macroeconomic guidelines (Rubery 1998). In other words, the EU policy-making has been strengthened in the field of employment. Nevertheless, the Maastricht Treaty continues to stress that:

> The primary objective of the ESCB shall be to maintain price stability. Without prejudice to the objective of the price stability, the ESCB shall support the general economic policies in the Community with a view to contributing to the achievement of the objectives of the Community as laid down in Article 2. (Maastricht Treaty 2000: Art. 105, Par. 1)

Many scholars thus conclude that the monetary decision-makers establish policy on the premise that monetary decisions have no influence on economic growth and employment policies (Huffschmid 2001).

Feminists have derived a more positive picture from the Amsterdam Treaty and conclude that with the Treaty the EU entered a new phase of European employment policy characterised by a growing recognition of the importance of gender issues. However, feminists disagree about the impact of the EU equal opportunities directives on women in member states. Scholars that work in the tradition of welfare policy overwhelmingly conclude that the EU equal opportunity policies have a mostly limited impact, or are ambivalent at best to their effect on women (Ostner and Lewis 1995). In contrast, Sylvia Walby (1999; 1997) presents the strongest defence of equal opportunity laws and argues that the EU has made significant changes to the governance of gender relations.

In this argument between European welfare specialists and labour market analysts, we face two different policy focuses. They draw on different political theories in regard to citizenship rights, and concepts of national sovereignty and the normativity that comes with it. In short, feminist welfare specialists are associated with social democracy and corporatism, while the issue of equal opportunities is situated within a liberal framework.

> Welfare has tended to make demands on the state, offer collective solutions to dilemmas, and be dependent upon taxation. Equal opportunities needs a more minimal type of regulatory state, ostensibly offers a more individualistic solution, and does not require taxation. (Walby 1999: 60)

Welfare policy analysts argue further that member states are an obstacle to the implementation of supranational regulation. In contrast, Walby focuses on the power of European law and suggests that many feminists have underestimated the power of European law to override national social regulation. The argument between welfare policy specialists and labour market analysts has provided important insights into different gender perspectives and approaches.

If we include a political economy approach, the focus shifts to the impact of the global macroeconomic environment that constrains both welfare and labour market policies. From this perspective, the Maastricht Agreements and EMU represent a dramatic shift towards a disciplinary neoliberal discourse of capitalism to produce the conditions for global economic production (Gill 1998; Young 2000). The implications of all of this for a social and gender-friendly Europe as the Danes and the Swedes seem to promise their female constituency are at best contradictory. At worst, the promises are quite unrealistic. The deflationary macroeconomic environment resulting from the Maastricht criteria is counter-posed to the social and employment guidelines enacted by the EU. Adopting the Maastricht guidelines has led to economic retrenchment in all member states, which has involved cutting, or at best stabilising, welfare and social expenditures (Teague 1998). Given the supply-side measures contained in the employment policies, it is difficult to see how effective the EU will be in creating higher rates of employment and thus fulfil the equal opportunity promises. Yet the equal opportunity employment agenda rests on the promotion of women's employment. The EU Commission has forgone, and even implicitly denied, any demand-side intervention in the economy. Instead, at the centre of the approach is a focus on the supply side. Improving the skills of the potential workers and facilitating easier access to the job market by providing childcare facilities is believed to promote the employment of women (Rubery 1998).

But here we confront a *Catch-22* situation. Women are entering the labour market in increasing numbers and the EU, rhetorically at least, encourages such a move particularly in the light of the Danish and Swedish recalcitrance to join the EMU. At the same time, the EMU creates the environment for a demand-constrained employment scenario. As Rubery (1998) has pointed out, these developments contribute to the problem of job shortage. To promote the employment of women in the absence of an active job-creating policy and in the context of a restrictive fiscal environment seems like trying to square a circle. Neither the employment guidelines nor the Joint Employment Report even mention the public sector as a vital promoter of women's employment and facilitator for labour-market integration and yet it is difficult to see how, in the absence of the revival of the public sector, the private sector can generate the required job growth to absorb the increased labour supply. The strict monetary goals of the EMU and fiscal targets circumscribe the policies that are needed to promote the EU's equal opportunity objectives. In other words, the neo-liberal macroeconomic environment shuts the door to a public sector employment strategy that, in fact, is the key to the Nordic equal employment model (Theobald 1999).

Concluding that the introduction of the EMU is commensurate with a new neo-liberal governance framework tells us little about the forces that drive these processes. The next section will thus place the EMU in the context of the political economy of globalisation.

## The EU as a strategic site of globalisation

The meaning of globalisation is central to the argument pursued in this chapter. We want to find out to what extent a particular discourse of economic globalisation serves to shape the European integration process, and how in turn the discursive practices influence the creation of new norms, values and practices within the EU. In other words, does a particular discursive construction of globalisation set the boundaries for the politically feasible within the EU? Which political strategies are thereby excluded, and which new opportunities are made possible? Political feasibility is understood not just as a question of objective and exogenous structures of the global economy. Political ability to act is a social construction, which is repeatedly redefined and constituted through a particular rhetoric of globalisation. Defining globalisation as a 'discourse of power' (Gill 1998) suggests that the present privileging of a particular reading of globalisation is, as Hay and Watson (1998) have pointed out, only tangentially related to the realities of the global economy. Although a particular neo-liberal version of globalisation has become hegemonic, this does not mean that alternative discourses do not exist that challenge the dominant assertions. The large demonstrations starting at the Ministerial Meeting of the World Trade Organisation (WTO) in Seattle in late 1999 and in Washington, DC, in the spring of 2000, continuing right up to the G-7/G-8 summit in Genoa in 2001 and in Brussels at the EU meeting in December 2001, have shown that many oppositional narratives to globalisation exist (Gill 2000).

In defining globalisation as a 'discourse of power', a particular reading of the materialist constructivist approach is suggested that maintains that there is an inherent connection between the social construction of the external environment and the interests that actors acquire (Wendt 1992; Ruggie 1998; Checkel 1999; Rosamond 1999). Unlike methodological individualism with its emphasis on rational actors that push the European integration process forward (Sandholtz and Zysman 1989),[6] constructivists focus on the complex effects of institutionalisation in shaping both the actors' expectations and in generating shared beliefs and norms within a policy context. In most economic analyses of the EMU, the role of institutions creating systems of beliefs and conventions play virtually no role (Checkel 1999; Christiansen *et al.* 1999). Realists assume that actors' interests are given. They arrive at this conclusion, because they assume a radical separation between subject and object (Kratochwil and Ruggie 1986). According to this logic, only objective forces have the power to influence the behaviour of actors. Constructivists on the other hand, attempt to dissolve the dualism between structure and agency. 'Agents' interests are not structured by their environment. They help to make their environment and their environment helps to make them' (Rosamond 1999: 659). Introducing an intersubjective meaning into the study of institutions opens a much needed space to raise questions about the origin and reconstruction of identities, the impact of institutional rules and norms and of political discourses. In other words, constructivists suggest that not only interests but also identities are important in explaining political processes (Christiansen *et al.* 1999).

If we apply this insight of a norm-creating process to the establishment of Economic and Monetary Union, then we can argue that the EMU is more than an economic project. The introduction of the Euro as a new European denomination has helped to create a world according to a particular neo-liberal logic which then shapes actors' behaviour according to this logic. Starting with the Maastricht convergence criteria and the Stability Pact, we can argue that these organisational structures have supplied a new ordering rationality that have subsequently defined the structural boundaries both in terms of its limits and opportunities in which actors can operate. One of the most powerful insights that constructivists provide is the inseparability between (economic) structures and the social construction of norms. According to this interpretation, the EMU is thus not only an important new institution that sets monetary policy for all member states. More importantly, the EMU and the introduction of the Euro helps to constitute a new European identity. That money is involved in constructing national identities is not exactly a new insight. Already Karl Marx had noted the close relationship between money and national identity. 'Money as money' functions not only as standard of value, as means of circulation and of payment, and as credit. Historically, money always had an identity-creating and a legitimating function in the development of the modern nation-states. 'Money thereby directly and simultaneously becomes the real community, since it is the general substance of survival for all, and at the same time the social product of all' (Marx 1996: 232). The introduction of the Euro as an identity creating entity is no exception. Thus the European Economic and Monetary Union can be seen as one, if not the central, constitutive moment of a common European identity.

## The new rules and norms of the EMU governance framework

If we conclude that Sweden and Denmark cannot reconcile the promise to maintain the present level of the universal welfare system and join the EMU, then we need to ask the role EMU plays in constructing new norms and conventions that effectively rule out a Keynesian-type demand management in the member states. In answering this question, it seems that the role of money and the definition of money in the neo-liberal orthodoxy play a central role. The role of money is important because at the centre of a monetary union is the definition of money. As pointed out earlier, money is not just an abstract measuring device. Much more important is the interest- and identity-forming effect that money generates. In order to explicate the norm-creating function of money, it may be helpful to compare the effects money, more precisely monetary theory, has in Keynesian economics and also in neoclassical economics. The intent of this exercise is to show that the orthodox monetary theory espoused by the EMU is based on assumptions that create norms favouring the interests of finance capitalism and contradict the Keynesian assumptions of a full employment economy.

According to classical theory, money does not enter into the 'real' economy. Neo-liberals have revived the classical orthodoxy about the neutrality of money (Hein 2000), which assumes that money supply and the rate of interest on money have no influence on the real factors of the economy (such as employment, production, and economic growth). Money only has an effect on the level of prices. It was John Maynard Keynes in *The General Theory of Employment, Interest, and Money* (1997) who challenged the classical assumptions of money as something separate from the general theory of supply and demand. According to Keynes, monetary and financial policies determine changes in the scale of output and employment as a whole. It is this conflict about the neutrality of money on the one side, and the influence of money on real economic variables on the other, which is at the centre of the normative construction of the neo-liberal globalisation discourses. Despite the existence of a large amount of quantitative econometric studies to justify one side or the other, it is not statistics that can resolve the puzzle. It is a question of the basic beliefs and theoretical foundations that underpin the two contrary positions (Flassbeck 1999).

More important than who is right and who is wrong in this historic struggle among economists about the role of money is the question about the effects of these two divergent monetary theories. Which shared norms, understandings and normative principles are mobilised and which ordering rationality is created that in turn shape interests and constrain the

behaviour of actors within the global economy? If we follow the fundamental assumptions of an expansive monetary theory, then money has a
double role in influencing the 'real' economy. First, the rate of interest on
the money influences the stability of wage income and economic growth
as was the case during the Fordist period after World War II. Here we have
a growth model that links real wage rates to productivity rates and to anti-
cyclical monetary and fiscal policy. The Keynesian welfare state had the
additional function to regulate demand and generalise norms of mass consumption and thereby contribute to full employment levels of demand. In
addition, the Bretton Woods monetary system and the GATT trade
regime meant that the circulation of free-floating international currencies
stabilised Keynesian economic management through state control over the
national money (Jessop 1994). In this Fordist model of managed economic growth, the level of interest rates played a major role in facilitating
full employment policies. Monetary institutions pursued a policy of
holding the real interest rate below the growth rate of the gross domestic
product (Hein 2000). A national distributional consensus was thus secured
through a corporatist male-dominated class compromise between capital
and labour. Not only did the Keynesian full employment model ensure a
certain level of economic stability, it also helped to foster an identity of
national citizenship within the redistributional model of European social
democracy.

In the present regime of a market-led global financial system or as
Giovanoli (2000) refers to it as a 'private international monetary system',
the geometry has been fundamentally altered. The drive toward deregulation and the creation of global financial markets has led to an increasing
competition on the exchange rate markets. To avoid capital flight, interest
rates are used to defend the national currency. In other words, the centre
of monetary policy pursued by central banks has shifted to securing assets
based on their own currency (Guttmann 2000b). With the transformation
of the credit system from commercial loans to securities as principal form
of credit, we also witness a change in monetary policy of the central banks
that favours the private commodity elements of money.

Increasingly, the social and the private dimensions of money are in
conflict with each other. Money as a social institution reveals itself as both
a public good and as a private commodity. It is a public good in that stable
valuation and smooth circulation is in the interest of all. It is a private
commodity inasmuch as it is created by private agents trying to gain
income from financial activities. If the private-commodity elements of
money become dominant, as is the case right now, the 'economic system
suffers from all the negative consequences of money's commodification
into a vehicle for bank profit – more pronounced cyclical fluctuations

punctuated by financial crises, greater price instability, and widening income-distribution gaps between rich and poor as the result of increasingly unequal access to money and credit' (Guttmann 2000a: 5). The bias towards private capital investors has shifted the emphasis in macroeconomic policy to price stability and the control against inflation (Soskice 1999).

In this exclusive emphasis on price stability, economic growth as a policy goal is not pursued by the ECB despite the risk of an economic slowdown and an incipient recession that started to confront Europe in the second half of 2001. The reasons are many: the rise of oil prices contributed to a reduction of domestic incomes as has the lack of productive investment that had a dampening effect on demand. Foreign trade was hit by a fall in exports since the end of 2000. The worldwide slowdown and the recession in the USA has weakened economic activity in all major parts of the global economy. Also, an inadequate increase in wages has weakened the growth of private consumption. As a result, unemployment has begun to rise again in many countries, particularly in Germany since the beginning of 2001 and France since the summer. Inequality of incomes and regional disparities which had remained high even prior to the recession, are again on the increase Huffschmid 2001). Despite these unfavourable economic data, Broad Economic Policy Guidelines for the Member States and the Community (BEPG) for 2001 has remained practically unchanged from those of previous years. In fact, the ECB raised its key interest rate six times in 2000 and hence contributed to a further decline in investment. Huffschmid (2001: 5) has pointed out 'it is hard to conceive of a less productive or more harmful policy-mix than to fetter national budgetary policies to the Stability and Growth Pact and at the same time impose an unnecessarily restrictive monetary policy'.

The paralysis of European economic policy is in sharp contrast to the strong response of the USA. Facing a cyclical downturn, the Federal Reserve Board lowered its interest rate ten times during 2001. The rapid loosening of monetary-policy in the US – despite a rate of inflation above 3 per cent – did little harm to the credibility of the Fed. The difference between the behaviour of the ECB and the Federal Reserve Board is this: the ECB punishes inflationary behaviour and fiscal looseness severely, and adopts virtually no stimulation in response to low inflation. The Fed is more even-handed, pushing up interest rates in response to inflationary signs, but bringing them down again as inflation subsides or as cyclical weaknesses appear (Soskice 1999). Unlike the ECB, the Fed has the double objective of keeping inflation low (without a maximum threshold being defined, as is the case in the EU) and preserving growth and full employment. In the ECB, there is no objective for growth or for employment. As a result, the small reductions of 0.25 per cent in interest rates in May and in August and of 0.5 per cent in September and November 2001 have come too late and have been too small to have any real impact on the economy (Huffschmid 2001).

If we compare the role of the Fed with the ECB after the shock of September 11, 2001, we witness, once again, the quick response of the Fed. It has responded with a large budgetary package in the order of 1.5 per cent of GNP, decreased interest rates and increased wages (Herr 2001). In contrast to this rapid reaction, the ECB only lowered euro interest rates by 0.5 per cent in September and November, and a small decrease in December. It did not – despite public demands from labour unions, social democratic and green parties, and small and medium firms – endorse a larger cut to counter the worldwide slowdown and the negative impacts Europe faced from the American recession.

The institutionalisation of restrictive monetary policy signals a fundamental shift in the theory of money in the Euro-zone from a belief in the power of money to influence economic variables to a belief in the neutrality of money in neo-liberal discourses. However, this shift in monetary policy is not restricted to monetary and economic variables. The particular discursive construction of globalisation in the EMU also supplied a new ordering rationality within the EU that helps to create a new world according to this rationality. Hans Tietmeyer, the former president of the German Bundesbank and one of the chief architects of the EMU expressed this new rationality very poignantly at the European University Institute in Florence in 1996:

> Therefore the fundamental truth holds: The members of the EMU will only have a chance to solve their problems if the Euro remains stable over the long run . . . Because financial markets judge countries. They do not only look at the actual data, they also try to estimate in as far as a country is able and prepared to solve its long-term problems . . . Financial markets can punish an expansive monetary policy and an undisciplined fiscal policy already at the start. They can disinvest capital from that country and charge a higher capital interest rate . . . The Monetary Union needs an implicit political 'quasi-union'. This means first the maintenance of a stability culture, and second the readiness of fiscal politics, if not to give up sovereignty, to regulate and set limits . . . The stability pact asks countries whether they are prepared to maintain the stability of the common currency at the expense of pursuing their own fiscal policies. (www.iue.it/ANN/tietspeechDE.html)

To invoke the power of neoclassical orthodoxy as the only reality for constructing the new EMU implies that the neo-liberal discourse of globalisation and the construction of the EMU are mutually constitutive processes. More importantly, the power of financial markets has been used, as Hay and Watson have pointed out, 'to act as an exogenous enforcement mechanism for domestic policies which aim to re-define existing notions of citizenship by limiting the state's role as guarantor of minimum social rights (Hay and Watson 1998: 8).

We can so far conclude that the Nordic promise to its female constituency to safeguard the present social and employment system cannot be sustained within the context of the restrictive monetary regime institutionalised by the EMU. The question now arises whether European citizens have to subordinate themselves to the dictates of the private commodity elements of money, or whether there is an alternative that would lead to a more gender-friendly Europe. This issue will be addressed in the next section.

### A feminist alternative: deconstructing macroeconomic assumptions

Feminist economists (Bakker 1994; 1999; Elson 1995; 2000; Elson and Cagatay 1999, 2000; Beneria 2000; Young 2001c) have called for a paradigmatic shift to 'engender the macro-economy' arguing that gender is a major factor in reconstituting the 'new geography of power' in a globalised economy. From the perspective of a gendered political economy, markets and states are viewed as institutions imbued with structural power relations that have asymmetrical class and gender dimensions. Markets are 'embedded' in social relations, and cooperation, reciprocity, trust, redistribution, care are vital to the functioning of any market economy. Missing from standard economic narratives are the 'non-market relations' which structure all markets and are important for the conditions under which people come to the market. As Isabella Bakker (1994: 4) reminds us, 'markets are as much political and cultural institutions as they are economic entities'. An engendered view of macroeconomics would not only include markets and states. It would also include social reproduction made up of non-monetised and non-market activities that provide the necessary conditions for production and exchange relations to take place.

As a first step in engendering macroeconomics, we need to *demystify* the economic rhetoric and ask whether the highly technical language in the Maastricht Treaty and in the Stabilisation Pact signed in Dublin in 1996 is not also a weapon to fight against an alternative vision of globalisation. Hans Tietmeyer and others may speak about the disciplinary effects of the market on nations. Yet we need to ask what 'prudent' monetary policy means? Who are the winners and losers from this finance-led globalisation, and how can globalisation and European integration benefit the many instead of the few? An emerging issue is the gender dimensions of international financial markets and feminist economists have started to articulate their ideas of how the global financial architecture has to be changed to provide alternative political spaces for inclusive class, gender and race relations.

Diane Elson and Nilufur Cagatay (2000) have in their recent work identified and critiqued three interlinked assumptions upon which macroeconomics rests:

1   *The first is the deflationary bias*: overemphasis on deflating the economy whenever the markets show any signs of rising inflation or whenever short-term capital is pulled out of mostly developing countries.
2   *The second bias is the commodification bias*: the bias that turns many public services into privatised commodities, to be sold to the public by newly privatised businesses, or to be delivered by a public sector operating on business principles and levying user fees for its services.
3   *The third is the male-breadwinner bias*: the assumption that women are dependent on males. Built on this bias are entire social service systems and tax systems that have created a 'two-channel welfare state' (Nelson 1990), carved out of a set of specific gender, race and class relationships. At an empirical level, the breadwinner model is breaking down in virtually all European countries. The important point is not its disappearance. Much more important is its continued reference system for economic theory. Virtually all economic theories to this date are based on the private/public dichotomy that is gender-based.

These three biases are mutually interlinked. For example, the commodification bias fuels the growth of financial institutions as pensions and health insurances are increasingly privatised; and the growth of financial institutions in search of high interest rates fuels the deflationary bias in monetary policy. In terms of the deflationary bias much has been said in the previous section on the negative distributional effects that are the result of the central banks' singular focus on price stability. Given that the EMU does not have an equivalent EU fiscal institution, the member states have to subordinate their fiscal policies, as Tietmeyer so clearly pointed out, to the restrictive monetary policy set by the EMU. In other words, the macroeconomic policies do not only have a negative distributional impact in that social expenditures either decline or at best are stabilised at the present level. They embody a profoundly unjust social content in that they favour the financial interests at the expense of the majority of its citizens. The development of a social welfare state was the major advance in social organisations in European development in the second half of the twentieth century. This welfare state has become increasingly under attack and it now faces some major challenges and pressures. Women, older people, ethnic minorities and children are particularly hard hit by the increasing privatisations of social policies. It is this scenario of growing inequalities and disparities, and endangering both employment opportunities and social services, that has made Swedish and Danish women so sceptical about joining the EMU.

Intertwined with the deflationary bias in macroeconomic policy is also the breadwinner bias. The particular Fordist compromise of the World War II period between capital and labour stipulated that the workplace and the 'family wage' were tailored to the needs and interests of the male worker and 'his' dependent family. It is true that the strong breadwinner models associated with the continental Catholic societies are not found in the Scandinavian countries (Pfau-Effinger 2000). However, even in Nordic countries, labour markets are highly segregated into private markets mainly reserved for males, and a public market occupied largely by women. The important aspect of the breadwinner bias is its normative content that males have a 'natural right' to the role of breadwinner, and that women have to justify their labour market integration. As a result, economic narratives do not take into account the unpaid work done in the home by women, because this type of work is regarded as 'natural' (Becker 1974). Despite the massive integration of women into the labour markets since the 1970s, the economic discourse and the public policies have continued to draw on the separation between family and work (Young 2001a; 2001b). Most importantly, the economic models are still based on the breadwinner bias despite its sharp decline since the 1970s. In other words, economic decisions about the failure to integrate women fully into the labour market and paying them wages equal with men are still justified on the grounds that women are not the main breadwinners.

In addition to the deflationary and the breadwinner bias, there is also the increasing commodification discourse that is linked to the deflationary bias. Many public services are turned into market-based, and individualised services available to those who can afford them. These changes have produced new social hierarchies based not just on gender but also on class and race. The 'reprivatisation discourse' (Fraser 1989) seeks to repatriate the economic and social to the domestic enclave. Reprivatisation of the domestic means that many of the social services once again become part of the non-monetised private sphere. The commodification bias has thus fundamentally challenged the very notion of what is public and what is private. In the process, it has worsened gender-specific social divisions. The growing participation of professional women in the labour market is accompanied by the largely 'invisible' development of a 'service class' that is involved in cleaning, as child caretakers, and in many other household-oriented service jobs. Growing numbers of migrant and immigrant women are involved in the informal labour market to provide these services. An invisible link has thus emerged between women's increasing participation in the formal labour market and the informal labour market roles of migrant and immigrant women. In the process of scaling back the social state, women have responded differently according to their social and class position. Either they are forced to work double or triple shifts to accommodate these added care functions at the household level. Or, for women in the lower skilled professions, the loss of publicly provided care services often make the difference between seeking employment or staying home. In the case of business and professional women, they increasingly 'solve' the marketisation bias by relying on inexpensive undocumented migrant women creating a new international division of labour at the level of the household. On the one side is the 'mistress' and on the other stands the 'maid', separated by different racial, ethnic, class and national belongings and backgrounds (Young 2001b).

## Conclusion

The general scepticism voiced by Danish and Swedish women that by joining the European Economic and Monetary Union the social Europe may be a thing of the past is certainly well-founded. A Fed-style ECB would do more for European economic growth and stimulate demand to prevent an aggravation of the present recession. In fairness it has to be said that the EMU is still a project under construction. The institutional structure, its operational dimensions, and its functional scope are not yet fully in place. Despite the 'institutional underdevelopment', the present construction of the EMU provides a new constitutionalism (Gill 1998) which shifts the European social norms of a stakeholder society to a disciplinary market-based capitalism.

The triple bias of deflation, commodification, and breadwinner are built into the theoretical frameworks of economics. In terms of practice, the 'costs' of these biases are largely distributed along ethnic, gender and class lines. With globalisation and European integration, the democratic aspects of economic decision-making have largely been moved to the transnational and international level and removed from the national level. Democratising the process of macroeconomic policy-making is, as Elson and Cagatay (2000) point out, a crucial element of a 'transformative' approach to macroeconomics. Transformative implies that democratising the economic process is more than adding the 'social' or gender dimensions to the macroeconomic framework. It means to change the fundamental assumptions of macroeconomic policy-making in the context of the global challenges.

## Notes

This chapter is a revised version of the article 'European Central Bank, monetary policy and the "social Europe"', published in *The International Feminist Journal of Politics* 4(3): December 2002, 295–314. The publisher gratefully acknowledges the co-operation of Taylor and Francis in granting permission to publish this revised version of the work.

1 The Danish activity rate of women in the labour market, with Sweden and Finland, is among the highest in Europe: Denmark 78.2 per cent, Finland 70.4 per cent, and Sweden 73.2 per cent. European average activity rate for women is 58.1 per cent, *Eurostat 1998.*
2 A solution was found that during the discussions of the Finance Ministers of the Euro-twelve group, the Swedish finance minister Bosse Ringholm had to leave the room when issues of monetary and interest rate policies were debated. The chair of the Finance Ministers passed then to the Belgian Finance Minister, since Belgium was in line for the next EU presidency in the summer of 2001.
3 For a detailed list of goals, see the Swedish website: www.eu2001.se.
4 It is important to point out that other European countries, such as the UK, Ireland, Greece and also Spain benefit from the gender equality measures enacted by the EU. However, the traditional lower social protection in these countries should not be allowed to lead to a 'race to the bottom' of social welfare systems in Europe. Rather the goal for a 'social Europe' is to strive for the standards of Nordic countries.
5 There are some exceptions to this automatic fine, if countries encounter a 'natural disaster' or if they experience a fall in GDP in excess of 2 per cent in the one year (Teague 1998: 125).
6 For Sandholtz and Zysman (1998) the driving force for the introduction of the Single European Market of the EU was the increasing economic internationalisation and the changing domestic constellations of the European nation-states starting in the 1970s.

## References

Altvater, Elmar and Birgit Mahnkopf. 1996. *Grenzen der Globalisierung. Ökonomie, Ökologie und Politik in der Weltgesellschaft.* Münster: Westfälisches Dampfboot.
Bakker, Isabella (ed.). 1994. *The Strategic Silence.* London: Zed Books.
Bakker, Isabella. 1999. 'Neoliberal Governance and the New Gender Order', *Working Papers in Local Governance and Democracy* 99 (1): 49–59.
Becker, Gary S. 1974. 'A Theory of Marriage: Part II', *Journal of Political Economy* 82 (2): 11–26.
Beneria, Lourdes. 2000. 'Globalization, Gender and the Davos Man', *Feminist Economics* 5 (3): 61–83.
Checkel, Jeffrey T. 1999. 'Social Construction and Integration', *Journal of European Public Policy* 6 (4): 545–60.

Christiansen, Thomas, Knud Erik Jørgensen and Antje Wiener. 1999. 'The Social Construction of Europe', *Journal of European Public Policy* 6 (4): 528–44.

Cook, Joanne. 1998. 'Flexible Employment: Implications for Gender and Citizenship in the European Union', *New Political Economy* 3 (2): 261–77.

Elman, Amy (ed.). 1996. *Sexual Politics and the European Union*. Oxford: Berghahn Books.

Elson, Diane. (ed.). 1995. *Male Bias in the Development Process*. Manchester: Manchester University Press.

Elson, Diane. 2000. *Progress of the World's Women 2000*, United Nations Development Fund for Women, Biennal Report, New York.

Elson, Diane and Nilufer Cagatay. 1999. 'Engendering Macroeconomic Policy and Budgets for Sustainable Development'. Paper presented at the First Global Forum on Human Development, New York.

Elson, Diane and Nilufer Cagatay. 2000. 'The Social Content of Macroeconomic Policies', *World Development Report* 28 (7): 1347–64.

Flassbeck, Heiner. 1999. 'Markt und Gerechtigkeit', *Blätter für deutsche und Internationale Politik* 12: 1450–9.

*Frankfurter Rundschau*. 2000a. 'Buhlen um die skeptischen Frauen' ('Courting the Sceptical Women') 11 September: 2.

*Frankfurter Rundschau*. 2000b. 'Im Zeichen des E. Unter Schwedens EU-Präsidentschaft geht es im kommenden Halbjahr um Eingemachtes wie Erweiterung und Euro' ('In the Symbol of E. During the Coming Swedish Presidency of the EU: The Central Issues Tackled will be Enlargement and the Euro') 21 September: 6.

Fraser, Nancy. 1989. *Unruly Practices: Power, Discourse and Gender in Contemporary Social Theory*. Minneapolis, MN: University of Minnesota Press.

Gill, Stephen. 1998. 'European Governance and New Constitutionalism: Economic and Monetary Union and Alternatives to DisciplinaryNeoliberalism in Europe', *New Political Economy* 3 (1): 5–26.

Gill, Stephen. 2000. *Toward a Postmodern Prince? The Battle in Seattle as a Moment in the New Politics of Globalisation*, www.sussex.ac.uk.

Giovanoli, Mario. 2000. *International Monetary Law. Issues for the New Millennium*. Oxford: Oxford University Press.

Guttmann, Robert. 2000a. *Reform des internationalen Währungssystems*. Paper for the Enquete-Commission of the German Parliament, 'Globalisierug der Weltwirtschaft', Berlin, Germany.

Guttmann, Robert. 2000b. *Investment- und Pensionsfonds*. Paper for the enquete-Commission of the German Parliament, Globalization of the World Economy, 'Globalisierug der Weltwirtschaft', Berlin Germany.

Hay, Colin and Matthew Watson. 1998. 'Rendering the Contingent Necessary: New Labour's Neo-Liberal Conversion and the Discourse of Globalization'. Paper presented at the American Political Science Association Conference, Boston, MA.

Hein, Eckhard. 2000. 'Zentralbankpolitik, Arbeitsmarktinstitutionen und Makroökonomische Resultate', *WSI-Mitteilungen* 2: 107–17.

Herr, Hansjörg. 2001. 'Das Kaninchen vor der Schlange. Europäische Wirtschaft-spolitiknach dem Anschlag vom 11. September', *PROKLA* 125: 637–48.

Hoskyns, Catherine. 1996. *Integrating Gender: Women, Law and Politics in the European Union*. London: Verso.

Huffschmid, Jörg. 2001. *Economic Policy against Recession and Polarisation in Europe*! Paper prepared for the European Economists for an Alternative Economic Policy in Europe.

Jessop, Bob. 1994. 'Post-Fordism and the State', in Ash Amin (ed.) *Post-Fordism: A Reader*, pp. 251–79. Oxford: Blackwell Publishing.

Jørgensen, Knud Erik. 1999. 'The Social Construction of the Acquis Communautaire: A Cornerstone of the European Edifice', *European Integration Online Papers* 6: 5.

Kratochwil, Friedrich and John Gerard Ruggie. 1986. 'International Organization: A State of the Art on an Art of the State', *International Organization* 40: 753–75.

Keynes, John Maynard. 1997. *The General Theory of Employment, Interest, and Money*. New York: Prometheus Books.

Maastricht Treaty Provisions. 2000. In Tommaso Padoa-Schioppa (ed.) *The Road to Monetary Union in Europe*. Oxford: Oxford University Press.

Marx, Karl. 1996. *Foundations of the Critique of Political Economy*. London: Penguin Classic Paperback.

Nelson, Barbara. 1990. 'The Origins of the Two-channel Welfare State: Workmen's Compensation and Mothers' Aid', in Linda Gordon (ed.) *Women, the State, and Welfare*. Madison, WI: University of Wisconsin Press.

Ostner, Ilona and Jane Lewis. 1995. 'Gender and the Evolution of Europeansocial Policies', in Stephan Leibfried and Paul Pierson (eds) *European Social Policy: Between Fragmentation and Integration*, pp. 159–93. Washington, DC: Brookings Institution.

Pfau-Effinger, Birgit. 2000. 'Gender Culture and Social Change in the European Context', in Simon S. Duncan and Birgit Pfau-Effinger (eds) *Gender Work and Culture in the European Union*. London: Routledge.

Rosamond, Ben. 1999. 'Discourses of Globalization and the Social Construction of European Identities', *Journal of European Public Policy* 6 (4): 652–68.

Rossilli, Mariagrazia. 1997. 'The European Community's Policy on the Equality of Women: From the Treaty of Rome to the Present', *European Journal of Women's Studies* 4 (1): 63–82.

Rubery, Jill. 1998. 'Equity and Employment: Complementary or Competitive Objectives of European Policy?' Paper presented to the IAFFE Conference, University of Amsterdam, NL.

Rubery, Jill, Mark Smith, Colette Fagan and Damian Grimshaw. 1998. *Women and European Employment*. London: Routledge.

Ruggie, John G. 1998. *Constructing the World Polity: Essays on International Institutionalization*. New York: Routledge.

Sandholtz, Wayne and John Zysman. 1989. 'Recasting the European Bargain', *World Politics* 42: 95–128.

Sassen, Saskia. 1998. *Globalization and Its Discontents*. New York: New Press.
Shaw, Jo. 1999. 'Constitutional Settlements and the Citizen after the Treaty of Amsterdam', in Karlheinz Neunreither and Antje Wiener (eds) *European Integration after Amsterdam*. Oxford: Oxford University Press.
Soskice, David. 1999. *The Political Economy of EMU: Rethinking the Effects of Monetary Integration on Europe*. Discussion paper. Wissenschaftszentrum Berlin.
Teague, Paul. 1998. 'Monetary Union and Social Europe', *Journal of European Social Policy* 8 (2): 117–37.
Theobald, Hildegard. 1999. *Geschlecht, Qualifikation und Wohlfahrtsstaat: Deutschland und Schweden im Vergleich*. Berlin: Sigma.
Tietmeyer, Hans. 1996. 'Die europäische Wirtschaft zwischen globalen Märkten und Internen Herausforderungen'. Jean Monnet Lecture, European University Institute.
Walby, Sylvia. 1997. *Gender Transformations*. New York: Routledge.
Walby, Sylvia. 1999. 'Changes in Women's Employment in the United Kingdom', *New Political Economy* 4 (2): 195–213.
Wendt, Alexander. 1992. 'Anarchy Is What States Make of It: The Social Construction of Power Politics', *International Organization* 46: 391–407.
Young, Brigitte. 2000. 'Disciplinary Neoliberalism in the European Union and Gender Politics', *New Political Economy* 5 (1): 77–98.
Young, Brigitte, 2001a. Globalization and Gender: A European Perspective, in RitaMae Kelly, Jane Bayes, Mary Hawkesworth, and Brigitte Young (eds) *Gender, Globalization and Democratization*, Lanham, MD: Rowman and Littlefield Publishers, pp. 27–47.
Young, Brigitte. 2001b. 'The "Mistress" and the "Maid" in the Globalized Economy', *Socialist Register 2001*, 264–76.
Young, Brigitte. 2001c. 'Genderdemokratische Governance der Finanzpolitik in der Europäischen Währungsunion', *Zeitschrift fuer Frauenforschung. Geschlechterstudien* 1 (2): 79–91.

# 13

# Private pain/public peace: women's rights as human rights and Amnesty International's report on violence against women

## Gillian Youngs

This is a case study of Amnesty International's 2001 report *Broken Bodies, Shattered Minds: Torture and Ill-treatment of Women*[1] in relation to women's rights as human rights. In linking questions of private pain to public peace, the research continues a well-established feminist tradition of focusing on gendered private/public connections as both historically and institutionally constructed, as well as socially dynamic in their potential for challenge and change. Women experience and tackle oppressive structures and relationships, and direct and indirect forms of exploitation and violence, across private (domestic, familial, personal) and public spheres of state and market (Gibson-Graham 1996; Jones 2000; Peterson 2003). Patriarchal systems have traditionally classified violence against women as private, denoting its distance, and to some degree protection, from the legal gaze and thereby from accountability and punishment. The protection of the private sphere from the intrusion of public (state) interference has historically worked against women exposed to the excesses of unfettered male dominance and violence. Where laws against domestic violence are in force there remain problems with their effectiveness related to broad and diverse private/public issues of gender inequality. The British Crime survey 2004 on domestic violence, sexual assault and stalking, points out that only a small fraction of such cases are reported to the police (Walby and Allen 2004). Even in cases where the police are called in, numerous assaults are likely to have already taken place, and focus is increasingly being placed in crime prevention on the problem of repeat offences.[2] Increasing attention to domestic violence in national contexts, such as the UK, indicates that the issue is gaining some ground as one of general public concern. This case study looks at how campaigning by Amnesty International (AI) is pressing such developments at the international level.

I undertake a critical reading of *Broken Bodies, Shattered Minds: Torture and Ill-treatment of Women* in the context of long-standing feminist campaigning against violence against women. I connect the report's findings to feminist efforts to politicize, and therefore make of public concern, all forms of oppression and cruelty toward women, whether this occurs in public or private settings. I argue that the report marks an important development in AI's established strategy for campaigning against the practice of torture by integrating private as well as public forms of violence against women into the general or universal definition of torture.

I explain that this ties issues of private pain to public peace by identifying a holistic definition of torture as acts by public officials *or* private individuals across all settings, including the home and community. This definition of torture adds force to feminist arguments that violence against women is violence against women, regardless of the setting. Feminist campaigns, at local, national and international levels, have successfully politicised this private pain suffered by women, arguing that it is a matter of public concern, affecting the nature of society as a whole and the rights and freedoms of all individuals. In this regard, women's rights have come to be explicitly understood and institutionalised as part of human rights.[3] If we are to have a peaceful world where all rights are recognised, then the private pain of violence against women must be taken into account and addressed. There can be no peace in its full sense while violence against women continues.

In what follows, I investigate the specific contributions that the AI report on violence against women has made to this ongoing campaign. My discussion covers the nature of AI as an NGO, its traditional orientation toward the state and public forms of torture, and the role of the report in signalling an expansion in its own approach to torture as well as its campaigning role in enlarging the scope of the women's-rights-as human-rights debate. The AI report challenges, to some extent, AI's own historical focus on a delimited (public) approach to the state and torture, and the campaigning perspectives, organisational structure and approaches suited to that focus. *Broken Bodies, Shattered Minds* tells us as much about the gender politics of institutional change within AI as about its evolving role within wider gender-sensitive debates about human rights.

My methodology seeks to contribute to broader thinking about public/private linkages and the inner dynamics of peace building. I argue that the internal (private) developments within an organisation such as AI may be integral to our understanding of the organisation's external (public) activities related to gender issues. The research interrogates a number of public and private and theory and practice connections – the public of torture and the private of violence against women, the theory and practice of women's rights as human rights, the public of NGO campaigning on gender and the private of the NGO's internal processes of change regarding gender politics. I bring into relation a critical assessment of the AI report and interview material relating to AI itself in the context of long-standing feminist work on women's rights as human rights.

My arguments are divided into four sections. The first explores how the report links private pain to public peace. The state is the core focus in AI's report, and this demonstrates a strong continuity in terms of its traditions of campaigning. However, in line with feminist critiques stressing the political nature of private as well as public forms of violence against women, the report reconfigures state accountability into the expanded sphere of private as well as public domains. The second section further unpacks the concept of torture as the means by which AI relates private and public forms of violence. Since torture traditionally has been defined as occurring in public spaces (police stations, secret service cells, prisons, etc.), what does it mean to incorporate private forms of violence against women within the definition? The third section addresses problems surrounding the state as an agent of its own change. Amnesty International makes the concept of 'due diligence' central in the report because it places a burden on states to both actively protect individuals from abuses of their rights and fully address breaches of rights through legal process, 'reparation' and 'redress' (AI 2001: 7). Due diligence extends state accountability to the actions of private individuals who deprive a person of his or her human rights. 'AI considers that acts of violence against women in the home or the community constitute torture for which the state is accountable when they are of the nature and severity envisaged by the concept of torture in international standards and the state has failed to fulfil its obligation to provide effective protection' (8).[4] The fourth section considers AI as a site of change in relation to gender politics and discusses the connections between private institutional change and public political campaigning.

## Private pain and public peace

Violence against women falls into the realm of the private in a number of ways. It is private because it frequently takes place in the private sphere of intimate relations between men and women, husbands and wives, and in the physical locations of those relations, notably the home. Violence against women has socio-spatial characteristics. Even when a man attacks a woman in a public space, if he is perceived to be her intimate partner the private patriarchal boundary around them as a social unit may serve to keep others from interfering. The violence in such instances is regarded as a private matter, and much institutional change, including police action, has revolved around the recognition that violence against women is a public offence and one that should be dealt with and punished accordingly.

There are also socio-spatial dimensions affecting women's exposure to violence in public: rape or other forms of attack; sexual harassment or other forms of abuse by men in positions of power. Women's social identification with the private sphere leads to their being at risk from the exertion of male power, including its most violent manifestations, in public spaces. Feminists have therefore mapped the diverse forms of women's vulnerability to violence across public and private settings as intrinsic to an understanding of patriarchal oppression and gendered identities. The operation of male power across public and private spheres frames women as under the control (or protection) of men. The patriarchal state serves to entrench this situation.

Feminist ambivalence about the state runs deep. As Jan Jindy Pettman (1996: 9) has explained, 'There is a very complex politics here, as women's organisations and feminists direct demands at the state, for more services or protection, while many are profoundly suspicious of the state and its implication in the reproduction of unequal gender relations.' The state is at once representative of institutionalised inequalities between men and women and a powerful site of actual or potential change (see Pateman 1988; MacKinnon 1989). As the sole legitimate user of force to maintain internal and external order, the state also expresses patriarchal power as violence, for example through masculinist cultures of militarism (Cohn 1999). Therefore, feminist interrogation of the state involves a critical assessment of patriarchy and force (Hoffman 2001). This approach links the private pain of women to questions of public peace. Affirming the theoretical and policy-oriented feminist debates about women's rights as human rights, the Amnesty report articulates that wherever and however violence against women occurs it is a matter of general (public) concern.

*Broken Bodies, Shattered Minds* maintains AI's traditional orientation toward state accountability. In other words, it could be argued that AI does not fundamentally diverge from its state-centred focus. Indeed, it reaffirms that focus while refashioning it, working from the public to the private and back to the public again, to track state responsibility in a holistic fashion and to elaborate it in terms of private as well as public acts of torture against women.

> Sometimes the perpetrators of acts of violence against women are agents of the state, such as police officers, prison guards or soldiers. Sometimes they are members of armed groups fighting against the government. However, much of the physical, mental and sexual abuse faced by women is at the hands of people they know, such as husbands, fathers, employers or neighbours.

> States have a duty to ensure that no one is subjected to torture or ill-treatment, whether inflicted by agents of the state or by private individuals. Yet far from protecting women, states all around the world have allowed beatings, rape and other acts of torture to continue unchecked. When a state fails to take effective measures to protect women from torture, it shares responsibility for the suffering these women endure.[5] (www.amnesty.org 2001)

The report attempts to raise the accountability threshold of states by going beyond the public boundaries of the official arms of the state, such as police and prison officers, or groups resistant to the state, to include private individuals.

> AI applies a human rights framework to combat violence against women and insists that under international human rights law, states have a responsibility to protect women from violence, whether the acts are committed by state officials, at the instigation of state officials or by private individuals . . . As part of its campaign for an end to torture, AI holds states accountable for all acts of torture of women, whatever the context in which they are committed and whoever is the perpetrator. (AI 2001; see Bunch 1993; Peters and Wolper 1995).

AI is undergoing change as an organisation as an intrinsic part of linking its campaigning on torture more effectively to global campaigning on women and human rights. AI holds firm to its established campaigning terrain in relation to torture – one historically focused on state (public) forms of torture – while also moving toward a more holistic (public/private) approach with regard to women. It therefore maintains its traditional campaigning ground while working for further change on the basis of it.

In this process, past and present policy conditions are considered, alongside strategies ultimately aimed at transforming those conditions. A cornerstone of AI's work in this regard is the UN Convention against Torture, on the basis of which states can be called to account for severe acts of cruelty by or on behalf of the state or acquiesced to by it. The report retains the central place of the Convention but goes beyond it to cite international human rights law's identification of state 'responsibility for human rights abuses committed by non-state actors' (AI 2001: 6). Focus is on the permissive role of the state, or 'failure of state protection.'

The report goes on to note that, 'The [UN] Special Rapporteur on violence against women has held that "a State can be held complicit where it fails systematically to provide protection from private actors who deprive any person of his/her human rights" ' (7). Amnesty International seeks to set the predominantly 'public' interpretation of torture in the Convention against Torture within an extended private/public definition that recognises torture as 'acts of violence against women in the home or the community' (8).

Statements within the report directly link the social (public) and individual (private) forms of 'vulnerability' affecting women with the exacerbated impact for 'poor and socially marginalized women' (10). Such stances have been central to feminist analysis of the structural disadvantages of women in socio-economic terms. These perspectives identify women's vulnerability as grounded in socio-economic inequalities. As Michelle Fine and Lois Weis argued in the context of the United States at the turn of the century:

> We exit this century and enter another with violence against women smarting, bound to another form of violence. That is, State-sponsored violence by which the public sphere, the State-sponsored safety net (always frayed and inadequate), has rapidly been dismantled, first by right-wing Republicans and soon thereafter by 'moderate' Democrats, as poor and working-class women and their children fall through the huge holes in the webbing. And yet today, with no public accountability, working-class and poor women (and men) have been tossed from our collective moral community, in particular by severe curtailments in their access to welfare, shelter and higher education. These very well traveled exit ramps from domestic abuse are under intensive and deliberate destruction. (2000: 1140–1)

By identifying 'a twinning of State and domestic violence against women' (1141), Fine and Weis emphasise the degree to which the overall social conditions confronting women in relation to violence, and, importantly, the constraints on the possibilities for them escaping it, are configured within a public/private dynamic that is evident in women's embodied experience of multiple 'spaces of danger and threat' with 'few exits' (1144).

Fine and Weis posit 'a restored feminist public sphere that recognizes the ravaged and intimate connections among the economy, public support for education, violence against women, and a restored welfare state' (1144). As an integrated approach to the public and private in the state, this resonates with Jan Jindy Pettman's (1996: 185–207) powerful analysis of 'an international political economy of sex.' As Pettman very clearly states: 'There is a close, though by no means fixed or uncontested, connection between social control of women and violence against them, and between these and the wider structures of gender/gendered power' (186). The vulnerability of women to violence is socially constructed across the public and private spheres and patriarchally performed, directly and indirectly, by agents and processes of the state and by private individuals. With the growth of migratory female workforces, notably in domestic service, diverse public and private settings come into play for the women involved, with multiple forms of vulnerability involving cross-cultural and racialised (including colonial and postcolonial) contexts (188–93).

Feminist perspectives disrupt the abstractions of local politics, international politics and international political economy by, among other things, writing the body into them. They replace male-centred limitations of the hierarchical public-over-private interpretation of social reality with gendered explorations of the structures, processes, and identities that relate public and private, implicitly and explicitly. The gendered body is an intrusion into the disembodied world of mainstream masculinist theory, and this intrusion reveals the expressions or manifestations of gendered forms of power, including (sexualised and racialised) violence (Youngs 2000). Lived reality, rather than being framed within the assumed neatness of patriarchal 'order', is negotiated on the basis of the conflicts (including those articulated brutally) that at least partly result from the unequal bases and implications of that 'order'.

In such terms, *Broken Bodies, Shattered Minds* can be understood as a gendered intervention in the debate on torture. It gives priority to the embodied experiences of women across public and private settings. Rather than working with the traditional abstractions of public from private and vice versa, it focuses on the linkages between public and private, that women's experiences of violence evidence. The report is another contribution to the growing international recognition of this dimension of women's lives as key to the human rights cause. The report makes specific reference to the UN Declaration on the Elimination of Violence against Women's definition of such violence

> As 'any act of gender-based violence that results in, or is likely to result in, physical, sexual, or psychological harm or suffering to women, including threats of such acts, coercion or arbitrary deprivation of liberty, whether occurring in public or private life'. It includes 'violence perpetrated or condoned by the State, wherever it occurs' and 'violence occurring in the family' and the 'general community'. (AI 2001: 65)

As such statements make clear, the social and global contextualisation of violence against women is central to 'locating' it within the human rights framework. Amnesty International is a notable campaigning organisation in this context because of its clearly delineated human rights focus, its independence from governments, and its grassroots orientations.[6]

### Torture and violence against women: making the links

Amnesty International's reputation is for working to free prisoners of conscience and political prisoners and states are the key targets in such work.

Its campaigning on the torture and ill-treatment of women maintains that focus on the state, while challenging the ways in which states (and the Convention against Torture) would generally identify torture as a 'public' rather than a 'private' form of mistreatment of women. Part of the politics of AI's campaign is the connections it makes between dominant framings of torture and wider human rights perspectives, including those focused specifically on women's rights. As Edna O. Aquino, campaign coordinator for women's rights at AI's International Secretariat explained to me:

> In this report, AI tried to reconcile the UN Convention against Torture which has yet to formally acknowledge gender-based violations against women as 'torture' and those advances being made, on the other hand, by other UN bodies which have acquired and applied a gender analysis in their monitoring and reporting of human rights violations against women. (personal communication, 15 October 2001)

The report's social and global contextualization of violence against women is a fundamental aspect of AI's detailed efforts to 'reconcile' the tensions between the public and private framings of violence against women. The report challenges the separations and distinctions between these public and private framings, and instead emphasises continuities of violence against women across public and private. But, in so doing, AI treads a difficult line, which, for grounded campaign and policy reasons, involves the need to avoid any danger of undermining the Convention against Torture as it stands, with all its importance to the core of the organisation's work.

> We tried to integrate the definition of torture with the conceptual framework of 'violence against women' and highlighted the pervasiveness of discrimination in many societies, which underpins women's vulnerabilities to torture and ill-treatment. This report is groundbreaking for AI especially when one considers its foundations on 'classic' international law . . . Human rights concepts on 'torture' evolved from the classic legal principle that law operates solely in the public sphere and that the state is only accountable for acts of torture committed by its own agents. Acts against individuals which are of the same nature and effects as 'torture' but which take place in the so-called private sphere (e.g., home) and are committed by someone related or close to the victim ('non state actor' as in 'domestic violence') would not necessarily have a place within the classic definition of 'torture'. (Edna O. Aquino, personal communication, 15 October 2001)

*Broken Bodies, Shattered Minds* begins by making the public/private connection through the association of three cases of violence against women: rape by soldiers, torture and rape by police officers, and a refugee woman who fled domestic violence only to be refused asylum in the United States.

> A woman in a village in a war-torn European country, a young Kurdish woman in Turkish police custody, a battered mother of two from Central America seeking asylum in the USA. On the surface, little links these three women other than their gender and their suffering: they come from different countries and dissimilar communities, and the men who assaulted them have very different backgrounds. What connects these three cases is that all three women have been the victims of torture. All three women have had to contend not only with violent physical abuses, but also with official silence or indifference. In all three cases, the men who abused them committed their crimes with impunity. In all three cases, the state failed to take the basic steps needed to protect women from physical and sexual abuse. The state there-fore shares responsibility for the suffering these women have endured, whether the perpetrator was a soldier, a police officer or a violent husband.
> (AI 2001: 1–2)

Working from case-based, practice- and policy-oriented perspectives, the report identifies links between individuals in different roles – soldiers, police officers, husbands, judges – and different public and private settings – war, prison, home, courtroom. And, importantly, the cases illus-trate the national and international contexts of violence against women, as well as the various boundaries within these contexts between public and private and between factions and states. Social and global contextualisa-tion of violence against women locates the problem firmly within the con-cerns of national and international law, bringing state accountability into play. This is pivotal for AI's campaigning concerns because it maintains the organisation's established focus on the state. The diverse social mani-festations of inequality between men and women, including different forms of violence against women, are part of 'a global culture'. Thus patriarchal abuse is a global problem cutting across public/private divides and state boundaries.

> Torture of women is rooted in a global culture which denies women equal rights with men, and which legitimizes the violent appropriation of women's bodies for individual gratification or political ends . . . for all the gains that women around the world have made in asserting their rights, women world-wide still earn less than men, own less property than men, and have less access to education, employment and health care. Pervasive discrimination continues to deny women full political and economic equality with men. Violence against women feeds off this discrimination and serves to reinforce it. When women are abused in custody, when they are raped by armed forces as 'spoils of war', when they are terrorized by violence in the home, unequal power relations between men and women are both manifested and enforced.

> Violence against women is compounded by discrimination on grounds of race, ethnicity, sexual orientation, social status, class and age. Such *multiple discrimination* [italics added] further restricts women's choices, increases their vulnerability to violence and makes it even harder for them to gain redress. (AI 2001: 2)

As feminists have frequently stressed, the oppression of women is a systemic condition, and it comes in a range of individualised and institutionalised forms that impact on women's life opportunities or lack of them, their physical freedoms, constraints and identities. Overt acts of violence against women may be among the most extreme demonstrations of their oppression but cannot be fully understood outside the pervasive and multi-faceted context in which these acts occur. The 'relational' emphases of feminist approaches to the ontological realm are key here, particularly with regard to the kinds of critique and advocacy that have challenged the traditional limitations of human rights discourse. As V. Spike Peterson has argued:

> The feminist critique of human rights practices reminds us that good intentions and liberal commitments are not in themselves sufficient. Although the liberal rights tradition (admirably) serves to minimize the incidence of direct violence, it stops short of challenging structural violence. In one sense, the relegation of women's rights is simply indicative of the 'acceptance' more generally of structural violence within the reigning normative order. But in other – and, I believe, more significant – senses, the relegation of women's rights is directly entailed by the domination dynamic embedded in our world view and its moral philosophy. The feminist critique of theoretical foundations reveals a masculinist ontology – an understanding of human nature imposed by taking the standpoint of men (more specifically, elite, white men) as generic. (1990: 306)

Amnesty International's report on violence against women as torture can be directly related to such a feminist focus on ontological concerns. The critique of torture, explicit and implicit in the report, inherently criticises the 'androcentrism' (Peterson 1990: 306) of the traditional orientation toward torture within the dominant political and legalistic discourses. It also criticises the 'atomistic' (304) nature of this traditional public-over-private approach based on notions of the abstract (public, male) individual. The critique is productive in feminist terms because it links the interpretation of torture to the structural conditions of inequality, which provide the direct and indirect bases for violence against women:

> The model of human nature currently presupposed is inadequate for eliminating structural violence (because that model presupposes domination), but it is also decisively inaccurate as a model of human nature. The world's

majority (*all* who are 'marginalized') are excluded from this model; their experiences provide alternative models; and these alternatives must be acknowledged and drawn upon if we are to achieve global solidarity and a just world order. (Peterson 1990: 306)

Amnesty International's gendered application of torture offers an alternative model that is relational in terms of men and women and that recognises structural (institutionalised) forms of violence as well as individual acts of violence against women. But it is important to see AI's stance as campaigning-driven and pragmatic and to realise that there are some tensions behind its adoption of the rather dualistic position described above. Amnesty International holds on to the Convention against Torture – which does not address all forms of violence against women as torture – as a key framework for the pursuit of human rights breaches related to torture. At the same time, AI's gendered framing of *torture* asserts the need for a transformed understanding of the term.

We see here the politics of practice. Amnesty International is working with the policy and legal imperatives and safeguards of the current system while at the same time campaigning for the system to be transformed into one that is better, more effective, and inclusive. The scenario is particularly interesting in that it highlights the contrasting circumstances for theoretical (philosophical) – vs. practice (policy) – based efforts toward change. Theoretical analysis can (and often needs to) posit the possibility of complete transformation – that is the move from an abstract (male-centred) to a gendered approach to human rights. This places no (practice-oriented) constraints on the depth of critique and transformative ideas associated with it. It allows for philosophical interrogation of what is masked or avoided by masculinist normative orders. Such theoretical groundwork is relevant to, but often distinct from, the kind of applied thinking necessary to strategic (legal, etc.) moves toward real inclusive change.

### The state as pivotal to change

The imperatives of practice- and policy-based activity include as a working priority holding on to ground that has been won toward change, and using effective tools that exist (e.g. the Convention against Torture), while campaigning for further change that may ultimately have transformative impact. The present conditions and the future possibilities may be in tension, but this is a tension that must be worked with, actively and carefully, to safeguard the actual and likely benefits of both.

We remain mindful of the value of the Convention against Torture. It is still one of the most viable instruments we could use to monitor and pin down states' responsibilities in upholding international human rights standards, which their governments are supposed to adhere to. Despite being one of the most widely ratified UN conventions, however, torture continues to be rampant in most parts of the world and the Convention Against Torture is the most important internationally accepted standard against which states' international obligations would be measured. (Edna O. Aquino, personal communication, 15 October 2001)

The present conditions affirm the political and legal importance of linking the concept of torture directly to violence against women. Through this linkage the public sphere of international law and the public sphere of states are linked to the public and private spheres of gendered realities. Hence a major focus of *Broken Bodies, Shattered Minds* is the violence and inequality that women experience across the private and public circumstances of their lives.

Our documentation of cases in this report illustrates the existence of a *continuum* between those acts of violence committed against women by state agents (when they come into contact with the law) and those committed by persons close to them in their homes or in their community. The *continuum* is about their common vulnerabilities – the risks, the type or the nature of human rights violations they face – in the hands of the state agent or members of their family or community and in the confines of their homes or in prisons or in the refugee camps, in armed conflict situations or in custody of the state. This *continuum* is maintained and reinforced by women's status in society and how society regards them as women. (Edna O. Aquino, personal communication, 15 October 2001)

The notion of continuum takes on particular political significance in this context. Continuum is, in a sense, the dual site of present conditions and future possibilities. In order to stress the private as well as public nature of torture against women and thus the continuum of state accountability, the report focuses on the severity of harm and intentional infliction:

The severity of the harm inflicted upon women by private individuals can be as damaging as that inflicted on women who are tortured by agents of the state. The *long-term effects* of repeated battering in the home are physically and psychologically devastating. Women are traumatized and injured by rape, *wherever the crime takes place*. The medical consequences include psychological trauma, wounds, unwanted pregnancies, infertility and life-threatening diseases. Many abuses in the family or the community are intentionally inflicted. In addition, *such abuses are often inflicted for similar reasons to torture in custody*. Torture in custody is often used not only to extract confessions but also to instil profound dread into victims, to break their will, to punish them and to demonstrate the power of the perpetrators. Similar purposes characterize acts of torture in the family or the community. The perpetrators may seek to intimidate women into obedience or to punish women for allegedly bringing shame on relatives by their disobedience. (AI2001: 5, italics added)

Such an assessment of torture and violence against women is an applied explanation of why public forms of violence against women cannot be regarded as distinct from private forms of violence against women, of why approaches that abstract the public from the private (politically and legally) are incomplete and distorted. *Broken Bodies, Shattered Minds* links structural factors (public and private) established over time with more immediate and evident (public and private) actions. As feminist critiques have emphasised, the structural conditions of women's lives operate across the historically established conditions of public and private existence.

Amnesty International's assessment explores these connections in precise ways – by equating the degree of harm that can be caused by private individuals with that of agents of the state, by linking the long-term effects of domestic violence with traditional interpretations of torture, and by breaching the public/private divide in illustrating that wherever the abuse takes place, it remains abuse. The brutal aims of control and intimidation cross the public and private in violence against women.

In terms of states' capacities to recognise and act on the public/private continuum of violence against women, there are also a number of important points relating to the concept of 'due diligence' AI is relying on. The concept is applied in deeply structural ways, and this is logical in relation to the areas discussed above. *Broken Bodies, Shattered Minds* draws as much attention to the social circumstances, parameters and constraints women confront as to the mechanisms, legal or otherwise, that may be available to address violence against women. State inaction, the report explains, involves such factors as 'inadequate preventive measures; police indifference to abuses; failure to define abuses as criminal offences; gender bias in the court system; and legal procedures which hamper fair criminal prosecution' (AI 2001: 7).

Problems such as police indifference and gender bias can clearly be addressed by legal and institutional change, but they can also be linked to wider social (structural) manifestations of gender discrimination. This is the case with the difficulties women may encounter in getting their plight recognised or addressed. 'Many women victims of violence find access to legal redress and reparations difficult, if not impossible. Impunity and indifference habitually surround many acts of violence against women' (7). Making violence against women visible as something that should be confronted and tackled is also part of the challenge of transcending the limitations of established definitions of torture.

Feminists, as I earlier indicated, have long struggled with the contradictions in the state's two roles of perpetuating patriarchal power as well as being a key site, in institutional and legal terms, for exposing and attacking it. In this sense, feminist activists have confronted similar problems to those outlined above relating to AI: working for change while at the same time drawing on the institutions (e.g., the state) and legal frameworks already in place. As Karen Engle has explained:

> Regardless of the approaches they take, women's human rights advocates confront a difficult task in attempting to secure women's place in the international human rights framework. Explicitly or implicitly, they challenge traditional notions of human rights for failing to take women into account adequately. At the same time, though, they rely on international legal instruments and human rights law and language as vehicles for achieving women's equality. Thus, *a tension emerges* [italics added], an ambivalence about whether and how women's rights can become a part of human rights. (1992: 521)

Amnesty International and *Broken Bodies, Shattered Minds* are clearly working for change within the system, with the state as pivotal in bringing about the transformation to a holistic (public and private) approach to torture. The report calls into question the limited (public) definition of torture and identifies states as accountable for the operation of an expanded (public and private) definition of torture and, importantly, action against it (AI 2001: 3). The recommendations in the report are directed primarily at states and their governments, covering areas such as: the condemnation of all acts of violence against women; the prohibition of acts of violence against women and the establishment of adequate legal protection against such acts; the investigation of all allegations of violence against women; prosecution, punishment, and reparation; protection against torture in custody; and prevention of torture of women in armed conflicts.

There is clearly tension in identifying the state as both part of the problem and the main guarantor of change in relation to women's rights as human rights. To what extent does the actual patriarchal nature of states work against such change or, equally importantly, even full recognition of the need for it? These are deep structural questions and not ones the AI report can open up in any major way. But they remain key questions for feminist critique of the state, patriarchy, and force and the relationship among them. As John Hoffman has argued:

> Not only are all states sovereign (in their own eyes), but this sovereignty helps to explain why the force of the state permeates social relations as a

whole. Male violence is not just analogous to the force of the state: it is part of the state, authorized by the state, and although some women may be attacked by men who are not themselves state functionaries, this violence is still state-related in character. Patriarchy is linked to force, which in turn is linked to the state. (2001: 109)

Deep critique of and debate about these areas remains high on feminist agendas, and the AI report falls largely outside of such developments, though it has some relevance to them. It is useful to explore in this regard AI's own climate for change in relation to gender, to recognize such organisations as part of change themselves, rather than solely as campaigners for change.

## Gender and Amnesty International

Amnesty International has an established international place at the forefront of NGO activity to combat torture. As such, its campaigning work interrogates state activity and its legitimacy. A major part of AI's profile is its orientation toward calling states to account for the detentions and acts of violence they commit, notably against prisoners of conscience and political prisoners. It has a strong reputation in the arena of work against torture as it has been traditionally defined.

How significant is it therefore that AI should be making specific contributions to the efforts to gain greater recognition of and action against violence against women? Indeed, how significant is it that it should be explicitly addressing the transformation of the abstract 'public' definition of torture into a grounded public/private one? There are a number of areas that can be considered in relation to this question. Aquino of AI described *Broken Bodies, Shattered Minds* as 'groundbreaking' for the organisation. The report signifies that in working for external change and a new understanding of torture, that incorporates violence against women, AI is also, to some degree, undergoing change itself as an organisation.

To put it simply, as AI works to contribute to the gendering of international human rights law the organisation itself is being gendered. And AI is undertaking this work from a specific campaigning location, that has not been primarily gender-oriented in the past. Could this be considered a strength in prioritising the kinds of connections it has set out in the report between public and private forms of violence? In working from a specific, predominantly 'public'-oriented site and moving into an overtly public/private one, does AI have a particular contribution to make?

Aspects of the analysis presented here have addressed such questions in certain ways. They are not easy or appropriate to answer in any complete sense, but they do draw our attention to the diversity and contrasts in the nature of campaigning for women's rights and, to some extent, the wider implications of those contrasts. This includes change within NGOs themselves. Because of their functions within global processes, NGOs can be notable sites for investigating how transformational politics are becoming institutionalised. In this sense, I am interested in looking not just at what they are doing or saying but why and how they have come to do and say it, and what the meanings behind it may be.

The grassroots linkages to *Broken Bodies, Shattered Minds* are interesting in this context too. To some degree, the report is a concrete representation of the activities and preoccupations of AI's global network and the growing importance of gender issues within it.

> We have a network of committed professionals and volunteers at all levels of the organisation who are the catalysts in bringing AI to challenge some dominant albeit gender-blind human rights concepts. We have a network of focal points for AI's work on women's rights in more than 60 countries. So many of the case examples in the report featured some groundbreaking issues (e.g. human rights violations against dalit[7] women in India, honour killings in Pakistan, trafficked women to Israel) by colleagues who have applied gender sensitive methodology in their research and reporting. (Edna O. Aquino, personal communication, 15 October 2001)

The interactions between the activities and concerns of activists on the ground and the institutional processes of AI as an NGO are part of gender politics. The networking and organisational processes behind *Broken Bodies, Shattered Minds* are as much a part of those politics as the final document itself and the processes to which it contributes.

> The next phase of strengthening AI's work in this area will be through the creation of the Gender Unit which will be tasked to mainstream the gender analysis in the internal processes of the organisation; and enhancing a gender sensitive methodology in our research and action. Efforts will also be taken to help empower our women activists situated in all countries where we have a presence and to help them become more effective in their collective role as the 'public face' of AI on women's rights issues. (Edna O. Aquino, personal communication, 15 October 2001)[8]

### Private pain/public peace: concluding thoughts

*Broken Bodies, Shattered Minds* is just one intervention in the global campaign for recognition of women's rights, and as such its importance lies at least in part in its connections with wider debates and strategies. Amnesty International adopts a specific campaigning approach in the report consistent with its own traditions as a human rights organisation. In considering the private as well as the public nature of torture and examining in some detail the joint impact of both forms, as well as the motivation driving them, AI is working with the legitimacy that instruments such as the Convention against Torture provide, while critiquing the limitations of traditional dominant ('public') interpretations of torture.

Such a dual position involves two major moves. One retains the Convention against Torture definition of torture as severe physical or mental pain or suffering. The other entails careful elaboration of why private forms of violence against women can be considered torture. The state and its enhanced accountability in relation to private as well as public forms of torture are central to the report. Thus AI affirms women's rights as human rights in terms of international law, and campaigns for states to be fully accountable across public–private divides, which means ensuring 'effective protection' against violence against women (AI 2001: 5).

The report focuses on structural conditions of violence as well as on acts of violence. This is the case with its discussion of 'due diligence' in relation to state accountability, and the socio-cultural and economic conditions of gender inequalities. The report is thus concerned with social and institutional processes and parameters. 'The failure of the state to ensure women's enjoyment of social, economic and cultural rights further hinders their access to redress for acts of violence and facilitates continuing torture and ill-treatment' (AI 2001: 39).

The report elaborates an alternative model of human nature, one that replaces the abstract (masculinist) atomistic individual of liberal legal traditions with gendered and unequal relational individuals. In this regard, it is a policy-oriented, practice-based assessment that has much in common with feminist perspectives. There are tensions, particularly with regard to the state, in the report as a whole. These signal the degree to which AI is working both within existing state and legal frameworks and advocating for some measure of change in the workings of those frameworks. The report clearly engages in a critique of the state while at the same time maintaining the state as the agent of its own change.

It is important to recognise the limitations of this critique in feminist terms. These would call to account the patriarchal limitations of states' capacities to both re-vision themselves through a gender lens (Peterson 1992) and act accordingly to effect change that would genuinely enforce women's rights as human rights. The arguments presented here, however, also stress that feminist activists face tensions similar to those confronted by AI in working for practical policy change and a similar imperative to use the existing means of change, however flawed they may be. Feminists might be working, in various forms of theory and practice, toward an entirely different kind of state, but we cannot wait for that to arrive before taking incremental steps to improve the lives of women in the meantime.

Radical feminist critiques of the state stress the need for new relational approaches to the individual, autonomy and power, which are based on relations within and between genders rather than abstract individuals (see Jones 1993; Youngs 1999; Hoffman 2001). The duality of AI's position lies in its working within established circumstances and maintaining its ability to do so while also working toward change. This practice is distinct from theoretical endeavours, which are not so tied by the pragmatics of such imperatives but freer, importantly so, to think critically about existing situations and their transformations.

I began my research on *Broken Bodies, Shattered Minds* by concentrating on AI's 'public' role as a campaigning organisation. Questions relating to the gendering of AI itself were, if anything, on the edges of this picture. But as the research progressed it became clear that both areas were important and that the linkages between AI's external campaigning and its own internal developments were worthy of close consideration. Indeed, AI's focus on women's rights is closely related to the organisation's own internal linkages to global women's movements. Its activist communities are a vital resource both for policy developments in preparing a report such as *Broken Bodies, Shattered Minds* and for AI's capacity to evolve as an organisation, with new structures to facilitate work in such areas.

My conclusions demonstrate that there are things to be learned about theory and practice from investigating *Broken Bodies, Shattered Minds*. They suggest that theoretical concerns when put into practice will have specific applications, often based on the strategic issues in play. They also suggest that assessing the specifics of practice can provide reflective resources for thinking through theory.

*Broken Bodies, Shattered Minds* makes direct contributions to a deeper political understanding of the reasons why addressing the private pain of violence against women is intrinsic to moves toward public peace on the basis of rights for all. It makes these contributions in the context of international law on torture and thus utilizes an identifiable and well-established terrain related to the Convention against Torture to put forward its case. This relies heavily on making effective connections between public and private forms of violence against women, which the report engages in at length in general and in case-related terms. As another step in the global campaign for women's rights, the report has its place, and it is interesting to note that it is as much part of AI's own (private or internal) journey in this regard as it is a (public or external) campaigning strategy.

## Notes

This chapter is a revised version of the article 'Private Pain/Public Peace: Women's Rights as Human Rights and Amnesty International's Report on Violence Against Women' published in *Signs: Journal of Women in Culture and Society*, 28(4), summer 2003, 1209–29. I am grateful to Edna Aquino for her time and her interest in this research. I would also like to thank the editors and anonymous reviewers of *Signs: Journal of Women in Culture and Society*, and the editors of this collection for the detailed and helpful comments that contributed to the clarification of the arguments presented. This project was in part inspired by the methodological innovation of Kathleen B. Jones in her work *Living Between Danger and Love: The Limits of Choice* (New Brunswick, NJ: Rutgers University Press, 2000).

1 The report is one of a series of publications issued by Amnesty International as part of its worldwide campaign against torture launched in October 2000. These include *Hidden Scandal, Secret Shame: Torture and Ill-treatment of Children* (London: Amnesty International Publications, 2000) and *Stopping the Torture Trade* (London: Amnesty International Publications, 2001). See other relevant materials at www.amnesty.org including campaign information, country links, and resources on AI's 'Stop Violence Against Women' site, http://web.amnesty.org/actforwomen/index-eng, last accessed 23 March 2005.
2 In addition to Walby and Allen (2004) see, for example, Hanmer, Griffiths and Jerwood (1999).
3 See, for example, Mertus and Goldberg (1994), Peters and Wolper (1995), UN Committee on the Elimination of Discrimination Against Women (CEDAW) www.un.org/womenwatch/daw/cedaw/committee, last accessed 23 March 2005.
4 UN Convention against Torture. Article 1: 'For the purposes of this Convention, the term "torture" means any act by which severe pain or suffering, whether physical or mental, is intentionally inflicted on a person for such purposes as obtaining from him or a third person information or a confession, punishing him for an act he or a third person has committed or is suspected of having committed, or intimidating or coercing him or a third person, or for any reason based on discrimination of any kind, when such pain or suffering is inflicted by or at the instigation of or with the consent or acquiescence of a public official or other person acting in an official capacity. It does not include pain or suffering arising only from, inherent in or incidental to lawful sanctions' (AI 2001: 4).
5 Introduction to the report, www.amnesty.org/ai.nsf/print/ACT400012001), accessed 26 November 2001.
6 'AI is a voluntary, democratic, self-governing movement with more than a million members and supporters in more than 140 countries and territories. It is funded largely by its worldwide membership and by donations from the public. No funds are sought or accepted from governments for AI's work in documenting and campaigning against human rights violations' (Introduction to the report, www.amnesty.org/ai.nsf/print/ACT400012001), accessed 26 November 2001.
7 '*Dalit* literally means "broken people", a term used to describe members of the Scheduled Castes, formerly known as "untouchables". *Dalits* are a

disadvantaged social group, and violence against *dalit* women is common' (AI 2001, 9).

8 See country links on AI's 'Stop Violence Against Women' site, http://web. amnesty.org/actforwomen/index-eng, accessed 23 March 2005.

## References

Amnesty International (AI). 2001. *Broken Bodies, Shattered Minds: Torture and Ill-treatment of Women*. London: Amnesty International Publications.

Bunch, Charlotte. 1993. 'Women's Rights as Human Rights: An International Lobbying Success Story', *Human Rights Tribune* 2(12): 29–32.

Cohn, Carol. 1999. 'Missions, Men and Masculinities: Carol Cohn Discusses "Saving Private Ryan" with Cynthia Weber', *International Feminist Journal of Politics* 1(3): 460–75.

Engle, Karen. 1992. 'International Human Rights and Feminism: When Discourses Meet', *Michigan Journal of International Law* 13: 517–610.

Fine, Michelle and Lois Weis. 2000. 'Disappearing Acts: The State and Violence against Women in the Twentieth Century', *Signs: Journal of Women in Culture and Society* 25(4): 1139–46.

Gibson-Graham, J. K. 1996. *The End of Capitalism (As We Knew It): A Feminist Critique of Political Economy*. Oxford: Blackwell.

Hanmer, Jalna, Griffiths, Sue and Jerwood, David. 1999. 'Arresting Evidence: Domestic Violence and Repeat Victimisation'. Police Research Series Paper 104.UK Home Office Policing and Reducing Crime Unit. London: Home Office Research, Development and Statistics Institute, www.homeoffice.gov.uk/rds/prgpdfs/fprs104.pdf, accessed 23 March 2005.

Hoffman, John. 2001. *Gender and Sovereignty: Feminism, the State and International Relations*. London: Palgrave.

Jones, Kathleen B. 1993. *Compassionate Authority: Democracy and the Representation of Women*. London: Routledge.

Jones, Kathleen B. 2000. *Living between Danger and Love: The Limits of Choice*. New Brunswick, NJ: Rutgers University Press.

MacKinnon, Catharine. 1989. *Toward a Feminist Theory of the State*. Cambridge MA: Harvard University Press.

Mertus, Julie, and Pamela Goldberg. 1994. 'A Perspective on Women and International Human Rights after the Vienna Declaration: The Inside/Outside Construct', *International Law and Politics* 26 (1): 201–34.

Pateman, Carole. 1988. *The Sexual Contract*. Cambridge: Polity.

Peters, Julie and Andrea Wolper (eds) 1995. *Women's Rights, Human Rights: International Feminist Perspectives*. London: Routledge.

Peterson, V. Spike. 1990. 'Whose Rights? A Critique of the "Givens" in Human Rights Discourse', *Alternatives* 15: 303–44.

Peterson, V. Spike (ed.). 1992. *Gendered States: Feminist (Re)Visions of International Relations Theory*. Boulder, CO: Lynne Rienner.

Peterson, V. Spike. 2003. *A Critical Rewriting of Global Political Economy:*

*Integrating Reproductive, Productive and Virtual Economies*. London: Routledge.

Pettman, Jan Jindy. 1996. *Worlding Women: A Feminist International Politics*. London: Routledge.

UN Committee on the Elimination of Discrimination Against Women. www.un.org/womenwatch/daw/cedaw/committee, accessed 23 March 2005.

Youngs, Gillian. 1999. *International Relations in a Global Age: A Conceptual Challenge*. Cambridge: Polity.

Youngs, Gillian (ed.). 2000. *Political Economy, Power and the Body: Global Perspectives*. London: Macmillan.

Walby, Sylvia and Allen, Jonathan. 2004. 'Domestic Violence, Sexual Assault and Stalking: Findings from the British Crime Survey.' UK Home Office Research Study 276. London: Home Office Research, Development and Statistics Directorate, March 2004, www.homeoffice.gov.uk/rds/pdfs04/hors276.pdf, accessed 23 March 2005.

# Index

Note: 'n.' after a page number indicates the number of a note on that page.